MW01142189

# Gifts for God's People

# Gifts for God's People

Compiled from the writings of
## Ellen G. White

*The gifts of the Spirit are promised to*
*every believer according to his need for the Lord's*
*work. The promise is just as strong and trustworthy*
*now as in the days of the apostles.*

—*The Desire of Ages,* p. 823.

REFORMATION HERALD PUBLISHING ASSOCIATION
ROANOKE, VA 24019

**Reformation Herald Cataloging Service**
White, Ellen Gould Harmon, 1827–1915.
    Gifts for God's People

    1. Daily Devotionals—Adventists. 2. Christian Prayers and Meditations for Daily Use. 3. Devotional Literature—Christian I. Reformation Herald Publishing. II. title.
                                    242.2

PRINTED IN U.S.A.

ISBN 1-934308-00-5
ISBN 13: 978-1-934308-00-4

# FOREWORD

Every fresh, new morning is a reminder of the precious gift of life given by our wonderful God. The first thoughts of our day should focus on His glory and goodness. This morning devotional book is designed to inspire our thoughts upward—to help us appreciate all that God gives. We are to make the best use of the gifts and talents He freely offers.

Every person is given life, and the Lord of life "maketh his sun to rise on the evil and on the good, and sendeth rain on the just and on the unjust" (Matthew 5:45). God is immensely generous to the whole human race. Yet there are special gifts uniquely promised to those specifically called His children. His loving hand is warmly out-stretched to all mankind, although only a few actually respond to take hold of that hand. Fewer still press on to follow in close harmony with the Master. Through God's great mercy, "you, that were sometime alienated and enemies in your mind by wicked works, yet now hath he reconciled in the body of his flesh through death, to present you holy and unblameable and unreproveable in his sight: if ye continue in the faith grounded and settled, and be not moved away from the hope of the gospel" (Colossians 1:21–23).

Those who accept God's grace and continue to walk with Him become privileged to enjoy additional gifts. "When [Christ] ascended up on high, he led captivity captive, and gave gifts unto men. . . . He gave some, apostles; and some, prophets; and some, evangelists; and some, pastors and teachers; for the perfecting of the saints, for the work of the ministry, for the edifying of the body of Christ: till we all come in the unity of the faith, and of the knowledge of the Son of God, unto a perfect man, unto the measure of the stature of the fulness of Christ" (Ephesians 4:8, 11–13). "God hath set some in the church, first apostles, secondarily prophets, thirdly teachers, after that miracles, then gifts of healings, helps, governments, diversities of tongues" (1 Corinthians 12:28). "Now there are diversities of gifts, but the same Spirit. And there are differences of administrations, but the same Lord. And there are diversities of operations, but it is the same God which worketh all in all. But the manifestation of the Spirit is given to every man to profit withal. For to one is given by the Spirit the word of wisdom; to another the word of knowledge by the same Spirit; to another faith by the same Spirit; to another the gifts of healing by the same Spirit; to another the working of miracles; to another prophecy; to another discerning of spirits; to another divers kinds of tongues; to another the interpretation of tongues: but all these worketh that one and the selfsame Spirit, dividing to every man severally as he will" (vs. 4–11).

The above passages from Ephesians 4 and 1 Corinthians 12 form the inspiration for this compilation. As we compare ourselves with the early Christians, we cannot help but wonder one thing: perhaps we may be coming short of truly appreciating and making the wisest use of the talents God offers. Remember, just as your fingerprint is unique to you, so are your talents unique! There is only one "you," so do not be discouraged that you are not the same as everyone else. "For the body is not one member, but many. If the foot shall say, Because I am not the hand, I am not of the body; is it therefore not of the body? And if the ear shall say, Because I am not the eye, I am not of the body; is it therefore not of the body? If the whole body were an eye, where were the hearing? If the whole were hearing, where were the smelling? But now hath God set the members every one of them in the body, as it hath pleased him" (1 Corinthians 12:14–18). We may actually be misunderstanding or passing by some of those special gifts of His Spirit.

We should prayerfully consider the sacredness of the gifts of the Holy Spirit. Let us eagerly tap into the rich resources abundantly available through them! "Then shall we know, if we follow on to know the Lord: his going forth is prepared as the morning; and he shall come unto us as the rain, as the latter and former rain unto the earth" (Hosea 6:3). This is the earnest desire of

*The Publishers*

# Monthly Topics

**JANUARY**
*Gifts Available to All*

**FEBRUARY**
*The Holy Spirit Helps the Willing to Obey*

**MARCH**
*The Gift of Truth*

**APRIL**
*Apostleship*

**MAY**
*The Gift of Prophecy*

**JUNE**
*Evangelists, Pastors, Teachers*

**JULY**
*Miracles*

**AUGUST**
*Faith as a Gift to Develop*

**SEPTEMBER**
*The Gift of Healing*

**OCTOBER**
*Helps, Governments, Discerning of Spirits*

**NOVEMBER**
*Inspired Communication Skills*

**DECEMBER**
*Edification, Unity, Perfection!*

*God bestows His gifts upon us that
we may minister to others, and thus become like
Him. Those who receive His gifts that they may
impart to others, become like Christ.
It is in helping and uplifting others that we become
ennobled and purified. This is the work that causes
glory to flow back to God. We must become intelligent upon these points. Our souls must be purified
from all selfishness; for God desires to use
His people as representatives of the
heavenly kingdom.*

—*Testimonies*, vol. 6, p. 190.

# Let's Go to the Source!

*"Every good gift and every perfect gift is from above, and cometh down from the Father of lights, with whom is no variableness, neither shadow of turning" (James 1:17).*

God is love. Like rays of light from the sun, love and light and joy flow out from Him to all His creatures. It is His nature to give. His very life is the outflow of unselfish love.[1]

A selfish man will grant an urgent request, in order to rid himself of one who disturbs his rest. But God delights to give. He is full of compassion, and He longs to grant the requests of those who come unto Him in faith. He gives to us that we may minister to others and thus become like Himself.[2]

God wants His children to ask for those things that will enable Him to reveal His grace through them to the world. He wants them to seek His counsel, to acknowledge His power. Christ lays loving claims on all for whom He has given His life; they are to obey His will if they would share the joys that He has prepared for all who reflect His character here. It is well for us to feel our weakness, for then we shall seek the strength and wisdom that the Father delights to give to His children for their daily strife against the powers of evil.

While education, training, and the counsel of those of experience are all essential, the workers are to be taught that they are not to rely wholly upon any man's judgment. As God's free agents, all should ask wisdom of Him.[3]

The Lord is under no obligation to grant us His favors, yet He has pledged His word that if we will comply with the conditions stated in the Scriptures, He will fulfill His part of the contract. Men often make promises, but do not live up to them. Often we have found that in trusting to men we have leaned upon broken reeds; but the Lord will never disappoint the soul that believes in Him.[4]

# Life Given for a Purpose

*"And the Lord God formed man of the dust of the ground, and breathed into his nostrils the breath of life; and man became a living soul" (Genesis 2:7).*

As possessors of God's free gift of life, we should do all in our power to reach the highest degree of usefulness. Those who do not possess a well-balanced mind in a sound body will fail in their life-work.[5]

Life is given us for wise improvement of the talents we possess. The greater our opportunities, the greater is our responsibility to the Giver of all good gifts. We are God's property, and must render an account of all our actions to Him. How poor will our lives appear in His sight if they are destitute of noble, unselfish actions; if they have been spent in idleness, pleasure seeking, and frivolity.

Adam was placed in glorious Eden as the king of the whole earth; yet there was given him a work to do; the Creator required him to dress and take care of the garden. Thus divine wisdom saw it was best for sinless man to have employment; how much more necessary, then, is it for the fallen race to occupy their time with useful labor, thus shutting the door against many temptations, and guarding against the encroachments of the evil one.

Those who have nothing to do are the most miserable of mortals. It is an unsatisfying life that is guided only by inclination and love of pleasure, in which we look in vain for some generous deed, some earnest, active work, that has blessed the world. In looking over the record of each day, we should be able to find a balance to our account above selfish gratification; something accomplished that elevates ourselves, benefits our fellow creatures, and is acceptable to God.[6]

Every receiver should hold himself accountable to God, and use his talents for God's glory.[7]

# Perfect Instruction

*"The law of the Lord is perfect, converting the soul: the testimony of the Lord is sure, making wise the simple" (Psalm 19:7).*

In the day of final reckoning, Christ does not present before men the great work He has done for them in giving His life for their redemption. He presents before them the faithful work they have done for him. What surpassing love is this! He even mentions the work of the heathen, who have no intelligent knowledge of the law of the Lord, but who have done the very things the law required, because they have heeded the voice speaking to them in the things of nature. When the Holy Spirit implants Christ's Spirit in the heart of the savage, and he befriends God's servants, the quickening of the heart's sympathy is contrary to his nature, contrary to his education. The grace of God, working upon the darkened mind, has softened the savage nature untaught by the wisdom of men. And these un-educated heathen, in all their cruelty, are regarded in a more favorable light than are those who have had great light and evidence, but who have rejected the mercy and reproof of God.

Christ implants His grace in the heart of the savage, and he min-isters to the necessity of the missionary, even before he has heard or comprehended the words of truth and life. Behold that crowd collect-ed about God's servant to harm him! But the Lord is working upon the heart and mind of perhaps one man to plead in behalf of His ser-vant; and when the war council has determined the destruction of the Christian's life, the intercession of that savage turns the decision, and his life is spared. O, the love that goes forth to the savage for this one act! To such Christ says, in the Judgment: "I was an hungred, and ye gave me meat: I was thirsty, and ye gave me drink: I was a stranger, and ye took me in: naked, and ye clothed me: I was sick, and ye visit-ed me: I was in prison, and ye came unto me." "Come, ye blessed of my Father, inherit the kingdom prepared for you from the foundation of the world" (Matthew 25:35, 36, 34).[8]

# God's Justice a Blessing

*"Thy throne, O God, is for ever and ever: a sceptre of righteousness is the sceptre of thy kingdom" (Hebrews 1:8).*

[God] desires that all the inhabitants of the universe shall be convinced of His justice in the final overthrow of rebellion and the eradication of sin. He purposes that the real nature and direful effects of sin shall be clearly manifested to the end that all may be assured of the wisdom and justice of the divine government.[9]

In matters concerning the kingdom of Christ no compulsion or forcing of conscience is permitted. No blood is to be shed, no force of arms employed, no prison is to be opened for the incarceration of one who does not choose the kingdom of God and His righteousness. Christ will accept only of the voluntary service of the heart which has been sanctified through the truth.[10]

The judgment scene will take place in the presence of all the worlds; for in this judgment the government of God will be vindicated, and His law will stand forth as "holy, and just, and good" (Romans 7:12). Then every case will be decided, and sentence will be passed upon all. Sin will not then appear attractive, but will be seen in all its hideous magnitude. . . .

Every deed, small and great, is to be brought into recognition. That which has been considered trivial here will then appear as it is. The two mites of the widow will be recognized. The cup of cold water offered, the prison visited, the hungry fed—each will bring its own reward. And that unfulfilled duty, that selfish act, will not be forgotten. In the open court around the throne of God it will appear a very different thing from what it did when it was performed. . . .

The character which we now manifest is deciding our future destiny. The happiness of heaven will be found by conforming to the will of God. . . . God knows who are the loyal and true subjects of His kingdom on earth, and those who do His will upon earth, as it is done in heaven, will be made the members of the royal family above.[11]

# Mercy

*"The Lord is merciful and gracious, slow to anger, and plenteous in mercy" (Psalm 103:8).*

It is a marvel to me that God will bear with the perversity of the children of men so long, bearing with their disobedience and yet suffering them to live, abusing His mercies, bearing false witness against Him in most wicked statements. But God's ways are not as our ways, and we will not marvel at His loving forbearance and tender pity and infinite compassion, for He has given an unmistakable evidence that this is just like His character—slow to anger, showing mercy unto thousands of those who love Him and keep His commandments.[12]

God is merciful. His requirements are reasonable, in accordance with the goodness and benevolence of His character.[13]

Were the Lord to deal with us as we deserve, would we not be punished in many ways as stubborn, ungrateful children? But He is long-suffering, He does not deal with us according to our perversity. Instead of this, He offers to take us into partnership with Himself and with His Son. All may have life who will accept it; the world has been invited to the gospel feast.[14]

The Lord is merciful. He does not chastise His people because He hates them, but because He hates the sins they are committing. He must chastise them, that they may return to their loyalty. He designs their punishment to be a warning to them and to others. No one need walk in darkness. No one need say, "Specify to me the precise wrongs of which I am guilty." To those who say this, I give the word of the Lord: "Search prayerfully, and you will know."

If the warnings and reproofs given in the Word of God and in the testimonies of His Spirit are not plain enough, what words would be sufficiently plain to bring about a revival and a reformation?[15]

[The Lord] waits long for His erring people to repent, that He may remove the rod from them, and grant them His forgiveness and love, filling their hearts with His peace and joy.[16]

# Preservation

*"Thou, even thou, art Lord alone; thou hast made heaven, the heaven of heavens, with all their host, the earth, and all things therein, . . . and thou preservest them all" (Nehemiah 9:6).*

As regards this world, God's work of creation is completed. For "the works were finished from the foundation of the world" (Hebrews 4:3). But His energy is still exerted in upholding the objects of His creation. It is not because the mechanism that has once been set in motion continues to act by its own inherent energy that the pulse beats and breath follows breath; but every breath, every pulsation of the heart, is an evidence of the all-pervading care of Him in whom "we live, and move, and have our being" (Acts 17:28). It is not because of inherent power that year by year the earth produces her bounties and continues her motion around the sun. The hand of God guides the planets and keeps them in position in their orderly march through the heavens. He "bringeth out their host by number: he calleth them all by names by the greatness of his might, for that he is strong in power; not one faileth" (Isaiah 40:26). It is through His power that vegetation flourishes, that the leaves appear and the flowers bloom. He "maketh grass to grow upon the mountains," and by Him the valleys are made fruitful. "All the beasts of the forest . . . seek their meat from God," and every living creature, from the smallest insect up to man, is daily dependent upon His providential care. In the beautiful words of the psalmist, "These wait all upon thee. . . . That thou givest them they gather; thou openest thine hand, they are filled with good" (Psalm 147:8; 104:20, 21, 27, 28). His word controls the elements; He covers the heavens with clouds and prepares rain for the earth. . . . "When he uttereth his voice, there is a multitude of waters in the heavens, and he causeth the vapours to ascend from the ends of the earth; he maketh lightnings with rain, and bringeth forth the wind out of his treasures" (Jeremiah 10:13).[17]

# A Measure of Health

*"Why art thou cast down, O my soul? and why art thou disquieted within me? hope thou in God: for I shall yet praise him, who is the health of my countenance, and my God" (Psalm 42:11).*

Health is a blessing of which few appreciate the value; yet upon it the efficiency of our mental and physical powers largely depends. Our impulses and passions have their seat in the body, and it must be kept in the best condition physically and under the most spiritual influences in order that our talents may be put to the highest use.

Anything that lessens physical strength enfeebles the mind and makes it less capable of discriminating between right and wrong. We become less capable of choosing the good and have less strength of will to do that which we know to be right.

The misuse of our physical powers shortens the period of time in which our lives can be used for the glory of God. And it unfits us to accomplish the work God has given us to do. By allowing ourselves to form wrong habits, by keeping late hours, by gratifying appetite at the expense of health, we lay the foundation for feebleness. By neglecting physical exercise, by overworking mind or body, we unbalance the nervous system. Those who thus shorten their lives and unfit themselves for service by disregarding nature's laws, are guilty of robbery toward God. And they are robbing their fellow men also. The opportunity of blessing others, the very work for which God sent them into the world, has by their own course of action been cut short. And they have unfitted themselves to do even that which in a briefer period of time they might have accomplished. The Lord holds us guilty when by our injurious habits we thus deprive the world of good.

Transgression of physical law is transgression of the moral law; for God is as truly the author of physical laws as He is the author of the moral law. His law is written with His own finger upon every nerve, every muscle, every faculty, which has been entrusted to man. And every misuse of any part of our organism is a violation of that law.[18]

# The Beauty of Nature

*"O Lord, how manifold are thy works! in wisdom hast thou made them all: the earth is full of thy riches" (Psalm 104:24).*

Nature testifies that One infinite in power, great in goodness, mercy, and love, created the earth, and filled it with life and gladness. Even in their blighted state, all things reveal the handiwork of the great Master Artist. Wherever we turn, we may hear the voice of God, and see evidences of His goodness.

From the solemn roll of the deep-toned thunder and old ocean's ceaseless roar, to the glad songs that make the forests vocal with melody, nature's ten thousand voices speak His praise. In earth and sea and sky, with their marvelous tint and color, varying in gorgeous contrast or blended in harmony, we behold His glory. The everlasting hills tell us of His power. The trees that wave their green banners in the sunlight, and the flowers in their delicate beauty, point to their Creator. The living green that carpets the brown earth tells of God's care for the humblest of His creatures. The caves of the sea and the depths of the earth reveal His treasures. He who placed the pearls in the ocean and the amethyst and chrysolite among the rocks is a lover of the beautiful. The sun rising in the heavens is a representative of Him who is the life and light of all that He has made. All the brightness and beauty that adorn the earth and light up the heavens speak of God.[19]

All created things declare the glory of [God's] excellence. There is nothing, save the selfish heart of man, that lives unto itself. No bird that cleaves the air, no animal that moves upon the ground, but ministers to some other life. There is no leaf of the forest, or lowly blade of grass, but has its ministry. . . . The flowers breathe fragrance and unfold their beauty in blessing to the world. The sun sheds its light to gladden a thousand worlds. The ocean, itself the source of all our springs and fountains, receives the streams from every land, but takes to give. The mists ascending from its bosom fall in showers to water the earth, that it may bring forth and bud.[20]

16

# God's Written Word

*"The words of the Lord are pure words: as silver tried in a furnace of earth, purified seven times" (Psalm 12:6).*

There is no need for us to trust to uncertainty. We pass by the Fathers to learn of God out of His Word. This is life eternal, to know God. Oh, how thankful we should be that the Bible is the inspired word of God. Holy men of old wrote this Word as they were moved by the Spirit. God did not leave His Word to be preserved in the memories of men and handed down from generation to generation by oral transmission and traditional unfolding. Had He done this, the Word would gradually have been added to by men. We would have been asked to receive that which is not inspired. Let us thank God for His written word.

The commentaries written about the Word do not all agree. Often they come into collision with one another. God does not ask us to be guided by them. It is His Word with which we have to deal. All can search this Word for themselves. And they may know that the teaching of this precious book is unchangeable. The opinions of human beings differ, but the Bible always says the same thing. The Word of God is from everlasting to everlasting.

The Bible was not given only for ministers and learned men. Every man, woman, and child should read the Scriptures for himself or herself. Do not depend on the minister to read it for you. The Bible is God's word to *you*. The poor man needs it as much as the rich man, the unlearned as much the learned. And Christ has made this Word so plain that in reading it no one need stumble. Let the humble cottager read and understand the Word given by the wisest Teacher the world has ever known, and among kings, governors, statesmen, and the world's most highly educated men there is none greater than He.

To search means to look diligently for something which has been lost. Search yourself for the hidden treasure. Do not leave this work to the minister. You cannot afford to be ignorant of the Word of God.[21]

# Time

*"He hath made every thing beautiful in his time: also he hath set the world in their heart, so that no man can find out the work that God maketh from the beginning to the end" (Ecclesiastes 3:11).*

Time brings to every human being a responsibility; and the youth are to use the faculties of mind and body in accomplishing the work that God has given them to do. They are required to use every hour in doing good in the service of the Master. Every passing day brings us nearer to the time when we shall see Him whom our souls love. Beyond this present is the eternal future. Just now is the time of our test and trial. Now is the seedtime of grace and the ripening harvest. Time is very precious. Days and weeks and months are filling up the year; and as they pass, we have one day, one week, one month less in which to prepare for the future life. Yet thousands are lingering in careless and heedless indifference, feeling no need of bearing responsibilities, spending their precious time as if it were of no value. This pleasure, this excursion, they say, will pass away time. This is not the true view of life. Time is a precious talent, for which they must render an account to God.[22]

Christ bids us, "Gather up the fragments that remain, that nothing be lost" (John 6:12). While thousands are every day perishing from famine, bloodshed, fire, and plague, it becomes every lover of his kind to see that nothing is wasted, that nothing is needlessly expended, whereby he might benefit a human being.

It is wrong to waste our time, wrong to waste our thoughts. We lose every moment that we devote to self-seeking. If every moment were valued and rightly employed, we should have time for everything that we need to do for ourselves or for the world. In the expenditure of money, in the use of time, strength, opportunities, let every Christian look to God for guidance. "If any of you lack wisdom, let him ask of God, that giveth to all men liberally, and upbraideth not; and it shall be given him" (James 1:5).[23]

# Opportunity

*"Behold, now is the accepted time; behold, now is the day of salvation" (2 Corinthians 6:2).*

Beware of procrastination. Do not put off the work of forsaking your sins and seeking purity of heart through Jesus. Here is where thousands upon thousands have erred to their eternal loss. I will not here dwell upon the shortness and uncertainty of life; but there is a terrible danger—a danger not sufficiently understood—in delaying to yield to the pleading voice of God's Holy Spirit, in choosing to live in sin; for such this delay really is. Sin, however small it may be esteemed, can be indulged in only at the peril of infinite loss. What we do not overcome, will overcome us and work out our destruction.[24]

It is not pleasing to God that we defer present opportunities for doing good, in hope of accomplishing a greater work in the future. Each should follow the leadings of Providence, not consulting self-interest, and not trusting wholly to his own judgment. Some may be so constituted as to see failure where God intends success; they may see only giants and walled cities, where others, with clearer vision, see also God and angels ready to give victory to His truth.[25]

What a victory you will gain when you learn to follow the opening providences of God with a grateful heart and a determination to live with an eye single to His glory, in sickness or health, in abundance or want.[26]

Shall we not individually make the best possible use of the natural powers of mind and body? Shall we not carefully treasure every entrusted talent, and by exercise strengthen every faculty, and live in such a way that the young and inexperienced and the aged and experienced shall be benefited by association with us?[27]

Every opportunity that presents itself to serve God must be improved. By use our gifts will increase.[28]

# Some Amount of Material Goods

*"Jesus beholding [the rich young man] loved him, and said unto him, One thing thou lackest: go thy way, sell whatsoever thou hast, and give to the poor, and thou shalt have treasure in heaven: and come, take up the cross, and follow me. And he was sad at that saying, and went away grieved: for he had great possessions" (Mark 10:21, 22).*

To [the rich young man] riches were honor and power; and the great amount of his treasure made such a disposal of it seem almost an impossibility.

This world-loving man desired heaven; but he wanted to retain his wealth, and he renounced immortal life for the love of money and power. Oh, what a miserable exchange! Yet many who profess to be keeping all the commandments of God are doing the same thing.

Here is the danger of riches to the avaricious man; the more he gains, the harder it is for him to be generous. To diminish his wealth is like parting with his life; and he turns from the attractions of the immortal reward, in order to retain and increase his earthly possessions. Had he kept the commandments, his worldly possessions would not have been so great. How could he, while plotting and striving for self, love God with all his heart, and with all his mind, and with all his strength, and his neighbor as himself? Had he distributed to the necessities of the poor as their wants demanded, he would have been far happier, and would have had greater heavenly treasure, and less of earth upon which to place his affections.

Christ has committed to each of us talents of means and of influence; and when He shall come to reckon with His servants, and all are called to the strictest account as to the use made of the talents entrusted to them, how will you, my brother, my sister, bear the investigation? Will you be prepared to return to the Master His talents doubled, laying before Him both principal and interest, thus showing that you have been a judicious as well as faithful and persevering worker in His service?[29]

# The Gift of a Sound Mind

*"For God hath not given us the spirit of fear; but of power, and of love, and of a sound mind" (2 Timothy 1:7).*

Man may have brilliant intellect; he may be rich in the possession of natural endowments. But these are all given him by God, his Maker. God can remove the gift of reason, and in a moment man will become as Nebuchadnezzar, degraded to the level of the beasts of the field.[30]

My dear Henry: My heart has been pained to witness the movements of an unfortunate child, without a mind. His skin is fair, his features good; but he has no intellect. Dear Henry, how thankful I felt to the Lord that my dear boys were blessed with intellect. I would not have you, my Henry, like that poor boy, for a house full of gold. How thankful should you be that the Lord has blessed you with quite good health, and with your reason.

If you only take a noble, manly course, you will make our hearts glad. Our dear children are precious jewels to us. We dedicated you to God as soon as you were born. We prayed earnestly from your earliest infancy for you, that your dispositions would be tempered. We wept for you, when you, dear Henry, lay an unconscious babe in our arms. We plead with the Lord to put within you a right spirit, to lead you to His own fold. And now our greatest anxiety is for you. We love you, we want you saved. We want your conduct to be right, governed by a sense of duty, and you have a principle, a determination of your own, that you will do right—not because you are obliged to, but because you love to. For in right-doing there is no sting, no self-reproach, no self-condemnation, but a pleasing consciousness of rightdoing.

Dear Henry, acquaint yourself with your own faults. . . . Ask yourself, Is this right? will it lead to evil? will it lead to unfaithfulness? will it lead to deception, or falsehood? shall I feel just as happy after I do this as before?[31]

# Reasoning Power

*"Come now, and let us reason together, saith the Lord: though your sins be as scarlet, they shall be as white as snow; though they be red like crimson, they shall be as wool" (Isaiah 1:18).*

Of all the creatures that God has made upon the earth, man alone is rebellious. Yet he possesses reasoning powers to understand the claims of the divine law and a conscience to feel the guilt of transgression and the peace and joy of obedience. God made him a free moral agent, to obey or disobey. The reward of everlasting life—an eternal weight of glory—is promised to those who do God's will, while the threatenings of His wrath hang over all who defy His law.[32]

God expects men to use the intellect He has given them. He expects them to use every reasoning power for Him. They are to give the conscience the place of supremacy that has been assigned to it.[33]

The government of God is not, as Satan would make it appear, founded upon a blind submission, an unreasoning control. It appeals to the intellect and the conscience. "Come now, and let us reason together" is the Creator's invitation to the beings He has made (Isaiah 1:18). God does not force the will of His creatures. He cannot accept an homage that is not willingly and intelligently given. A mere forced submission would prevent all real development of mind or character; it would make man a mere automaton. Such is not the purpose of the Creator. He desires that man, the crowning work of His creative power, shall reach the highest possible development. He sets before us the height of blessing to which He desires to bring us through His grace. He invites us to give ourselves to Him, that He may work His will in us. It remains for us to choose whether we will be set free from the bondage of sin, to share the glorious liberty of the sons of God.[34]

# The Gift of a Saviour

*"[Mary] shall bring forth a son, and thou shalt call his name Jesus: for he shall save his people from their sins" (Matthew 1:21).*

We may have flattered ourselves, as did Nicodemus, that our life has been upright, that our moral character is correct, and think that we need not humble the heart before God, like the common sinner: but when the light from Christ shines into our souls, we shall see how impure we are; we shall discern the selfishness of motive, the enmity against God, that has defiled every act of life. Then we shall know that our own righteousness is indeed as filthy rags, and that the blood of Christ alone can cleanse us from the defilement of sin, and renew our hearts in His own likeness.[35]

There is but one power that can break the hold of evil from the hearts of men, and that is the power of God in Jesus Christ. Only through the blood of the Crucified One is there cleansing from sin. His grace alone can enable us to resist and subdue the tendencies of our fallen nature.[36]

All who have a sense of their deep soul poverty, who feel that they have nothing good in themselves, may find righteousness and strength by looking unto Jesus. . . . We are not worthy of God's love, but Christ, our surety, is worthy, and is abundantly able to save all who shall come unto Him. Whatever may have been your past experience, however discouraging your present circumstances, if you will come to Jesus just as you are, weak, helpless, and despairing, our compassionate Saviour will meet you a great way off, and will throw about you His arms of love and His robe of righteousness. He presents us to the Father clothed in the white raiment of His own character. He pleads before God in our behalf, saying: I have taken the sinner's place. Look not upon this wayward child, but look on Me. Does Satan plead loudly against our souls, accusing of sin, and claiming us as his prey, the blood of Christ pleads with greater power.[37]

# Forgiveness

*"If thou, Lord, shouldest mark iniquities, O Lord, who shall stand? But there is forgiveness with thee, that thou mayest be feared"* (Psalm 130:3, 4).

There are today thousands suffering from physical disease who, like the paralytic, are longing for the message, "Thy sins are forgiven." The burden of sin, with its unrest and unsatisfied desires, is the foundation of their maladies. They can find no relief until they come to the Healer of the soul. The peace which He alone can impart would restore vigor to the mind and health to the body.[38]

Your motives are impure; your heart is unclean. You see that your life has been filled with selfishness and sin. You long to be forgiven, to be cleansed, to be set free. Harmony with God, likeness to Him—what can you do to obtain it?

It is peace that you need—Heaven's forgiveness and peace and love in the soul. Money cannot buy it, intellect cannot procure it, wisdom cannot attain to it; you can never hope, by your own efforts, to secure it. But God offers it to you as a gift, "without money and without price" (Isaiah 55:1). It is yours if you will but reach out your hand and grasp it. The Lord says, "Though your sins be as scarlet, they shall be as white as snow; though they be red like crimson, they shall be as wool" (Isaiah 1:18). "A new heart also will I give you, and a new spirit will I put within you" (Ezekiel 36:26).

You have confessed your sins, and in heart put them away. You have resolved to give yourself to God. Now go to Him, and ask that He will wash away your sins and give you a new heart. Then believe that He does this *because He has promised*. This is the lesson which Jesus taught while He was on earth, that the gift which God promises us, we must believe we do receive, and it is ours.[39]

# Cleansing

*"Purge me with hyssop, and I shall be clean: wash me, and I shall be whiter than snow" (Psalm 51:7).*

You are a sinner. You cannot atone for your past sins; you cannot change your heart and make yourself holy. But God promises to do all this for you through Christ. You *believe* that promise. You confess your sins and give yourself to God. You *will* to serve Him. Just as surely as you do this, God will fulfill His word to you. If you believe the promise—believe that you are forgiven and cleansed—God supplies the fact; you are made whole, just as Christ gave the paralytic power to walk when the man believed that he was healed. It is so if you believe it.

Do not wait to *feel* that you are made whole, but say, "I believe it; it is so, not because I feel it, but because God has promised."

Jesus says, "What things soever ye desire, when ye pray, believe that ye receive them, and ye shall have them" (Mark 11:24). There is a condition to this promise—that we pray according to the will of God. But it is the will of God to cleanse us from sin, to make us His children, and to enable us to live a holy life. So we may ask for these blessings, and believe that we receive them, and thank God that we *have* received them. It is our privilege to go to Jesus and be cleansed, and to stand before the law without shame or remorse. "There is therefore now no condemnation to them which are in Christ Jesus, who walk not after the flesh, but after the Spirit" (Romans 8:1).

Henceforth you are not your own; you are bought with a price. "Ye were not redeemed with corruptible things, as silver and gold; . . . but with the precious blood of Christ, as of a lamb without blemish and without spot" (1 Peter 1:18, 19). Through this simple act of believing God, the Holy Spirit has begotten a new life in your heart. You are as a child born into the family of God, and He loves you as He loves His Son.[40]

# The Blessing of Confession

*"If we confess our sins, he is faithful and just to forgive us our sins, and to cleanse us from all unrighteousness" (1 John 1:9).*

Those who have not humbled their souls before God in acknowledging their guilt, have not yet fulfilled the first condition of acceptance. . . . The only reason why we do not have remission of sins that are past is that we are not willing to humble our hearts and comply with the conditions of the word of truth. Explicit instruction is given concerning this matter. Confession of sin, whether public or private, should be heartfelt and freely expressed. It is not to be urged from the sinner. It is not to be made in a flippant and careless way, or forced from those who have no realizing sense of the abhorrent character of sin. The confession that is the outpouring of the inmost soul finds its way to the God of infinite pity. The psalmist says, "The Lord is nigh unto them that are of a broken heart; and saveth such as be of a contrite spirit" (Psalm 34:18).

True confession is always of a specific character, and acknowledges particular sins. They may be of such a nature as to be brought before God only; they may be wrongs that should be confessed to individuals who have suffered injury through them; or they may be of a public character, and should then be as publicly confessed. But all confession should be definite and to the point, acknowledging the very sins of which you are guilty.[41]

The examples in God's word of genuine repentance and humiliation reveal a spirit of confession in which there is no excuse for sin or attempt at self-justification. Paul did not seek to shield himself; he paints his sin in its darkest hue, not attempting to lessen his guilt. . . .

The humble and broken heart, subdued by genuine repentance, will appreciate something of the love of God and the cost of Calvary; and as a son confesses to a loving father, so will the truly penitent bring all his sins before God.[42]

# What a Friend!

*"A man that hath friends must shew himself friendly: and there is a friend that sticketh closer than a brother" (Proverbs 18:24).*

[Jesus] has borne the burden of our guilt. He will take the load from our weary shoulders. He will give us rest. The burden of care and sorrow also He will bear. He invites us to cast all our care upon Him; for He carries us upon His heart.

The Elder Brother of our race is by the eternal throne. He looks upon every soul who is turning his face toward Him as the Saviour. He knows by experience what are the weaknesses of humanity, what are our wants, and where lies the strength of our temptations; for He was "in all points tempted like as we are, yet without sin" (Hebrews 4:15). He is watching over you, trembling child of God. Are you tempted? He will deliver. Are you weak? He will strengthen. Are you ignorant? He will enlighten. Are you wounded? He will heal. The Lord "telleth the number of the stars"; and yet "He healeth the broken in heart, and bindeth up their wounds" (Psalm 147:4, 3).

Whatever your anxieties and trials, spread out your case before the Lord. Your spirit will be braced for endurance. The way will be open for you to disentangle yourself from embarrassment and difficulty. The weaker and more helpless you know yourself to be, the stronger will you become in His strength. The heavier your burdens, the more blessed the rest in casting them upon your Burden Bearer.

Circumstances may separate friends; the restless waters of the wide sea may roll between us and them. But no circumstances, no distance, can separate us from the Saviour. Wherever we may be, He is at our right hand, to support, maintain, uphold, and cheer. Greater than the love of a mother for her child is Christ's love for His redeemed. It is our privilege to rest in His love, to say, "I will trust Him; for He gave His life for me."

Human love may change, but Christ's love knows no change. When we cry to Him for help, His hand is stretched out to save.[43]

# An Example for Us

*"Trust in him at all times; ye people, pour out your heart before him: God is a refuge for us" (Psalm 62:8).*

After Christ rose up from the water and from the hand of John, He walked out to the bank of Jordan, and bowed in the attitude of prayer. The eyes of John were fastened upon Christ with the deepest interest and amazement. His heart was stirred with emotion as he looked upon Him thus bowed as a suppliant. Christ's hands were raised upward, and His gaze seemed to penetrate Heaven. As the believer's example, His sinless humanity supplicated support and strength from His heavenly Father, as He was about to commence His public labors as the Messiah. Jesus poured out His soul in earnest prayer. A new and important era was opening before Him. His former peaceful, quiet life is to here end. He had been happy in a life of industry and toil, while fulfilling the duties devolving on a son. He was an example to those in childhood, youth, and manhood. His deportment showed that He felt the importance and solemnity of the hour. He knew that trials, toils, conflicts, sufferings, and death were in the path His feet had entered. He felt the weight of the responsibilities He must bear. He was about to engage in new and arduous duties. A sense of the sinfulness of men and the hardness of their hearts, which separated them from God, convinced Him that but few would discern His merciful mission, and accept the salvation He came from Heaven to bring them.

Never before had angels listened to such a prayer as Christ offered at His baptism, and they were solicitous to be the bearers of the message from the Father to His Son. But, no; direct from the Father issues the light of His glory.[44]

If you will find heart and voice to pray, [God] will be sure to hear, and an arm will be reached down to save you. There is a God that hears prayer, and when all other resources fail, He is your refuge, a very present help in time of trouble.[45]

# The Great Burden Bearer

*"Humble yourselves therefore under the mighty hand of God, that he may exalt you in due time: casting all your care upon him; for he careth for you" (1 Peter 5:6, 7).*

Whether [every human being] knows it or not, all are weary and heavy-laden. All are weighed down with burdens that only Christ can remove. The heaviest burden that we bear is the burden of sin. If we were left to bear this burden, it would crush us. But the Sinless One has taken our place. "The Lord hath laid on Him the iniquity of us all" (Isaiah 53:6). He has borne the burden of our guilt. He will take the load from our weary shoulders. He will give us rest. The burden of our care and sorrow also He will bear. He invites us to cast our cares upon Him; for He carries us upon His heart. Not until we stand face to face with God, when we shall see as we are seen and know as we are known, shall we know how many burdens the Saviour has borne for us, and how many burdens He would have been glad to bear, had we brought them to Him.

The Elder Brother of our race is by the eternal throne. He looks upon every soul who is turning his face toward Him as the Saviour. He knows by experience what are the weaknesses of humanity, what are our wants, and where lies the strength of our temptations; for "He was in all points tempted like as we are, yet without sin" (Hebrews 4:15). "Come unto Me," is His invitation. The weaker and more helpless you know yourself to be, the stronger will you become in His strength. "In all things it behoved Him to be made like unto His brethren, that He might be a merciful and faithful high priest in things pertaining to God, to make reconciliation for the sins of the people. For in that He Himself hath suffered being tempted, He is able to succour them that are tempted" (Hebrews 2:17, 18).

Human love may change, but Christ's love knows no change. When we cry to Him for help, His hand is stretched out to save.[46]

# Spiritual Sustenance

*"Cast thy burden upon the Lord, and he shall sustain thee"* (Psalm 55:22).

Many of Christ's followers forget the lesson He has bidden us learn from the flowers of the field. They do not trust to His constant care. Christ cannot carry their burden, because they do not cast it upon Him. Therefore the cares of life, which should drive them to the Saviour for help and comfort, separate them from Him.[47]

It is trial that leads us to see what we are. It is the season of temptation that gives a glimpse of one's real character and shows the necessity for the cultivation of good traits. Trusting in the blessing of God, the Christian is safe anywhere. In the city he will not be corrupted. In the counting room he will be marked for his habits of strict integrity. In the mechanic's shop every portion of his work will be done with fidelity, with an eye single to the glory of God.[48]

Do not think that by placing your burdens on others, you can find relief. Come right to the Burden Bearer, and tell Him about them. Believe that He is able and willing to meet the circumstances of your case. When in contrition you come to the foot of the cross, when you have faith in the merits of a crucified and risen Saviour, you will receive power through Him. As you cast your helpless soul upon Him, He gives you peace and joy and strength and courage. Then you are able to tell someone else how precious Christ is to you. You can say, "I sought Him, and found Him precious to my soul." . . .

Those who learn His meekness and lowliness learn also how to love one another as He has loved them. They reach the place where they refuse to criticize and condemn others. They learn that there is committed to them a work that no one else can do for them—the work of learning of Christ. When we place ourselves in His hands, He shows us the possibilities and probabilities before us, and bids us go for help to One infinitely higher than erring human beings.[49]

# The Protection of Angels

*"O Lord, thou preservest man and beast. How excellent is thy lov-*
*ingkindness, O God! therefore the children of men put their trust under*
*the shadow of thy wings" (Psalm 36:6, 7).*

How graciously and tenderly our heavenly Father deals with His children! He preserves them from a thousand dangers to them unseen and guards them from the subtle arts of Satan, lest they should be destroyed. Because the protecting care of God through His angels is not seen by our dull vision, we do not try to contemplate and appreciate the ever-watchful interest that our kind and benevolent Creator has in the work of His hands; and we are not grateful for the multitude of mercies that He daily bestows upon us.[50]

Satan is even now seeking by disasters upon sea and land to seal the fate of as many as possible. What is the defense of the people of God at this time? It is a living connection with heaven. If we would dwell in safety from the noisome pestilence, if we would be preserved from dangers seen and unseen, we must hide in God; we must secure the protecting care of Jesus and holy angels. In these days of peril, the Lord would have us walk before Him in humility. Instead of trying to cover our sins, He would have us confess them.[51]

In all ages, angels have been near to Christ's faithful followers. The vast confederacy of evil is arrayed against all who would overcome; but Christ would have us look to the things which are not seen, to the armies of heaven encamped about all who love God, to deliver them. From what dangers, seen and unseen, we have been preserved through the interposition of the angels, we shall never know, until in the light of eternity we see the providences of God. Then we shall know that the whole family of heaven was interested in the family here below, and that messengers from the throne of God attended our steps from day to day.[52]

31

# Power to Resist Temptation

*"There hath no temptation taken you but such as is common to man: but God is faithful, who will not suffer you to be tempted above that ye are able; but will with the temptation also make a way to escape, that ye may be able to bear it" (1 Corinthians 10:13).*

It is not the absence of temptation or trial that is most favorable for the development of Christian character. Where there are fewest difficulties to meet, the Christian is in the greatest danger of spiritual slothfulness. The God of all grace has promised that His people shall not be tempted above that which they are able to bear, but that with the temptation he will make a way of escape. Constant exposure to rebuffs and opposition will lead the Christian to greater watchfulness and more earnest prayer to the mighty Helper. Extraordinary trials, endured through the grace of God, will give him a deeper experience and greater spiritual strength, as vigilance, patience, and fortitude are called into exercise.[53]

Let not the weakest be discouraged because they are assailed by temptation. The best men who ever lived have been grievously assaulted by Satan and his agents. Unless we yield to its power, temptation is not sin. The armor of truth will prove a sure defense against all the fiery darts of the enemy.

Yet the Christian should not place himself needlessly in the way of temptation.[54]

Remember that temptation is not sin. Remember that however trying the circumstances in which a man may be placed, nothing can really weaken his soul so long as he does not yield to temptation but maintains his own integrity. The interests most vital to you individually are in your own keeping. No one can damage them without your consent. All the satanic legions cannot injure you unless you open your soul to the arrows of Satan. As long as you are firm to do right, your ruin can never take place. If there is not pollution of mind in yourself, all the surrounding pollution cannot taint and defile you.[55]

# Investing in Security

*"The Lord knoweth how to deliver the godly out of temptations"* (2 Peter 2:9).

Jesus was holy and pure; yet He was tempted in all points as we are, but with a strength and power that man will never be called upon to endure. In His successful resistance He has left us a bright example, that we should follow His steps. If we are self-confident or self-righteous we shall be left to fall under the power of temptation; but if we look to Jesus and trust in Him we call to our aid a power that has conquered the foe on the field of battle, and with every temptation He will make a way of escape. When Satan comes in like a flood, we must meet his temptations with the sword of the Spirit, and Jesus will be our helper and will lift up for us a standard against him. The father of lies quakes and trembles when the truth of God, in burning power, is thrown in his face.

Satan makes every effort to lead people away from God; and he is successful in his purpose when the religious life is drowned in business cares, when he can so absorb their minds in business that they will not take time to read their Bibles, to pray in secret, and to keep the offering of praise and thanksgiving burning on the altar of sacrifice morning and evening. How few realize the wiles of the arch-deceiver! how many are ignorant of his devices! When our brethren voluntarily absent themselves from religious meetings, when God is not thought of and reverenced, when He is not chosen as their counselor and their strong tower of defense, how soon secular thoughts and wicked unbelief come in, and vain confidence and philosophy take the place of humble, trusting faith. Often temptations are cherished as the voice of the True Shepherd because men have separated themselves from Jesus. . . .

Whatever position in life we may occupy, whatever our business, we must be humble enough to feel our need of help; we must lean implicitly on the teachings of God's word, acknowledge His providence in all things, and be faithful in pouring out our souls in prayer.[56]

# The Promise of Eternity

*"God hath given to us eternal life, and this life is in his Son. He that hath the Son hath life; and he that hath not the Son of God hath not life"* (1 John 5:11, 12).

Now is the time for us to make sure work for eternity. Christ is pleading in our behalf. Shall we offer ourselves as a free, acceptable sacrifice? Shall we cover up our sins, or shall we confess them, that we may find mercy and grace to help in every time of need? While Christ is pleading in our behalf, shall we not put away and loathe the sins that caused the Son of God such great suffering and death? While Jesus is showing compassion for us, shall we not have compassion for ourselves? Shall we not pour out our souls in repentance and contrition, and receive the promise of a new heart? God says, "As far as the east is from the west, so far hath he removed our transgressions from us" (Psalm 103:12).

If you are violating the law in the least, you stand under the wrath of an offended God. You may have the mercy of God. If you plead for it, you will obtain it. Cast yourself just as you are upon His mercy and compassion. Lay hold of Him by faith. Put away all selfishness, all covetousness. By faith in the blood of Jesus cleanse your soul from moral defilement. Full and free salvation is offered to every one who will fall on the Rock and be broken. There are many who are saying, Lord, Lord, but they trust to their own self-righteousness. Every day they are practicing sin. They are no honor to God; for wherever they go they are like evil leaven.

Why do you not cease from sin? You may overcome if you will cooperate with God. Christ's promise is sure.[57]

Those who believe in Christ derive their motive power and the texture of their characters from Him in whom they believe.[58]

Lift up the man of Calvary. Talk of His love, tell of His power. All the universe is watching to see if you prize the gift of eternal life that has been purchased for you at an infinite cost.[59]

# "Godliness With Contentment"

*"Godliness with contentment is great gain" (1 Timothy 6:6).*

Be less greedy of gain, less self-caring. Redeem your godlike manhood, your noble womanhood, by noble acts of disinterested benevolence. Heartily despise your former avaricious spirit and regain true nobility of soul. From what God has shown me, unless you zealously repent, Christ will spew you out of His mouth. . . .

I appeal to all who profess to believe the truth, to consider the character and life of the Son of God. He is our example. His life was marked with disinterested benevolence. He was ever touched with human woe. He went about doing good. There was not one selfish act in all His life.[60]

Through pride men and women are led to take the position that rendering service to a brother or sister in certain ways has a degrading tendency; but it is just as commendable to serve in what are called menial positions as to minister from the pulpit. There is no degradation in doing the duties that must be done in the house, and there is no humiliation in being able to do well and thoroughly the duties that devolve on a housemaid or a man of all work. It will never injure self-respect to be a good servant if the right view is taken of the subject.

But in whatever branch of the Lord's work you are, you should study to show yourself approved unto God, a workman that needeth not to be ashamed, willing to be taught, ready to learn, faithful in your work, and ever growing in power and efficiency.[61]

Oh, that we could be satisfied with less heart-longings, less striving for things difficult to obtain wherewith to beautify our homes, while that which God values above jewels, the meek and quiet spirit, is not cherished. The grace of simplicity, meekness, and true affection would make a paradise of the humblest home. It is better to endure cheerfully every inconvenience than to part with peace and contentment.[62]

# In Any Situation

*"I have learned, in whatsoever state I am, therewith to be content. I know both how to be abased, and I know how to abound: every where and in all things I am instructed both to be full and to be hungry, both to abound and to suffer need. I can do all things through Christ which strengtheneth me" (Philippians 4:11–13).*

If Paul, troubled on every side, perplexed, persecuted, could call his trials light afflictions, of what has the Christian of today to complain? How trifling are our trials in comparison with Paul's many afflictions! They are not worthy to be compared with the eternal weight of glory awaiting the overcomer. They are God's workmen, ordained for the perfection of character. However great the deprivation and suffering of the Christian, however dark and inscrutable may seem the way of providence, he is to rejoice in the Lord, knowing that all is working for his good.[63]

Whatever may be your circumstances, however dark and mysterious may be the ways of Providence, though the path may be through the deep waters, and trials and bereavements may afflict again and again, the assurance still comes, "All things work together for good to them that love God" (Romans 8:28). "I know whom I have believed, and am persuaded that he is able to keep that which I have committed unto him against that day" (2 Timothy 1:12).[64]

No one is qualified for great and important work unless he has been faithful in the performance of little duties. It is by degrees that the character is formed and that the soul is trained to put forth effort and energy proportionate to the task which is to be accomplished. If we are creatures of circumstance, we shall surely fail of perfecting Christian characters. You must master circumstances, and not allow circumstances to master you. You can find energy at the cross of Christ. You can now grow by degrees, and conquer difficulties, and overcome force of habit. You need to be stimulated by the life-giving force of Jesus.[65]

# The Gift of Trial

*"Our light affliction, which is but for a moment, worketh for us a far more exceeding and eternal weight of glory" (2 Corinthians 4:17).*

While in Portland, . . . I visited localities of special interest in connection with my early life, among them the spot where I met with the accident that has made me a lifelong invalid. This misfortune, which for a time seemed so bitter and was so hard to bear, has proved to be a blessing in disguise. The cruel blow which blighted the joys of earth was the means of turning my eyes to heaven. I might never have known Jesus, had not the sorrow that clouded my early years led me to seek comfort in Him.

I have read of a little bird that while his cage is full of light never sings the songs his master would teach him. He will listen, and learn a snatch of this, a trill of that, but never a separate and entire melody. But the master covers his cage, and then, in the dark, he listens to the one song he is to sing. He tries and tries again to sing that song, until it is learned, and he breaks forth in perfect melody; and then the cage is uncovered, and ever after he can sing it in the light. Thus God deals with His creatures. He has a song to teach us, and when we have learned it amid the deep shadows of affliction, we can sing it ever afterward.[66]

In the future we shall see how closely all our trials were connected with our salvation, and how these light afflictions worked out for us "a far more exceeding and eternal weight of glory" (2 Corinthians 4:17).[67]

Trials . . . are an evidence that we are children of God. Paul passed through great trials, but he did not despair as though his Father in heaven were dead. He rejoiced in tribulation; for he desired, through participation in the sufferings of Christ, to be conformed to His image. Let this hero of faith speak for himself. He says, "I take pleasure in infirmities, in reproaches, in necessities, in persecution, in distresses for Christ's sake" (2 Corinthians 12:10).[68]

# Sure Victory

*"Thanks be to God, which giveth us the victory through our Lord Jesus Christ. Therefore, my beloved brethren, be ye stedfast, unmoveable, always abounding in the work of the Lord, forasmuch as ye know that your labour is not in vain in the Lord" (1 Corinthians 15:57, 58).*

In order to overcome . . . wrong habits, you must watch unto prayer. You should now be thoroughly in earnest, for you have little time in which to work. Do not feel that you are sufficient in your own strength. Only in the name of the mighty Conqueror can you gain the victory. In conversation with others dwell upon the mercy, goodness, and love of God instead of upon His strict judgment and justice. Cling fast to His promises. You can do nothing in your own strength, but in the strength of Jesus you can do all things. If you are in Christ, and Christ is in you, you will be transformed, renewed, and sanctified. "If ye abide in Me, and My words abide in you, ye shall ask what ye will, and it shall be done unto you" (John 15:7). Be sure that Christ is in you, that your heart is broken and submissive and humble. God will accept only the humble and contrite. Heaven is worth a lifelong, persevering effort; yes, it is worth everything.[69]

Could we but behold the joy in the heavenly courts at the news that one sinner has repented and turned to God, could we hear the anthems of praise ascend before the throne with the music of the angel harpers, we would not be so listless, so indifferent in the work which God has left for us to do.[70]

Shall we obtain strength from God, and win victory after victory, or shall we try in our own strength, and at last fall back defeated, worn out by vain effort? Victory is sure when self is surrendered to God. . . .

And when we obtain the blessing, let us not selfishly hoard it. Let us use for the help of some struggling fellow being the strength that we have gained.[71]

# Opportunities to Serve Others

*"I heard the voice of the Lord, saying, Whom shall I send, and who will go for us? Then said I, Here am I; send me" (Isaiah 6:8).*

It is not more mighty men, not more talented men, not more learned men, that we need in the presentation of the truth for this time; but men who have a knowledge of God and Jesus Christ, whom He has sent. Personal piety will qualify any worker, for the Holy Spirit takes possession of him, and the truth for this time becomes a power, because his everyday thoughts, and all his activities are running in Christ's lines. He has an abiding Christ; and the humblest soul, linked with Christ Jesus, is a power, and his work will abide.[72]

Many do not realize their accountability to God. They are handling their Lord's talents; they have powers of mind, that, if employed in the right direction, would make them coworkers with Christ and His angels. Many souls might be saved through their efforts, to shine as stars in the crown of their rejoicing. But they are indifferent to all this. Satan has sought, through the attractions of this world, to enchain them and paralyze their moral powers, and he has succeeded only too well.

How can houses and lands compare in value with precious souls for whom Christ died? Through your instrumentality, dear brethren and sisters, these souls may be saved with you in the kingdom of glory; but you cannot take with you there the smallest portion of your earthly treasure. Acquire what you may, preserve it with all the jealous care you are capable of exercising, and yet the mandate may go forth from the Lord, and in a few hours a fire which no skill can quench, may destroy the accumulations of your entire life, and lay them a mass of smoldering ruins. You may devote all your talent and energy to laying up treasures on earth; but what will they advantage you when your life closes or Jesus makes His appearance?"[73]

# A Gift for Those Willing to Obey

*"The God of our fathers raised up Jesus, . . . and we are his witnesses of these things; and so is also the Holy Ghost, whom God hath given to them that obey him"* (Acts 5:30, 31).

"You have the word of the living God, and for the asking you may have the gift of the Holy Spirit to make that word a power to those who believe and obey."[1]

There is truth in Jesus that is terrible to the ease-loving, do-nothing ones. There is truth in Jesus that is full of soothing joy to the obedient. It is the joy of the Holy Ghost.[2]

There are three living persons of the heavenly trio. In the name of these three great powers—the Father, the Son, and the Holy Ghost, those who receive Christ by living faith are baptized and these powers will cooperate with the obedient subjects of heaven in their efforts to live the new life in Christ.[3]

There is a class of persons who are not following the example of Christ in keeping God's law, yet they claim to be holy. They are ready to appropriate the promises of God without fulfilling the conditions upon which they are given. But their faith has no foundation; it is like sliding sand. There is another class who see the claims of the law of God, and, although it involves a cross, they choose the path of obedience, coming out and separating themselves from the world. They do not consult convenience, nor shrink from accepting the truth for fear of reproach. They step out from the path of transgression, and place their feet in the way of God's commandments. The promises of God, which are given on condition of obedience, are for those who walk in the light of His holy word. Those who do His will may claim all the benefits the Lord has promised.[4]

We can receive of heaven's light only as we are willing to be emptied of self. We cannot discern the character of God, or accept Christ by faith, unless we consent to the bringing into captivity of every thought to the obedience of Christ. To all who do this the Holy Spirit is given without measure.[5]

# Power Gained by Trusting

*"What the law could not do, in that it was weak through the flesh, God sending his own Son in the likeness of sinful flesh, and for sin, condemned sin in the flesh: that the righteousness of the law might be fulfilled in us, who walk not after the flesh, but after the Spirit"* (Romans 8:3, 4).

The terms of the "old covenant" were, Obey and live: "If a man do, he shall even live in them" (Ezekiel 20:11; Leviticus 18:5); but "cursed be he that confirmeth not all the words of this law to do them" (Deuteronomy 27:26). The "new covenant" was established upon "better promises"—the promise of forgiveness of sins and of the grace of God to renew the heart and bring it into harmony with the principles of God's law. "This shall be the covenant that I will make with the house of Israel; after those days, saith the Lord, *I will put my law* in their inward parts, *and write it in their hearts. . . .* I will *forgive* their iniquity, and will remember their sin no more" (Jeremiah 31:33, 34).

The same law that was engraved upon the tables of stone is written by the Holy Spirit upon the tables of the heart. Instead of going about to establish our own righteousness we accept the righteousness of Christ. His blood atones for our sins. His obedience is accepted for us. Then the heart renewed by the Holy Spirit will bring forth "the fruits of the Spirit." Through the grace of Christ we shall live in obedience to the law of God written upon our hearts. Having the Spirit of Christ, we shall walk even as He walked.[6]

The Saviour overcame to show man how he may overcome. All the temptations of Satan, Christ met with the word of God. By trusting in God's promises, He received power to obey God's commandments, and the tempter could gain no advantage.[7]

By His humanity, Christ touched humanity; by His divinity, He lays hold upon the throne of God. As the Son of man, He gave us an example of obedience; as the Son of God, He gives us power to obey.[8]

# What Does the Holy Spirit Do?

*"When [the Comforter] is come, he will reprove the world of sin, and of righteousness, and of judgment" (John 16:8).*

It is through the mighty agency of the Holy Spirit that the government of Satan is to be subdued and subjected. It is the Holy Spirit that convinces of sin and expels it from the soul by the consent of the human agent. The mind is then brought under a new law, and that law is the royal law of liberty. Jesus came to break the shackles of sin-slavery from the soul; for sin can triumph only when the liberty of the soul is extinguished. Jesus reached to the very depth of human woe and misery, and His love attracts man to Himself. Through the agency of the Holy Spirit, He lifts the mind up from its degradation, and fastens it upon the eternal reality. Through the merits of Christ man may be able to exercise the noblest powers of his being and expel sin from his soul.[9]

The Holy Spirit flatters no man, neither does [He] work according to the devising of any man. Finite, sinful men are not to work the Holy Spirit. When [He] shall come as a reprover, through any human agent whom God shall choose, it is man's place to hear and obey [His] voice.[10]

We are not in the place where our fathers were. Advanced light is shining upon us in these last days. We cannot be accepted of God; we cannot honor Him by rendering the same service, doing the same work that our fathers did. In order to be accounted guiltless before God, we must be as faithful in our time in following and obeying our light, as they were faithful in following and obeying the light that shone upon them. Of every individual member of His church, our heavenly Father requires faith and fruits according to the grace and light given. God cannot accept less.[11]

There is no help for man, woman, or child who will not hear and obey the voice of duty; for the voice of duty is the voice of God.[12]

# A Peculiar, Happy Life

*"They that are Christ's have crucified the flesh with the affections and lusts. If we live in the Spirit, let us also walk in the Spirit" (Galatians 5:24, 25).*

The converted will feel a continual longing desire that their friends shall forsake all for Christ, knowing that, unless they do, there will be a final and eternal separation. The true Christian cannot, while with unbelieving friends, be light and trifling. The value of the souls for whom Christ died is too great.

He "that forsaketh not all that he hath," says Jesus, "cannot be My disciple" (Luke 14:33). Whatever shall divert the affections from God must be given up. Mammon is the idol of many. Its golden chain binds them to Satan. Reputation and worldly honor are worshiped by another class. The life of selfish ease and freedom from responsibility is the idol of others. These are Satan's snares, set for unwary feet. But these slavish bands must be broken; the flesh must be crucified with the affections and lusts. We cannot be half the Lord's and half the world's.[13]

You gave yourself to God, to be His wholly, to serve and obey Him, and you took Christ as your Saviour. You could not yourself atone for your sins or change your heart; but having given yourself to God, you believe that He for Christ's sake did all this for you. By *faith* you became Christ's, and by faith you are to grow up in Him—by giving and taking. You are to give all—your heart, your will, your service—give yourself to Him to obey all His requirements; and you must *take* all—Christ, the fullness of all blessing, to abide in your heart, to be your strength, your righteousness, your everlasting helper—to give you power to obey.[14]

Those who are connected with Christ have happiness at their command. They follow in the path where their Saviour leads, for His sake crucifying self with the affections and lusts. These persons have built their hopes on Christ, and the storms of earth are powerless to sweep them from the sure foundation.[15]

# Keep His Words—Reap a Blessing!

*"If a man love me, he will keep my words: and my Father will love him, and we will come unto him, and make our abode with him. . . . The Holy Ghost, whom the Father will send in my name, he shall teach you all things, and bring all things to your remembrance, whatsoever I have said unto you" (John 14:23, 26).*

Obedience is doing the word of Christ. The word of God is a channel of communication with the living God. He who feeds upon the word will become fruitful in all good works. He who labors together with God will be the discoverer of rich mines of truth which he must work to find the hidden treasure. When surrounded with temptations, the Holy Spirit will bring to his mind the very words with which to meet the temptation at the very moment when they are most needed, and he can use them effectually with commanding power.[16]

Christ gives us direction as to how we should pray. We are to come to our heavenly Father with the simplicity of a child, asking Him for the gift of the Holy Spirit. Jesus says again, "When ye pray, believe that ye receive the things ye ask for, and ye shall have them." You are to come to the Father repenting and confessing your sins, emptying the soul of every sin and defilement, and it is your privilege to prove the promises of the Lord. You cannot indulge your own temper, and have your own way, and still remain the children of God. We shall have to struggle with our hereditary tendencies, that we may not yield to temptation, and become angry under provocation. I have to battle every day with things that trouble, perplex, and annoy me, and which, if I would permit, would destroy my peace. But I dare not yield to temptation; I have riveted my soul to the eternal Rock, and Christ must be my helper at every point, so that Satan may not keep me in a state of perplexity and trouble. Jesus has said, "My peace I give unto you." As surely as we seek for the peace of Christ by faith, we shall obtain it. Jesus says, "Ask, and ye shall receive" (John 14:27; 16:24).[17]

# Ask for the Gift;
# Comply With the Conditions

*"He that keepeth his commandments dwelleth in him, and he in him. And hereby we know that he abideth in us, by the Spirit which he hath given us" (1 John 3:24).*

A revival of true godliness among us is the greatest and most urgent of all our needs. To seek this should be our first work. There must be earnest effort to obtain the blessing of the Lord, not because God is not willing to bestow His blessing upon us, but because we are unprepared to receive it. Our heavenly Father is more willing to give His Holy Spirit to them that ask Him, than are earthly parents to give good gifts to their children. But it is our work, by confession, humiliation, repentance, and earnest prayer, to fulfill the conditions upon which God has promised to grant us His blessing.[18]

Jesus says: "Follow me." "He that followeth me shall not walk in darkness, but shall have the light of life" (John 8:12). Consider it not a hard duty. The commandments of God are His expressed character flowing out of a heart of love in thoughtful plans that man may be preserved from every evil. They are not to exercise an arbitrary authority over man, but the Lord would have men act as His obedient children, members of His own family. Obedience is the outgrowth and fruit of oneness with Christ and the Father. . . .

When we unmistakably hear His voice and obey, every murmuring thought will be repressed; and we will leave all consequences with Him who gave the commandment. If, as we see the footprints of Jesus, we step in them and follow Him, we shall have love and power.[19]

We are to watch and to pray, to keep our souls in the love of God, that we may render unto Him willing obedience. We are to cherish every ray of light received through searching the Scriptures. The Holy Spirit will work upon the heart of him who is sincere and earnest in seeking for God's blessing, and will enable him to resist temptation.[20]

# The True Metal of Character

*"The Holy Ghost . . . is a witness to us: for after that he had said before, This is the covenant that I will make with them after those days, saith the Lord, I will put my laws into their hearts, and in their minds will I write them" (Hebrews 10:15, 16).*

Those who exercise true faith in Christ make it manifest by holiness of character, by obedience to the law of God. They realize that the truth as it is in Jesus reaches heaven, and compasses eternity. They understand that the Christian's character should represent the character of Christ, and be full of grace and truth. To them is imparted the oil of grace, which sustains a never-failing light. The Holy Spirit in the heart of the believer makes him complete in Christ. It is not a decided evidence that a man or a woman is a Christian because he [or she] manifests deep emotion when under exciting circumstances. He who is Christlike has a deep, determined, persevering element in his soul, and yet has a sense of his own weakness, and is not deceived and misled by the devil, and made to trust in himself. He has a knowledge of the word of God, and knows that he is safe only as he places his hand in the hand of Jesus Christ and keeps firm hold upon Him.

Character is revealed by a crisis. When the earnest voice proclaimed at midnight, "Behold, the bridegroom cometh; go ye out to meet him" (Matthew 25:6). the sleeping virgins roused from their slumbers, and it was seen who had made preparation for the event. Both parties were taken unawares, but one was prepared for the emergency, and the other was found without preparation. Character is revealed by circumstances. Emergencies bring out the true metal of character. Some sudden and unlooked-for calamity, bereavement, or crisis, some unexpected sickness or anguish, something that brings the soul face to face with death, will bring out the true inwardness of the character. It will be made manifest whether or not there is any real faith in the promises of the word of God.[21]

# Obeying From the Depth of the Heart

*"Obey my voice, and I will be your God, and ye shall be my people: and walk ye in all the ways that I have commanded you, that it may be well unto you" (Jeremiah 7:23).*

We may each obey and live, or we may transgress God's law, defy His authority, and receive the punishment that is meet. Then to every soul the question comes home with force, Shall I obey the voice from heaven, the ten words spoken from Sinai, or shall I go with the multitude who trample on that fiery law? To those who love God it will be the highest delight to keep His commandments, and to do those things that are pleasing in His sight. But the natural heart hates the law of God, and wars against its holy claims. Men shut their souls from the divine light, refusing to walk in it as it shines upon them. They sacrifice purity of heart, the favor of God, and their hope of heaven, for selfish gratification or worldly gain.

Says the psalmist, "The law of the Lord is perfect" (Psalm 19:7). How wonderful in its simplicity, its comprehensiveness and perfection, is the law of Jehovah! It is so brief that we can easily commit every precept to memory, and yet so far-reaching as to express the whole will of God, and to take cognizance, not only of the outward actions, but of the thoughts and intents, the desires and emotions, of the heart. Human laws cannot do this. They can deal with the outward actions only. A man may be a transgressor, and yet conceal his misdeeds from human eyes; he may be a criminal—a thief, a murderer, or an adulterer—but so long as he is not discovered, the law cannot condemn him as guilty. The law of God takes note of the jealousy, envy, hatred, malignity, revenge, lust, and ambition that surge through the soul, but have not found expression in outward action, because the opportunity, not the will, has been wanting.[22]

Let all remember that there is not a motive in the heart of any man that the Lord does not clearly see. The motives of each one are weighed as carefully as if the destiny of the human agent depended upon this one result.[23]

# Take Heed to That Still, Small Voice

*"Whether it be good, or whether it be evil, we will obey the voice of the Lord our God, to whom we send thee; that it may be well with us, when we obey the voice of the Lord our God" (Jeremiah 42:6).*

Take heed today to the voice of the Holy Spirit. Thank God it is not too late for wrongs to be righted. Now is the accepted time, now is the day of salvation.[24]

The Spirit of God does not interfere with the freedom of the human agent. The Holy Spirit is given to be a helper, so that the human agent may cooperate with the divine intelligences, and it is its province to draw the soul but never to force obedience. Christ is ready to impart all heavenly influences. He knows every temptation that comes to man, and the capabilities of every human agent. He knows every temptation that comes to man, and the capabilities of every human agent. He weighs his strength. He sees the present and the future, and presents before the mind the obligations that should be met, and urges that common, earthly things shall not be permitted to be so absorbing that eternal things shall be lost out of the reckoning. The Lord has fulness of grace to bestow on every one that will receive the heavenly gift. The Holy Spirit will bring the God-entrusted capabilities into Christ's service, and will mold and fashion the human agent according to the divine Pattern, in proportion as the human agent shall earnestly desire the transformation.[25]

No one can abide in Christ and treat the law of God with indifference and disrespect; for this would be arraying Christ against Christ. In a heart renewed by the Spirit of truth there will be love for all the commandments of God. . . . Jesus plainly stated that when we treasure up His words and do them, we give evidence that we have that genuine love which makes us one with the Father. We are one in taste and inclination. The Spirit of Jesus fills the Christian with His love, His obedience, His joy.[26]

# The Result of Surrendering

*"If ye love me, keep my commandments. And I will pray the Father, and he shall give you another Comforter, that he may abide with you for ever; even the Spirit of truth" (John 14:15–17).*

Christ has promised the gift of the Holy Spirit to His church, and the promise belongs to us as much as to the first disciples. But like every other promise, it is given on conditions. There are many who believe and profess to claim the Lord's promise; they talk *about* Christ and *about* the Holy Spirit, yet receive no benefit. They do not surrender the soul to be guided and controlled by the divine agencies. We cannot use the Holy Spirit. The Spirit is to use us. Through the Spirit God works in His people "to will and to do of His good pleasure" (Philippians 2:13). But many will not submit to this. They want to manage themselves. This is why they do not receive the heavenly gift. Only to those who wait humbly upon God, who watch for His guidance and grace, is the Spirit given. The power of God awaits their demand and reception. This promised blessing, claimed by faith, brings all other blessings in its train. It is given according to the riches of the grace of Christ, and He is ready to supply every soul according to the capacity to receive.[27]

God has given us specific directions so that no one need err. "Man shall not live by bread alone," He says, "but by every word that proceedeth out of the mouth of God" (Matthew 4:4). The truth given by inspiration "is profitable for doctrine, for reproof, for correction, for instruction in righteousness" (2 Timothy 3:16). Not by one word, not by many words, but by *every word* that God has spoken, shall man live. You cannot disregard one word, a single injunction that He has given, however trifling it may seem to you, and be safe.[28]

The impartation of the Spirit is the impartation of the life of Christ. Those only who are thus taught of God, those only who possess the inward working of the Spirit, and in whose life the Christ-life is manifested, can stand as true representatives of the Saviour.[29]

# Strengthened for Spiritual Victory

*"If ye will obey my voice indeed, and keep my covenant, then ye shall be a peculiar treasure unto me above all people: for all the earth is mine: and ye shall be unto me a kingdom of priests, and an holy nation"* *(Exodus 19:5, 6).*

God takes men as they are, and educates them for His service, if they will yield themselves to Him. The Spirit of God, received into the soul, quickens all its faculties. Under the guidance of the Holy Spirit, the mind that is devoted unreservedly to God, develops harmoniously, and is strengthened to comprehend and fulfil the requirements of God. The weak, vacillating character becomes changed to one of strength and steadfastness. Continual devotion establishes so close a relation between Jesus and His disciples that the Christian becomes like his Master in character. He has clearer, broader views. His discernment is more penetrative, his judgment better balanced. So quickened is he by the life-giving power of the Sun of Righteousness, that he is enabled to bear much fruit to the glory of God.

Christ promised that the Holy Spirit should abide with those who wrestle for victory over sin, to demonstrate the power of divine might by endowing the human agent with supernatural strength and instructing the ignorant in the mysteries of the kingdom of God. Of what avail would it be to us that the only begotten Son of God humbled Himself, endured the temptations of the wily foe, and died, the just for the unjust, if the Spirit had not been given as a constant, working, regenerating agent, to make effectual in each individual case what has been wrought out by the world's Redeemer? . . .

Today this Spirit is constantly at work, seeking to draw the attention of men to the great sacrifice made upon the cross of Calvary, to unfold to the world the love of God to man, and to open to the convicted soul the promises of the Scriptures.[30]

# Walking in the Spirit

*"Walk in the Spirit, and ye shall not fulfil the lust of the flesh"*
*(Galatians 5:16).*

When one is fully emptied of self, when every false god is cast out of the soul, the vacuum is filled by the inflowing of the Spirit of Christ. Such a one has the faith that purifies the soul from defilement. He is conformed to the Spirit, and he minds the things of the Spirit. He has no confidence in self. Christ is all and in all. He receives with meekness the truth that is constantly being unfolded, and gives the Lord all the glory, saying, "God hath revealed them unto us by His Spirit." "Now we have received, not the spirit of the world, but the spirit which is of God; that we might know the things that are freely given to us of God" (1 Corinthians 2:10, 12).

The Spirit that reveals, also works in him the fruits of righteousness. Christ is in him, "a well of water springing up into everlasting life" (John 4:14). He is a branch of the True Vine, and bears rich clusters of fruit to the glory of God. What is the character of the fruit borne? The fruit of the Spirit is "love," not hatred; "joy," not discontent and mourning; "peace," not irritation, anxiety, and manufactured trials. It is "long suffering, gentleness, goodness, faith, meekness, temperance" (Galatians 5:22, 23).[31]

It is the Spirit that causes to shine into darkened minds the bright beams of the Sun of Righteousness; that makes men's hearts burn within them with an awakened realization of the truths of eternity; that presents before the mind the great standard of righteousness, and convinces of sin; that inspires faith in Him who alone can save from sin; that works to transform character by withdrawing the affections of men from those things which are temporal and perishable, and fixing them upon the eternal inheritance. The Spirit recreates, refines, and sanctifies human beings, fitting them to become members of the royal family, children of the heavenly King.[32]

51

# A Thorough Purging

*"He shall baptize you with the Holy Ghost, and with fire: whose fan is in his hand, and he will thoroughly purge his floor" (Matthew 3:11, 12).*

Already the judgments of God are abroad in the land, as seen in storms, in floods, in tempests, in earthquakes, in perils by land and by sea. The great I AM is speaking to those who make void His law. When God's wrath is poured out upon the earth, who will then be able to stand? Now is the time for God's people to show themselves true to principle. When the religion of Christ is most held in contempt, when His law is most despised, then should our zeal be the warmest and our courage the most unflinching. To stand in defense of truth and righteousness when the majority forsake us, to fight the battles of the Lord when champions are few—this will be our test. At this time we must gather warmth from the coldness of others, courage from their cowardice, and loyalty from their treason. The nation will be on the side of the great rebel leader.

The days of purification of the church are hastening on space. God will have a people pure and true. In the mighty sifting soon to take place, we shall be better able to measure the strength of Israel. The signs reveal that the time is near when the Lord will manifest that His fan is in His hand, and that He soon will thoroughly purge His floor.

The days are fast approaching when there will be great perplexity and confusion. Satan, clothed in angel robes, will deceive, if possible, the very elect. There will be gods many and lords many. Every wind of doctrine will be blowing. . . .

In the time when [God's] wrath shall go forth in judgments, the humble, devoted followers of Christ will be distinguished from the rest of the world by their soul anguish, which will be expressed in lamentation and weeping, reproofs and warnings. While others try to throw a cloak over the existing evil, and excuse the great wickedness everywhere prevalent, those who have a zeal for God's honor and a love for souls will not hold their peace to obtain favor of any.[33]

# Reproof That Reforms

*"Turn you at my reproof: behold, I will pour out my spirit unto you, I will make known my words unto you" (Proverbs 1:23).*

To effect the salvation of men, God employs various agencies. He speaks to them by His word and by His ministers, and He sends by the Holy Spirit messages of warning, reproof, and instruction. These means are designed to enlighten the understanding of the people, to reveal to them their duty and their sins, and the blessings which they may receive, to awaken in them a sense of spiritual want, that they may go to Christ and find in Him the grace they need. But many choose to follow their own way instead of God's way. They are not reconciled to God, neither can be, until self is crucified and Christ lives in the heart by faith.[34]

Every warning, reproof, and entreaty in the word of God or through His messengers is a knock at the door of the heart. It is the voice of Jesus asking for entrance. With every knock unheeded, the disposition to open becomes weaker. The impressions of the Holy Spirit if disregarded today, will not be as strong tomorrow. The heart becomes less impressible, and lapses into a perilous unconsciousness of the shortness of life, and of the great eternity beyond. Our condemnation in the judgment will not result from the fact that we have been in error, but from the fact that we have neglected heaven-sent opportunities for learning what is truth.[35]

In seeking to correct or reform others we should be careful of our words. They will be a savor of life unto life or of death unto death. In giving reproof or counsel, many indulge in sharp, severe speech, words not adapted to heal the wounded soul. By these ill-advised expressions the spirit is chafed, and often the erring ones are stirred to rebellion. All who would advocate the principles of truth need to receive the heavenly oil of love. Under all circumstances reproof should be spoken in love. Then our words will reform but not exasperate. Christ by His Holy Spirit will supply the force and the power. This is His work.[36]

# Spiritual Nourishment

*"It is the spirit that quickeneth; the flesh profiteth nothing: the words that I speak unto you, they are spirit, and they are life" (John 6:63).*

There is danger of those in our ranks making a mistake in regard to receiving the Holy Ghost. Many suppose an emotion or a rapture of feeling to be an evidence of the presence of the Holy Spirit. There is danger that right sentiments will not be understood, and that Christ's words, "Teaching them to observe all things whatsoever I have commanded you" (Matthew 28:20), will lose their significance. There is danger that original devisings and superstitious imaginings will take the place of the Scriptures. Tell our people: "Be not anxious to bring in something not revealed in the Word. Keep close to Christ."[37]

It is in eating the words of Christ that we eat the flesh and drink the blood of the Son of God. In obedience to His word, we become partakers of His divine nature in the same way in which we are composed of the food we eat. Those who eat the flesh and drink the blood of the Son of God become one in spiritual life with Christ. No human being can be nourished by the food which another eats. He must eat for himself.[38]

The creative energy that called the worlds into existence is in the word of God. This word imparts power; it begets life. Every command is a promise; accepted by the will, received into the soul, it brings with it the life of the Infinite One. It transforms the nature and re-creates the soul in the image of God.

The life thus imparted is in like manner sustained. "By every word that proceedeth out of the mouth of God" (Matthew 4:4) shall man live.

The mind, the soul, is built up by that upon which it feeds; and it rests with us to determine upon what it shall be fed. It is within the power of everyone to choose the topics that shall occupy the thoughts and shape the character.[39]

# Creative Power Available

*"The spirit of God hath made me, and the breath of the Almighty hath given me life" (Job 33:4).*

Men and women are to begin at the beginning, seeking God most earnestly for a true Christian experience. They are to feel the creative power of the Holy Spirit. They are to receive the new heart, that is kept soft and tender by the grace of heaven. The selfish spirit is to be cleansed from the soul. They are to labor earnestly and with humility of heart, each one looking to Jesus for guidance and encouragement. Then the building, fitly framed together, will grow into a holy temple in the Lord.[40]

As the man is converted by the truth, the work of transformation of character goes on. He has an increased measure of understanding, in becoming a man of obedience to God. The mind and will of God become his will, and by constantly looking to God for counsel, he becomes a man of increased understanding. There is a general development of the mind that is unreservedly placed under the guidance of the Spirit of God. This is not a one-sided education, which develops a one-sided character; but there is revealed a harmoniously developed character. Weaknesses that have been seen in the powerless, vacillating character are overcome, and continual devotion and piety bring the man in such close relation to Jesus Christ that he has the mind of Christ. He is one with Christ, having soundness and strength of principle, and clearness of perception, which is that wisdom that comes from God, who is the source of all light and understanding. The grace of God has fallen upon the humble, obedient, conscientious soul like the Sun of righteousness, strengthening the mental faculties, and in the most astonishing manner making those who long to use their capacity in the Master's service, small though it may be, strong continually by obedience and practice, and grow in grace and in the knowledge of Jesus Christ, and be bearers of much fruit to the glory of God, in good works.[41]

# Walking After the Spirit

*"That which is born of the flesh is flesh; and that which is born of the Spirit is spirit" (John 3:6).*

God is clothed with power; He is able to take those who are dead in trespasses and sins, and by the operation of the Spirit which raised Jesus from the dead, transform the human character, bringing back to the soul the lost image of God. Those who believe in Jesus Christ are changed from being rebels against the law of God into obedient servants and subjects of His kingdom. They are born again, regenerated, sanctified through the truth.[42]

In order to serve [God] aright, we must be born of the divine Spirit. This will purify the heart and renew the mind, giving us a new capacity for knowing and loving God. It will give us a willing obedience to all His requirements. This is true worship. It is the fruit of the working of the Holy Spirit.[43]

As many as are led by the Spirit of God, they are the sons of God. They are united to Christ as the branches are united to the one living vine. They walk not after the flesh, but after the Spirit. These are living examples of Christianity in the world. They are called Christians because they are like Christ and because Christ is in them. Of a truth they are the light of the world and the salt of the earth. The help of the Spirit and the words of eternal life are their wisdom and their strength. And they are led into all truth because they are willing and obedient.[44]

The willing and obedient who have received the teaching of the Holy Spirit will rejoice in the Lord, saying, 'O give thanks unto the Lord; for he is good: for his mercy endureth forever' (Psalm 106:1). If the people of God rightly appreciated the temporal and spiritual blessings which the Lord has poured upon them through Jesus Christ, continual praise would be upon their lips. We have had an experience in being relieved from spiritual bondage similar to that of the Israelites who were set free from the bondage of Egypt. Have we not had chains of oppression broken, and Red Seas of impossibilities opened up before us?[45]

# The Spirit Given for Missionary Labor

*"He that believeth on me, as the scripture hath said, out of his belly shall flow rivers of living water. (But this spake he of the Spirit, which they that believe on him should receive: for the Holy Ghost was not yet given; because that Jesus was not yet glorified)" (John 7:38, 39).*

Do we believe on Him who is the light of the world? and is Jesus in us a well of water springing up into life eternal? Are we endowed with the Holy Spirit, so that with heavenly wisdom we may meet the emergencies of this age, and counteract as far as possible the movements of the world? It is no time now for the watchman to become sleepy, and cease to be a sentinel upon the walls of Zion. Peculiar and rapid changes will soon take place, and if the church is not asleep, if the followers of Christ watch and pray, they may have light to comprehend and appreciate the movements of the enemy. It is now time earnestly to seek the Lord that every one of you may know what is the will of God in reference to the part you shall act in the conflict; and when you see an opportunity for labor, obey the indication of the Lord. Christ is saying to His people, "Can ye discern the signs of the times?" It is the duty of the watchman to mark these signs, and at the cry of the church, "Watchman, what of the night?" give the correct signal, and not present that which will be misleading and ruinous. Those who have been, and who still are, diligent students of prophecy, are to "prepare the way of the Lord, and to make his paths straight."

God has given to every man a work to do in connection with His kingdom. Each one professing the name of Christ is to be an interested worker, ready to defend the principles of righteousness. The work of the gospel is not to depend solely upon the ministers; every soul should take an active part in advancing the cause of God. . . . In whatever calling the Christian is found, he has his work to do for the Lord in representing Christ to the world. Whatever may be our occupation, we are to be missionaries, having for our chief aim the winning of souls to Christ.[46]

# Protection From Counterfeits

*"When the enemy shall come in like a flood, the Spirit of the Lord shall lift up a standard against him" (Isaiah 59:19).*

I was pointed back to the time of Moses and saw the signs and wonders which God wrought through him before Pharaoh, most of which were imitated by the magicians of Egypt; and that just before the final deliverance of the saints, God would work powerfully for His people, and these modern magicians would be permitted to imitate the work of God.

That time will soon come, and we shall have to keep hold of the strong arm of Jehovah; for all these great signs and mighty wonders of the devil are designed to deceive God's people and overthrow them. Our minds must be stayed upon God, and we must not fear the fear of the wicked, that is, fear what they fear, and reverence what they reverence, but be bold and valiant for the truth. Could our eyes be opened, we should see forms of evil angels around us, trying to invent some new way to annoy and destroy us. And we should also see angels of God guarding us from their power; for God's watchful eye is ever over Israel for good, and He will protect and save His people, if they put their trust in Him. When the enemy shall come in like a flood, the Spirit of the Lord will lift up a standard against him.

Said the angel, "Remember, thou art on the enchanted ground." I saw that we must watch and have on the whole armor and take the shield of faith, and then we shall be able to stand, and the fiery darts of the wicked cannot harm us.[47]

God's people are to keep His commandments, discarding all worldly policy. Having adopted right principles of action, they are to reverence these principles; for they are heaven-born. Obedience to God is of more value to you than gold or silver. Yoking up with Christ, learning His meekness and lowliness, cuts short many a conflict; for when the enemy comes in like a flood, the Spirit of the Lord lifts up a standard against him.[48]

# Teaching Obedience as God Directs

*"Truly I am full of power by the spirit of the Lord, and of judgment, and of might, to declare unto Jacob his transgression, and to Israel his sin" (Micah 3:8).*

In the name and strength of my Redeemer I shall do what I can. I shall warn and counsel and reprove and encourage as the Spirit of God dictates, whether men will hear or whether they will forbear. My duty is not to please myself, but to do the will of my heavenly Father, who has given me my work.[49]

Men hear the words of Christ, but they are not doers of His words. The progressive character of the life of godliness is not agreeable to their ease-loving, selfish habits and desires. They do not partake of the broken body and shed blood of the Saviour of men. They are not willing to crucify "the flesh with the affections and lusts" (Galatians 5:24), that they may be renewed in true holiness, after the image of the Son of God. The word of God that tries the hearts of men, proves them wanting. They have no part in the Saviour's grace, no foundation for hope in His salvation. Says Jesus, "He that is of God heareth God's words" (John 8:47). Those who receive the law and the testimony, and assimilate the truth of God, are partaking of the divine nature, growing up unto the full stature of men and women in Christ Jesus, and the word of truth is working their sanctification. Though they make no boasting profession of holiness, but manifest a meek and quiet spirit, working the works of Christ, they will stand before the throne of God, without spot or wrinkle or any such thing. They will be sanctified and glorified through obedience to the commandments of God, wrought by divine power, through the faith of the Son of God.[50]

You may be assured that so long as my life is spared, I shall not cease to lift a warning voice as I am impressed by the Spirit of God, whether men will hear or whether they will forbear. I have no special wisdom in myself; I am only an instrument in the Lord's hands to do the work He has set for me to do.[51]

# The Secret of True Prosperity

*"Not by might, nor by power, but by my spirit, saith the Lord of hosts" (Zechariah 4:6).*

In the great and measureless gift of the Holy Spirit are contained all of heaven's resources. It is not because of any restriction on the part of God that the riches of His grace do not flow earthward to men. If all were willing to receive, all would become filled with His Spirit.[52]

As the chosen people of God we cannot copy the habits, aims, practices, or fashions of the world. We are not left in darkness to pattern after worldly models and to depend on outward appearance for success. The Lord has told us whence comes our strength. [Zechariah 4:6 quoted.] As the Lord sees fit, He imparts to those who keep His way, power that enables them to exert a strong influence for good. On God they are dependent, and to Him they must give an account of the way in which they use the talents He has entrusted to them. They are to realize that they are God's stewards and are to seek to magnify His name.

Those whose affections are set on God will succeed. They will lose sight of self in Christ, and worldly attractions will have no power to allure them from their allegiance. They will realize that outward display does not give strength. It is not ostentation, outward show, that gives a correct representation of the work that we, as God's chosen people, are to do. . . .

So long as those who claim to believe the truth for this time walk in the way of the Lord, to do justice and judgment, they may expect that the Lord will give them prosperity. But when they choose to wander from the narrow way, they bring ruin upon themselves and upon those who look to them for guidance.[53]

It is only those who render perfect and thorough obedience to God that He will choose. Those who follow the Lord are to be firm and straightforward in obeying His directions. Any deviation to follow human devising or planning disqualifies them from being trustworthy.[54]

# Mental and Moral Vigor

*"Gird up the loins of your mind, be sober, and hope to the end for the grace that is to be brought unto you at the revelation of Jesus Christ; as obedient children" (1 Peter 1:13, 14).*

The wicked one is ever watching for a chance to misrepresent God and to attract the mind to that which is forbidden. If he can, he will fasten the mind upon the things of the world. He will endeavor to excite the emotions, to arouse the passions, to fasten the affections on that which is not for your good; but it is for you to hold every emotion and passion under control, in calm subjection to reason and conscience. Then Satan loses his power to control the mind. The work to which Christ calls us is to the work of progressive conquest over spiritual evil in our characters. Natural tendencies are to be overcome for the natural disposition is to be transformed by the grace of Christ. Appetite and passion must be conquered, and the will must be placed wholly on the side of Christ. This will not be a painful process, if the heart is opened to receive the impression of the Spirit of God.[55]

Though men have fallen through transgression, they may receive moral power from Christ and return to their allegiance. They may receive the Holy Spirit as the representative of the Lord. If they believe the testimony of the Spirit, obey the requirements of the Gospel, following on in the ways of purity and holiness, they shall know that "his going forth is prepared as the morning" (Hosea 6:3).[56]

When I look upon Him whom my sins have pierced, the inspiration from on high comes upon me; and this inspiration may come upon each one of you through the Holy Spirit. Unless you receive the Holy Spirit, you cannot have the love of God in the soul; but through a living connection with Christ, we are inspired with love and zeal and earnestness. We are not as a block of marble, which may reflect the light of the sun, but cannot be imbued with life. We are capable of responding to the bright beams of the Sun of righteousness; for as Christ illuminates our souls, He gives light and life.[57]

# The Spirit Requires Surrender

*"God hath not called us unto uncleanness, but unto holiness. He therefore that despiseth, despiseth not man, but God, who hath also given unto us his holy Spirit" (1 Thessalonians 4:7, 8).*

Paul's sanctification was a constant conflict with self. "I die daily" (1 Corinthians 15:31), he said. Every day his will and his desires conflicted with duty and the will of God. But instead of following inclination, he did the will of God, however unpleasant and crucifying to his nature. If we would press forward to the mark of our high calling in Christ Jesus, we must show that we are emptied of all self, and supplied with the golden oil of grace. God is dealing with us through His providence. From eternity He has chosen us to be His obedient children. He gave His Son to die for us, that we might be sanctified through obedience to the truth, cleansed from all the littleness of self. Now He requires of us a personal work, a personal self-surrender. We are to be controlled by the Holy Spirit. God can be honored only when we who profess to believe in Him are conformed to His image. We are to represent to the world the beauty of holiness, and we shall never enter the gates of the city of God until we perfect a Christlike character. If we, with trust in God, strive for sanctification, we shall receive it. Then, as witnesses for Christ, we may make known what the grace of God has wrought in us.[58]

To have the religion of Christ means that you have absolutely surrendered your all to God, and consented to the guidance of the Holy Spirit. Through the gift of the Holy Spirit moral power will be given you, and not only will you have your former entrusted talents for the service of God, but their efficiency will be greatly multiplied. The surrender of all our powers to God greatly simplifies the problem of life. It weakens and cuts short a thousand struggles with the passions of the natural heart. Religion is as a golden cord that binds the souls of both youth and aged to Christ. Through it the willing and obedient are brought safely through dark and intricate paths to the city of God.[59]

# Evidence of Conversion

*"Hereby know we that we dwell in him, and he in us, because he hath given us of his Spirit" (1 John 4:13).*

Those who exercise true faith in Christ make it manifest by holiness of character, by obedience to the law of God. They realize that the truth as it is in Jesus reaches heaven, and compasses eternity. They understand that the Christian's character should represent the character of Christ, and be full of grace and truth. To them is imparted the oil of grace, which sustains a never-failing light. The Holy Spirit in the heart of the believer, makes him complete in Christ. It is not a decided evidence that a man or a woman is a Christian because he [or she] manifests deep emotion when under exciting circumstances. He who is Christlike has a deep, determined, persevering element in his soul, and yet has a sense of his own weakness, and is not deceived and misled by the devil, and made to trust in himself. He has a knowledge of the word of God, and knows that he is safe only as he places his hand in the hand of Jesus Christ, and keeps firm hold upon Him.[60]

Wherever the holy precepts of God are observed, it is an evidence that the word and the Spirit of God have penetrated the human heart and transformed the natural character.[61]

There must be in the experience that faith that works by love and purifies the soul. The love of Christ will subdue the carnal propensities. The truth not only bears within itself the evidence of its heavenly origin, but proves that by the grace of God's Spirit it is effectual in the purification of the soul. The Lord would have us come to Him daily with all our troubles and confessions of sin, and He can give us rest in wearing His yoke and bearing His burden. His Holy Spirit, with its gracious influences, will fill the soul, and every thought will be brought into subjection to the obedience of Christ.[62]

The Spirit of Jesus fills the Christian with His love, His obedience, His joy.[63]

# What Does the Spirit Reveal?

*"Now we have received, not the spirit of the world, but the spirit which is of God; that we might know the things that are freely given to us of God" (1 Corinthians 2:12).*

When one is fully emptied of self, when every false god is cast out of the soul, the vacuum is filled by the inflowing of the Spirit of Christ. Such a one has the faith that purifies the soul from defilement. He is conformed to the Spirit, and he minds the things of the Spirit. He has no confidence in self. Christ is all and in all. He receives with meekness the truth that is constantly being unfolded, and gives the Lord all the glory.[64]

Let all who understand the abiding claims of the law of God yield implicit obedience to every requirement given in the Word. The convictions of the Holy Spirit are warnings which it is dangerous to disregard.[65]

While the Spirit of God is convicting you of the truth, do not stop to cavil, but believe. Do not find fault, but listen to evidence. Yield your pride to humility, and exchange your prejudice for candor. Confer not with flesh and blood, but surrender all to God. Take the Bible as your guide, and earnestly inquire, "Lord, what wilt thou have me to do?" (Acts 9:6). When you once yield your natural independence and self-will for a childlike, submissive obedience, and are willing to be taught, you will hear the voice of the true Shepherd saying, "This is the way, walk ye in it" (Isaiah 30:21). Christ does not propose to teach the self-conceited and self-willed. It is only the meek whom He pledges to guide in judgment, and to whom He will teach His way. If you are in search of truth, obedience will not be difficult. If you really want to know the Master's will, you will thankfully receive it. We are learners in the school of Christ. A genuine love for Jesus will of necessity create a love for the truth. Treasure up the truth in your heart. Seek knowledge. Make this your daily prayer: "With my whole heart have I sought thee: O let me not wander from thy commandments. . . . Open thou mine eyes, that I may behold wondrous things out of thy law" (Psalm 119:10, 18).[66]

# A Commission and a Comforter

*"When they shall lead you, and deliver you up, take no thought beforehand what ye shall speak, neither do ye premeditate: but whatsoever shall be given you in that hour, that speak ye: for it is not ye that speak, but the Holy Ghost" (Mark 13:11).*

We are not willing enough to trouble the Lord with our petitions, and to ask Him for the gift of the Holy Spirit. The Lord wants us to trouble Him in this matter. He wants us to press our petitions to the throne. The converting power of God needs to be felt throughout our ranks. The most valuable education that can be obtained will be found in going out with the message of truth to the places that are now in darkness. We should go out just as the first disciples went out in obedience to the commission of Christ. . . . "I send you forth," He said, "as sheep in the midst of wolves: be ye therefore wise as serpents, and harmless as doves" (Matthew 10:16). . . .

The Lord wants us to come into harmony with Him. If we will do this, His Spirit can rule our minds.[67]

There is need of close self-examination in the light of the word of God, that we may do the work essential to be done.[68]

The revelation of the Son of God upon the cross, dying for the sins of men, draws the hearts of men by the power of infinite love, and convinces the sinner of sin. Christ died because the law was transgressed, that guilty man might be saved from the penalty of his enormous guilt. But history has proved that it is easier to destroy the world than to reform it; for men crucified the Lord of glory, who came to unite earth with heaven, and man with God.[69]

[Christ] promised His followers that when they should stand before councils and judges, they were to take no thought what they should speak. I will instruct you, He said. I will guide you. Knowing what it is to be taught of God, when words of heavenly wisdom are brought to our mind, we shall distinguish them from our own thoughts. We shall understand them as the words of God, and we shall see in the words of God wisdom and life and power.[70]

# Under the Power of the Holy Spirit

*"The spirit of the Lord God is upon me; because the Lord hath anointed me to preach good tidings unto the meek" (Isaiah 61:1).*

Christ reached the people where they were. He presented the plain truth to their minds in the most forcible and simple language. The humble poor, the most unlearned, could comprehend, through faith in Him, the most exalted truths of God. No one needed to consult the learned doctors as to His meaning. He did not perplex the ignorant with mysterious inferences, or use unaccustomed and learned words, of which they had no knowledge. The greatest Teacher the world has ever known, was the most definite, simple, and practical in His instruction.

Jesus labored constantly for one object; all His powers were employed for the salvation of men, and every act of His life tended to that end. He traveled on foot, teaching His followers as He went. His garments were dusty and travel-stained, and His appearance was uninviting. But the simple, pointed truths which fell from His divine lips soon caused His hearers to forget His appearance, and to be charmed, not with the man, but with the doctrine He taught.[71]

Many in the world set their affections on things that in themselves are not evil; but they become satisfied with these things, and do not seek the greater and higher good that Christ desires to give them. Now we must not rudely seek to deprive them of what they hold dear. Reveal to them the beauty and preciousness of truth. Lead them to behold Christ in His loveliness; then they will turn from everything that would draw their affections away from Him. This is the principle of the Saviour's dealing with men; it is the principle that must be brought into the church. . . .

The world is full of men and women who are carrying a heavy burden of sorrow and suffering and sin. God sends His children to reveal to them Him who will take away the burden and give them rest. It is the mission of Christ's servants to help, to bless, and to heal.[72]

66

# Prerequisites and Promises

*"If ye be willing and obedient, ye shall eat the good of the land"*
*(Isaiah 1:19).*

We need to walk carefully every moment, keeping close to the side of Christ. The spirit and grace of Christ are needed in the life, and the faith that works by love and purifies the soul.

We need to understand clearly the divine requirements that God makes of His people. The law, which is the transcript of His character, no one need fail to understand. The words written by the finger of God on tables of stone so perfectly reveal His will concerning His people that none need make any mistake.[73]

Love for a lost world was manifested every day, in every act of [Christ's] life. Those who are imbued by His Spirit will work in the same lines as those in which Christ worked. . . .

It is through the grace of Christ that the soul sees his need of repentance toward God because of the transgression of His law, and is led to look to Christ by faith, realizing that His merit is efficacious to save to the uttermost all who come unto God by Him.[74]

It is important that all now come up to the work and act as though they were living men, laboring for the salvation of souls who are perishing. If all in the church would come up to the help of the Lord, we would see such a revival of His work as we have not hitherto witnessed. God requires this of you and of each member of the church. It is not left with you to decide whether it is best for you to obey the call of God. Obedience is required; and unless you obey you will stand on worse than neutral ground. Unless you are favored with the blessing of God you have His curse. He requires you to be willing and obedient, and says that you shall eat the good of the land. . . .

You have an individual work in the vineyard of the Lord. You have thought and cared too much for yourselves. Set your hearts in order, and then be in earnest. Inquire: "Lord, what wilt Thou have me to do?" (Acts 9:6).[75]

# A Pure, Honest Government

*"[The Lord] is the Rock, his work is perfect: for all his ways are judgment: a God of truth and without iniquity, just and right is he"* *(Deuteronomy 32:4).*

Every manifestation of creative power is an expression of infinite love. The sovereignty of God involves fullness of blessing to all created beings. The psalmist says: "Strong is Thy hand, and high is Thy right hand. Righteousness and judgment are the foundation of Thy throne: mercy and truth go before Thy face" (Psalm 89:13, 14, RV).[1]

He that ruleth in the heavens is the one who sees the end from the beginning—the one before whom the mysteries of the past and the future are alike outspread, and who, beyond the woe and darkness and ruin that sin has wrought, beholds the accomplishment of His own purposes of love and blessing. Though "clouds and darkness are round about Him: righteousness and judgment are the foundation of His throne" (Psalm 97:2, RV). And this the inhabitants of the universe, both loyal and disloyal, will one day understand.[2]

Our probation is of more value to us than all the gold and silver of the world. Man has been given a second trial; but it was at an infinite cost to heaven that we were granted another opportunity to form characters of which God can approve. Christ united His divinity with humanity. He possessed the qualities of infinite and finite. In His person all excellence dwells. His sacrifice was our ransom from the slavery of sin. By His atonement we are enabled to sit with Him on His throne, and share His glory. Then shall we, with such possibilities before us, show ourselves incapable of appreciating the heavenly gift? As the recipients of His grace, shall we not do our part by working out our salvation with fear and trembling? It is God that works in us both to will and to do of His good pleasure. Man works, and God works; but God can do nothing without man's cooperation.[3]

# A Perfect, Honest Law

*"Thy righteousness is an everlasting righteousness, and thy law is the truth" (Psalm 119:142).*

God gave man a perfect law.[4]

God is omnipotent, omniscient, immutable. He always pursues a straightforward course. His law is truth—immutable, eternal truth. His precepts are consistent with His attributes. But Satan makes them appear in a false light. By perverting them, he seeks to give human beings an unfavorable impression of the Lawgiver. Throughout his rebellion he has sought to represent God as an unjust, tyrannical being.

In the beginning it was Satan's purpose to separate man from God. And this purpose he has carried out in every age. Constantly he is at work among the children of men. He sways all classes. The same method of deception, the same logic, that he used to deceive the holy pair in Eden, he has used in all succeeding ages. His plan of work has ever been one of deception. At times he assumes a cloak of piety, purity, and holiness. Often he transforms himself into an angel of light. He has blinded the eyes of men so that they can not see beneath the surface and discern his real purpose. As a result of Adam's disobedience every human being is a transgressor of the law, sold under sin. Unless he repents and is converted, he is under bondage to the law, serving Satan, falling into the deceptions of the enemy, and bearing witness against the precepts of Jehovah. But by perfect obedience to the requirements of the law, man is justified. Only through faith in Christ is such obedience possible. Men may comprehend the spirituality of the law, they may realize its power as a detector of sin, but they are helpless to withstand Satan's power and deceptions, unless they accept the atonement provided for them in the remedial sacrifice of Christ, who is our Atonement—our At-one-ment—with God.

Those who believe on Christ and obey His commandments are not under bondage to God's law; for to those who believe and obey, His law is not a law of bondage, but of liberty.[5]

# Pure, Flawless Commandments

*"Thou art near, O Lord; and all thy commandments are truth"* *(Psalm 119:151).*

With His own finger God wrote His commandments on two tables of stone. These tables were not left in the keeping of men, but were placed in the ark; and in the great day when every case is decided, these tables, inscribed with the commandments, will be placed so that all the world will see and understand. The witness against them will be unanswerable. . . . The pure truth for this time requires a reformation in the life.[6]

The Lord designed that His church should not receive the commandments of men, but acknowledge His law alone. He designed that the pure, unadulterated truth should be proclaimed in the world. Self-denial and cross-bearing was to characterize His children. They were to represent to the world the character of Christ, and keep before the world a representation of the eternal world; for among them was to be found the spirit, the character, that should be developed by coming under the control of the divine government. They were to be obedient to higher laws than the princes of this world originate, and yield submission to a greater power than kings can command.

While all the world is under the care of God, and angels are commissioned to do service in all parts of it, yet the church is the special object of God's love and care. In the church, He is making experiments of mercy and love, and drawing men to Himself. Through the grace of Christ an amazing transformation is taking place in the corrupt hearts of men. The work wrought in the characters of sinners through the grace of Christ is a greater work than to perform a miracle upon the bodies of men. The old, carnal nature dies, and a new creature appears after the likeness of Christ. At this mighty work, angels look and rejoice. They see that upon this sin-cursed earth, Christ has His training schools. He takes the ignorant children of darkness and of wrath, and brings them as willing subjects to His feet to learn of Him.[7]

# Perfect Guidance

*"When he, the Spirit of truth, is come, he will guide you into all truth" (John 16:13).*

The needed knowledge will be given to all who come to Christ, receiving and practicing His teachings, making His word a part of their lives. The Holy Spirit teaches the student of the Scriptures to judge all things by the standard of righteousness and truth and justice. The divine revelation supplies him with the knowledge that he needs.[8]

The Holy Spirit will guide those who prize the wisdom of God above the deceptive sophistries of satanic agencies. Let there be much praying, not in human lines but under the inspiration and love of the truth as it is in Jesus Christ. The families who believe the truth are to speak words of wisdom and intelligence—words that will come to them as the result of searching the Scriptures. Now is our time of test and trial. Now is the time when the members of every believing family must close their lips against speaking words of accusation concerning their brethren. Let them speak words that impart courage, and strengthen the faith which works by love and purifies the soul.[9]

By faith let the Holy Spirit instruct you, that you may not only receive but impart the heavenly grace.

All is to be surrendered to Christ. There must be no reservation. God expects more of us than we give Him. It is an insult to Jehovah to claim to be Christians and yet speak and act as worldlings. We cannot yield the smallest place to worldly policy. We need to be sanctified every hour through the belief of the truth.[10]

The Holy Spirit will guide and direct those who stand ready to go where God calls, and to speak the words He gives them. The humble, patient, Christlike worker will have something to show for his labors. Everyone who goes forth seeking to do his best will have the support of the One who can supply all his necessities.[11]

# Facing Ourselves Honestly

*"Behold, thou desirest truth in the inward parts: and in the hidden part thou shalt make me to know wisdom" (Psalm 51:6).*

In order to manifest the character of God, in order that we may not deceive ourselves, the church, and the world by a counterfeit Christianity, we must become personally acquainted with God.[12]

What a diligent, constant work is the work of the true Christian. Ever he wears the yoke of Christ. Evil surmisings are not allowed to take root in his heart. He has genuine modesty, and does not talk of his qualifications and accomplishments. Self-admiration is not a part of his experience. There is much to learn in regard to what comprises true Christian character. It certainly is not self-inflation. The true Christian keeps his eyes fixed on Him who searches the heart and tries the reins, who requires truth in the inward parts.[13]

If Christ be in us the hope of glory, we shall discover such matchless charms in Him that the soul will be enamored. It will cleave to Him, choose to love Him, and in admiration of Him, self will be forgotten. Jesus will be magnified and adored, and self abased and humbled. But a profession, without this deep love, is mere talk, dry formality, and heavy drudgery. Many of you may retain a notion of religion in the head, an outside religion, when the heart is not cleansed. God looks at the heart; "all things are naked and opened unto the eyes of Him with whom we have to do" (Hebrews 4:13). Will He be satisfied with anything but truth in the inward parts? Every truly converted soul will carry the unmistakable marks that the carnal mind is subdued. . . .

Determine to know the worst of your case. Ascertain if you have an inheritance on high. Deal truly with your own soul. Remember that a church without spot, or wrinkle, or any such thing, will Jesus present to His Father.

How are you to know that you are accepted of God? Study His word prayerfully. Lay it not aside for any other book. This Book convinces of sin. It plainly reveals the way of salvation.[14]

# Freedom From Fallacy

*"Ye shall know the truth, and the truth shall make you free"* (John 8:32).

Let no one think that he can permit himself to indulge in any sin, however secret it may be, for God requires truth in the inward parts, and in the hidden part wisdom. You need not feel complacency because you are sure that your brethren do not know of your misdeeds. Does not One who is acquainted with your brethren know all about your life? Does not He read your heart as an open book? You cannot indulge in sin and still be a witness for the Lord, for in works you deny Him. Where is the holy boldness that should characterize your faith and prayers because you are not under condemnation before man or God? Where is your ringing testimony on the side of truth?

If you are indulging in any known sin, you cannot utter words to the glory of God, because there is something in your heart that condemns you. The Spirit of God is not in your soul. But let the heart, with all its affections, be surrendered to God, and you will have joy and peace in the Holy Ghost. Your intellect, your ability, your soul, body, and spirit have been purchased at an infinite price by the Son of God, and all belong to Him. And yet, though Christ has redeemed men, how few render to Him that which is His own. How many rob Him in thought. Oh, shall we not gird up the loins of our minds, and bring into captivity every thought to the obedience of Christ, and hope unto the end for grace that shall be given unto us at the revelation of Jesus Christ?[15]

Truth has a spiritual influence. It enters the mind, direct and uncorrupted, from One who is truth. The reception of truth in the inward parts is charged with the greatest results. Truth is to be received into the heart and developed and expressed in the character.

No lie is of the truth. On every occasion possible Satan is on hand to introduce the leaven of his deceptive fallacies. Listen not a moment to the interpretations that would loosen one pin, remove one pillar, from the platform of truth.[16]

# Preserved by Truth in Action

*"Let thy lovingkindness and thy truth continually preserve me"* (*Psalm 40:11*).

The law of self-sacrifice is the law of self-preservation. The seed buried in the ground produces fruit, and in turn this is planted. Thus the harvest is multiplied. The husbandman preserves his grain by casting it away. So in human life, to give is to live. The life that will be preserved is the life that is freely given in service to God and man. Those who for Christ's sake sacrifice their life in this world, will keep it unto life eternal.[17]

The people of God are to preserve the world from complete corruption by their own moral characteristics; but if they lose their moral qualities, they have no value to restore the world from its state of moral pollution. He who preserves his saving qualities and exercises them in benefiting humanity is shedding forth the light of truth and cooperating with Christ. But those who lose their spirituality, whose love waxes cold because of the iniquity that abounds, have a sickly piety, and are as salt when it has lost its savor. Their energy and efficiency are gone.[18]

We have no time now, and should have no disposition, to stand as spectators of the great warfare between good and evil. We should be actively engaged in fighting the good fight of faith, and this will demand all the energies of the mind, all the capabilities and powers of the being. We are to be faithful soldiers, obeying the orders of the Captain of our salvation. We are not to take the Captain's place, but hourly to live in constant contact with Christ. We must know, individually, that we know the truth, not only theoretically, but practically. We must bring its divine principles into our daily life. God requires truth in the inward parts, and in the hidden part wisdom. He requires us to practice righteousness, to manifest patience, mercy, and love. We should carefully review our character in the light of the character of God, as expressed in His holy law. There should be no deviating from the perfect standard.[19]

# A Shield of Protection

*"[The Lord's] truth shall be thy shield and buckler" (Psalm 91:4).*

In the truths of His word, God has given to men a revelation of Himself; and to all who accept them they are a shield against the deceptions of Satan. It is a neglect of these truths that has opened the door to the evils which are now becoming so widespread in the religious world. The nature and the importance of the law of God have been, to a great extent, lost sight of. A wrong conception of the character, the perpetuity, and the obligation of the divine law has led to errors in relation to conversion and sanctification, and has resulted in lowering the standard of piety in the church. Here is to be found the secret of the lack of the Spirit and power of God in the revivals of our time.

There are, in the various denominations, men eminent for their piety, by whom this fact is acknowledged and deplored. Professor Edwards A. Park, in setting forth the current religious perils, ably says: "One source of danger is the neglect of the pulpit to enforce the divine law. In former days the pulpit was an echo of the voice of conscience. . . . Our most illustrious preachers gave a wonderful majesty to their discourses by following the example of the Master, and giving prominence to the law, its precepts, and its threatenings. They repeated the two great maxims, that the law is a transcript of the divine perfections, and that a man who does not love the law does not love the gospel; for the law, as well as the gospel, is a mirror reflecting the true character of God. This peril leads to another, that of underrating the evil of sin, the extent of it, the demerit of it. In proportion to the rightfulness of the commandment is the wrongfulness of disobeying it. . . .

"Affiliated to the dangers already named is the danger of underestimating the justice of God. The tendency of the modern pulpit is to strain out the divine justice from the divine benevolence, to sink benevolence into a sentiment rather than exalt it into a principle. The new theological prism puts asunder what God has joined together."[20]

# The Secret Is to Surrender

*"Into thine hand I commit my spirit: thou hast redeemed me, O Lord God of truth" (Psalm 31:5).*

How many today see the force and beauty of the truth; but they cannot serve God and mammon, and they hold to the world. The truth requires the sacrifice of the world's honor, their position in business, their daily bread; and they falter and fail. They do not consider the promises of God to those who seek first the kingdom of heaven. They raise the excuse, "I cannot be different from those around me. What will people say?" . . . We must not study how to serve ourselves, but how to do the will of God. Christ left His glory, and clothed His divinity with humanity. He was a man of sorrows, and acquainted with grief. For our sakes He became poor, that we through His poverty might be made rich. And yet, after this great manifestation of love on the part of Heaven, we are reluctant to yield our meager treasures, so soon to pass away.[21]

We lie down to rest at night, but in the morning the same old worldly train of thought to which we have been accustomed comes back to our minds, and instead of resting everything in the hands of God, we become troubled about many things, the peace and joy that we had the night before are gone, and we feel desolate and unblessed. Then what shall we do? Let us go to God, and say, "I commit all my troubles and perplexities to Thee, and I know that I shall have Thy help in all my tribulation, because Thou hast promised it unto me. Thou hast said, 'Lo, I am with you alway, even unto the end of the world' (Matthew 28:20). 'I am at your right hand to help you.'" Believe these words, trust in the promise of Jesus, and do your duty as it comes to you. If we manifested as much distrust of our friends as we do of God, they would feel that we had greatly wronged them; but we do not treat our friends in the way we treat our God.[22]

When the Bible is made the study book, with earnest supplication for the Spirit's guidance, and with a full surrender of the heart to be sanctified through the truth, all that Christ has promised will be accomplished.[23]

# Facing Reality

*"If we say that we have no sin, we deceive ourselves, and the truth is not in us" (1 John 1:8).*

We are blind to our own deficiencies. We are not easily impressed with our weakness and the necessity of seeing as far as possible our errors, not to discourage our efforts, but to bring us to reform and thorough reformation.[24]

The more clearly fallen man comprehends the character of Christ, the more distrustful will he be of himself, and the more imperfect will his works appear to him, in contrast with those which marked the life of the spotless Redeemer. But those who are far from Jesus, those whose spiritual perceptions are so clouded by error that they cannot comprehend the character of the great Exemplar, conceive of Him as altogether such a one as themselves.[25]

When we were looking for the Saviour to come in 1844, how great was the anxiety of each to know that his own heart was right before God. When we met together, the question would be asked by one and another, "Brethren, have you seen anything in me that is not right? I know that we are often blind to our own faults, and if you have seen anything wrong in me, I want you to tell me." Sometimes errors would be pointed out, and we would all bow before God and seek forgiveness. If any variance or alienation existed, we felt that we could not separate until all were in harmony. Sometimes brethren who had difficulty would be seen going away together to some secret place to plead with God, and they would return with their hearts knit together in love. The sweet spirit of peace was in our assemblies, and the glory of God was around us. The faces of the believers shone with the light of heaven.[26]

When the enemy comes in like a flood, and seeks to overwhelm you with the thought of your sin, tell him: "I know I am a sinner; if I were not, I could not go to the Saviour, for he says, 'I am not come to call the righteous, but sinners to repentance.' And because I am a sinner, I am entitled to come to Christ." In this way you will have power to overcome the wicked one. Keep looking up, for your faith has bound you to the throne of God.[27]

# Real Charity Based on Real Truth

*"[Charity] rejoiceth not in iniquity, but rejoiceth in the truth"* (1 Corinthians 13:6).

I was shown the necessity of those who believe that we are having the last message of mercy, being separate from those who are daily imbibing new errors. I saw that neither young nor old should attend their meetings; for it is wrong to thus encourage them while they teach error that is a deadly poison to the soul and teach for doctrines the commandments of men. The influence of such gatherings is not good. If God has delivered us from such darkness and error, we should stand fast in the liberty wherewith He has set us free and rejoice in the truth. God is displeased with us when we go to listen to error, without being obliged to go; for unless He sends us to those meetings where error is forced home to the people by the power of the will, He will not keep us. The angels cease their watchful care over us, and we are left to the buffetings of the enemy, to be darkened and weakened by him and the power of his evil angels; and the light around us becomes contaminated with the darkness.

I saw that we have no time to throw away in listening to fables. Our minds should not be thus diverted, but should be occupied with the present truth, and seeking wisdom that we may obtain a more thorough knowledge of our position, that with meekness we may be able to give a reason of our hope from the Scriptures. While false doctrines and dangerous errors are pressed upon the mind, it cannot be dwelling upon the truth which is to fit and prepare the house of Israel to stand in the day of the Lord.[28]

Withhold not the testing truths that should come to every soul at this time, and which must be practiced by those who would find acceptance with God. We are to let the word of God come to every appointed agency, for there is a crisis before the people of God. Labor that souls may receive that word of truth that refines and sanctifies the soul, finding delight in the truth because Christ is identified with truth.[29]

# Walking in the Pathway of Light

*"All the paths of the Lord are mercy and truth unto such as keep his covenant and his testimonies" (Psalm 25:10).*

Do not look down, as though you were bound to earth. Do not keep pulling up your faith to see if it has any root. Faith grows imperceptibly, and when the enemy rallies his forces to bring you into a critical place, the angels of God will be roundabout you, and you will have help from on high; for your prayer will be answered in the conflict. If you have genuine faith, you will praise God, from whom all blessings flow; and as you praise Him, you will realize more of His blessing.

> *"What doth much increase the store,*
> *When I thank Him, He gives me more."*

As God gives us light, we should make use of it; God will not give us a second ray, while the first is not appreciated. We must praise the Lord for the light already graciously given, and reflect it upon those around us. Then more light will shine upon us, and as we praise, we shall know that "the path of the just is as a shining light, that shineth more and more unto the perfect day." Do not say, I will praise the Lord when the Holy Spirit is poured out upon us. How will you know when the Holy Spirit is poured out, unless you walk in the light day by day? You are to go about your duties, advancing step, by step, according to the counsel of the Lord, and you will find that you will have light and peace and joy, and will make melody in your heart unto the Lord. Thus the people of God will mingle their praises with those of the hosts of heaven, and sing songs of thanksgiving with the angels of God.[30]

There is a great work to be done in our world, and we are accountable for every ray of light that shines upon our pathway. Impart that light, and you will receive more light to impart. Great blessing will come to those who use their talents aright.[31]

# Open to All the Truth

*"Lead me in thy truth, and teach me: for thou art the God of my salvation; on thee do I wait all the day" (Psalm 25:5).*

How dangerous is the position of men who, while claiming sanctification, still will not receive the light of the law by which sin is detected! Sanctification is conformity to the will of God, and the will of God is expressed in His holy law. Those only are truly sanctified who live by every word that proceedeth out of the mouth of God.[32]

You should cultivate a spirit of entire submission to the will of God, earnestly, humbly seeking to know His ways and to follow the leadings of His Spirit. You must not lean to your own understanding. You should have deep distrust of your own wisdom and supposed prudence. Your condition demands these cautions. It is unsafe for man to confide in his own judgment. He has limited capacities at best, and many have received, as their birthright, both strong and weak points of character, which are positive defects. These peculiarities color the entire life.

The wisdom which God gives will lead men to self-examination. The truth will convict them of their errors and existing wrongs. The heart must be open to see, realize, and acknowledge these wrongs, and then, through the help of Jesus, each must earnestly engage in the work of overcoming them. The knowledge gained by the wise of the world, however diligent they may be in acquiring it, is, after all, limited and comparatively inferior. . . .

Sometimes a course of conduct is pursued every day, and persisted in, because it is a habit, and not because the judgment approves. In these cases, feeling, rather than duty, bears sway.

If we could understand our own weakness, and see the sharp traits in our character which need repressing, we should see so much to do for ourselves that we would humble our hearts under the mighty hand of God. Hanging our helpless souls upon Christ, we should supplement our ignorance with His wisdom, our weakness with His strength, our frailty with His enduring might, and, connected with God, we should indeed be lights in the world.[33]

# Creative Power in the Word of Truth

*"Of his own will begat he us with the word of truth" (James 1:18).*

The new birth is accomplished by the reception of the word of God.[34]

The creative energy that called the worlds into existence is in the word of God. This word imparts power; it begets life. Every command is a promise; accepted by the will, received into the soul, it brings with it the life of the Infinite One. It transforms the nature and re-creates the soul in the image of God.

The life thus imparted is in like manner sustained. "By every word that proceedeth out of the mouth of God" (Matthew 4:4) shall man live.[35]

Consider, says Jesus, how the lilies grow; how, springing from the cold, dark earth, or from the mud of the river bed, the plants unfold in loveliness and fragrance. Who would dream of the possibilities of beauty in the rough brown bulb of the lily? But when the life of God, hidden therein, unfolds at His call in the rain and the sunshine, men marvel at the vision of grace and loveliness. Even so will the life of God unfold in every human soul that will yield itself to the ministry of His grace, which, free as the rain and the sunshine, comes with its benediction to all. It is the word of God that creates the flowers, and the same word will produce in you the graces of His Spirit.[36]

The Lord has given His life to the trees and vines of His creation. His word can increase or decrease the fruit of the land. . . . Without the life of God, nature would die. His creative works are dependent on Him. He bestows life-giving properties on all that nature produces. We are to regard the trees laden with fruit as the gift of God, just as much as though He placed the fruit in our hands.[37]

Let Christ be daily made manifest in you, and He will reveal through you the creative energy of His word—a gentle, persuasive, yet mighty influence to recreate other souls in the beauty of the Lord our God.[38]

# True Worship

*"The hour cometh, and now is, when the true worshippers shall wor-*
*ship the Father in spirit and in truth: for the Father seeketh such to wor-*
*ship him. God is a Spirit: and they that worship him must worship him*
*in spirit and in truth" (John 4:23, 24).*

It is not enough to argue in defense of the truth. The most telling
evidence of its worth is seen in a godly life; and without this the most
conclusive statements will be lacking in weight and prevailing power;
for our strength lies in being connected with God by His Holy Spirit,
and transgression severs us from this sacred nearness with the Source
of our might and wisdom. We are to bring to the attention of the
world the truth for this time; and if we should see the work advance,
we must be sure that there is no accursed thing among us. . . .

The Israelites forgot that their strength was in God, and not in the
ark, and those who advocate the truth today, will have to learn that
their power is not in the clearness of their arguments; not in the rea-
sonableness of their doctrines, though these be sustained by the word
of God; not in their belief in the law and the truth of its claims, but in
obedience to all of its requirements, through the faith of the Son of
God.

Let us take heed to the warning of the past, remembering that
God requireth truth in the secret hearts of His followers; for only that
worship is acceptable that is rendered in spirit and in truth. He that
hath clean hands and a pure heart will realize the aid of heavenly
power, and will see of the salvation of God; but let no one think that
God will favor those who go contrary to His word; for He says, "Thou
canst not stand before thine enemies, until ye take away the accursed
thing from among you" (Joshua 7:13).[39]

Are we worshiping the Lord in spirit and in truth? Everything is
to be held in subordination to the service of God. The temptation is
presented to us from every side to serve ourselves, to serve the world,
to serve Satan; but we are to overcome as Christ also overcame.[40]

# Walking in the Truth

*"I beseech thee, O Lord, remember now how I have walked before thee in truth and with a perfect heart, and have done that which is good in thy sight"* (*2 Kings 20:3*).

It is in looking to Jesus and beholding His loveliness, having our eyes steadfastly fixed upon Him, that we become changed into His image. He will give grace to all that keep His way, and do His will, and walk in truth. But those who love their own way, who worship their idols of opinion, and do not love God and obey His word, will continue to walk in darkness. O, how terrible is unbelief! As well let light be poured upon the blind, as to present truth to these souls; the one cannot see, and the other will not see.

I beseech you whose names are registered on the church book as worthy members, to be indeed worthy, through the virtue of Christ. Mercy and truth and the love of God are promised to the humble and contrite soul. The displeasure and judgments of God are against those who persist in walking in their own ways, loving self, loving the praise of men. They will certainly be swept into the satanic delusions of these last days, because they received not the love of the truth. Because the Lord has, in former days, blessed and honored them, they flatter themselves that they are chosen and true, and do not need warning and instruction and reproof.[41]

God's Word tells us that faith without works is dead, being alone. Many refuse to obey God's commandments, yet they make a great deal of faith. But faith must have a foundation. God's promises are all made upon conditions. If we do His will, if we walk in truth, then we may ask what we will, and it shall be done unto us. While we earnestly endeavor to be obedient, God will hear our petitions; but He will not bless us in disobedience. . . . You are not to sit in indolence, waiting for some great occasion, in order to do a great work for the Master. You are not to neglect the duty that lies directly in your pathway; but you are to improve the little opportunities that open around you.[42]

# Honesty From the Inside Out

*"Lord, who shall abide in thy tabernacle? who shall dwell in thy holy hill? He that walketh uprightly, and worketh righteousness, and speaketh the truth in his heart" (Psalm 15:1, 2).*

The purpose of all God's commandments is to reveal man's duty not only to God, but to his fellowman. In this late age of the world's history, we are not, because of the selfishness of our hearts, to question or dispute the right of God to make these requirements, or we will deceive ourselves, and rob our souls of the richest blessings of the grace of God. Heart and mind and soul are to be merged in the will of God. Then the covenant, framed from the dictates of infinite wisdom, and made binding by the power and authority of the King of kings and Lord of lords, will be our pleasure.[43]

The Lord has graciously given man a time of probation in which to perfect a character for eternal life; but those who are selfish, those who exalt self by seeking to abase another, making the most of every mote and defect in his character, prove that there is a beam in their own eye which unfits them for an entrance into the abode of life. The principles of divine goodness must dwell in the heart, in order that pure, generous, kindly thoughts and actions shall be manifested in the life. Everything like secret working, like deception, like anxiety to discover a mote in our brother's eye, like officious effort to remove the mote when a beam is in our own eye, is abhorrent to God. Until the accuser discovers the evil of his own heart, and feels sincere repentance for his sin, and makes confession of his wrong, he can have no clear vision to pull the mote out of his brother's eye. It is easy to deceive ourselves, but we cannot deceive God, to whose ears smooth words and fair speeches, which are only pretensions to piety, are as sounding brass or a tinkling cymbal. Unless the principles of heaven are inwrought in the heart, all outward profession is pretension and deception. God measures every man's piety by the character of his motives.[44]

# Not a Taint of Guile

*"He that speaketh truth sheweth forth righteousness: but a false witness deceit" (Proverbs 12:17).*

In this age, just prior to the second coming of Christ in the clouds of heaven, the Lord calls for men who will be earnest and prepare a people to stand in the great day of the Lord. The men who have spent long terms in the study of books are not revealing in their lives that earnest ministry which is essential for this last time. They do not bear a simple, straightforward testimony.[45]

Truth is of God; deception in all its myriad forms is of Satan, and whoever in any way departs from the straight line of truth is betraying himself into the power of the wicked one. Those who have learned of Christ will "have no fellowship with the unfruitful works of darkness" (Ephesians 5:11). In speech, as in life, they will be simple, straightforward, and true, for they are preparing for the fellowship of those holy ones in whose mouth is found no guile. See Revelation 14:5.[46]

A course of obedience to God is the wisest course for us to pursue; for it brings peace, content, and happiness as the sure result.

If the lips were constantly guarded so that no guile could corrupt them, what an amount of suffering, degradation, and misery might be prevented. If we would say nothing to wound or grieve, except in necessary reproof of sin, that God might not be dishonored, how much misunderstanding, bitterness, and anguish would be prevented. If we would speak words of good cheer, words of hope and faith in God, how much light we might shed upon the pathway of others, to be reflected in still brighter beams upon our own souls. The path of obedience to God is the path of virtue, of health, and happiness. The plan of salvation, as revealed in the Holy Scriptures, opens up a way whereby man may secure happiness and prolong his days upon the earth, as well as enjoy the favor of Heaven and secure that future life which measures with the life of God. The words of inspiration will never fail. Whenever we comply with the conditions, the Lord will surely fulfill His promises.[47]

# Trustworthy, Dependable Promises

*"The lip of truth shall be established for ever: but a lying tongue is but for a moment" (Proverbs 12:19).*

Promises are estimated by the truth of the one who makes them. Many men make promises only to break them, to mock the heart that trusted in them. Those who lean upon such men lean upon broken reeds. But God is behind the promises He makes. He is ever mindful of His covenant, and His truth endures to all generations.[48]

Truth makes its impression upon the heart, and is recommended by the conscience. But men begin to speculate. Why are there so few who believe this truth? they ask. Have any of the ministers or learned men believed it?

Many refuse to obey the truth through fear that they will lose their standing in the world. They allow the inconveniences in the pathway of truth to prevent them from following the Saviour. They do not realize that to reject truth means to lose eternal life.

The heavenly intelligences watch with intense interest the struggle between tempter and tempted. It is a life-and-death question that is being settled. Christ knows this, and before those whose souls are trembling in the balance, He holds up the sure test of obedience or disobedience, saying, "He that loveth his life"—his good name, his reputation, his money, his property, his business—"shall lose it; and he that hateth his life in this world shall keep it unto life eternal" (John 12:25). He who hates the life which is lived in transgression of God's law, he who accepts the divine requirements, leaving God to take care of the consequences, will gain eternal life.[49]

It is our duty to love Jesus as our Redeemer. He has a right to command our love, but He invites us to give Him our heart. He calls us to walk with Him in the path of humble, truthful obedience. . . . If we choose to live with Christ through the ceaseless ages of eternity, why not choose Him now as our most loved and trusted friend, our best and wisest Counselor?[50]

# Sanctified by the Word of Truth

*"Sanctify them through thy truth: thy word is truth" (John 17:17).*

Instead of looking at the lives of your fellow men, look to Jesus. There you will see no imperfection, but perfection, righteousness, goodness, mercy, and truth.[51]

No error can sanctify the soul; we must bear this in mind. Sanctification comes not through error, but through belief of the truth. We need to possess a faith that is based upon the sure word of promise.[52]

How many of us place a right estimate upon the Word of God? Do we receive the testimony of the Scriptures as the voice of God? Through the Scriptures the voice of God comes to us as veritably as it came to Israel when He spoke on Sinai in the audience of all the people. How many of us regard it in this light? If we did regard it thus, what a change would be seen in our daily words and actions. With what reverence and awe would we search the Word of God to know the truth, the medium through which the soul's sanctification is accomplished. No indifference, no carelessness, is allowed in our searching of the Scriptures. Our spiritual development depends upon our knowledge of the truth, upon our practice of its divine principles as embodied in the precepts of the law and in the teaching of our Lord.[53]

The Word of God specifies the quality of the faith that will distinguish between the sacred and the common, and will render the life well-pleasing to Him who has purchased the powers of our being by the redemption price of His blood. All men have a certain kind of faith; but it is that faith which works by love that purifies the soul. This faith cleanses the life from all self-serving, from all acquiescence to man's arbitrary exactions. It is a genuine faith that is revealed in the spirit, in the speech, and in the actions. In the life of the one who possesses such a faith as this the will of Christ will be daily carried out.[54]

# Sanctification Means Purification

*"He that saith, I know him, and keepeth not his commandments, is a liar, and the truth is not in him" (1 John 2:4).*

Men may cry, Holiness! holiness! sanctification! sanctification! consecration! consecration! and yet know no more by experience of what they talk than the sinner with his corrupt propensities. God will soon tear off this whitewashed garb of professed sanctification which some who are carnally minded have thrown around them to hide the deformity of the soul.

A faithful record is kept of the acts of the children of men. Nothing can be concealed from the eye of the high and holy One. Some take a course directly opposed to the law of God, and then, to cover up their sinful course, they profess to be consecrated to God. This profession of holiness does not make itself manifest in their daily lives. It does not have a tendency to elevate their minds.[55]

Faith in Christ is demonstrated by works; it produces a transformation of character through the effectual working of God's Holy Spirit. Selfishness and pride, with all their force, will make a stand against anything that would show them to be sinful. But all who shall endure as seeing Him who is invisible, will have to lie very low at the foot of the cross. Contrition of soul will mark the experience of every one who has received the grace of Christ.[56]

When our hearts kindle up as we read the claims of the law of God in His word, when we can pray with the psalmist, "Open thou mine eyes, that I may behold wondrous things out of thy law" (Psalm 119:18), we are in a position to claim the merits of the blood of a crucified and risen Saviour, and may fully rely upon the prayer of Christ to His Father for the sanctification which comes through the belief of the truth.[57]

Sanctification means purification. The wisdom that comes from above is first pure, then peaceable. It is only thus that they can be qualified to do the work that Christ did in the world in proclaiming the truth.[58]

True sanctification comes through willing obedience.[59]

# Pure Truth Has Power

*"I have not written unto you because ye know not the truth, but because ye know it, and that no lie is of the truth" (1 John 2:21).*

No lie is of the truth. If we follow cunningly devised fables, we unite with the enemy's forces against God and Christ. God calls upon those who have been wearing a yoke of human manufacture to break this yoke, and no longer be the bond servants of men.

The battle is on. Satan and his angels are working with all deceivableness of unrighteousness. They are untiring in their efforts to draw souls away from the truth, away from righteousness, to spread ruin throughout the universe. They work with marvelous industry to furnish a multitude of deceptions to take souls captive. Their efforts are unceasing. The enemy is ever seeking to lead souls into infidelity and skepticism. He would do away with God, and with Christ, who was made flesh and dwelt among us, to teach us that in obedience to God's will we may be victorious over sin.

Every form of evil is waiting for an opportunity to assail us. Flattery, bribes, inducements, promises of wonderful exaltation, will be most assiduously employed.

What are God's servants doing to raise the barrier of a "Thus saith the Lord" against this evil? The enemy's agents are working unceasingly to prevail against the truth. Where are the faithful guardians of the Lord's flocks? Where are His watchmen? . . . Where are the medical missionaries? Are they coworkers with Christ, wearing His yoke, or are they wearing a yoke of human manufacture?[60]

On our knees we are to claim the promises of God's Word, asking that we may receive pure, unadulterated truth, and that we may realize the necessity of giving this truth to others. Then men and women will be converted. The hand of God will be recognized in the raising up of new churches. The Lord will baptize with the apostolic spirit many who will go forth to do missionary work in places where the people know not the truth.[61]

# True Love

*"My little children, let us not love in word, neither in tongue; but in deed and in truth" (1 John 3:18).*

All selfishness is condemned by the law of God, and we are made stewards of God, and should not be neglectful of, or indifferent to, our brethren. We cannot love God unless we love those about us. A man will reveal just what is in his heart. Words are of but little value. Love should be expressed in acts of sympathy, in kindness to those who are oppressed, or in poverty, or affliction, or temptation. God's deeds are the fruits of sanctification. If we are waiting and watching for opportunities to do good, to infuse light, to impart tangible blessings, we shall not feel that in doing so we have done any great things: yet Jesus will reckon every act of kindness done to others as done to Himself.

He who seeks to walk by the rule of God's law, will care for the interests of his brethren as he would care for his own interests. Genuine piety manifested in this manner is of more value in the sight of God, who readeth the thoughts and intents of the heart, than all manner of boasting professions. Those who are genuine Christians can say, "Whatsoever we ask, we receive of Him, because we keep His commandments, and do those things that are pleasing in His sight."

How carefully should we examine the motives which prompt us to actions! When we follow the inclination of the natural heart, we separate our souls from God, although the lips may declare that we are wholly the Lord's. With the Bible open before us, let us look into God's holy mirror, and see whether our practices and plans are holy. Let us ask the question, Is this the way of the Lord? If we do an injury to our brother or neighbor, we shall have to meet the injured one before the throne of God. No difference in belief will justify us in invading another's rights, in neglecting to do justice and judgment. . . . Is the mind of God, as revealed in the holy law, the guide of our life? If so, love, joy, peace—yes, heaven—is brought into our life here below.[62]

# "Girt About With Truth"

*"Stand therefore, having your loins girt about with truth"*
*(Ephesians 6:14).*

Christ maintained an all-sided, firm self-possession in His remarkable sympathy for others. He did good with a tranquillity and patient continuance never equaled by any human being. The Pharisees and Sadducees were always on His track; and many of them, as they listened to His words, and noted His calmness, even when assailed by passionate, uncourteous men, believed on Him. Constantly Christ had to meet the underhand, deceptive opposition of the very men who should gladly have received and acknowledged Him. But He was ever calm, while His adversaries, because they could not prevail against Him, were in a fever of indignant excitement. Their indignation and malignity showed what spirit they were of.

All the contempt and bitterness that Christ met day by day could not rob Him of His self-possession. When He was reviled, He reviled not again. He was not roused by passion to revile those who made use of every opportunity to revile Him. He never overstepped the bounds of decorum. Who was He? The Majesty of heaven, the King of glory. The storm raised by His opponents beat about Him, but He heeded it not. He could afford to be calm; for He was the living embodiment of truth.

And those today who bear the message of truth to the world should study the life of Christ, and practice His lessons. Never forget that you are children of the heavenly King, sons and daughters of the Lord of hosts. Maintain a calm repose in God, even when meeting with those who are moved by a power from beneath to uphold falsehood. Be sure that the best weapons they possess are not able to destroy the truth, however they may strive to blacken it by misrepresentation. "If God be for us, who can be against us?" (Romans 8:31).

Christ spoke no words revealing His importance, or showing His superiority. . . . His words and actions showed Him to be possessed of a knowledge of His mission and character.[63]

91

# On to Battle, Armed With Truth

*"O send out thy light and thy truth: let them lead me; let them bring me unto thy holy hill, and to thy tabernacles" (Psalm 43:3).*

Those who are truly the followers of Christ love as brethren, and are the salt of the earth, the light of the world. Every true believer catches the beams from the Morning Star, and transmits the light to those who sit in darkness. Not only do they shine amid the darkness in their own neighborhoods, but as a church they go forth to regions beyond. The Lord expects every man to do his duty. Everyone who unites with the church is to be one with Christ, diffusing the beams of the Morning Star, and becoming the light of the world. Christ and His people are to be copartners in the great work of saving the world.

The churches have not been educated altogether as they should have been educated. They have been educated to depend upon the ministers to pray and to open the Scriptures to the people who assemble to worship God. God would have the people hear the voice of God, and go to work for the Master. Thousands might be at work who are not ordained to preach the gospel. If the love of God was a living, abiding element in the soul, there would be love among the brethren, and many who have been indifferent to the great Teacher's commandment, who now bite and devour one another, would be convinced of their mistake, and [would be] draw[n] into fellowship. God has made every provision for better things. God's people have close, severe battles to fight; but these battles are not to be against their brethren. All desire to hurt and weaken and destroy the influence of even the weakest of God's workers is registered in the books of heaven as desire to weaken the influence of Jesus Christ. The warfare we are to undertake is to be waged against the confederacy of evil, which is arrayed against the people of God. But woe unto those who shall turn their implements of warfare against their own brethren. God reminds us that we are to fight in unison with the angels of heaven, and that more than angels are engaged in the warfare.[64]

# Lift Up the Banner of Truth

*"Thou hast given a banner to them that fear thee, that it may be dis-
played because of the truth" (Psalm 60:4).*

Everyone who has heard and accepted the third angel's message
is to hold the banner of truth, unstained and uncorrupted, higher and
still higher. I was shown large numbers engaged in work for the outcasts, while all through God's moral vineyard were fields white for
the harvest, destitute of the truth. Every organization among our people, as well as every individual, is responsible to God to give the last
message of warning to the world with a loud voice. Strong, decided
appeals are to be made in the very best way.[65]

The Holy Spirit, Christ's representative, arms the weakest with
might to press forward unto victory. God has organized His instrumentalities to draw all men unto Him. He sends forth to His work
many who have not been dedicated by the laying on of hands. He
answers objections that would arise against this method of labor, even
before they arise. God sees the end from the beginning. He knows and
anticipates every want, and provides for every emergency.[66]

True missionary work will furnish the churches with a sure foundation, a foundation having this seal, "The Lord knoweth them that
are his" (2 Timothy 2:19). Then God will be glorified in His people.
Christian missions will be built upon Jesus Christ. Under the supervision of God the work will go forward, and innumerable evidences
will be given of the genuineness of the work. The workers will not
seek to glorify self, but will praise God as the designer and organizer
of every holy, ennobling work. They not only *profess* to be believers;
they *are* believers. They are sanctified by the truth; for truth *acted* as
well as *preached* has a purifying influence upon the character.[67]

We are to raise the banner on which is inscribed, "The commandments of God, and the faith of Jesus" (Revelation 14:12). Obedience to
God's law is the great issue. Let it not be put out of sight.[68]

# "Truth Unto the Clouds"

*"I will praise thee, O Lord, among the people: I will sing unto thee among the nations. For thy mercy is great unto the heavens, and thy truth unto the clouds" (Psalm 57:9, 10).*

Christ has commissioned us to sow the seeds of truth, and to urge upon our people the importance of the work to be done by those who are living amidst the closing scenes of this earth's history. As the words of truth are proclaimed in the highways and the byways, there is to be a revelation of the working of the Spirit of God on human hearts.

Oh, how much good might be accomplished if all who have the truth, the Word of life, would labor for the enlightenment of those who have it not! When the Samaritans came to Christ at the call of the Samaritan woman, Christ spoke of them to His disciples as a field of grain ready for harvesting. . . . Christ abode with the Samaritans for two days; for they were hungry to hear the truth. And what busy days they were! As a result of those days of labor, "many more believed because of his own word." This was their testimony: "We have heard him ourselves, and know that this is indeed the Christ, the Saviour of the world" (John 4:41, 42).

Who among God's professing people will take up this sacred work, and labor for the souls who are perishing for lack of knowledge? The world must be warned. Many places are pointed out to me as in need of consecrated, faithful, untiring effort. Christ is opening the hearts and minds of many in our large cities. These need the truths of God's Word; and if we will come into a sacred nearness with Christ, and will seek to draw near to these people, impressions for good will be made. We need to wake up, and enter into sympathy with Christ and with our fellow men. The large and small cities, and places nigh and afar off, are to be worked, and worked intelligently. Never draw back. The Lord will make the right impressions upon hearts, if we will work in unison with His Spirit. [69]

# Grab Every Opportunity

*"These are the things that ye shall do; Speak ye every man the truth to his neighbour" (Zechariah 8:16).*

We should treat as a sacred treasure every line of printed matter containing present truth. Even the fragments of a pamphlet or of a periodical should be regarded as of value. Who can estimate the influence that a torn page containing the truths of the third angel's message may have upon the heart of some seeker after truth? Let us remember that somebody would be glad to read all the books and papers we can spare.[70]

To all who are working with Christ I would say, Wherever you can gain access to the people by the fireside, improve your opportunity. Take your Bible, and open before them its great truths. Your success will not depend so much upon your knowledge and accomplishments as upon your ability to find your way to the heart. By being social and coming close to the people, you may turn the current of their thoughts more readily than by the most able discourse.

Take along the publications and ask them to read. When they see that you are sincere they will not despise any of your efforts. There is a way to reach the hardest hearts. Approach in the simplicity and sincerity and humility that will help us to reach the souls of them for whom Christ died.

Allow no opportunity to pass unimproved. Visit those who live near you, and by sympathy and kindness try to reach their hearts. Visit the sick and suffering and show a kindly interest in them. If possible, do something to make them more comfortable. Through this means you can reach their hearts and speak a word for Christ. Eternity alone will reveal how far reaching such a line of labor can be.

Those who do not take up this work, those who act with the indifference that some have manifested, will soon lose their first love and will begin to censure, criticize, and condemn their own brethren.

Those who go forth in the spirit of the Master, seeking to reach souls with the truth, will . . . become more and more vitalized as they give themselves to the service of God. It is a joyous work to open the Scriptures to others.[71]

# Self-Supporting Missionaries

*"Mercy and truth shall be to them that devise good" (Proverbs 14:22)*

Self-supporting missionaries are often very successful. Beginning in a small, humble way, their work enlarges as they move forward under the guidance of the Spirit of God. Let two or more start out together in evangelistic work. They may not receive any particular encouragement from those at the head of the work that they will be given financial support; nevertheless let them go forward, praying, singing, teaching, living the truth. They may take up the work of canvassing, and in this way introduce the truth into many families. As they move forward in their work they gain a blessed experience. They are humbled by a sense of their helplessness, but the Lord goes before them, and among the wealthy and the poor they find favor and help. Even the poverty of these devoted missionaries is a means of finding access to the people. As they pass on their way they are helped in many ways by those to whom they bring spiritual food. They bear the message God gives them, and their efforts are crowned with success. Many will be brought to a knowledge of the truth who, but for these humble teachers, would never have been won to Christ.

God calls for workers to enter the whitening harvest field. Shall we wait because the treasury is exhausted, because there is scarcely sufficient to sustain the workers now in the field? Go forth in faith, and God will be with you. . . . [Psalm 126:6 quoted.]

Nothing is so successful as success. Let this be secured by persevering effort, and the work will move forward. New fields will be opened. Many souls will be brought to a knowledge of the truth. What is needed is increased faith in God.[72]

As humble, God-fearing men and women consecrate themselves to the Lord, He will accept them and work through them. As they place themselves in right relation to Him, light from the throne above will shine upon them, making them channels of blessing to others.[73]

# For Now and for Eternity

*"The truth of the Lord endureth for ever. Praise ye the Lord"* (Psalm 117:2).

Through the ages that have passed since the days of the apostles, the building of God's temple has never ceased. We may look back through the centuries and see the living stones of which it is composed gleaming like jets of light through the darkness of error and superstition. Throughout eternity these precious jewels will shine with increasing luster, testifying to the power of the truth of God. The flashing light of these polished stones reveals the strong contrast between light and darkness, between the gold of truth and the dross of error.

Paul and the other apostles, and all the righteous who have lived since then, have acted their part in the building of the temple. But the structure is not yet complete. We who are living in this age have a work to do, a part to act. . . . The Christian who faithfully presents the word of life, leading men and women into the way of holiness and peace, is bringing to the foundation material that will endure, and in the kingdom of God he will be honored as a wise builder.

Of the apostles it is written, "They went forth, and preached every where, the Lord working with them, and confirming the word with signs following" (Mark 16:20). As Christ sent forth His disciples, so today He sends forth the members of His church. The same power that the apostles had is for them. If they will make God their strength, He will work with them, and they shall not labor in vain. . . .

Christ has given to the church a sacred charge. Every member should be a channel through which God can communicate to the world the treasures of His grace, the unsearchable riches of Christ. There is nothing that the Saviour desires so much as agents who will represent to the world His Spirit and His character. There is nothing that the world needs so much as the manifestation through humanity of the Saviour's love. All heaven is waiting for men and women through whom God can reveal the power of Christianity.[74]

# The Reward of Presenting the Truth

*"Open ye the gates, that the righteous nation which keepeth the truth may enter in" (Isaiah 26:2).*

Jesus' silver trumpet sounded, as He descended on the cloud, wrapped in flames of fire. He gazed on the graves of the sleeping saints, then raised His eyes and hands to heaven, and cried: "Awake! Awake! Awake! ye that sleep in the dust, and arise." Then there was a mighty earthquake. The graves opened, and the dead came up clothed with immortality. The 144,000 shouted, "Alleluia!" as they recognized their friends who had been torn from them by death, and in the same moment we were changed, and caught up together with them to meet the Lord in the air.

We all entered the cloud together, and were seven days ascending to the sea of glass, when Jesus brought the crowns, and with His own right hand placed them on our heads. He gave us harps of gold and palms of victory. Here on the sea of glass the 144,000 stood in a perfect square. Some had very bright crowns, others not so bright. Some crowns appeared heavy with stars, while others had but few. All were perfectly satisfied with their crowns. And they were all clothed with a glorious white mantle from their shoulders to their feet. Angels were all about us as we marched over the sea of glass to the gate of the city. Jesus raised His mighty, glorious arm, laid hold of the pearly gate, swung it back on its glittering hinges, and said to us: "You have washed your robes in My blood, stood stiffly for My truth, enter in." We all marched in and felt we had a perfect right there.

Within the city we saw the tree of life and the throne of God. Out of the throne came a pure river of water, and on either side of the river was the tree of life. On one side of the river was a trunk of a tree, and a trunk on the other side of the river, both of pure, transparent gold. At first I thought I saw two trees; I looked again, and saw that they were united at the top in one tree. So it was the tree of life on either side of the river of life. Its branches bowed to the place where we stood; and the fruit was glorious, which looked like gold mixed with silver.[75]

# The Call of the Twelve

*[Jesus] called unto him his disciples: and of them he chose twelve, whom also he named apostles (Luke 6:13).*

For the carrying on of His work, Christ did not choose the learning or eloquence of the Jewish Sanhedrin or the power of Rome. Passing by the self-righteous Jewish teachers, the Master Worker chose humble, unlearned men to proclaim the truths that were to move the world. These men He purposed to train and educate as the leaders of His church. They in turn were to educate others and send them out with the gospel message. That they might have success in their work they were to be given the power of the Holy Spirit. Not by human might or human wisdom was the gospel to be proclaimed, but by the power of God.

For three years and a half the disciples were under the instruction of the greatest Teacher the world has ever known. By personal contact and association, Christ trained them for His service. Day by day they walked and talked with Him, hearing His words of cheer to the weary and heavy-laden, and seeing the manifestation of His power in behalf of the sick and the afflicted. . . . He did not command the disciples to do this or that, but said, "Follow Me." . . .

It was at the ordination of the Twelve that the first step was taken in the organization of the church that after Christ's departure was to carry on His work on the earth. . . .

Look upon the touching scene. Behold the Majesty of heaven surrounded by the Twelve whom He has chosen. He is about to set them apart for their work. By these feeble agencies, through His word and Spirit, He designs to place salvation within the reach of all.

With gladness and rejoicing, God and the angels beheld this scene. The Father knew that from these men the light of heaven would shine forth; that the words spoken by them as they witnessed for His Son, would echo from generation to generation till the close of time.[1]

# The Gospel Minister

*"When [Christ] ascended up on high, he led captivity captive, and gave gifts unto men. . . . And he gave some, apostles" (Ephesians 4:8, 11).*

While Christ is the minister in the sanctuary above, He is also, through His delegates, the minister of His church on earth. He speaks to the people through chosen men, and carries forward His work through them, as when in the days of His humiliation He moved visibly upon the earth. Although centuries have passed, the lapse of time has not changed His parting promise to His disciples. "Lo, I am with you alway, even unto the end of the world" (Matthew 28:20). From Christ's ascension to the present day, men ordained of God, deriving their authority from Him, have become teachers of the faith. Christ, the True Shepherd, superintends His work through the instrumentality of these undershepherds. Thus the position of those who labor in word and doctrine becomes very important. In Christ's stead they beseech the people to be reconciled to God.

The people should not regard their ministers as mere public speakers and orators, but as Christ's ambassadors, receiving their wisdom and power from the great Head of the church.[2]

Theoretical discourses are essential, that all may know the form of doctrine and see the chain of truth, link after link, uniting in a perfect whole. But no discourse should ever be delivered without presenting Christ and Him crucified as the foundation of the gospel, making a practical application of the truths set forth, and impressing upon the people the fact that the doctrine of Christ is not Yea and Nay, but Yea and Amen in Christ Jesus.

After the theory of truth has been presented, then comes the laborious part of the work. The people should not be left without instruction in the practical truths which relate to their everyday life. They must see and feel that they are sinners and need to be converted to God. What Christ said, what He did, and what He taught should be brought before them in the most impressive manner.[3]

# Watchmen Upon the Walls

*"God hath set some in the church, first apostles"* (1 Corinthians 12:28).

The watchmen anciently placed upon the walls of Jerusalem and other cities occupied a most responsible position. Upon their faithfulness depended the safety of all within those cities. When danger was apprehended, they were not to keep silent day nor night. Every few moments they were required to call to one another to see if all were awake and no harm had come to any. Sentinels were stationed upon some eminence overlooking the important posts to be guarded, and the cry of warning or of good cheer was sounded from them. This was borne from one to another, each repeating the words, till it went the entire rounds of the city.

These watchmen represent the ministry, upon whose fidelity depends the salvation of souls. The stewards of the mysteries of God should stand as watchmen upon the walls of Zion; and if they see the sword coming, they should sound the note of warning. If they are sleepy sentinels, if their spiritual senses are so benumbed that they see and realize no danger, and the people perish, God will require their blood at the watchmen's hands.[4]

It is the privilege of the watchmen on the walls of Zion to live so near to God, and to be susceptible to the impressions of His Spirit, that He can work through them to tell men and women of their peril and point them to the place of safety. Faithfully are they to warn them of the sure result of transgression, and faithfully are they to safeguard the interests of the church. At no time may they relax their vigilance. Theirs is a work requiring the exercise of every faculty of the being. In trumpet tones their voices are to be lifted, and never are they to sound one wavering, uncertain note. Not for wages are they to labor, but because they cannot do otherwise, because they realize that there is a woe upon them if they fail to preach the gospel. Chosen of God, sealed with the blood of consecration, they are to rescue men and women from impending destruction.[5]

# The Humblest Servants

*"Ye know that the princes of the Gentiles exercise dominion over them, and they that are great exercise authority upon them. But it shall not be so among you: but whosoever will be great among you, let him be your minister; and whosoever will be chief among you, let him be your servant: even as the Son of man came not to be ministered unto, but to minister, and to give his life a ransom for many" (Matthew 20:25–28).*

[Christ] came not to be ministered unto, but to minister to others. He pleased not Himself. He made Himself of no reputation, but took upon Himself the form of a servant, and spent His life in doing good. He could have spent His days on earth in ease and plenty, and have appropriated to Himself the enjoyments of this life. But He lived not to enjoy, He lived to do good and to save others from suffering, and His example is for us to follow.[6]

Those who profess to be servants of the living God must be willing to be servants of all, instead of being exalted above the brethren, and they must possess a kind, courteous spirit. If they err, they should be ready to confess thoroughly. Honesty of intention cannot stand as an excuse for not confessing errors. Confession would not lessen the confidence of the church in the messenger, and he would set a good example; a spirit of confession would be encouraged in the church, and sweet union would be the result. Those who profess to be teachers should be patterns of piety, meekness, and humility, possessing a kind spirit, to win souls to Jesus and the truth of the Bible. A minister of Christ should be pure in conversation and in actions. He should ever bear in mind that he is handling words of inspiration, words of a holy God. He must also bear in mind that the flock is entrusted to his care, and that he is to bear their cases to Jesus, and plead for them as Jesus pleads for us with the Father.[7]

[Ministers] will be called to a strict account for the manner in which they have discharged their responsibility. If they do not tell the people of the binding claims of God's law, if they do not preach the Word with clearness, but confuse the minds of the people by their own interpretations, they are shepherds who feed themselves, but neglect to feed the flock.[8]

# Undivided Attention

*"Neglect not the gift that is in thee, which was given thee by prophecy, with the laying on of the hands of the presbytery. Meditate upon these things; give thyself wholly to them; that thy profiting may appear to all" (1 Timothy 4:14, 15).*

The reason why ministers of Christ are no more successful in their labors is that they are not unselfishly devoted to the work. The interest of some is divided; they are double-minded. The cares of this life engage their attention, and they do not realize how sacred is the work of the minister. Such may complain of darkness, of great unbelief, of infidelity. The reason for this is, they are not right with God; they do not see the importance of making a full and entire consecration to Him. They serve God a little, but themselves more. They pray but little.

The Majesty of heaven, while engaged in His earthly ministry, prayed much to His Father. He was frequently bowed all night in prayer. His spirit was often sorrowful as He felt the powers of the darkness of this world, and He left the busy city and the noisy throng, to seek a retired place to make His intercessions. The Mount of Olives was the favorite resort of the Son of God for His devotions. Frequently after the multitude had left Him for the retirement of the night, He rested not, though weary with the labors of the day. In the Gospel of John we read: "And every man went unto his own house. Jesus went unto the Mount of Olives" (John 7:53; 8:1). While the city was hushed in silence, and the disciples had returned to their homes to obtain refreshment in sleep, Jesus slept not. His divine pleadings were ascending to His Father from the Mount of Olives that His disciples might be kept from the evil influences which they would daily encounter in the world, and that His own soul might be strengthened and braced for the duties and trials of the coming day. All night, while His followers were sleeping, was their divine Teacher praying. The dew and frost of night fell upon His head bowed in prayer. His example is left for His followers.[9]

# Evidence of This Calling

*"Not that we are sufficient of ourselves to think any thing as of ourselves; but our sufficiency is of God; who also hath made us able ministers of the new testament" (2 Corinthians 3:5, 6).*

The conversion of sinners and their sanctification through the truth is the strongest proof a minister can have that God has called him to the ministry. The evidence of his apostleship is written upon the hearts of those converted, and is witnessed to by their renewed lives. Christ is formed within, the hope of glory. A minister is greatly strengthened by these seals of his ministry.

Today the ministers of Christ should have the same witness as that which the Corinthian church bore to Paul's labors. But though in this age there are many preachers, there is a great scarcity of able, holy ministers—men filled with the love that dwelt in the heart of Christ. Pride, self-confidence, love of the world, faultfinding, bitterness, envy, are the fruit borne by many who profess the religion of Christ. Their lives, in sharp contrast to the life of the Saviour, often bear sad testimony to the character of the ministerial labor under which they were converted.

A man can have no greater honor than to be accepted by God as an able minister of the gospel. But those whom the Lord blesses with power and success in His work do not boast. They acknowledge their entire dependence on Him.[10]

If the man who feels that he is called of God to be a minister will humble himself and learn of Christ, he will become a true preacher. If his lips are touched with a live coal from the altar, he will lift up Jesus as the sinner's only hope. When the heart of the speaker is sanctified through the truth, his words will be living realities to himself and to others. Those who hear him will know that he has been with God, and has drawn near to him in fervent, effectual prayer. The Holy Spirit has fallen upon him, his soul has felt the vital, heavenly fire, and he is able to compare spiritual things with spiritual. Power will be given him to tear down the strongholds of Satan. Hearts will be broken by his presentation of the love of God, and many will inquire. "What must I do to be saved?" (Acts 16:30).[11]

# The Mark of a Gentleman

*"I think that God hath set forth us the apostles last, as it were appointed to death: for we are made a spectacle unto the world, and to angels, and to men" (1 Corinthians 4:9).*

The consecrated messengers . . . in the early days of Christianity . . . allowed no thought of self-exaltation to mar their presentation of Christ and Him crucified. They coveted neither authority nor preeminence.[12]

Paul regarded the occasion of his formal ordination as marking the beginning of a new and important epoch in his lifework. It was from this time that he afterward dated the beginning of his apostleship in the Christian church.[13]

Lifting up his toil-worn hands, Paul makes his appeal to the elders of Ephesus: "Ye yourselves know, that these hands have ministered unto my necessities, and to them that were with me" (Acts 20:34). Those hands speak to us with remarkable impressiveness. Paul is not speaking mysteries. He is appealing to their knowledge of his manner of life. The great apostle was not ashamed nor afraid of work, and he did not treat this subject as in any way lowering to his work in the ministry.

The opinion of men has, in many minds, changed the order of God, and men have come to think that it is not fitting for a man who works with his hands to take his place among gentlemen. The Lord's purposes are not the thoughts and purposes of men. In the beginning God created man a gentleman, which means a man who can do work cheerfully. Men have worked hard to obtain money; and having gained wealth, they suppose that their money will make their sons gentlemen. But many such men fail to train their sons as they themselves were trained, to hard, useful labor.[14]

If ministers feel that they are suffering hardship and privation in the cause of Christ, let them in imagination visit the workshop where Paul labored. Let them bear in mind that while this chosen man of God is fashioning the canvas, he is working for bread which he has justly earned by his labors as an apostle.[15]

# Misunderstood and Maligned

*"We are fools for Christ's sake, but ye are wise in Christ; we are weak, but ye are strong; ye are honourable, but we are despised" (1 Corinthians 4:10).*

There was a small minority of the Corinthians who stubbornly resisted all efforts of the apostle [Paul] for the purification of the church; but their course was such that none could be deceived in them. They displayed a most bitter spirit, and were bold in denunciation of Paul, accusing him of mercenary motives, and craft in preaching the gospel and dealing with the churches. They charged him with receiving personal advantage from the means contributed by the brethren for various benevolent purposes. On the other hand, some challenged his claims to apostleship, because he did not demand support from the churches which he had raised up. Thus the accusations of his opposers were conflicting and without a shadow of foundation.

Just such unreasonable persons are to be met in our times, men who set themselves against the progress of the work of God, while professing to believe the truth. They refuse to come into harmony with the body of the church, the burden of their work being to dissect the characters of their brethren, to raise dark suspicions, and circulate covert insinuations. . . .

The apostle mentions his distress because of the burden of the churches. The pressure was sometimes so great that he could scarcely endure it. Outward dangers and inward fears had harassed him beyond his own power to bear. False teachers had prejudiced his brethren against him; they had made false charges against him to destroy his influence among the churches which he had raised up. But, amid all his persecutions and discouragements, he could rejoice in the consolation which he found in Christ.

His conscience did not accuse him of dishonesty or unfaithfulness to his trust. It was a cause of joy to him that he had been enabled, through the grace of God, to labor in the ministry, not using his natural eloquence, to receive the praise of men, but with simplicity and pureness, in the Spirit of God, his only aim being the good of souls.[16]

# The Life of a Hero of Faith

*"We both hunger, and thirst, and are naked, and are buffeted, and have no certain dwellingplace; and labour, working with our own hands: being reviled, we bless; being persecuted, we suffer it: being defamed, we intreat: we are made as the filth of the world, and are the offscouring of all things unto this day" (1 Corinthians 4:11–13).*

Amid the constant storm of opposition, the clamor of enemies, and the desertion of friends, the intrepid apostle [Paul] at times almost lost heart. But he looked back to Calvary, and with new ardor pressed on to spread the knowledge of the Crucified. He was but treading the blood-stained path which Christ had trodden before him. He sought no discharge from the warfare till he should lay off his armor at the feet of his Redeemer.

Eighteen centuries have passed since the apostle rested from his labors; yet the history of his toils and sacrifices for Christ's sake are among the most precious treasures of the church. That history was recorded by the Holy Spirit, that the followers of Christ in every age might thereby be incited to greater zeal and faithfulness in the cause of their Master.

How does this hero of faith tower above the self-indulgent, easeloving men who are today crowding the ranks of the ministry. When subjected to the ordinary difficulties and trials of life, many feel that their lot is hard. But what have they done or suffered for the cause of Christ? How does their record appear when compared with that of this great apostle? What burden of soul have they felt for the salvation of sinners? They know little of self-denial or sacrifice. They are indebted to the grace of Christ for all the excellences of character which they possess, for every blessing which they enjoy. All that they are, and all that they have, is the purchase of the blood of Christ. As the servants of Christ encounter opposition and persecution, they should not permit their faith to grow dim or their courage to fail. With Christ as a helper, they can resist every foe, and overcome every difficulty. The same obligation rests upon them which impelled the apostle to his unwearied labors. Only those who emulate his fidelity, will share with him the crown of life.[17]

# The Life of the Minister

*"Giving no offence in any thing, that the ministry be not blamed: but in all things approving ourselves as the ministers of God, in much patience, in afflictions, in necessities, in distresses, in stripes, in imprisonments, in tumults, in labours, in watchings, in fastings; by pureness, by knowledge, by longsuffering, by kindness, by the Holy Ghost, by love unfeigned, by the word of truth, by the power of God, by the armour of righteousness on the right hand and on the left, by honour and dishonour, by evil report and good report: as deceivers, and yet true; as unknown, and yet well known; as dying, and, behold, we live; as chastened, and not killed; as sorrowful, yet alway rejoicing; as poor, yet making many rich; as having nothing, and yet possessing all things"* (2 Corinthians 6:3–10).

There is nothing more precious in the sight of God than His ministers, who go forth into the waste places of the earth to sow the seeds of truth, looking forward to the harvest. None but Christ can measure the solicitude of His servants as they seek for the lost. He imparts His Spirit to them, and by their efforts souls are led to turn from sin to righteousness.

God is calling for men who are willing to leave their farms, their business, if need be their families, to become missionaries for Him. And the call will be answered. In the past there have been men who, stirred by the love of Christ and the needs of the lost, have left the comforts of home and the society of friends, even that of wife and children, to go into foreign lands, among idolaters and savages, to proclaim the message of mercy. Many in the attempt have lost their lives, but others have been raised up to carry on the work. Thus step by step the cause of Christ has progressed, and the seed sown in sorrow has yielded a bountiful harvest. The knowledge of God has been widely extended and the banner of the cross planted in heathen lands.

For the conversion of one sinner the minister should tax his resources to the utmost. . . . If Christ left the ninety and nine that He might seek and save one lost sheep, can we be justified in doing less?[18]

# The Secret of Paul's Strength

*"Are they ministers of Christ? (I speak as a fool) I am more; in labours more abundant, in stripes above measure, in prisons more frequent, in deaths oft. Of the Jews five times received I forty stripes save one. Thrice was I beaten with rods, once was I stoned, thrice I suffered shipwreck, a night and a day I have been in the deep; in journeyings often, in perils of waters, in perils of robbers, in perils by mine own countrymen, in perils by the heathen, in perils in the city, in perils in the wilderness, in perils in the sea, in perils among false brethren; in weariness and painfulness, in watchings often, in hunger and thirst, in fastings often, in cold and nakedness. Beside those things that are without, that which cometh upon me daily, the care of all the churches" (2 Corinthians 11:23–28).*

A more hearty, persevering, energetic disciple of Jesus Christ than was Paul has never been upon the earth. He counted all things but loss, for the excellency of the knowledge of Christ. He had one aim before him, and that was, that from his lips should go forth the tidings of redemption to perishing souls, that they might be brought into acquaintance with the Redeemer of the world. His whole soul was wrapped up in Jesus, and in the light of truth received from the Source of all light.[19]

Is not a neglect to work as Christ worked, to sacrifice as He sacrificed, a betrayal of sacred trusts, an insult to God?

The heart of the true minister is filled with an intense longing to save souls. Time and strength are spent, toilsome effort is not shunned; for others must hear the truths that brought to his own soul such gladness and peace and joy. The Spirit of Christ rests upon him. He watches for souls as one that must give an account. With his eyes fixed on the cross of Calvary, beholding the uplifted Saviour, relying on His grace, believing that He will be with him until the end, as his shield, his strength, his efficiency, he works for God. With invitations and pleadings, mingled with the assurances of God's love, he seeks to win souls to Jesus, and in heaven he is numbered among those who are "called, and chosen, and faithful" (Revelation 17:14).[20]

# Way Beyond Mere Preaching

*"It is now revealed unto his holy apostles and prophets by the Spirit; that the Gentiles should be fellowheirs, and of the same body, and partakers of his promise in Christ by the gospel: whereof I was made a minister, according to the gift of the grace of God given unto me by the effectual working of his power"* (Ephesians 3:5–7).

If one enters upon this work [of ministry] choosing the least self-sacrificing part of it, contenting himself with preaching, and leaving the work of ministering for some one else to do, he need not expect that his labors will be acceptable to God. Souls for whom Christ has died are perishing for want of well-directed personal labor, and when the minister is not willing to be a servant of the people, as Jesus has directed in His word, then he has mistaken his calling. Those who minister in the sacred desk should fall upon the Rock and be broken, that the Lord may put His superscription upon them and fashion them as vessels unto honor. If those engaged in the work of the ministry were indeed laborers together with God, we should see a solid and beautiful work wrought in all countries for the saving of the souls for whom Christ has died.

God calls for consecrated men, who are willing to deny self. The work of the heavenly intelligences is constant and earnest, for they are intent upon drawing men to Jesus. This is the manner in which ministers should labor. Their message should be, "Whosoever will, let him take the water of life freely" (Revelation 22:17). In the ministration of angels, they do not labor so as to shut any soul out, but rather to gather them all in; but if the message of the gospel is to go to all men, human agents must cooperate with the angel workers. Divine and human agencies must combine in order to accomplish the great work of saving the souls of the lost. Man cannot work out his own salvation without divine aid, and God will not save him without willing, decided cooperation. Human agencies must be educated; they must become sufficient for this great work, and their growth and education depend upon their union with divine forces.[21]

# A Good Work

*"This is a true saying, If a man desire the office of a bishop, he desireth a good work" (1 Timothy 3:1).*

There must be no belittling of the gospel ministry. No enterprise should be so conducted as to cause the ministry of the word to be looked upon as an inferior matter. It is not so. Those who belittle the ministry are belittling Christ. The highest of all work is ministry in its various lines, and it should be kept before the youth that there is no work more blessed of God than that of the gospel minister.

Let not our young men be deterred from entering the ministry. There is danger that through glowing representations some will be drawn away from the path where God bids them walk. Some have been encouraged to take a course of study in medical lines who ought to be preparing themselves to enter the ministry. The Lord calls for more ministers to labor in His vineyard. The words were spoken: "Strengthen the outposts; have faithful sentinels in every part of the world." God calls for you, young men. He calls for whole armies of young men who are largehearted and large-minded, and who have a deep love for Christ and the truth.

The measure of capacity or learning is of far less consequence than is the spirit with which you engage in the work. It is not great and learned men that the ministry needs; it is not eloquent sermonizers. God calls for men who will give themselves to Him to be imbued with His Spirit. The cause of Christ and humanity demands sanctified, self-sacrificing men, those who can go forth without the camp, bearing the reproach. . . .

How many of our young men will enter the service of God, not to be served, but to serve? In times past there were those who fastened their minds upon one soul after another, saying: "Lord, help me to save this soul." But now such instances are rare. How many act as if they realized the peril of sinners? How many take those whom they know to be in peril, presenting them to God in prayer and supplicating Him to save them?[22]

# Caution Needed

*"A bishop then must be blameless" (1 Timothy 3:2).*

[Titus 1:5–7 quoted.] It would be well for all our ministers to give heed to these words and not to hurry men into office without due consideration and much prayer that God would designate by His Holy Spirit whom He will accept.

Said the inspired apostle: "Lay hands suddenly on no man" (1 Timothy 5:22). In some of our churches the work of organizing and of ordaining elders has been premature; the Bible rule has been disregarded, and consequently grievous trouble has been brought upon the church. There should not be so great haste in electing leaders as to ordain men who are in no way fitted for the responsible work—men who need to be converted, elevated, ennobled, and refined before they can serve the cause of God in any capacity.

The gospel net gathers both good and bad. It takes time for character to be developed; there must be time to learn what men really are.[23]

We profess to be the depositaries of God's law; we claim to have greater light and to aim at a higher standard than any other people upon the earth; therefore we should show greater perfection of character and more earnest devotion.[24]

In the days of the apostles the ministers of God did not dare to rely upon their own judgment in selecting or accepting men to take the solemn and sacred position of mouthpiece for God. They selected the men whom their judgment would accept, and then they placed them before the Lord to see if He would accept them to go forth as His representatives. No less than this should be done now.

In many places we meet men who have been hurried into responsible positions as elders of the church, when they are not qualified for such a position. . . .

Ministers of God should be of good repute, capable of discreetly managing an interest after they have aroused it. We stand in great need of competent men who will bring honor instead of disgrace upon the cause which they represent.[25]

# A Case of Eligibility Lost

*"Now the sons of Reuben the firstborn of Israel, (for he was the first-born; but, forasmuch as he defiled his father's bed, his birthright was given unto the sons of Joseph the son of Israel)" (1 Chronicles 5:1).*

"Reuben, thou art my firstborn, my might, and the beginning of my strength, the excellency of dignity, and the excellency of power." Thus the father [Jacob] pictured what should have been the position of Reuben as the firstborn son; but his grievous sin at Edar [Genesis 35:21, 22] had made him unworthy of the birthright blessing. Jacob continued—"Unstable as water, thou shalt not excel" (Genesis 49:3, 4).

The priesthood was apportioned to Levi, the kingdom and the Messianic promise to Judah, and the double portion of the inheritance to Joseph.[26]

We must guard against the sins of this degenerate age. Let not Christ's ambassadors descend to trifling conversation, to familiarity with women, married or single. Let them keep their proper place with becoming dignity; yet at the same time they may be sociable, kind, and courteous to all. They must stand aloof from everything that savors of commonness and familiarity. This is forbidden ground, upon which it is unsafe to set the feet. Every word, every act, should tend to elevate, to refine, to ennoble. There is sin in thoughtlessness about such matters. . . .

Is there not enough taking place around us to show the need for this caution? Everywhere are seen wrecks of humanity, broken-down family altars, ruined homes. There is a strange abandonment of principle, the standard of morality is lowered, and the earth is fast becoming a Sodom. The practices which brought the judgment of God upon the antediluvian world, and which caused Sodom to be destroyed by fire, are fast increasing. We are nearing the end, when the earth is to be purified by fire.[27]

God will not entrust the care of His precious flock to men whose mind and judgment have been weakened by former errors that they have cherished such as so-called perfectionism and Spiritualism.[28]

# An Issue of Character

*"A bishop then must be . . . the husband of one wife" (1 Timothy 3:2).*

Do we consider and realize that the greatest influence to recommend Christianity to our world is a well-ordered and well-disciplined Christian family? The world sees that they believe God's Word.[29]

The greatest evidence of the power of Christianity that can be presented to the world is a well-ordered, well-disciplined family. This will recommend the truth as nothing else can, for it is a living witness of its practical power upon the heart.

The best test of the Christianity of a home is the type of character begotten by its influence. Actions speak louder than the most positive profession of godliness.[30]

Every Christian family should illustrate to the world the power and excellence of Christian influences.

The home in which the members are kindly, courteous Christians exerts a far-reaching influence for good. Other families mark the results attained by such a home and follow the example set, in their turn guarding their homes against evil influences. Angels of heaven often visit the home in which the will of God bears sway. Under the power of divine grace such a home becomes a place of refreshing to worn, weary pilgrims. Self is kept from asserting itself. Right habits are formed. There is a careful recognition of the rights of others. The faith that works by love and purifies the soul stands at the helm, presiding over the entire household. One well-ordered, well-disciplined family tells more in behalf of Christianity than all the sermons that can be preached.[31]

You will know whether or not a man is a Christian, for actions speak louder than words or profession. The spirit that characterizes the action represents the man, and the work will be in accordance with the mold he gives it. God will have it made manifest by test and trial who will stand connected with Christ in the end in the great plan of salvation. We are to act as reformers in every branch of our work; for then Christ works with us.[32]

# Guard Against Pride

*"A bishop then must be . . . vigilant" (1 Timothy 3:2).*

There are many who are always ready to flatter and praise a minister who can talk. A young minister is ever in danger of being petted and applauded to his own injury, while at the same time he may be deficient in the essentials which God requires of everyone who professes to be a mouthpiece for Him. . . . It requires a constant, earnest, and vigilant effort to watch and control self, to keep Jesus prominent and self out of sight.

It is necessary for you to watch for the weak points in your character, to restrain wrong tendencies, and to strengthen and develop noble faculties that have not been properly exercised. The world will never know the work secretly going on between the soul and God, nor the inward bitterness of spirit, the self-loathing, and the constant efforts to control self; but many of the world will be able to appreciate the result of these efforts. . . .

"Learn of Me," said Christ; "for I am meek and lowly in heart: and ye shall find rest unto your souls" (Matthew 11:29). He will instruct those who come to Him for knowledge. There are multitudes of false teachers in the world. The apostle declares that in the last days men will "heap to themselves teachers, having itching ears" (2 Timothy 4:3), because they desire to hear smooth things. . . . "Beware of false prophets, which come to you in sheep's clothing, but inwardly they are ravening wolves. Ye shall know them by their fruits" (Matthew 7:15, 16). The class of religious teachers here described profess to be Christians. They have the form of godliness and appear to be laboring for the good of souls, while they are at heart avaricious, selfish, ease-loving, following the promptings of their own unconsecrated hearts. They are in conflict with Christ and His teachings, and are destitute of His meek and lowly spirit.

The preacher who bears the sacred truth for these last days must be the opposite of all this and, by his life of practical godliness, plainly mark the distinction existing between the false and the true shepherd.[33]

# Cultivating Sobriety

*"A bishop then must be . . . sober" (1 Timothy 3:2).*

There are men working in the capacity of teachers of the truth who need to learn their first lessons in the school of Christ. The converting power of God must come upon the hearts of the ministers, or they should seek some other calling. If Christ's ambassadors realize the solemnity of presenting the truth to the people, they will be sober, thoughtful men, workers together with God. If they have a true sense of the commission which Christ gave to His disciples, they will with reverence open the word of God, and listen for instruction from the Lord, asking for wisdom from heaven that, as they stand between the living and the dead, they may realize that they must render an account to God for the work coming forth from their hands.

What can the minister do without Jesus? Verily, nothing. Then if he is a frivolous, joking man, he is not prepared to perform the duty laid upon him by the Lord. "Without me," says Christ, "ye can do nothing" (John 15:5). The flippant words that fall from his lips, the trifling anecdotes, the words spoken to create a laugh, are all condemned by the word of God, and are entirely out of place in the sacred desk. . . .

Unless the ministers are converted, our churches will be sickly and ready to die. God's power alone can change the human heart and imbue it with the love of Christ. God's power alone can correct and subdue the passions and sanctify the affections. All who minister must humble their proud hearts, submit their will to the will of God, and hide their life with Christ in God.

What is the object of the ministry? Is it to mix the comical with the religious? The theater is the place for such exhibitions. If Christ is formed within, if the truth with its sanctifying power is brought into the inner sanctuary of the soul, you will not have jolly men, neither will you have sour, cross, crabbed men to teach the precious lessons of Christ to perishing souls.[34]

# Intense Spiritual Life

*"A bishop then must be . . . of good behaviour" (1 Timothy 3:2).*

The Lord sets before His ministers the divine standard and instructs them that they are to be shepherds of the flock of God and ensamples of good behavior, that the ministry be not blamed, or brought down to a low, common level, and shaped according to the desires of the natural, unconverted heart. The ministers are not to carry into their sacred office their own defective spirits and faulty characters; for in all things they are to fulfill the word, and be found approving themselves "as the ministers of God."[35]

The ministry is no place for idlers. God's servants are to make full proof of their ministry. They will not be sluggards, but as expositors of His word they will put forth their utmost energies to be faithful. They should never cease to be learners. They are to keep their own souls alive to the sacredness of the work and to the great responsibilities of their calling, that they may at no time or place bring to God a maimed sacrifice, an offering which has cost them neither study nor prayer. The Lord has need of men of intense spiritual life.[36]

The work to be done calls for self-sacrifice at every step; but go forward. The worker who reveals a right spirit and consistent behavior under trying circumstances is proving his adaptability for his work. . . .

The knowledge that souls are perishing in their sins should arouse every worker to greater fervor in giving the light of present truth to all within his reach. He should never forget that whenever a soul is truly converted, God is glorified and angels in heaven burst forth into singing.

All who would have success in the work must tarry long with God. The story is told of an old Lancashire woman who was listening to the reasons her neighbors gave for their minister's success. They spoke of his gifts, of his style of address, of his manners. "Nay" said the old woman. "I will tell you what it is. Your man is very *thick* with the Almighty."[37]

# Hospitality

*"A bishop then must be . . . given to hospitality" (1 Timothy 3:2).*

There is altogether too little sociability, too little of a disposition to make room for two or three more at the family board, without embarrassment or parade. Some plead that "it is too much trouble." It would not be if you would say: "We have made no special preparation, but you are welcome to what we have." By the unexpected guest a welcome is appreciated far more than is the most elaborate preparation.

It is a denial of Christ to make preparation for visitors which requires time that rightly belongs to the Lord. In this we commit robbery of God. And we wrong others as well. In preparing an elaborate entertainment, many deprive their own families of needed attention, and their example leads others to follow the same course.

Needless worries and burdens are created by the desire to make a display in entertaining visitors. In order to prepare a great variety for the table, the housewife overworks; because of the many dishes prepared, the guests overeat; and disease and suffering, from overwork on the one hand and overeating on the other, are the result. These elaborate feasts are a burden and an injury.

But the Lord designs that we shall care for the interests of our brethren and sisters.[38]

Ministers, do not confine your work to giving Bible instruction. Do practical work. Seek to restore the sick to health. This is true ministry.[39]

Our work in this world is to live for others' good, to bless others, to be hospitable; and frequently it may be only at some inconvenience that we can entertain those who really need our care and the benefit of our society and our homes. Some avoid these necessary burdens. But someone must bear them; and because the brethren in general are not lovers of hospitality, and do not share equally in these Christian duties, a few who have willing hearts, and who cheerfully make the cases of those who need help their own, are burdened. A church should take special care to relieve its ministers of extra burdens in this direction.[40]

# A Work of Teaching

*"A bishop then must be . . . apt to teach" (1 Timothy 3:2).*

Some who enter the field are mere novices in the Scriptures. In other things also they are incompetent and inefficient. They cannot read the Scriptures without hesitating, miscalling words, and jumbling them together in such a manner that the word of God is abused. Those who are not qualified to present the truth in a proper manner need not be perplexed with regard to their duty. Their place is that of learners, not teachers. Young men who wish to prepare for the ministry are greatly benefited by attending our college; but advantages are still needed that they may be qualified to become acceptable speakers. A teacher should be employed to educate the youth to speak without wearing the vocal organs. The manners also should receive attention.

Some young men who enter the field are not successful in teaching the truth to others because they have not been educated themselves. Those who cannot read correctly should learn, and they should become apt to teach before they attempt to stand before the public. . . .

Ministers should be examined especially to see if they have an intelligent understanding of the truth for this time, so that they can give a connected discourse upon the prophecies or upon practical subjects. If they cannot clearly present Bible subjects they need to be hearers and learners still. They should earnestly and prayerfully search the Scriptures, and become conversant with them, in order to be teachers of Bible truth to others. All these things should be carefully and prayerfully considered before men are hurried into the field of labor.[41]

There should be less preaching and more teaching—teaching the people, and also teaching young men how to labor successfully. Ministers should become efficient in teaching others how to study the Bible, and in training the minds and manners of those who would become workers in the cause of God.[42]

# Setting the Example in Temperance

*"A bishop must be . . . not given to wine, . . . just, holy, temperate"*
*(Titus 1:7, 8).*

Ministers of the gospel are engaged in a most solemn work. They should be encouraged to deny themselves on the point of appetite, refusing to eat anything that will work an injury to their physical and mental powers. It is their privilege to have physical strength, which they may use to the honor of God in carrying forward His work. The fact that a man preaches the gospel does not give him license to indulge in selfish practices that will imperil his health. The ministers should set an example of temperance before the church members. They should keep their physical and mental powers in the very best condition, that they may do the greatest amount of good.[43]

We have had the light of health reform, and the Lord requires us to live that light. God will not daily work a miracle to counteract the unhealthful, selfish doings of man. . . . Our ministers must become increasingly intelligent in regard to their bodies and how to treat them.[44]

There is a solemn responsibility upon all, especially upon ministers who teach the truth, to overcome upon the point of appetite. Their usefulness would be much greater if they had control of their appetites and passions, and their mental and moral powers would be stronger if they combined physical labor with mental exertion. With strictly temperate habits, and with mental and physical labor combined, they could accomplish a far greater amount of labor and preserve clearness of mind. If they would pursue such a course, their thoughts and words would flow more freely, their religious exercises would be more energized, and the impressions made upon their hearers would be more marked.[45]

The destiny of souls hangs upon the course [ministers] pursue and the decisions they make. How important then that they should be temperate in *all* things, not only in their eating, but in their labor, that their strength may be unabated and devoted to their sacred calling.[46]

# Calm, Self-Possessed

*"A bishop must be . . . not soon angry, . . . no striker" (Titus 1:7).*

If the minister, when before his congregation, sees a disbelieving smile upon the faces of opponents, let him be as one who sees not. If any should be so impolite as to laugh and sneer, let not the minister, by voice or attitude, reflect the same spirit. Show that you handle no such weapons. . . .

The Holy Spirit does not work with men who love to be sharp and critical. That Spirit has been cherished in meeting debaters, and some have formed the habit of squaring for a combat. God is dishonored in this. Keep back the sharp thrusts; do not learn in Satan's school his methods of warfare. The Holy Spirit does not inspire the words of censure. A time of trouble is before us, and every honest soul who has not had the light of truth will then take a stand for Christ. Those who believe the truth are to be newly converted every day. Then they will be vessels unto honor.[47]

Ministers of calm contemplation, of thought and devotion, of conscience and faith, combined with activity and zeal, are wanted in this age. The two qualities, thought and devotion, activity and zeal, should go together.

Debating ministers are the most unreliable among us, because they cannot be depended upon when the work goes hard. Bring them into a place where there is but little interest, and they manifest a want of courage, zeal, and real interest. They depend as much upon being enlivened and invigorated by the excitement created by debate or opposition as does the inebriate upon his dram. These ministers need to be converted anew.[48]

Ministers who are preaching present truth were held up to me in contrast with the leading men of the Reformation; especially was Luther's devoted, zealous life placed beside the lives of some of our preachers. He proved his undying love for the truth by his courage, his calm firmness, his self-denial. He encountered trials and sacrifices, and at times suffered the deepest anguish of soul, while standing in defense of the truth; yet he murmured not. He was hunted like a wild beast of prey, yet for Christ's sake he endured all cheerfully.[49]

# Wages Are Not the Priority

*"A bishop then must be . . . not greedy of filthy lucre; . . . not covetous" (1 Timothy 3:2, 3).*

Too often the minister [of popular churches] has not the courage to stand for the right. He does not declare to his people what God has said. . . . To speak plainly would mean the offending of his congregation, the sacrifice of his popularity, the loss of his salary.[50]

It is not God's will that [our ministers] should seek to be rich. They should not engage in worldly enterprises; for this disqualifies them for giving their best powers to spiritual things. But they are to receive wages enough to support themselves and their families. They are not to have so many burdens laid upon them that they cannot give proper attention to the church in their own family; for it is their special duty to train their children for the Lord.[51]

It is a great mistake to keep a minister constantly at work in business lines, going from place to place, and sitting up late at night in attendance at board meetings and committee meetings. This brings upon him weariness and discouragement. Ministers should have time to rest, to obtain from God's word the rich nourishment of the bread of life. They should have time to drink refreshing drafts of consolation from the stream of living water.[52]

No man should be granted an exorbitant salary, even though he may possess special capabilities and qualifications. The work done for God and His cause is not to be placed on a mercenary basis. . . .

Those who labor wholeheartedly in the Lord's vineyard, working to the utmost of their ability, are not the ones to set the highest estimate on their own services. Instead of swelling with pride and self-importance, and measuring with exactness every hour's work, they compare their efforts with the Saviour's work and account themselves unprofitable servants.

Brethren, do not study how little you may do in order to reach the very lowest standard; but arouse to grasp the fullness of Christ, that you may do much for Him.[53]

# Patient With Opposers

*"A bishop then must be . . . patient, not a brawler" (1 Timothy 3:2, 3).*

The servants of God who teach the truth should be men of judgment. They should be men who can bear opposition and not get excited; for those who oppose the truth will pick at those who teach it, and every objection that can be produced will be brought in its worst form to bear against the truth. The servants of God who bear the message must be prepared to remove these objections with calmness and meekness, by the light of truth. Frequently opposers talk to ministers of God in a provoking manner, to call out something from them of the same nature, that they can make as much of it as possible and declare to others that the teachers of the commandments have a bitter spirit and are harsh, as has been reported. I saw that we must be prepared for objections, and with patience, judgment, and meekness, let them have the weight they deserve, not throw them away or dispose of them by positive assertions, and then bear down upon the objector, and manifest a hard spirit toward him; but give the objections their weight, then bring forth the light and the power of the truth, and let it outweigh and remove the errors. Thus a good impression will be made.[54]

Let all who are in error be treated with the gentleness of Christ. If those for whom you labor do not immediately grasp the truth, do not censure, do not criticize or condemn. Remember that you are to represent Christ in His meekness and gentleness and love. We must expect to meet unbelief and opposition. The truth has always had to meet these elements. But though you should meet the bitterest opposition, do not denounce your opponents. They may think, as did Paul, that they are doing God's service, and to such we must manifest patience, meekness, and long-suffering.

Let us not feel that we have heavy trials to bear, severe conflicts to endure, in representing unpopular truth. Think of Jesus and what He has suffered for you, and be silent. Even when abused and falsely accused, make no complaint; speak no word of murmuring; let no thought of reproach or discontent enter your mind.[55]

# Sound Family Management

*"A bishop then must be . . . one that ruleth well his own house, hav-ing his children in subjection with all gravity; (for if a man know not how to rule his own house, how shall he take care of the church of God?)"* (1 Timothy 3:2, 4, 5).

The family of the one suggested for office should be considered. Are they in subjection? Can the man rule his own house with honor? What character have his children? Will they do honor to the father's influence? If he has no tact, wisdom, or power of godliness at home in managing his own family, it is safe to conclude that the same defects will be carried into the church, and the same unsanctified management will be seen there. It will be far better to criticize the man before he is put into office than afterward, better to pray and counsel before taking the decisive step than to labor to correct the conse-quences of a wrong move.[56]

If a man does not show wisdom in the management of the church in his own house, how can he show wisdom in the management of the larger church outside? How can he bear the responsibilities which mean so much, if he cannot govern his own children? Wise discrimi-nation is not shown in this matter. God's blessing will not rest upon the minister who neglects the education and training of his children. He has a sacred trust, and he should in no case set before church members a defective example in the management of his home.[57]

Ministers' children are in some cases the most neglected children in the world, for the reason that the father is with them but little, and they are left to choose their own employment and amusement. If a minister has a family of boys, he should not leave them wholly to the care of the mother. This is too heavy a burden for her. He should make himself their companion and friend. He should exert himself to keep them from evil associates, and should see that they have useful work to do. It may be hard for the mother to exercise self-control. If the hus-band sees this, he should take more of the burden upon himself, doing all in his power to lead his boys to God.[58]

# Humble, Reputable, Exemplary

*"A bishop then must be . . . not a novice, lest being lifted up with pride he fall into the condemnation of the devil. Moreover he must have a good report of them which are without; lest he fall into reproach and the snare of the devil" (1 Timothy 3:2, 6, 7).*

Men will arise who claim that God has laid upon them the burden of teaching the truth to others. All such should be proved and tried. They should not be relieved from all care, neither should they be lifted into responsible positions at once; but they should be encouraged if they deserve encouragement, to give full proof of their ministry. It would not be the best course for such ones to pursue, to enter into other men's labors. Let them first labor in connection with one of experience and wisdom, and he can soon see whether they are capable of exerting an influence that will be saving.[59]

There should be a thorough investigation of the cases of those who present themselves to labor in the cause. The apostle warns you to "lay hands suddenly on no man" (1 Timothy 5:22). If the life is not what God can accept, the labors will be worthless; but if Christ is abiding in the heart by faith, every wrong will be made right, and those who are soldiers of Christ will be willing to prove it by a well-ordered life. There are many who enter the ministry, and their influence demoralizes the churches; and when they are rejected, they take their dismissal as a personal wrong. They have not Christ in the soul, as a well of water springing up unto everlasting life. . . .

We want men who are willing to go into new fields, and to do hard service for the Lord.[60]

In Timothy Paul saw one who appreciated the sacredness of the work of a minister; who was not appalled at the prospect of suffering and persecution; and who was willing to be taught. Yet the apostle did not venture to take the responsibility of giving Timothy, an untried youth, a training in the gospel ministry, without first fully satisfying himself in regard to his character and his past life.[61]

# Stewards of God

*"A bishop must be . . . as the steward of God; not self-willed" (Titus 1:7).*

Ministers have been presented to me, with their course of action and their character before they were converted—the hardest and most incorrigible, the most unbending, the most stubborn—and yet, every one of these traits of character was what they needed in the work of God. We don't want to kill that. It is needed in order to fill important positions of trust in the cause of God. There must be a transformation of character. The leaven must work in the human heart, until every action is in conformity to the will of God, and they are sanctified; then they become the most valuable.[62]

[Ezekiel 33:7–9 quoted.] The words of the prophet declare the solemn responsibility of those who are appointed as guardians of the church of God, stewards of the mysteries of God. They are to stand as watchmen on the walls of Zion, to sound the note of alarm at the approach of the enemy. Souls are in danger of falling under temptation, and they will perish unless God's ministers are faithful to their trust. If for any reason their spiritual senses become so benumbed that they are unable to discern danger, and through their failure to give warning the people perish, God will require at their hands the blood of those who are lost.

It is the privilege of the watchmen on the walls of Zion to live so near to God, and to be susceptible to the impressions of His Spirit, that He can work through them to tell men and women of their peril and point them to the place of safety. Faithfully are they to warn them of the sure result of transgression, and faithfully are they to safeguard the interests of the church. At no time may they relax their vigilance. Theirs is a work requiring the exercise of every faculty of the being. In trumpet tones their voices are to be lifted, and never are they to sound one wavering, uncertain note. Not for wages are they to labor, but because they cannot do otherwise, because they realize that there is a woe upon them if they fail to preach the gospel.[63]

# Praying in Anguish of Soul

*"Let the priests, the ministers of the Lord, weep between the porch and the altar, and let them say, Spare thy people, O Lord, and give not thine heritage to reproach, that the heathen should rule over them: wherefore should they say among the people, Where is their God? Then will the Lord be jealous for his land, and pity his people" (Joel 2:17, 18).*

Our ministers need a transformation of character. They should feel that if their works are not wrought in God, if they are left to their own imperfect efforts, they are of all men the most miserable. Christ will be with every minister who, although he may not have attained to perfection of character, is seeking most earnestly to become Christlike. Such a minister will pray. He will weep between the porch and the altar, crying in soul anguish for the Lord's presence to be with him; else he cannot stand before the people, with all heaven looking upon him, and the angel's pen taking note of his words, his deportment, and his spirit.

Oh, that men would fear the Lord! Oh, that they would love the Lord! Oh, that the messengers of God would feel the burden of perishing souls! Then they would not merely speechify; but they would have the power of God vitalizing their souls, and their hearts would glow with the fire of God's love. Out of weakness they would become strong; for they would be doers of the word. They would hear the voice of Jesus: "Lo: I am with you alway" (Matthew 28:20). . . . Just in proportion as the speaker appreciates the divine presence, and honors and trusts the power of God, is he acknowledged as a laborer together with God. Just in this proportion does he become mighty through God.

There needs to be an elevating, uplifting power, a constant growth in the knowledge of God and the truth, on the part of one who is seeking the salvation of souls. If the minister utters words drawn from the living oracles of God; if he believes in and expects the cooperation of Christ, whose servant he is; if he hides self and exalts Jesus, the world's Redeemer; his words will reach the hearts of his hearers, and his work will bear the divine credentials.[64]

# The Final Work of a Purified Ministry

*"[The Lord] shall purify the sons of Levi, and purge them as gold and silver, that they may offer unto the Lord an offering in righteousness" (Malachi 3:3).*

God will have order in His work. There are unfaithful men in the ministry, but this does not make the ministry any less the Lord's means for doing a great work. Those who accuse and disparage the ministry because the work done does not appear to be the work that should be done, are not wise men.

Those who think they are pleasing God by obeying some other law than His, and by performing works other than those the gospel has enjoined, are mocking God. They are insulting the Holy One of Israel. Warning after warning has been given. Appeal after appeal is made in the last message of mercy given to the world. Loath to give up, hoping, sorrowfully hoping, Christ knocks for the last time at the door of the heart. Men and women are given a final test. The worst of sinners are to hear the message of mercy. God will prove who will receive His seal or mark.[65]

I am instructed to say to our ministers, Be careful that the work of cleansing and sanctifying shall go on in your own individual souls. Let your first thought be to make your calling and election sure. Your example is to be full of kindness and encouragement. No masterful spirit is to come in, but let the heart be filled with the tenderness and love and compassion of Christ. Work every day for sanctification of the spirit through belief of the truth. Let all realize that they are chosen of God to reveal that they understand the mystery of godliness.

As a people we are to be purified from our natural evil habits and desires. Our hearts must be changed, or we cannot correctly represent the Lord Jesus, who gave His life for us. The Son of God took humanity upon Him that He might make it possible for humanity to take hold upon divinity through the exercise of a perfect faith. Christ is our example for the development of a perfect character. Through the strength we receive from Him, we may be overcomers.[66]

# A Vital Gift to Edify the Church

*"God hath set some in the church, first apostles, secondarily prophets" (1 Corinthians 12:28).*

Christ coming at the time and in the manner which He did was a direct and complete fulfillment of prophecy. The evidence of this, given to the world through the testimony of the apostles and that of their contemporaries, is among the strongest proofs of the Christian faith. We were not eyewitnesses of the miracles of Jesus, which attest His divinity; but we have the statements of His disciples who were eyewitnesses of them, and we see by faith through their eyes, and hear through their ears; and our faith with theirs grasps the evidence given.[1]

The apostles accepted Jesus upon the testimony of prophets and righteous men, stretching over a period of many centuries. The Christian world have a full and complete chain of evidence running through both the Old and the New Testament; in the one pointing to a Saviour to come, and in the other fulfilling the conditions of that prophecy. All this is sufficient to establish the faith of those who are willing to believe.[1]

The apostle cautioned the Thessalonians not to despise the gift of prophecy, and in the words, "Quench not the Spirit. Despise not prophesyings. Prove all things; hold fast that which is good" (1 Thessalonians 5:19–21), he enjoined a careful discrimination in distinguishing the false from the true.[2]

Until Christ shall appear in the clouds of heaven with power and great glory, men will become perverse in spirit and turn from the truth to fables. The church will yet see troublous times. She will prophesy in sackcloth. But although she must meet heresies and persecutions, although she must battle with the infidel and the apostate, yet by the help of God she is bruising the head of Satan. The Lord will have a people as true as steel, and with faith as firm as the granite rock. They are to be His witnesses in the world, His instrumentalities to do a special, a glorious work in the day of His preparation.[3]

# Counterfeits: a Sampling

*"If there arise among you a prophet, or a dreamer of dreams, and giveth thee a sign or a wonder, and the sign or the wonder come to pass, whereof he spake unto thee, saying, Let us go after other gods, which thou hast not known, and let us serve them; thou shalt not hearken unto the words of that prophet, or that dreamer of dreams: for the Lord your God proveth you, to know whether ye love the Lord your God with all your heart and with all your soul" (Deuteronomy 13:1–3).*

The Lord requires His people to use their reason, and not lay it aside for impressions. His work will be intelligible to all His children. His teaching will be such as will commend itself to the understanding of intelligent minds. It is calculated to elevate the mind. God's power is not manifested upon every occasion. Man's necessity is God's opportunity.

I was shown companies in confusion exercised by a wrong spirit, all making loud prayers together, some crying one thing and some another; and it was impossible to tell what was piped and what was harped. "God is not the author of confusion, but of peace" (1 Corinthians 14:33). Satan stepped in and controlled matters as he pleased. Reason and health were sacrificed to this delusion.

God does not require His people to imitate Baal's prophets, to afflict their bodies and cry out and shout, and throw themselves into almost every attitude, having no regard for order, until their strength fails through sheer exhaustion. Religion does not consist in making a noise; yet when the soul is filled with the Spirit of the Lord, sweet, heartfelt praise to God glorifies Him. Some have professed to have great faith in God, and to have special gifts and special answers to their prayers, although the evidence was lacking. They mistook presumption for faith. The prayer of faith is never lost; but to claim that it will be always answered in the very way and for the particular thing we have expected, is presumption. . . .

The greater the light which the people reject, the greater will be the power of deception and darkness which will come upon them. The rejection of truth leaves men captives, the subjects of Satan's deception.[4]

# Developing Discernment

*"When a prophet speaketh in the name of the Lord, if the thing follow not, nor come to pass, that is the thing which the Lord hath not spoken, but the prophet hath spoken it presumptuously: thou shalt not be afraid of him" (Deuteronomy 18:22).*

We need to know for ourselves what voice we are heeding, whether it is the voice of the true and living God, or the voice of the great apostate. Eternal life is of value to each of us, and we must take heed how we hear. We need sound doctrine, pure faith.[5]

Dishes of fables are presented to us on every hand, and men choose to believe error rather than truth, because the acceptance of the truth involves a cross. Self must be denied; self must be crucified. Therefore Satan presents to them an easier way by making void the law of God. When God lets man have his own way, it is the darkest hour of his life. For a willful, disobedient child to be left to have his own way, to follow the bent of his own mind and gather the dark clouds of God's judgment about him, is a terrible thing. But Satan has his agents who are too proud to repent and who are constantly at work to tear down the cause of Jehovah and trample it under their feet. What a day of sorrow and despair when these meet their work with all its burden of results! Souls who might have been saved to Jesus Christ have been lost through their teachings and influence. Christ died for them that they might have life. He opened before them the way whereby they might, through His merits, keep the law of God.[6]

Have we given ourselves up to do God's will? Are we transformed by the grace of Christ? Some claim to be in Christ, while their special work is to make void the law of Jehovah. Shall we take their word for it? Shall we accept their assertions? How shall we distinguish God's true servants from the false prophets who Christ said should arise to deceive many? There is only one test of character—the law of Jehovah.[7]

# Deborah the Prophetess

*"Deborah, a prophetess, the wife of Lapidoth, she judged Israel at that time. And she dwelt under the palm tree of Deborah between Ramah and Bethel in mount Ephraim: and the children of Israel came up to her for judgment" (Judges 4:4, 5).*

For twenty years, the Israelites groaned under the yoke of the oppressor; then they turned from their idolatry, and with humiliation and repentance cried unto the Lord for deliverance. They did not cry in vain. There was dwelling in Israel a woman illustrious for her piety, and through her the Lord chose to deliver His people. Her name was Deborah. She was known as a prophetess, and in the absence of the usual magistrates, the people had sought to her for counsel and justice.

The Lord communicated to Deborah His purpose to destroy the enemies of Israel, and bade her send for a man named Barak, of the tribe of Naphtali, and make known to him the instructions which she had received. She accordingly sent for Barak, and directed him to assemble ten thousand men of the tribes of Naphtali and Zebulun, and make war upon the armies of King Jabin.

Barak knew the scattered, disheartened, and unarmed condition of the Hebrews, and the strength and skill of their enemies. Although he had been designated by the Lord Himself as the one chosen to deliver Israel, and had received the assurance that God would go with him and subdue their enemies, yet he was timid and distrustful. He accepted the message from Deborah as the word of God, but he had little confidence in Israel, and feared that they would not obey his call. He refused to engage in such a doubtful undertaking unless Deborah would accompany him, and thus support his efforts by her influence and counsel. Deborah consented, but assured him that because of his lack of faith, the victory gained should not bring honor to him; for Sisera would be betrayed into the hands of a woman. . . .

The Israelites acted with courage and promptness; but God alone could have discomfited the enemy, and the victory could be ascribed to Him alone.[8]

# The Spirit Manifested at Ramah

*"Saul sent messengers to take David: and when they saw the company of the prophets prophesying, and Samuel standing as appointed over them, the Spirit of God was upon the messengers of Saul, and they also prophesied. . . . Then went he also to Ramah . . . and the Spirit of God was upon him also, and he went on, and prophesied"* (1 Samuel 19:20, 22, 23).

As Saul went on to Gibeah in Benjamin, he perceived a company of prophets returning from the high place where they had been to worship; and as they went, they sang the praise of God to the music of the pipe and the harp, the psaltery and the tabret. Then the Spirit of God rested upon Saul, and he joined the prophets, and with them sang the praise of the Most High and declared the wonders of divine truth. He spoke with so great fluency and wisdom, and joined so earnestly in the services of prayer and praise, that those who had known him only as the untaught husbandman exclaimed in wonder, "What is this that is come unto the son of Kish? Is Saul also among the prophets?" (1 Samuel 10:11). They could not understand how so great a transformation had been effected.

Samuel had founded the first regular establishments for religious instruction and the unfolding of the prophetic gifts. Among the chief subjects of study were the law of God with the instructions given to Moses, sacred history, sacred music, and poetry. In these "schools of the prophets" young men were educated by those who were not only well versed in divine truth, but who themselves maintained close communion with God and had received the special endowment of His Spirit. These educators enjoyed the respect and confidence of the people both for learning and piety. The power of the Holy Spirit was often strikingly manifest in their assemblies, and the exercise of the prophetic gift was not infrequent. These schools, or colleges, were of untold value to Israel, not only as providing for the dissemination of religious truth, but as preserving the spirit of vital godliness. As Saul united with the prophets in their worship, a great change was wrought in him by the renewing power of the Holy Spirit.[9]

# The Example of Micaiah

*"The messenger that was gone to call Micaiah spake unto him, saying, Behold now, the words of the prophets declare good unto the king with one mouth: let thy word, I pray thee, be like the word of one of them, and speak that which is good. And Micaiah said, As the Lord liveth, what the Lord saith unto me, that will I speak"* (1 Kings 22:13, 14).

While many of the professed followers of Christ have lapsed away into error and apostasy, those who have walked in the light, not only hear, but read and understand the prophecies of His word. The law of God will be made void in the world; its authority will be despised just as it was in heaven in the first great rebellion; and God would have us intelligent to note the movement of the nations, so that we may see the signal of danger, and recognize the warnings that He has given us, that we may not be found on the side of the great deceiver in the crisis that is just before us. . . .

If we are anxious to understand our duty, [God] will not leave us to be enshrouded in darkness, but will enlighten our understanding so that we shall know for ourselves what is truth. We do not want to be found receiving dangerous error as truth. We do not wish to imperil our souls by rejection of God's messages of warning and counsel. Our greatest danger lies in our tendency to refuse increased light, and our only safety is to see and understand for ourselves "what saith the Lord." . . . The controversy in regard to the law of God has begun, and we must be prepared to give a reason of the hope that is in us, with meekness and fear. We must know where our feet are standing.

Although the law of God will be almost universally made void in the world, there will be a remnant of the righteous that will be obedient to God's requirements. . . .

The winds of doctrine will blow fiercely about us, but we should not be moved by them. God has given us a correct standard of righteousness and truth—the law and the testimony.[10]

# Disappointments for the Best

*"Now it came to pass, as David sat in his house, that David said to Nathan the prophet, Lo, I dwell in an house of cedars, but the ark of the covenant of the Lord remaineth under curtains. Then Nathan said unto David, Do all that is in thine heart; for God is with thee. And it came to pass the same night, that the word of God came to Nathan, saying, Go and tell David my servant, Thus saith the Lord, Thou shalt not build me an house to dwell in" (1 Chronicles 17:1–4).*

David knew that it would be an honor to his name and would bring glory to his government to perform the work that he had purposed in his heart to do, but he was ready to submit his will to the will of God. The grateful resignation thus manifested is rarely seen, even among Christians. How often do those who have passed the strength of manhood cling to the hope of accomplishing some great work upon which their hearts are set, but which they are unfitted to perform! God's providence may speak to them, as did His prophet to David, declaring that the work which they so much desire is not committed to them. It is theirs to prepare the way for another to accomplish it. But instead of gratefully submitting to the divine direction, many fall back as if slighted and rejected, feeling that if they cannot do the one thing which they desire to do, they will do nothing. Many cling with desperate energy to responsibilities which they are incapable of bearing, and vainly endeavor to accomplish a work for which they are insufficient, while that which they might do, lies neglected. And because of this lack of cooperation on their part the greater work is hindered or frustrated.[11]

All the difficulties, the backsets, the hardships, and the disappointments which God's servants will meet in active labor will only strengthen them in the formation of correct characters.[12]

Better far the cross and disappointed hopes, than to live with princes and forfeit heaven.[13]

# Huldah's Message

*"Thus saith the Lord, . . . because they have forsaken me, and have burned incense unto other gods, that they might provoke me to anger with all the works of their hands; therefore my wrath shall be kindled against this place, and shall not be quenched. But to the king of Judah which sent you to enquire of the Lord, thus shall ye say to him, Thus saith the Lord God of Israel, As touching the words which thou hast heard; because thine heart was tender, and thou hast humbled thyself before the Lord, when thou heardest what I spake against this place, and against the inhabitants thereof, that they should become a desolation and a curse, and hast rent thy clothes, and wept before me; I also have heard thee, saith the Lord" (2 Kings 22:16–19).*

God sent Josiah the word that Jerusalem's ruin could not be averted. Even if the people should humble themselves before God, they could not escape their punishment. So long had their senses been deadened by sinning against God that, if the judgments had not come upon them, they would soon have swung back into the same sinful course. But because the king humbled his heart before God, he received from Huldah the prophetess the word that the Lord would acknowledge his quickness in seeking God for forgiveness and mercy. . . .

The king, on his part, left undone nothing that might bring about a reformation. . . . In the place of making a speech to the people, Josiah ordered that the book of the law be read to them. So earnest did he feel that he himself read the law aloud. He was deeply affected, and he read with the pathos of a broken heart. . . .

What should we do, we who have had great light? The law has been kept constantly before us. Time and again we have heard it preached. The Lord's anger is kindled against His people because of their disregard of His Word. Conviction of soul should send us in penitence to the foot of the cross, there to pray with the whole heart, saying, "What shall we do to be saved? Wherewithal shall we come before the Lord?" My brethren, inquire quickly, before it is too late.[14]

# The Prophets as Examples

*"Take, my brethren, the prophets, who have spoken in the name of the Lord, for an example of suffering affliction, and of patience" (James 5:10).*

The unfaltering servants of God have usually suffered the bitterest persecution from false teachers of religion. But the true prophets will ever prefer reproach, and even death, rather than unfaithfulness to God. The Infinite Eye is upon the instruments of divine reproof, and they bear a heavy responsibility. But God regards the injury done to them through misrepresentation, falsehood, or abuse as though it were done unto Himself, and will punish accordingly.[15]

Jeremiah suffered the severest persecution from his own countrymen, because he bore a faithful message from God. Isaiah, who was permitted by the Lord to see wonderful things, was sawn asunder because he faithfully reproved the sins of the Jewish nation. The prophets who came to look after the Lord's vineyard were indeed beaten and killed.[16]

In every age God's chosen messengers have been reviled and persecuted, yet through their affliction the knowledge of God has been spread abroad. Every disciple of Christ is to step into the ranks and carry forward the same work, knowing that its foes can do nothing against the truth, but for the truth. God means that truth shall be brought to the front and become the subject of examination and discussion, even through the contempt placed upon it. The minds of the people must be agitated; every controversy, every reproach, every effort to restrict liberty of conscience, is God's means of awakening minds that otherwise might slumber.

How often this result has been seen in the history of God's messengers! When the noble and eloquent Stephen was stoned to death at the instigation of the Sanhedrin council, there was no loss to the cause of the gospel. The light of heaven that glorified his face, the divine compassion breathed in his dying prayer, were as a sharp arrow of conviction to . . . Saul, the persecuting Pharisee, [who] became a chosen vessel to bear the name of Christ.[17]

# A Similar Call Today

*"The word of the Lord came unto me, saying, Before I formed thee in the belly I knew thee; and before thou camest forth out of the womb I sanctified thee, and I ordained thee a prophet unto the nations. Then said I, Ah, Lord God! behold, I cannot speak: for I am a child. But the Lord said unto me, Say not, I am a child: for thou shalt go to all that I shall send thee, and whatsoever I command thee thou shalt speak. Be not afraid of their faces: for I am with thee to deliver thee, saith the Lord. Then the Lord put forth his hand, and touched my mouth. And the Lord said unto me, Behold, I have put my words in thy mouth"* (Jeremiah 1:4–9).

As Christ sent forth His disciples, so today He sends forth the members of His church. The same power that the apostles had is for them. If they will make God their strength, He will work with them, and they shall not labor in vain. Let them realize that the work in which they are engaged is one upon which the Lord has placed His signet. . . . [Jeremiah 1:7–9 quoted.] And He bids us go forth to speak the words He gives us, feeling His holy touch upon our lips.

Christ has given to the church a sacred charge. Every member should be a channel through which God can communicate to the world the treasures of His grace, the unsearchable riches of Christ. There is nothing that the Saviour desires so much as agents who will represent to the world His Spirit and His character. There is nothing that the world needs so much as the manifestation through humanity of the Saviour's love. All heaven is waiting for men and women through whom God can reveal the power of Christianity.

The church is God's agency for the proclamation of truth, empowered by Him to do a special work; and if she is loyal to Him, obedient to all His commandments, there will dwell within her the excellency of divine grace. If she will be true to her allegiance, if she will honor the Lord God of Israel, there is no power that can stand against her.[18]

# Prophecy Faithfully Spoken

*"The prophet that hath a dream, let him tell a dream; and he that hath my word, let him speak my word faithfully. What is the chaff to the wheat? saith the Lord" (Jeremiah 23:28).*

We have an abundance of weighty, solemn truths to proclaim from the Word of God without allowing the mind to devise and plan theories of human nothingness to present to the flock of God as testing truth. What is the chaff to the wheat?[19]

To John [the Revelator] the Lord opened the subjects that He saw would be needed by His people in the last days. The instruction that He gave is found in the book of Revelation. Those who would be co-workers with our Lord and Saviour Jesus Christ will show a deep interest in the truths found in this book. With pen and voice they will strive to make plain the wonderful things that Christ came from heaven to reveal. [Revelation 1:1–3 quoted.]

The solemn messages that have been given in their order in the Revelation are to occupy the first place in the minds of God's people. Nothing else is to be allowed to engross our attention.

Precious time is rapidly passing, and there is danger that many will be robbed of the time which should be given to the proclamation of the messages that God has sent to a fallen world. Satan is pleased to see the diversion of minds that should be engaged in a study of the truths which have to do with eternal realities.

The testimony of Christ, a testimony of the most solemn character, is to be borne to the world. All through the book of Revelation there are the most precious, elevating promises, and there are also warnings of the most fearfully solemn import. Will not those who profess to have a knowledge of the truth read the testimony given to John by Christ? Here is no guesswork, no scientific deception. Here are the truths that concern our present and future welfare. What is the chaff to the wheat?[20]

# Smooth Things Not of God

*"Now go, write it before them in a table, and note it in a book, that it may be for the time to come for ever and ever: that this is a rebellious people, lying children, children that will not hear the law of the Lord: which say to the seers, See not; and to the prophets, Prophesy not unto us right things, speak unto us smooth things, prophesy deceits: get you out of the way, turn aside out of the path, cause the Holy One of Israel to cease from before us" (Isaiah 30:8–11).*

There are many false prophets in these days, to whom sin does not appear specially repulsive. They complain that the peace of the people is unnecessarily disturbed by the reproofs and warnings of God's messengers. As for them, they lull the souls of sinners into a fatal ease by their smooth and deceitful teachings. Ancient Israel was thus charmed by the flattering messages of the corrupt priests. Their prediction of prosperity was more pleasing than the message of the true prophet, who counseled repentance and submission.

The servants of God should manifest a tender, compassionate spirit and show to all that they are not actuated by any personal motives in their dealings with the people, and that they do not take delight in giving messages of wrath in the name of the Lord. But they must never flinch from pointing out the sins that are corrupting the professed people of God, nor cease striving to influence them to turn from their errors and obey the Lord.

Those who seek to cloak sin and make it appear less aggravating to the mind of the offender are doing the work of the false prophets and may expect the retributive wrath of God to follow such a course. The Lord will never accommodate His ways to the wishes of corrupt men. . . .

God has no sympathy with the evildoer. He gives no one liberty to gloss over the sins of His people, nor to cry, "Peace, peace," when He has declared that there shall be no peace for the wicked. Those who stir up rebellion against the servants whom God sends to deliver His messages are rebelling against the word of the Lord.[21]

# An Imposter Destroyed

*"Then said the prophet Jeremiah unto Hananiah the prophet, Hear now, Hananiah; The Lord hath not sent thee; but thou makest this people to trust in a lie. Therefore thus saith the Lord; Behold, I will cast thee from off the face of the earth: this year thou shalt die, because thou hast taught rebellion against the Lord. So Hananiah the prophet died the same year in the seventh month" (Jeremiah 28:15–17).*

The lightest punishment that a merciful God could inflict upon so rebellious a people was submission to the rule of Babylon, but if they warred against this decree of servitude they were to feel the full vigor of His chastisement.

The amazement of the assembled council of nations knew no bounds when Jeremiah, carrying the yoke of subjection about his neck, made known to them the will of God.

Against determined opposition Jeremiah stood firmly for the policy of submission. Prominent among those who presumed to gainsay the counsel of the Lord was Hananiah, one of the false prophets against whom the people had been warned. Thinking to gain the favor of the king and of the royal court, he lifted his voice in protest, declaring that God had given him words of encouragement for the Jews. . . .

Jeremiah, in the presence of the priests and people, earnestly entreated them to submit to the king of Babylon for the time the Lord had specified. He cited the men of Judah to the prophecies of Hosea, Habakkuk, Zephaniah, and others whose messages of reproof and warning had been similar to his own. He referred them to events which had taken place in fulfillment of prophecies of retribution for unrepented sin. In the past the judgments of God had been visited upon the impenitent in exact fulfillment of His purpose as revealed through His messengers. . . .

The false prophet had strengthened the unbelief of the people in Jeremiah and his message. He had wickedly declared himself the Lord's messenger, and he suffered death in consequence.[22]

# God Is in Control

*"Son of man, set thy face against the Ammonites, and prophesy against them; and say unto the Ammonites, Hear the word of the Lord God; Thus saith the Lord God; Because thou saidst, Aha, against my sanctuary, when it was profaned; and against the land of Israel, when it was desolate; and against the house of Judah, when they went into captivity; behold, therefore I will deliver thee to the men of the east for a possession, and they shall set their palaces in thee, and make their dwellings in thee: they shall eat thy fruit, and they shall drink thy milk"* (Ezekiel 25:2–4).

Lot's only posterity, the Moabites and Ammonites, were vile, idolatrous tribes, rebels against God and bitter enemies of His people.[23]

Because of the cruelty and treachery of the Ammonites and Moabites toward Israel, God had declared through Moses that they should be forever shut out from the congregation of His people. See Deuteronomy 23:3–6.[24]

While nations have rejected God's principles, and in this rejection have wrought their own ruin, yet a divine, overruling purpose has manifestly been at work throughout the ages. It was this that the prophet Ezekiel saw in the wonderful representation given him during his exile in the land of the Chaldeans, when before his astonished gaze were portrayed the symbols that revealed an overruling Power that has to do with the affairs of earthly rulers.[25]

In the visions given to Isaiah, to Ezekiel, and to John we see how closely heaven is connected with the events taking place upon the earth and how great is the care of God for those who are loyal to Him. The world is not without a ruler. The program of coming events is in the hands of the Lord. The Majesty of heaven has the destiny of nations, as well as the concerns of His church, in His own charge. . . .

We need to trust in God, believe in Him, and go forward.[26]

# The Humble Called Unexpectedly

*"Amos . . . said to Amaziah, I was no prophet, neither was I a prophet's son; but I was an herdman, and a gatherer of sycomore fruit: and the Lord took me as I followed the flock, and the Lord said unto me, Go, prophesy unto my people Israel" (Amos 7:14, 15).*

How many useful and honored workers in God's cause have received a training amid the humble duties of the most lowly positions in life! Moses was the prospective ruler of Egypt, but God could not take him from the king's court to do the work appointed him. Only when he had been for forty years a faithful shepherd was he sent to be the deliverer of his people. Gideon was taken from the threshing-floor to be the instrument in the hands of God for delivering the armies of Israel. Elisha was called to leave the plow and do the bidding of God. Amos was a husbandman, a tiller of the soil, when God gave him a message to proclaim.

All who become coworkers with Christ will have a great deal of hard, uncongenial labor to perform, and their lessons of instruction should be wisely chosen, and adapted to their peculiarities of character, and the work which they are to pursue.[27]

As Elisha was called from following his oxen in the field, to receive the mantle of consecration to the prophetic office, so was William Miller called to leave his plow and open to the people the mysteries of the kingdom of God. With trembling he entered upon his work, leading his hearers down, step by step, through the prophetic periods to the second appearing of Christ. With every effort he gained strength and courage as he saw the widespread interest excited by his words.

Though he had little of the learning of the schools, he became wise because he connected himself with the Source of wisdom. He possessed strong mental powers, united with true kindness of heart, Christian humility, calmness, and self-control. He was a man of sterling worth, who could not but command respect and esteem wherever integrity of character and moral excellence were valued.[28]

# A Message From Haggai

*"Then came the word of the Lord by Haggai the prophet, saying, Is it time for you, O ye, to dwell in your cieled houses, and this house lie waste? Now therefore thus saith the Lord of hosts; Consider your ways" (Haggai 1:3–5).*

A striking illustration of the results of selfishly withholding even freewill offerings from the cause of God was given in the days of the prophet Haggai. After their return from the captivity in Babylon, the Jews undertook to rebuild the temple of the Lord; but meeting determined opposition from their enemies, they discontinued the work; and a severe drought, by which they were reduced to actual want, convinced them that it was impossible to complete the building of the temple. "The time is not come," they said, "the time that the Lord's house should be built" (Haggai 1:2). But a message was sent them by the Lord's prophet: [Haggai 1:4–6, 9–11; 12:16, 17 quoted].

Roused by these warnings, the people set themselves to build the house of God.[29]

Repentant sinners have no cause to despair because they are reminded of their transgressions and warned of their danger. These very efforts in their behalf show how much God loves them and desires to save them. They have only to follow His counsel and do His will, to inherit eternal life. God sets the sins of His erring people before them, that they may behold them in all their enormity under the light of divine truth. It is then their duty to renounce them forever.

God is as powerful to save from sin today as He was in the times of the patriarchs, of David, and of the prophets and apostles. The multitude of cases recorded in sacred history where God has delivered His people from their own iniquities should make the Christian of this time eager to receive divine instruction and zealous to perfect a character that will bear the close inspection of the judgment.[30]

Consider your ways. Take time to think. Weigh your actions.[31]

# Elijah's Message Returns

*"Behold, I will send you Elijah the prophet before the coming of the great and dreadful day of the Lord: and he shall turn the heart of the fathers to the children, and the heart of the children to their fathers, lest I come and smite the earth with a curse" (Malachi 4:5, 6).*

When the Spirit of God controls the mind and heart, [He] turns the hearts of the fathers to the children, and the disobedient to the wisdom of the just. The law of Jehovah will then be regarded as a transcript of the divine character, and a new song bursts forth from the heart that has been touched by divine grace; for he realizes that the promise of God has been fulfilled in his experience, that his transgression is forgiven, his sin covered. He has exercised repentance toward God for the violation of His law, and faith toward our Lord Jesus Christ who has died for his justification.[32]

There is nothing so ennobling and invigorating as a study of the great themes which concern our eternal life. Let students seek to grasp these God-given truths; let them seek to measure these precious things, and their minds will expand and grow strong in the effort. But a mind crowded with a mass of matter it will never be able to use is a mind dwarfed and enfeebled, because only put to the task of dealing with commonplace material. It has not been put to the task of considering the high, elevated disclosures coming from God. . . .

All unnecessary matters need to be weeded from the course of study, and only such studies placed before the student as will be of real value to him. With these alone he needs to become familiarized, that he may secure for himself that life which measures with the life of God. And as he learns of these, his mind will strengthen and expand as did the mind of Christ and of John the Baptist. What was it that made John great? He closed his mind to the mass of tradition taught by the teachers of the Jewish nation, opening it to the wisdom which cometh down from above.[33]

# Preparing a Prophet

*"The angel said . . . Fear not, Zacharias: for thy prayer is heard; and thy wife Elisabeth shall bear thee a son, and thou shalt call his name John. . . . And many of the children of Israel shall he turn to the Lord their God. And he shall go before him in the spirit and power of Elias, to turn the hearts of the fathers to the children, and the disobedient to the wisdom of the just; to make ready a people prepared for the Lord" (Luke 1:13, 16, 17).*

An angel from heaven came to instruct Zacharias and Elizabeth as to how they should train and educate their child, so as to work in harmony with God in preparing a messenger to announce the coming of Christ. As parents they were to faithfully cooperate with God in forming such a character in John as would fit him to perform the part God had assigned him as a competent worker. John was the son of their old age, he was a child of miracle, and the parents might have reasoned that he had a special work to do for the Lord and the Lord would take care of him. But the parents did not thus reason; they moved to a retired place in the country, where their son would not be exposed to the temptations of city life, or induced to depart from the counsel and instruction which they as parents would give him. They acted their part in developing a character in the child that would in every way meet the purpose for which God had designed his life. By no careless neglect on their part shall their son fail to become good and wise, "to give light to them that sit in darkness and in the shadow of death, and to guide our feet into the way of peace" (Luke 1:79). They sacredly fulfilled their obligation.[34]

The character and experience of John the Baptist, the forerunner of Christ, should be an encouragement to parents in the training of their children. John did not make his home in the cities and villages. From childhood to youth, and from youth to manhood, he lived in the wilderness. But he did not live thus for any selfish purpose.[35]

# Learning From the Prophet's Parents

*"He shall be great in the sight of the Lord, and shall drink neither wine nor strong drink; and he shall be filled with the Holy Ghost, even from his mother's womb" (Luke 1:15).*

The solemn responsibilities and duties enjoined upon us by our Lord are not to be ignored until our will and our circumstances are adjusted. The principle of self-denial and self-sacrifice, as revealed in the example of Christ, of John the Baptist, of Daniel and the three worthies, is to pass like a plowshare through hereditary and cultivated habits through all circumstances and surroundings.[36]

The Lord has died for children, and He is ready to do a great work for them if parents will cooperate with Him in training and educating their children according to the instruction that He has given. The character in childhood of John the Baptist should be an encouragement to parents in the training of their children.

To bring up the children in the nurture and admonition of the Lord is the greatest missionary work that parents can perform. The mother is entrusted with a greater work than is the king upon his throne. She has a class of duty to perform in connection with her children that no other one can perform. If she daily learns in the school of Christ, she will discharge her duty in the fear of God, and care for the children as the Lord's beautiful flock.

Mothers should forbear from fretting and scolding. It is not safe to practice habits of fretting and scolding, for you will become unpleasant and harsh in your home, and will be likely to burst into a passion at anything that displeases you. This would greatly injure your soul, and injure the souls of your family. Be patient, be kind, be gentle. Gain the confidence and love of your children, and it will not be difficult to control them. Never fret, never threaten, never make a promise to your children that you cannot fulfill. Your lack of fulfilling your word will weaken the confidence of your children in you. . . .

Do not treat them in such a way that they will think that there is no use trying to be good and to do right.[37]

# The Prophet's Own Preparation

*"And the child grew, and waxed strong in spirit, and was in the deserts till the day of his shewing unto Israel" (Luke 1:80).*

John the Baptist, the forerunner of Christ, received his early training from his parents. The greater portion of his life was spent in the wilderness, that he might not be influenced by beholding the lax piety of the priests and rabbis or by learning their maxims and traditions, through which right principles were perverted and belittled. The religious teachers of the day had become so blind spiritually that they could hardly recognize the virtues of heavenly origin. So long had they cherished pride, envy, and jealousy that they interpreted the Old Testament Scriptures in such a manner as to destroy their true meaning. It was John's choice to forgo the enjoyments and luxuries of city life for the stern discipline of the wilderness. Here his surroundings were favorable to habits of simplicity and self-denial. Uninterrupted by the clamor of the world, he could here study the lessons of nature, of revelation, and of providence. The words of the angel to Zacharias had been often repeated to John by his God-fearing parents. From his childhood his mission had been kept before him, and he accepted the holy trust. To him the solitude of the desert was a welcome escape from the society in which suspicion, unbelief, and impurity had become well-nigh all-pervading. He distrusted his own power to withstand temptation and shrank from constant contact with sin lest he should lose the sense of its exceeding sinfulness.

But the life of John was not spent in idleness, in ascetic gloom, or in selfish isolation. From time to time he went forth to mingle with men, and he was ever an interested observer of what was passing in the world. From his quiet retreat he watched the unfolding of events. With vision illuminated by the divine Spirit, he studied the characters of men, that he might understand how to reach their hearts with the message of heaven.[38]

# In the Wilderness With Power

*"In those days came John the Baptist, preaching in the wilderness of Judaea, and saying, Repent ye: for the kingdom of heaven is at hand. For this is he that was spoken of by the prophet Esaias, saying, The voice of one crying in the wilderness, Prepare ye the way of the Lord, make his paths straight" (Matthew 3:1–3).*

Amid discord and strife, a voice was heard from the wilderness, a voice startling and stern, yet full of hope: "Repent ye: for the kingdom of heaven is at hand" (Matthew 3:2). With a new, strange power it moved the people. Prophets had foretold the coming of Christ as an event far in the future; but here was an announcement that it was at hand. John's singular appearance carried the minds of his hearers back to the ancient seers. In his manner and dress he resembled the prophet Elijah. With the spirit and power of Elijah he denounced the national corruption, and rebuked the prevailing sins. His words were plain, pointed, and convincing. Many believed him to be one of the prophets risen from the dead. The whole nation was stirred. Multitudes flocked to the wilderness.

John proclaimed the coming of the Messiah, and called the people to repentance. As a symbol of cleansing from sin, he baptized them in the waters of the Jordan. Thus by a significant object lesson he declared that those who claimed to be the chosen people of God were defiled by sin, and that without purification of heart and life they could have no part in the Messiah's kingdom.[39]

The words of the preacher in the wilderness were with power. He bore his message unflinchingly, rebuking the sins of priests and rulers, and enjoining upon them the works of the kingdom of heaven. He pointed out to them their sinful disregard of their Father's authority in refusing to do the work appointed them. He made no compromise with sin, and many were turned from their unrighteousness.

Had the profession of the Jewish leaders been genuine, they would have received John's testimony and accepted Jesus as the Messiah. But they did not show the fruits of repentance and righteousness. The very ones whom they despised were pressing into the kingdom of God before them.[40]

# More Than a Prophet

*"Jesus began to say unto the multitudes concerning John, . . . What went ye out for to see? A prophet? yea, I say unto you, and more than a prophet. For this is he, of whom it is written, Behold, I send my messenger before thy face, which shall prepare thy way before thee. Verily I say unto you, Among them that are born of women there hath not risen a greater than John the Baptist: notwithstanding he that is least in the kingdom of heaven is greater than he" (Matthew 11:7, 9–11).*

For years the Lord has been calling the attention of His people to health reform. This is one of the great branches of the work of preparation for the coming of the Son of man. John the Baptist went forth in the spirit and power of Elijah to prepare the way of the Lord and to turn the people to the wisdom of the just. He was a representative of those living in these last days to whom God has entrusted sacred truths to present before the people to prepare the way for the second appearing of Christ. John was a reformer. The angel Gabriel, direct from heaven, gave a discourse upon health reform to the father and mother of John. He said that he should not drink wine or strong drink, and that he should be filled with the Holy Ghost from his birth.

John separated himself from friends and from the luxuries of life. The simplicity of his dress, a garment woven of camel's hair, was a standing rebuke to the extravagance and display of the Jewish priests, and of the people generally. His diet, purely vegetable, of locusts and wild honey, was a rebuke to the indulgence of appetite and the gluttony that everywhere prevailed. . . .

Those who are to prepare the way for the second coming of Christ are represented by faithful Elijah, as John came in the spirit of Elijah to prepare the way for Christ's first advent. The great subject of reform is to be agitated, and the public mind is to be stirred. Temperance in all things is to be connected with the message, to turn the people of God from their idolatry, their gluttony, and their extravagance in dress and other things.[41]

# Martyred for the Truth

*"Herod had laid hold on John, and bound him, and put him in prison for Herodias' sake, his brother Philip's wife. For John said unto him, It is not lawful for thee to have her" (Matthew 14:3, 4).*

John's life was sorrowful and self-denying. He heralded the first advent of Christ, but was not permitted to witness His miracles, and enjoy the power manifested by Him. When Jesus should establish Himself as a teacher, John knew that he himself must die. His voice was seldom heard, except in the wilderness. His life was lonely. He did not cling to his father's family, to enjoy their society, but left them in order to fulfill his mission. Multitudes left the busy cities and villages and flocked to the wilderness to hear the words of the wonderful prophet. John laid the ax to the root of the tree. He reproved sin, fearless of consequences, and prepared the way for the Lamb of God.

Herod was affected as he listened to the powerful, pointed testimonies of John, and with deep interest he inquired what he must do to become his disciple. John was acquainted with the fact that he was about to marry his brother's wife, while her husband was yet living, and faithfully told Herod that this was not lawful. Herod was unwilling to make any sacrifice. He married his brother's wife, and through her influence, seized John and put him in prison, intending however to release him. While there confined, John heard through his disciples of the mighty works of Jesus. He could not listen to His gracious words; but the disciples informed him and comforted him with what they had heard. Soon John was beheaded, through the influence of Herod's wife. I saw that the humblest disciples who followed Jesus, witnessed His miracles, and heard the comforting words which fell from His lips, were greater than John the Baptist; that is, they were more exalted and honored, and had more pleasure in their lives.[42]

# Prophecy for the Last Days

*"It shall come to pass in the last days, saith God, I will pour out of my Spirit upon all flesh: and your sons and your daughters shall prophesy, and your young men shall see visions, and your old men shall dream dreams: and on my servants and on my handmaidens I will pour out in those days of my Spirit; and they shall prophesy" (Acts 2:17, 18).*

We have the assurance that in this age of the world the Holy Spirit will work with mighty power, unless by our unbelief we limit our blessings, and thus lose the advantages we might obtain. . . .

In times past holy men of old spake as they were moved by the Holy Spirit. In ancient times the prophets searched what the Spirit of God which was in them signified. The Spirit was not then given in power because Jesus was not yet glorified. Dating from the day of Pentecost, the Holy Spirit was to be poured forth on sons and daughters, on servants and handmaidens.[43]

The second chapter of Acts records the experiences that came to the disciples when they received the Holy Ghost. . . . [Acts 2:12–21, quoted.]

If this prophecy of Joel met a partial fulfillment in the days of the apostles, we are living in a time when it is to be even more evidently manifest to the people of God. He will so bestow His Spirit upon His people that they will become a light amid the moral darkness; and great light will be reflected in all parts of the world. O that our faith might be increased, that the Lord might work mightily with His people.[44]

In ancient times God spoke to men by the mouth of prophets and apostles. In these days He speaks to them by the testimonies of His Spirit. There was never a time when God instructed His people more earnestly than He instructs them now concerning His will and the course that He would have them pursue. But will they profit by His teachings? will they receive His reproofs and heed His warnings? God will accept of no partial obedience; He will sanction no compromise with self.[45]

# Separate From Vanity

*"O Israel, thy prophets are like the foxes in the deserts. Ye have not gone up into the gaps, neither made up the hedge for the house of Israel to stand in the battle in the day of the Lord. They have seen vanity and lying divination, saying, The Lord saith: and the Lord hath not sent them: and they have made others to hope that they would confirm the word" (Ezekiel 13:4–6).*

The false shepherds were drunk, but not with wine; they stagger, but not with strong drink. The truth of God is sealed up to them; they cannot read it. When they are interrogated as to what the seventh-day Sabbath is, whether or not it is the true Sabbath of the Bible, they lead the mind to fables. . . . These prophets were like the foxes of the desert. They have not gone up into the gaps, they have not made up the hedge that the people of God may stand in the battle in the day of the Lord. When the minds of any get stirred up, and they begin to inquire of these false shepherds about the truth, they take the easiest and best manner to effect their object and quiet the minds of the inquiring ones, even changing their own position to do it. . . .

Many of the opposers of God's truth devise mischief in their heads upon their beds, and in the day they carry out their wicked devices to put down the truth and to get something new to interest the people and divert their minds from the precious, all-important truth. . . .

The different parties of professed Advent believers have each a little truth, but God has given all these truths to His children who are being prepared for the day of God. He has also given them truths that none of these parties know, neither will they understand. Things which are sealed up to them, the Lord has opened to those who will see and are ready to understand. If God has any new light to communicate, He will let His chosen and beloved understand it, without their going to have their minds enlightened by hearing those who are in darkness and error.[46]

# Prophecy Misapplied

*"The word of the Lord came unto me, saying, Son of man, prophesy against the prophets of Israel that prophesy, and say thou unto them that prophesy out of their own hearts, Hear ye the word of the Lord; Thus saith the Lord God; Woe unto the foolish prophets, that follow their own spirit, and have seen nothing!" (Ezekiel 13:1–3).*

The hardest task I ever had to do in this line [of speaking plainly to those who were leading away from right paths] was in dealing with one who, I knew, wanted to follow the Lord. For some time he had thought he was obtaining new light. He was very ill, and must soon die. And oh, how my heart hoped he would not make it necessary for me to tell him just what he was doing. Those to whom he presented his views listened to him eagerly, and some thought him inspired. He had a chart made, and reasoned from the Scriptures to show that the Lord would come at a certain date, in 1894, I think. To many his reasoning seemed to be without a flaw. They told of his powerful exhortations in his sickroom. Most wonderful views passed before him. But what was the source of his inspiration? It was the morphine given him to relieve his pain. . . .

The word of the Lord to me was, "This is not truth, but will lead into strange paths, and some will become confused over this representation, and will give up the faith.". . .

No one has a true message fixing the time when Christ is to come or not to come. Be assured that God gives no one authority to say that Christ delays His coming five years, ten years, or twenty years. "Be ye also ready: for in such an hour as ye think not the Son of man cometh" (Matthew 24:44). This is our message, the very message that the three angels flying in the midst of heaven are proclaiming.[47]

Again and again have I been warned in regard to time setting. There will never again be a message for the people of God that will be based on time. We are not to know the definite time either for the outpouring of the Holy Spirit or for the coming of Christ.[48]

# The Danger of Delusion

*"Thou son of man, set thy face against the daughters of thy people,*
*which prophesy out of their own heart; and prophesy thou against them"*
*(Ezekiel 13:17).*

Anna Phillips should not have been given the encouragement she
has had. It has been a great injury to her—fastened her in a deception.
I am sorry that any of our brethren and sisters are ready to take up
with these supposed revelations, and imagine they see in them the
divine credentials. These things are not of the right character to
accomplish the work essential for this time. Childish figures and illustrations are employed in describing sacred, heavenly things, and
there is a mingling of the sublime and the ridiculous. While the work
has an appearance of great sanctity, it is calculated to ensnare and
mislead souls.[49]

Anna Phillips is being injured; she is led on, encouraged in a work
which will not bear the test of God.

Anna Garmire was thus injured. Her father and mother made her
believe that her childish dreams were revelations from God. Her father
talked to the child as one chosen of God; all her fancies and dreams
were written down as Anna's visions. She had figures and symbols presented to her, and had reproofs for her mother and for her father. After
a scathing reproof, there followed the most flattering representations of
the wonderful things the Lord would do for them. . . .

A little party was formed who were apparently inspired by them,
and the visions were declared to be more spiritual than the visions of
Sister White.

Then Mr. Garmire issued tracts teaching that probation would
close at a certain time, and setting the time for the Lord to come.
Testimonies on moral purity were borne, and next came the most
loathsome theories concerning the third angel's message, theories too
revolting to place upon paper. Some honest, God-fearing, trembling
souls accepted these things, and some were defiled. One died broken-
hearted; another was within a hair's breadth of moral ruin, when a
testimony came from Sister White revealing the plottings of Satan and
breaking the spell.[50]

# A Species of Fanaticism

*"Beware of false prophets, which come to you in sheep's clothing, but inwardly they are ravening wolves. Ye shall know them by their fruits" (Matthew 7:15, 16).*

A sister, in a letter to her friends, speaks with much enthusiasm of a statement by Brother _____ that Sister White has seen that the time has come when, if we hold the right relation to God, all can have the gift of prophecy to the same extent as do those who are now having visions. Where is the authority for this statement? I must believe that the sister failed to understand Brother _____, for I cannot think that he made the statement. The writer continues: "Brother_____said last night that is the case, not that God will speak to all for the benefit of everyone else but to each for his own benefit, and this will fulfill the prophecy of Joel." He stated that this is already being developed in numerous instances. He spoke as if he thought none would hold such a leading position as Sister White had done and will still do. Referred to Moses as a parallel. He was a leader, but many others are referred to as prophesying, though their prophecies are not published. . . .

These statements, interwoven with other matter that professes to be from God, are misleading; many minds will eagerly seize upon them, and through false impressions will misapprehend our true position and work. With much that is truth, there is mingled error that is accepted in its extreme meaning, and acted upon by persons of excitable temperament. Thus fanaticism will take the place of well-regulated, well-disciplined, heaven ordained efforts to carry forward the work to its completion.

These ideas in relation to prophesying, I do not hesitate to say, might better never have been expressed. Such statements prepare the way for a state of things that Satan will surely take advantage of to bring in spurious exercises. There is danger, not only that unbalanced minds will be led into fanaticism, but that designing persons will take advantage of this excitement to further their own selfish purposes.[51]

# As a Thief in the Night

*"The day of the Lord so cometh as a thief in the night. For when they shall say, Peace and safety; then sudden destruction cometh upon them, as travail upon a woman with child; and they shall not escape"* (1 Thessalonians 5:2, 3).

Notwithstanding the fact that there are false prophets, there are also those who are preaching the truth as pointed out in the Scriptures. With deep earnestness, with honest faith, prompted by the Holy Spirit, they are stirring minds and hearts by showing them that we are living near the second coming of Christ. . . .

Prophecy is fast fulfilling. More, much more, should be said about these tremendously important subjects. The day is at hand when the destiny of every soul will be fixed forever. This day of the Lord hastens on apace. The false watchmen are raising the cry, "All is well;" but the day of God is rapidly approaching. Its footsteps are so muffled that it does not arouse the world from the death-like slumber into which it has fallen. While the watchmen cry, "Peace and safety," "sudden destruction" cometh upon them, and they shall not escape; "for as a snare shall it come on all them that dwell on the face of the whole earth" (1 Thessalonians 5:3; Luke 21:35). It overtakes the pleasure-lover and the sinful man as a thief in the night. When all is apparently secure, and men retire to contented rest, then the prowling, stealthy, midnight thief steals upon his prey. When it is too late to prevent the evil, it is discovered that some door or window was not secured. "Be ye also ready: for in such an hour as ye think not the Son of man cometh" (Matthew 24:44). People are now settling to rest, imagining themselves secure under the popular churches; but let all beware, lest there is a place left open for the enemy to gain an entrance. Great pains should be taken to keep this subject before the people. The solemn fact is to be kept not only before the people of the world, but before our own churches also, that the day of the Lord will come suddenly, unexpectedly. The fearful warning of the prophecy is addressed to every soul. Let no one feel that he is secure from the danger of being surprised.[52]

# A More Sure Word of Prophecy

*"We have also a more sure word of prophecy; whereunto ye do well that ye take heed, as unto a light that shineth in a dark place, until the day dawn, and the day star arise in your hearts: knowing this first, that no prophecy of the scripture is of any private interpretation. For the prophecy came not in old time by the will of man: but holy men of God spake as they were moved by the Holy Ghost" (2 Peter 1:19–21).*

Each of the ancient prophets spoke less for their own time than for ours, so that their prophesying is in force for us.[53]

The more fully we accept the light presented by the Holy Spirit through the consecrated servants of God, the deeper and surer, even as the eternal throne, will appear the truths of ancient prophecy; we shall be assured that men of God spake as they were moved upon by the Holy Ghost. Men must themselves be under the influence of the Holy Spirit in order to understand the Spirit's utterances through the prophets. These messages were given, not for those that uttered the prophecies, but for us who are living amid the scenes of their fulfillment.[54]

Through His Holy Spirit the voice of God has come to us continually in warning and instruction, to confirm the faith of the believers in the Spirit of prophecy. Repeatedly the word has come, Write the things that I have given you to confirm the faith of My people in the position they have taken. Time and trial have not made void the instruction given, but through years of suffering and self-sacrifice have established the truth of the testimony given. The instruction that was given in the early days of the message is to be held as safe instruction to follow in these its closing days. Those who are indifferent to this light and instruction must not expect to escape the snares which we have been plainly told will cause the rejecters of light to stumble, and fall, and be snared, and be taken.[55]

Let no one's interpretation of prophecy rob you of the conviction of the knowledge of events which show that this great event [the second time of Jesus' coming] is near at hand.[56]

# Life-Giving Power

*"Prophesy unto the wind, prophesy, son of man, and say to the wind, Thus saith the Lord God; Come from the four winds, O breath, and breathe upon these slain, that they may live. So I prophesied as he commanded me, and the breath came into them, and they lived, and stood up upon their feet, an exceeding great army" (Ezekiel 37:9, 10).*

When the hand of the Lord was upon the prophet Ezekiel in the vision of the valley of dry bones, he was commanded to prophesy to the wind; and in answer to his word, life was restored to the slain, and they stood up before him, an exceeding great army. This figure was presented before the prophet to show him that no work of restoration can be too hard for God to do.[57]

Take your stand on the Lord's side, and act your part as a loyal subject of the kingdom. Acknowledge the gift that has been placed in the church for the guidance of God's people in the closing days of earth's history. From the beginning the church of God has had the gift of prophecy in her midst as a living voice to counsel, admonish, and instruct.

We have now come to the last days of the work of the third angel's message, when Satan will work with increasing power because he knows that his time is short. At the same time there will come to us through the gifts of the Holy Spirit, diversities of operations in the outpouring of the Spirit. This is the time of the latter rain.[58]

It is now no time to relax our efforts, to become tame and spiritless; no time to hide our light under a bushel, to speak smooth things, to prophesy deceit. No, no; there is no place for sleepy watchmen on the walls of Zion. Every power is to be employed wholly and entirely for God. Maintain your allegiance, bearing testimony for God and for truth. Be not turned aside by any suggestion that the world may make. We can make no compromise. There is a living issue before us, which will be of vital importance to the remnant people of God, to the very close of this earth's history; for eternal interests are here involved. We are to look constantly to the Lord Jesus Christ.[59]

# Shepherding the Flock

*"[Christ] gave some, ... evangelists; and some, pastors and teachers"*
*(Ephesians 4:11).*

Let missionaries be laboring two and two in different parts of all our large cities. The workers in each city should frequently meet together for counsel and prayer, that they may have wisdom and grace to work together effectively and harmoniously. Let all be wide-awake to make the most of every advantage. Our people must gird the armor on and establish centers in all the large cities.[1]

Eloquent sermons will seldom do the work of breaking up long-established habits of selfishness, and leading the church to a deep Christian experience. The true servant of God will be in earnest. He will manifest humility of soul, and will labor untiringly for the church of God. He will reveal the attributes of the faithful shepherd, and will tenderly care for the sheep of the Lord's pasture. He will "be watchful, and strengthen the things which remain, that are ready to die" (Revelation 3:2).

A true shepherd of souls will care for the sheep and lambs of his flock; and the love of Christ, filling his own heart, will flow through him to them. He will guard them carefully. His tender love for his charge has been presented in a picture I have seen representing Christ, the true Shepherd. The shepherd is leading the way, while the flock follow closely behind. Carried in his arms, and enfolded in his robe, is a helpless lamb, while its mother walks trustingly by his side.

The prophet Isaiah, speaking of the work of the true Shepherd, says, "He shall gather the lambs with his arm, and carry them in his bosom" (Isaiah 40:11). The lambs need more than daily food. They look to the shepherd for protection. They need watchcare. The one that goes astray must be faithfully searched for until it is found and restored to the fold. The figure is a beautiful one, and well represents the faithful, loving service that the undershepherd of the flock of Christ is to give to those under his protection and care.[2]

# Evangelize!

*"Cast thy bread upon the waters: for thou shalt find it after many days. Give a portion to seven, and also to eight; for thou knowest not what evil shall be upon the earth" (Ecclesiastes 11:1, 2).*

We need men who will become leaders in home and foreign missionary enterprises. We need men whose sympathies are not congealed, but whose hearts go out to the perishing that are nigh and afar off. The ice that binds about souls that are frozen up with selfishness needs to be melted away, so that every brother shall realize that he is his brother's keeper. Then everyone will go forth to help his neighbor to see the truth and to serve God in an acceptable service. Then those who profess the name of Christ will aid others in the formation of a Christlike character. If everyone would work in Christ's lines, much would be done to change the condition that now exists among the poor and distressed. Pure religion and undefiled would gleam forth as a bright and shining light. God's love in the heart would melt away the barriers of race and caste and would remove the obstacles with which men have barred others away from the truth as it is in Jesus. True religion will induce its advocates to go forth into the highways and byways of life. It will lead them to help the suffering, and enable them to be faithful shepherds going forth into the wilderness to seek and to save the lost, to lead back the perishing sheep and lambs.

The most unfortunate may bear the image of God, and they are of value to God. Those who have true religion will realize that it is their supreme duty to reveal Christ to men, to make manifest the fact that they have learned in the school of Christ. O that we might individually realize that we are simply stewards in trust of God's means, and that we are to use the gifts God has given us as Christ used His eternal riches in seeking and saving that which is lost. We are only trustees, only stewards, and by and by we must give a reckoning to the Master. He will inquire how we have used His goods, and whether or not we have ministered to His family in the world.[3]

# Pastors According to God's Heart

*"Turn, O backsliding children, saith the Lord; for I am married unto you: and I will take you one of a city, and two of a family, and I will bring you to Zion: and I will give you pastors according to mine heart, which shall feed you with knowledge and understanding" (Jeremiah 3:14, 15).*

Again and again the voice of Christ is heard repeating the charge to His undershepherds, "Feed My lambs," "Feed My sheep."[4]

Those who occupy the position of undershepherds are to exercise a watchful diligence over the Lord's flock. This is not to be a dictatorial vigilance, but one that tends to encourage and strengthen and uplift. Ministry means more than sermonizing; it means earnest, personal labor. The church on earth is composed of erring men and women, who need patient, painstaking effort that they may be trained and disciplined to work with acceptance in this life, and in the future life to be crowned with glory and immortality. Pastors are needed—faithful shepherds—who will not flatter God's people, nor treat them harshly, but who will feed them with the bread of life—men who in their lives feel daily the converting power of the Holy Spirit and who cherish a strong, unselfish love toward those for whom they labor.

There is tactful work for the undershepherd to do as he is called to meet alienation, bitterness, envy, and jealousy in the church, and he will need to labor in the spirit of Christ to set things in order. Faithful warnings are to be given, sins rebuked, wrongs made right, not only by the minister's work in the pulpit, but by personal labor. . . .

The spirit of the true shepherd is one of self-forgetfulness. He loses sight of self in order that he may work the works of God. By the preaching of the word and by personal ministry in the homes of the people, he learns their needs, their sorrows, their trials; and, cooperating with the great Burden Bearer, he shares their afflictions, comforts their distresses, relieves their soul hunger, and wins their hearts to God.[5]

# Active Labor

*"Blessed are ye that sow beside all waters" (Isaiah 32:20).*

The time has come to make decided efforts to proclaim the truth in our large cities. The message is to be given with such power that the hearers shall be convinced. God will raise up laborers to do this work. Let no one hinder these men of God's appointment. Forbid them not. God has given them their work. They will occupy peculiar spheres of influence and will carry the truth to the most unpromising places. Some who were once enemies will become valuable helpers, advancing the work with their means and their influence.

In these large cities missions should be established where workers can be trained to present to the people the special message for this time. There is need of all the instruction that these missions can give.[6]

Let the canvasser remember that he has an opportunity to sow beside all waters. Let him remember, as he sells the books which give a knowledge of the truth, that he is doing the work of God and that every talent is to be used to the glory of His name. God will be with everyone who seeks to understand the truth that he may set it before others in clear lines. . . .

Where there is one canvasser in the field, there should be one hundred. Canvassers should be encouraged to take hold of this work, not to canvass for storybooks, but to bring before the world the books containing truth essential for this time.

Let canvassers go forth with the word of the Lord, remembering that those who obey the commandments and teach others to obey them will be rewarded by seeing souls converted, and one soul truly converted will bring others to Christ. Thus the work will advance into new territory.

The time has come when a large work should be done by the canvassers. The world is asleep, and as watchmen they are to ring the warning bell to awake the sleepers to their danger. The churches know not the time of their visitation. Often they can best learn the truth through the efforts of the canvasser.[7]

# A Challenge of Endurance

*"Watch thou in all things, endure afflictions, do the work of an evangelist, make full proof of thy ministry"* (2 Timothy 4:5).

The followers of Christ should expect to be regarded by the world with no more favor than was their Master. But he who has God for his friend and helper can afford to spend a long winter of chilling neglect, abuse, and persecution. By the grace which Christ imparts, he can maintain his faith and trust in God under the sorest trials. He recalls the Saviour's example, and he feels that he can endure affliction and persecution if he may thus gain simplicity of character, lowliness of heart, and an abiding trust in Jesus. The triumph of Christian faith is to suffer, and be strong; to submit, and thus conquer; to be killed all the day long, and yet to live; to bear the cross, and thus win the crown of immortal glory.[8]

He who takes up the work of canvassing as he should must be both an educator and a student. While he tries to teach others he himself must learn to do the work of an evangelist. As canvassers go forth into the field with humble hearts, full of earnest activity, they will find many opportunities to speak a word in season to souls ready to die in discouragement. After laboring for these needy ones they will be able to say: "Ye were sometimes darkness, but now are ye light in the Lord" (Ephesians 5:8). As they see the sinful course of others they can say: "Such were some of you: but ye are washed, but ye are sanctified, but ye are justified in the name of the Lord Jesus, and by the Spirit of our God" (1 Corinthians 6:11).

Those who work for God will meet with discouragement, but the promise is always theirs: "Lo, I am with you alway, even unto the end of the world" (Matthew 28:20). God will give a most wonderful experience to those who will say: "I believe Thy promise; I will not fail nor become discouraged." . . .

Let the canvasser tell of the joy and blessing he has received in his ministry as an evangelist. These reports should find a place in our papers, for they are far-reaching in their influence. They will be as sweet fragrance in the church, a savor of life unto life. Thus it is seen that God works with those who cooperate with Him.[9]

# Living What We Teach

*"There was a man of the Pharisees, named Nicodemus, a ruler of the Jews: the same came to Jesus by night, and said unto him, Rabbi, we know that thou art a teacher come from God" (John 3:1, 2).*

In the Teacher sent from God, heaven gave to men its best and greatest. He who had stood in the councils of the Most High, who had dwelt in the innermost sanctuary of the Eternal, was the One chosen to reveal in person to humanity the knowledge of God.

Through Christ had been communicated every ray of divine light that had ever reached our fallen world. It was He who had spoken through everyone that throughout the ages had declared God's word to man. Of Him all the excellences manifest in the earth's greatest and noblest souls were reflections. The purity and beneficence of Joseph, the faith and meekness and long-suffering of Moses, the steadfastness of Elisha, the noble integrity and firmness of Daniel, the ardor and self-sacrifice of Paul, the mental and spiritual power manifest in all these men, and in all others who had ever dwelt on the earth, were but gleams from the shining of His glory. In Him was found the perfect ideal.

To reveal this ideal as the only true standard for attainment; to show what every human being might become; what, through the indwelling of humanity by divinity, all who received Him would become—for this, Christ came to the world. He came to show how men are to be trained as befits the sons of God; how on earth they are to practice the principles and to live the life of heaven.

God's greatest gift was bestowed to meet man's greatest need.[10]

What [Christ] taught, He lived. "I have given you an example," He said to His disciples; "that ye should do as I have done." "I have kept My Father's commandments" (John 13:15; 15:10). Thus in His life, Christ's words had perfect illustration and support. And more than this; what He taught, He was. His words were the expression, not only of His own life experience, but of His own character. Not only did He teach the truth, but He was the truth. It was this that gave His teaching, power.[11]

# Seeking the Heavenly Standard

*"Preach the word; be instant in season, out of season; reprove, rebuke, exhort with all longsuffering and doctrine" (2 Timothy 4:2).*

Some ministers have adopted a style of preaching that has not the best influence. It has become a habit with them to weave anecdotes into their discourses. The impression thus made upon the hearers is not a savor of life unto life. Ministers should not bring amusing stories into their preaching. The people need pure provender, thoroughly winnowed from the chaff. "Preach the word" (2 Timothy 4:2), was the charge that Paul gave to Timothy, and this is our commission also.

The minister who mixes story-telling with his discourses is using strange fire. God is offended, and the cause of truth is dishonored, when His representatives descend to the use of cheap, trifling words.[12]

The satanic delusions of the age must be met clearly and intelligently with the sword of the Spirit, which is the word of God. The same unseen Hand that guides the planets in their courses, and upholds the worlds by His power, has made provision for man formed in His image, that he may be little less than the angels of God while in the performance of his duties on earth. God's purposes have not been answered by men who have been entrusted with the most solemn truth ever given to man. He designs that we should rise higher and higher toward a state of perfection, seeing and realizing at every step the power and glory of God. Man does not know himself. . . .

The precious book of God contains rules of life for men of every class and every vocation. Examples are here found which it would be well for all to study and imitate. "The Son of God came not to be ministered unto, but to minister" (Matthew 20:28). The true honor and glory of the servant of Christ consists, not in the number of sermons preached, nor in the amount of writing accomplished, but in the work of faithfully ministering to the wants of the people. If he neglects this part of his work he has no right to the name of minister.[13]

# Faithful Reproof to Promote Life

*"The commandment is a lamp; and the law is light; and reproofs of instruction are the way of life" (Proverbs 6:23).*

God holds His people, as a body, responsible for sins existing in individuals among them. If there is a neglect with the leaders of the church to diligently search out the sins which bring the displeasure of God upon His people as a body, they become responsible for these sins. But this is the nicest work that men ever engaged in, to deal with minds. All are not fitted to correct the erring. They have not wisdom to deal justly, while loving mercy. They will not be inclined to see the necessity of mingling love and tender compassion with faithful reproof of wrongs. Some will ever be needlessly severe, and will not feel the necessity of the injunction of the apostle, "And of some have compassion, making a difference: and others save with fear, pulling them out of the fire" (Jude 22, 23). There are many who do not have the discretion of Joshua and who have no special duty to search out wrongs and to deal promptly with the sins existing among them; let not such hinder those who have the burden of this work upon them; let them not stand in the way of those who have this duty to do. Some make it a point to question and doubt and find fault because others do the work that God has not laid upon themselves. These stand directly in the way to hinder those upon whom God has laid the burden of reproof and of correcting the sins that are prevailing, that His frown may be turned away from His people. . . .

God will not be trifled with. It is in the time of conflict when the true colors should be flung to the breeze. It is then that the standard-bearers need to be firm and let their true position be known. It is then that the skill of every true soldier for the right is tested. Shirkers can never wear the laurels of victory. Those who are true and loyal will not conceal the fact, but will put heart and might into the work, and venture their all in the struggle, let the battle turn as it will. God is a sin-hating God; and those who will encourage the sinner, saying, It is well with thee, God will curse.[14]

# The Basis of Doctrines and Reforms

*"All scripture is given by inspiration of God, and is profitable for doctrine, for reproof, for correction, for instruction in righteousness: that the man of God may be perfect, throughly furnished unto all good works" (2 Timothy 3:16, 17).*

The apostle Paul declared, looking down to the last days: "The time will come when they will not endure sound doctrine" (2 Timothy 4:3). That time has fully come. The multitudes do not want Bible truth, because it interferes with the desires of the sinful, world-loving heart; and Satan supplies the deceptions which they love.

But God will have a people upon the earth to maintain the Bible, and the Bible only, as the standard of all doctrines and the basis of all reforms. The opinions of learned men, the deductions of science, the creeds or decisions of ecclesiastical councils, as numerous and discordant as are the churches which they represent, the voice of the majority—not one nor all of these should be regarded as evidence for or against any point of religious faith. Before accepting any doctrine or precept, we should demand a plain "Thus saith the Lord" in its support.[15]

It is not new and fanciful doctrines which the people need. They do not need human suppositions. They need the testimony of men who know and practice the truth. . . .

Walk firmly, decidedly, your feet shod with the preparation of the gospel of peace. You may be sure that pure and undefiled religion is not a sensational religion. God has not laid upon anyone the burden of encouraging an appetite for speculative doctrines and theories. My brethren, keep these things out of your teaching. Do not allow them to enter into your experience. Let not your lifework be marred by them.[16]

A devoted, spiritual worker will avoid bringing up minor theoretical differences, and will devote his energies to the proclamation of the great testing truths to be given to the world. He will point the people to the work of redemption, the commandments of God, the near coming of Christ; and it will be found that in these subjects there is food enough for thought.[17]

# Rightly Dividing the Word

*"Speak thou the things which become sound doctrine" (Titus 2:1).*

"Sound doctrine" is Bible truth—truth that will promote piety and devotion, confirming God's people in the faith. Sound doctrine means much to the receiver; and it means much, too, to the teacher. . . .

Some who in Paul's day listened to the truth, raised questions of no vital importance, presenting the ideas and opinions of men, and seeking to divert the mind of the teacher from the great truths of the gospel, to the discussion of non-essential theories and the settlement of unimportant disputes. Paul knew that the laborer for God must be wise enough to see the design of the enemy, and refuse to be misled or diverted. The conversion of souls must be the burden of his work; he must preach the word of God, but avoid controversy.

"Study to shew thyself approved unto God," he wrote, "a workman that needeth not to be ashamed, rightly dividing the word of truth. But shun profane and vain babblings: for they will increase unto more ungodliness" (2 Timothy 2:15, 16).

The ministers of Christ today are in the same danger. Satan is constantly at work to divert the mind into wrong channels, so that the truth may lose its force upon the heart. And unless ministers and people practice the truth and are sanctified by it, they will allow speculation regarding questions of no vital importance to occupy the mind. This will lead to caviling and strife; for countless points of difference will arise.

Men of ability have devoted a lifetime of study and prayer to the searching of the Scriptures, and yet there are many portions of the Bible that have not been fully explored. Some passages of Scripture will never be perfectly comprehended until in the future life Christ shall explain them. There are mysteries to be unraveled, statements that human minds cannot harmonize. And the enemy will seek to arouse argument upon these points, which might better remain undiscussed.[18]

# Men of Mature Age

*"That the aged men be sober, grave, temperate" (Titus 2:2).*

May the Lord bless and sustain our old and tried laborers. May He help them to be wise in regard to the preservation of their physical, mental, and spiritual powers. I have been instructed by the Lord to say to those who bore their testimony in the early days of the message: "God has endowed you with the power of reason, and He desires you to understand and obey the laws that have to do with the health of the being. Do not be imprudent. Do not overwork. Take time to rest. God desires you to stand in your lot and place, doing your part to save men and women from being swept downward by the mighty current of evil. He desires you to keep the armor on till He bids you lay it off. Not long hence you will receive your reward."[19]

The most tender regard should be cherished for those whose life interest has been bound up with the work of God. These aged workers have stood faithful amid storm and trial. They may have infirmities, but they still possess talents that qualify them to stand in their place in God's cause. Though worn, and unable to bear the heavier burdens that younger men can and should carry, the counsel they can give is of the highest value.

They may have made mistakes, but from their failures they have learned to avoid errors and dangers, and are they not therefore competent to give wise counsel? They have borne test and trial, and though they have lost some of their vigor, the Lord does not lay them aside. He gives them special grace and wisdom.

Those who have served their Master when the work went hard, who endured poverty and remained faithful when there were few to stand for truth, are to be honored and respected. The Lord desires the younger laborers to gain wisdom, strength, and maturity by association with these faithful men. Let the younger men realize that in having such workers among them they are highly favored. Let them give them an honored place in their councils.[20]

# Teachers of Experience

*"That the aged men be . . . sound in faith, in charity, in patience"* (Titus 2:2).

When men come in who would move one pin or pillar from the foundation which God has established by His Holy Spirit, let the aged men who were pioneers in our work speak plainly, and let those who are dead speak also, by the reprinting of their articles in our periodicals. Gather up the rays of divine light that God has given as He has led His people on step by step in the way of truth. This truth will stand the test of time and trial.[21]

There are those who have some experience who should, with every effort they make in dying churches as well as in new places, select young men or men of mature age to assist in the work. Thus they will be obtaining knowledge by interesting themselves in personal effort, and scores of helpers will be fitting for usefulness as Bible readers, as canvassers, and as visitors in the families.[22]

The messengers sent by God are to act as true undershepherds. They are not true undershepherds who care only for those who do as they direct, who say of the people, They must do precisely as I command. If they do not follow my voice, I will have no love or care for them.[23]

The fruit Christ claims, after the patient care bestowed upon His church, is faith, patience, love, forbearance, heavenly-mindedness, meekness. These are clusters of fruit which mature amid storm and cloud and darkness, as well as in the sunshine.[24]

As those who have spent their lives in the service of Christ draw near to the close of their earthly ministry, they will be impressed by the Holy Spirit to recount the experiences they have had in connection with the work of God. The record of His wonderful dealings with His people, of His great goodness in delivering them from trial, should be repeated to those newly come to the faith. God desires the old and tried laborers to stand in their place, doing their part to save men and women from being swept downward by the mighty current of evil, He desires them to keep the armor on till He bids them lay it down.[25]

# Mature Women

*"The aged women likewise, that they be in behaviour as becometh holiness"* (Titus 2:3).

The sisters should encourage true meekness. They should not be forward, talkative, and bold, but modest and slow to speak. They should be courteous. To be kind, tender, pitiful, forgiving, and humble would be becoming and well pleasing to God. If they occupy this position, they will not be burdened with undue attention from gentlemen. It will be felt by all that there is a sacred circle of purity around these God-fearing women which shields them from any unwarrantable liberties. There is too much careless, loose, coarse freedom of manner by some women professing godliness, which leads to greater wrongs. Those godly women who occupy their minds and hearts in meditating upon themes which strengthen purity of life, which elevate the soul to commune with God, will not be easily led astray from the path of rectitude and virtue. They will be fortified against the sophistry of Satan and prepared to withstand his seductive arts.[26]

Women professing godliness generally fail to train the mind. They leave it uncontrolled, to go where it will. This is a great mistake. Many seem to have no mental power. They have not educated the mind to think; and because they have not done this, they suppose they cannot. Meditation and prayer are necessary to a growth in grace. Why there is no more stability among women is because of so little mental culture, so little reflection. Leaving the mind in a state of inaction, they lean upon others to do the brainwork, to plan, and think, and remember for them, and thus grow more and more inefficient. Some need to discipline the mind by exercise. They should force it to think. While they depend upon someone to think for them, to solve their difficulties, and they refuse to tax the mind with thought, the inability to remember, to look ahead and discriminate, will continue. Efforts must be made by every individual to educate the mind.[27]

# Tender Reproof, Not Accusation

*"The aged women likewise, that they be . . . not false accusers" (Titus 2:3).*

False accusers, though their names are on the church records, are under the control of Satan, and work as his agents to weaken and confuse the church, and divide the brethren of Christ on earth. When this has been accomplished, Satan exults over the divided state of the church, and points the world to the professed followers of Christ, thus bringing the name of Christ into dishonor before the world, and entrenching men in their unbelief and rebellion against God.[28]

We are to feed the hungry, clothe the naked, and comfort the suffering and afflicted. We are to minister to the despairing, and to inspire hope in the hopeless. . . . Often the heart that hardens under reproof will melt under the love of Christ.[29]

Always the words of rebuke that God finds it necessary to send are spoken in tender love and with the promise of peace to every penitent believer.[30]

Christ was a faithful reprover. Never lived there another who so hated evil; never another whose denunciation of it was so fearless. To all things untrue and base His very presence was a rebuke. In the light of His purity, men saw themselves unclean, their life's aims mean and false. Yet He drew them. He who had created man, understood the value of humanity. Evil He denounced as the foe of those whom He was seeking to bless and to save. In every human being, however fallen, He beheld a son of God, one who might be restored to the privilege of his divine relationship.

"God sent not His Son into the world to condemn the world; but that the world through Him might be saved" (John 3:17). Looking upon men in their suffering and degradation, Christ perceived ground for hope where appeared only despair and ruin. Wherever there existed a sense of need, there He saw opportunity for uplifting. Souls tempted, defeated, feeling themselves lost, ready to perish, He met, not with denunciation, but with blessing.[31]

# Experienced Women Teachers

*"The aged women likewise, that they be . . . teachers of good things"* *(Titus 2:3).*

The Lord has a work for women as well as men to do. They may accomplish a good work for God if they will first learn in the school of Christ the precious, all-important lesson of meekness. They must not only bear the name of Christ, but possess His Spirit. They must walk even as He walked, purifying their souls from everything that defiles. Then they will be able to benefit others by presenting the all-sufficiency of Jesus.

Women may take their places in the work at this crisis, and the Lord will work through them. If they are imbued with a sense of their duty, and labor under the influence of the Spirit of God, they will have just the self-possession required for this time. The Saviour will reflect upon these self-sacrificing women the light of His countenance, and this will give them a power which will exceed that of men. They can do in families a work that men cannot do, a work that reaches the inner life. They can come close to the hearts of those whom men cannot reach. Their labor is needed.[32]

Many youth as well as our older sisters manifest themselves shy of religious conversation. They do not take in the matter as it is. The word of God must be their assurance, their hope, their peace. They close the windows that should open heavenward, and open the windows wide earthward. But when they shall see the excellency of the human soul, they will close the windows earthward, cease depending on earthly amusements and associations, break away from folly and sin, and will open the windows heavenward, that they may behold spiritual things. Then can they say, I will receive the light of the Sun of Righteousness, that I may shine forth to others.[33]

Those who bear the last message of mercy to the world should feel it their duty to instruct parents in regard to home religion.[34]

174

# Teaching Women Sobriety

*"That [the aged women] may teach the young women to be sober"*
*(Titus 2:4).*

I am acquainted with a number of women who have thought their marriage a misfortune. They have read novels until their imaginations have become diseased, and they live in a world of their own creating. They think themselves women of sensitive minds, of superior, refined organizations, and imagine that their husbands are not so refined, that they do not possess these superior qualities, and therefore cannot appreciate their own supposed virtue and refined organizations. Consequently these women think themselves great sufferers, martyrs. They have talked of this and thought upon it until they are nearly maniacs upon this subject. They imagine their worth superior to that of other mortals, and it is not agreeable to their fine sensibilities to associate with common humanity. These women are making themselves fools; and their husbands are in danger of thinking that they do possess a superior order of mind.

From what the Lord has shown me, the women of this class have had their imaginations perverted by novel reading, daydreaming, and castle-building, living in an imaginary world. They do not bring their own ideas down to the common, useful duties of life. They do not take up the life burdens which lie in their path, and seek to make a happy, cheerful home for their husbands. They rest their whole weight upon them, not bearing their own burden. They expect others to anticipate their wants and do for them, while they are at liberty to find fault and to question as they please. These women have a lovesick sentimentalism, constantly thinking they are not appreciated, that their husbands do not give them all the attention they deserve. They imagine themselves martyrs.

The truth of the matter is, if they would show themselves useful their value might be appreciated; but when they pursue a course to constantly draw upon others for sympathy and attention, while they feel under no obligation to give the same in return . . . there can be in their lives but little that is valuable. . . . They have viewed things all wrong. They are unworthy of their husbands.[35]

# Teaching the Wives

*"That [the aged women] may teach the young women . . . to love their husbands" (Titus 2:4).*

Women who suppose they possess . . . sensitive, refined organizations make very useless wives and mothers. It is frequently the case that they withdraw their affections from their husbands, who are useful, practical men, and show much attention to other men, and with their lovesick sentimentalism draw upon the sympathies of others, tell them their trials, their troubles, their aspirations to do some elevated work, and reveal the fact that their married life is a disappointment, a hindrance to their doing the work they had hoped to do.

Oh, what wretchedness exists in families that might be happy! These women are a curse to themselves and a curse to their husbands. In supposing themselves to be angels, they make themselves fools, and are nothing but heavy burdens. The common duties of life which the Lord has left for them to do, they leave right in their path, and are restless and complaining, always looking for an easy, more exalted, and more agreeable work. Supposing themselves to be angels, they are found human after all.[36]

The wife may take her position in favor of truth, while the husband may oppose it. Here a trial comes in at once, the trial of separation in faith and feeling. Shall we say to that wife, "You should leave your husband because he does not keep the Sabbath?" No, indeed. If she was a faithful wife before she accepted the truth, and if she sees in her friends those for whom Christ has died, she will seek to discharge her duties with even greater fidelity after she accepts the truth, that if possible she may lead them to see the light. "But," it is asked, "should not the believing wife yield her convictions of duty because of her husband's unbelief?" By no means; because Christ is her Lord and Master. She cannot cast aside the claims of high heaven upon her.[37]

God knows your trials as you view the state of your husband and children, who so greatly lack saving faith. Much more depends upon you than you realize. You should put the armor on.[38]

# The First Missionary Field

*"That [the aged women] may teach the young women . . . to love their children" (Titus 2:4).*

There is a work for women that is even more important and elevating than the duties of the king upon his throne. They may mold the minds of their children and shape their characters so that they may be useful in this world and that they may become sons and daughters of God.[39]

You have a great work, a sacred, holy calling to exemplify the Christian graces as a faithful wife and mother; to be lovable, patient, kind, yet firm in your home life. To learn right methods and acquire tact for the training of your own little ones, that they may keep the way of the Lord. As a humble child of God, learn in the school of Christ, seek constantly to improve your powers to do the most perfect, thorough work at home, both by precept and example.

In this work you will have the help of the Lord; but if you ignore your duty as a wife and mother, and hold out your hands for the Lord to put another class of work in them, be sure that He will not contradict Himself; He points you to the duty you have to do at home. If you have the idea that some work greater and holier than this has been entrusted to you, you are under a deception. In neglecting your husband and children for what you suppose to be religious duties, either to attend meetings or to work for others, to give Bible readings or to have messages for others, you are going directly contrary to the words of inspiration in the instruction of Paul to Titus. . . .

The children need the watchful eye of the mother. They need to be instructed, to be guided in safe paths, to be kept from vice, to be won by kindness, and be confirmed in well doing, by diligent training. . . .

To those who forsake their homes, their companions and children, God will not entrust the work of saving souls, for they have proved unfaithful to their holy vows. They have proved unfaithful to sacred responsibilities. God will not entrust to them eternal riches.[40]

# A Work for Women, Not Men

*"That [the aged women] may teach the young women . . . to be discreet, chaste" (Titus 2:4, 5).*

It is time, my dear brother, that you looked at these matters [of guarding your reputation] in a right light. You have been called away from the word of God to serve tables. . . .

There are women who fasten themselves to someone to whom they tell their home difficulties. But there are two sides to every question, and often these women are themselves in need of reproof. They speak only of their side of the question, and words of sympathy that they do not deserve are given to them.

You are not to set such an example that women will feel at liberty to tell you the grievances of their home life, and to draw upon your sympathies. When a woman comes to you with her troubles, tell her plainly to go to her sisters, to tell her troubles to the deaconesses of the church. Tell her that she is out of place in opening her troubles to any man, for men are easily beguiled and tempted. Tell the one who has thrown her case upon you that God has not placed this burden upon any man. You are not wise to take these burdens upon yourself. It is not your appointed work.[41]

In the battle with inward corruptions and outward temptations, even the wise and powerful Solomon was vanquished. It is not safe to permit the least departure from the strictest integrity. "Abstain from all appearance of evil" (1 Thessalonians 5:22). When a woman relates her family troubles, or complains of her husband, to another man, she violates her marriage vows; she dishonors her husband and breaks down the wall erected to preserve the sanctity of the marriage relation; she throws wide open the door and invites Satan to enter with his insidious temptations. This is just as Satan would have it. If a woman comes to a Christian brother with a tale of her woes, her disappointments and trials, he should ever advise her, if she must confide her troubles to someone, to select sisters for her confidants, and then there will be no appearance of evil whereby the cause of God may suffer reproach.[42]

# Missionaries in the Highest Sense

*"That [the aged women] may teach the young women to be . . . keepers at home, good, obedient to their own husbands, that the word of God be not blasphemed" (Titus 2:4).*

The Lord has not called you to neglect your home and your husband and children. He never works in this way; and He never will. You have before your own door a little plot of ground to care for, and God will hold you responsible for this work which He has left in your hands. Through earnest prayer and study, you may become wise in your home, learning the different dispositions of your children, and carefully noting their behavior. You may have at home a little school, of which you shall be the teacher. If you seek wisdom from the Lord to understand His way, and to keep it, He will lead you, not away from your own home, but back to it. . . .

Never for a moment suppose that God has given you a work that will necessitate a separation from your precious little flock. Do not leave them to become demoralized by improper associations and to harden their hearts against their mother. . . .

When we give ourselves unreservedly to the Lord, the simple, commonplace duties of home life will be seen in their true importance, and we shall perform them in accordance with the will of God. Oh, my sister, you may be bound about with poverty, your lot in life may be humble, but Jesus does not forsake your family. . . .

Your husband has rights; your children have rights; and these must not be ignored by you. Whether you have one talent or three or five, God has given you your work. . . .

Scolding and fretting, gathering clouds and gloom about the soul, will bring only a shadow and discouragement in the home life. Mothers do not half appreciate their possibilities and privileges. They do not seem to understand that they can be in the highest sense missionaries, laborers together with God in aiding their children to build up a symmetrical character. This is the great burden of the work given them of God. The mother is God's agent to Christianize her family. She is to exemplify Bible religion, showing how its influence is to control us in its everyday duties and pleasures.[43]

# Young Men

*"Young men likewise exhort to be sober minded. In all things shew-ing thyself a pattern of good works: in doctrine shewing uncorruptness, gravity, sincerity" (Titus 2:6, 7).*

No matter who you are, it is the mind, the heart, the sincere pur-pose, and the daily life that mark the value of the man. Restless, talk-ative, dictatorial men are not needed in this work. There are too many of them springing up everywhere. Many youth who have but little experience, push themselves forward, manifest no reverence for age or office, and take offense if counseled or reproved. We have already more of these self-important ones than we want, God calls for mod-est, quiet, sober-minded youth, and men of mature age, who are well-balanced with principle, who can pray as well as talk, who will rise up before the aged, and treat gray hairs with respect.[44]

Young men are not to be lovers of pleasure, seekers for amusement, ready to squander time and money and influence in selfish gratifica-tion; but they are to cultivate sobriety and godliness. They should seek each day to realize that they are now in the sowing time, and that the harvest reaped will be according to the seed sown. Young men should form their plans of life with thoughtful deliberation, and subject their conduct to criticism, as they seek for integrity of heart and action that will stand the test of the judgment. They should be willing to receive counsel from those of experience, that they may be fortified to stand in the perils that will beset their pathway. They will be exposed to influ-ences which will lead them away from fidelity to God, unless they ever keep a realization of their responsibilities.

God wants the youth to become men of earnest mind, to be pre-pared for action in His noble work, and fitted to bear responsibilities. God calls for young men with hearts uncorrupted, strong and brave, and determined to fight manfully in the struggle before them, that they may glorify God, and bless humanity. If the youth would but make the Bible their study, would but calm their impetuous desires, and listen to the voice of their Creator and Redeemer, they would not only be at peace with God, but would find themselves ennobled and elevated.[45]

# Words That Teach Christ

*"Sound speech, that cannot be condemned; that he that is of the contrary part may be ashamed, having no evil thing to say of you"* (Titus 2:8).

The word of God coming from sanctified hearts and lips will soften and break hard hearts. And if ever there was a period of time when the words of Christ should be heard, it is now.

None but He who created man can effect a change in the human heart. Every teacher is to realize that he must be moved by divine agencies. The mind and judgment must be submitted to the Holy Spirit. Through the sanctification of the truth, we may bear a decided testimony for righteousness before both believers and unbelievers.

We are far behind what we should be in our experience. We are backward in pronouncing the testimony that should flow from sanctified lips. Even when sitting at the table, Christ taught truths that brought comfort and courage to the hearts of His hearers. Whenever it is possible, we are to present the words of Christ. If His love is in the soul, abiding there as a living principle, there will come forth from the treasure-house of the heart, words suitable to the occasion, not light, trifling words, but uplifting words, words of truth and spirituality.

Let teachers and students watch their opportunities whenever possible to confess Christ in their conversations, speaking of their experiences in following Christ, praying with their brethren for the Holy Spirit. Confessing Christ openly and bravely, exhibiting in the choice of words the simplicity of true godliness, will be more effective than many sermons. There are but few who give a true representation of the meekness of Christ. Oh, we need, and we must have, His meekness! Christ is to be formed within, the hope of glory.

We are preparing for translation to the heavenly world. Our conversation should be in heaven, from whence we look for the Lord Jesus. He is to be acknowledged as the Giver of every good and perfect gift, the Author of all our blessings, in whom is centered our hope of eternal life.[46]

181

# Feeding the Home Flock

*"Gather me the people together, and I will make them hear my words, that they may learn to fear me all the days that they shall live upon the earth, and that they may teach their children" (Deuteronomy 4:10).*

God had commanded the Hebrews to teach their children His requirements and to make them acquainted with all His dealings with their fathers. This was one of the special duties of every parent—one that was not to be delegated to another. In the place of stranger lips the loving hearts of the father and mother were to give instruction to their children. Thoughts of God were to be associated with all the events of daily life. The mighty works of God in the deliverance of His people and the promises of the Redeemer to come were to be often recounted in the homes of Israel; and the use of figures and symbols caused the lessons given to be more firmly fixed in the memory. The great truths of God's providence and of the future life were impressed on the young mind. It was trained to see God alike in the scenes of nature and the words of revelation. The stars of heaven, the trees and flowers of the field, the lofty mountains, the rippling brooks—all spoke of the Creator. The solemn service of sacrifice and worship at the sanctuary and the utterances of the prophets were a revelation of God.

Such was the training of Moses in the lowly cabin home in Goshen; of Samuel, by the faithful Hannah; of David, in the hill dwelling at Bethlehem; of Daniel, before the scenes of the captivity separated him from the home of his fathers. Such, too, was the early life of Christ at Nazareth; such the training by which the child Timothy learned from the lips of his grandmother Lois, and his mother Eunice (2 Timothy 1:5; 3:15), the truths of Holy Writ.[47]

Parents should be the only teachers of their children until they have reached eight or ten years of age. As fast as their minds can comprehend it, the parents should open before them God's great book of nature.[48]

# Daily Enthusiasm for God's Word

*"These words, which I command thee this day, shall be in thine heart: and thou shalt teach them diligently unto thy children, and shalt talk of them when thou sittest in thine house, and when thou walkest by the way, and when thou liest down, and when thou risest up"* *(Deuteronomy 6:6, 7).*

[Deuteronomy 6:7 quoted.] The use of object lessons, blackboards, maps, and pictures will be an aid in explaining these lessons, and fixing them in the memory. Parents and teachers should constantly seek for improved methods. The teaching of the Bible should have our freshest thought, our best methods, and our most earnest effort.

In arousing and strengthening a love for Bible study, much depends on the use of the hour of worship. The hours of morning and evening worship should be the sweetest and most helpful of the day. Let it be understood that into these hours no troubled, unkind thoughts are to intrude; that parents and children assemble to meet with Jesus, and to invite into the home the presence of holy angels. Let the services be brief and full of life, adapted to the occasion, and varied from time to time. Let all join in the Bible reading and learn and often repeat God's law. It will add to the interest of the children if they are sometimes permitted to select the reading. Question them upon it, and let them ask questions. Mention anything that will serve to illustrate its meaning. When the service is not thus made too lengthy, let the little ones take part in prayer, and let them join in song, if it be but a single verse.

To make such a service what it should be, thought should be given to preparation. And parents should take time daily for Bible study with their children. No doubt it will require effort and planning and some sacrifice to accomplish this; but the effort will be richly repaid. . . .

In order to interest our children in the Bible, we ourselves must be interested in it. To awaken in them a love for its study, we must love it. Our instruction to them will have only the weight of influence given it by our own example and spirit.[49]

# Teaching the Bible to Children

*"Train up a child in the way he should go: and when he is old, he will not depart from it" (Proverbs 22:6).*

God called Abraham to be a teacher of His word, He chose him to be the father of a great nation, because He saw that Abraham would instruct his children and his household in the principles of God's law. And that which gave power to Abraham's teaching was the influence of his own life. His great household consisted of more than a thousand souls, many of them heads of families, and not a few but newly converted from heathenism. Such a household required a firm hand at the helm. No weak, vacillating methods would suffice. Of Abraham God said, "I know him, that he will command his children and his household after him." Yet his authority was exercised with such wisdom and tenderness that hearts were won. The testimony of the divine Watcher is, "They shall keep the way of the Lord, to do justice and judgment" (Genesis 18:19). And Abraham's influence extended beyond his own household. Wherever he pitched his tent, he set up beside it the altar for sacrifice and worship. . . .

No less effective today will be the teaching of God's word when it finds as faithful a reflection in the teacher's life. . . .

In teaching children the Bible, we may gain much by observing the bent of their minds, the things in which they are interested, and arousing their interest to see what the Bible says about these things. He who created us, with our various aptitudes, has in His word given something for everyone. As the pupils see that the lessons of the Bible apply to their own lives, teach them to look to it as a counselor.

Help them also to appreciate its wonderful beauty. Many books of no real value, books that are exciting and unhealthful are recommended, or at least permitted to be used, because of their supposed literary value. Why should we direct our children to drink of these polluted streams when they may have free access to the pure fountains of the word of God?[50]

# Defeating Satan's Counterfeit

*"The king spake unto Ashpenaz the master of his eunuchs, that he should bring certain of the children of Israel, and of the king's seed, and of the princes; children in whom was no blemish, but well favoured, and skilful in all wisdom, and cunning in knowledge, and understanding science, and such as had ability in them to stand in the king's palace, and whom they might teach the learning and the tongue of the Chaldeans"* (Daniel 1:3, 4).

From the comparative simplicity of their Judean home these youth of royal line were transported to the most magnificent of cities, to the court of its greatest monarch, and were singled out to be trained for the king's special service. Strong were the temptations surrounding them in that corrupt and luxurious court. The fact that they, the worshipers of Jehovah, were captives to Babylon; that the vessels of God's house had been placed in the temple of the gods of Babylon; that the king of Israel was himself a prisoner in the hands of the Babylonians, was boastfully cited by the victors as evidence that their religion and customs were superior to the religion and customs of the Hebrews.[51]

Deeming it no longer safe to entrust our youth with infidels or with irreligious teachers or even with teachers who would poison their minds with doctrinal errors, we have erected our present commodious home and college in Healdsburg. We saw the necessity of religious training being interwoven with their education, also of their knowing something of the different trades and branches of business. In order for them to develop symmetrical characters they need not only the advantages of a thorough intellectual training but of a training of the physical powers. Then their mental capabilities will develop proportionately. It is painful to see how many one-sided, half-developed characters there are in our world. Our churches today show that these defects have been brought into the religious life to the great detriment of the church. There is a great work to be done for our youth.[52]

# Neglect of Instruction Fatal

*"[The wicked] shall die without instruction; and in the greatness of his folly he shall go astray" (Proverbs 5:23).*

All the miserable traits of character, all the depravity and over-flowing profligacy which prevails in our world is because the law of God is not made the standard of character.[53]

Education not only affects to a great degree the life of the student in this world, but its influence extends to eternity. How important, then, that the teachers be persons capable of exerting a right influence! They should be men and women of religious experience, daily receiving divine light to impart to their pupils.

But the teacher should not be expected to do the parent's work. There has been, with many parents, a fearful neglect of duty. Like Eli, they fail to exercise proper restraint; and then they send their undisciplined children to college, to receive the training which the parents should have given them at home. The teachers have a task which but few appreciate. If they succeed in reforming these wayward youth, they receive but little credit. If the youth choose the society of the evil-disposed, and go on from bad to worse, then the teachers are censured and the school denounced.

In many cases, the censure justly belongs to the parents. They had the first and most favorable opportunity to control and train their children, when the spirit was teachable, and the mind and the heart easily impressed. But through the slothfulness of the parents the children are permitted to follow their own will until they become hardened in an evil course.

Let parents study less of the world and more of Christ; let them put forth less effort to imitate the customs and fashions of the world, and devote more time and effort to molding the minds and characters of their children according to the divine model. Then they could send forth their sons and daughters fortified by pure morals and a noble purpose, to receive an education for positions of usefulness and trust. Teachers who are controlled by the love and fear of God could lead such youth still onward and upward, training them to be a blessing to the world, and an honor to their Creator.[54]

# Educating Our Young

*"Whosoever therefore shall break one of these least commandments, and shall teach men so, he shall be called the least in the kingdom of heaven: but whosoever shall do and teach them, the same shall be called great in the kingdom of heaven" (Matthew 5:19).*

Connected with God, every instructor will exert an influence to lead his pupils to study God's word and obey His law. He will direct their minds to the contemplation of eternal interests, and open before them vast fields for thought; grand and ennobling themes, which the most vigorous intellect may put forth all its powers to grasp, and yet feel that there is an infinity beyond.[55]

Every Christian family is a church in itself. The members of the family are to be Christlike in every action. The father is to sustain so close a relation to God that he realizes his duty to make provision for the members of his family to receive an education and training that will fit them for the future, immortal life. His children are to be taught the principles of heaven. He is the priest of the household, accountable to God for the influence that he exerts over every member of his family. He is to place his family under the most favorable circumstances possible, so that they shall not be tempted to conform to the habits and customs, the evil practices and lax principles, that they would find in the world.[56]

Our children should be removed from the evil influences of the public school and placed where thoroughly converted teachers may educate them in the Holy Scriptures. Thus students will be taught to make the word of God the grand rule of their lives. . . .

In planning for the education of their children outside the home, parents should realize that it is no longer safe to send them to the public school, and should endeavor to send them to schools where they will obtain an education based on a Scriptural foundation. Upon every Christian parent there rests the solemn obligation of giving to his children an education that will lead them to gain a knowledge of the Lord and to become partakers of the divine nature through obedience to God's will and way.[57]

# The Teacher's Curriculum

*"We both labour and suffer reproach, because we trust in the living God, who is the Saviour of all men, specially of those that believe. These things command and teach" (1 Timothy 4:10, 11).*

Teach fundamentals. Teach that which is practical. You should not make a great parade before the world, telling what you expect to do, as if you were planning something wonderful. No, indeed. Boast neither of the branches of study you expect to teach nor of the industrial work you hope to do; but tell everyone who inquires, that you intend to do the best you can to give your students a physical, mental, and spiritual training that will fit them for usefulness in this life and prepare them for the future immortal life.

What influence do you think it would have to publish in your announcement of the school that you will endeavor to give the students a training that will prepare them for the future, immortal life because you desire to see them live throughout the ceaseless ages of eternity? I believe such a statement would have a far greater influence upon the brethren and sisters of this conference, and upon the community in the midst of which the school is established, than would the display of a number of courses of study in ancient and modern languages and other higher branches of study.

Let the school prove itself. Then the patrons will not be disappointed, and the students will not claim that they were promised instruction in certain studies which, after entering the school, they were not permitted to take up.

Let it be understood at the beginning that the Bible lies at the foundation of all education. An earnest study of God's word, resulting in transformation of character and in a fitness for service, will make the Fernando school a power for good. My brethren who are connected with this school, your strength lies not in the number of languages you may teach, or in telling how large a "college" you have. Keep silent on these points. Silence in regard to the great things you plan to do will help you more than all the positive assertions and all the promises that you might publish in your announcements.[58]

# Ordained Unto Life and Ordained to Work

*"Take heed unto thyself, and unto the doctrine; continue in them: for in doing this thou shalt both save thyself, and them that hear thee"* (1 Timothy 4:16).

The Lord calls for pastors, teachers, and evangelists. From door to door His servants are to proclaim the message of salvation. To every nation, kindred, tongue, and people the tidings of pardon through Christ are to be carried. Not with tame, lifeless utterances is the message to be given, but with clear, decided, stirring utterances. Hundreds are waiting for the warning to escape for their lives. The world needs to see in Christians an evidence of the power of Christianity. Not merely in a few places, but throughout the world, messages of mercy are needed.

He who beholds the Saviour's matchless love will be elevated in thought, purified in heart, transformed in character. He will go forth to be a light to the world, to reflect in some degree this mysterious love. The more we contemplate the cross of Christ, the more fully shall we adopt the language of the apostle when he said, "God forbid that I should glory, save in the cross of our Lord Jesus Christ" (Galatians 6:14).[59]

Rich and poor, high and low, are calling for light. Men and women are hungering for the truth as it is in Jesus. When they hear the gospel preached with power from on high, they will know that the banquet is spread for them, and they will respond to the call: "Come; for all things are now ready" (Luke 14:17).

The words "Go ye into all the world, and preach the gospel to every creature" (Mark 16:15) are spoken to each one of Christ's followers. All who are ordained unto the life of Christ are ordained to work for the salvation of their fellow men. The same longing of soul that He felt for the saving of the lost is to be manifest in them. Not all can fill the same place, but for all there is a place and a work. All upon whom God's blessings have been bestowed are to respond by actual service; every gift is to be employed for the advancement of His kingdom.[60]

# Fourth on the List of Gifts

*"God hath set some in the church, first apostles, secondarily prophets, thirdly teachers, after that miracles" (1 Corinthians 12:28).*

We are living in a special period of this earth's history. A great work must be done in a very short time, and every Christian is to act a part in sustaining this work.

God is calling for men who will consecrate themselves to the work of soulsaving. Those who desire to be regarded by God as liberal should devote mind and heart—the entire being—to His service. When we begin to comprehend what a sacrifice Christ made in order to save a perishing world, there will be seen a mighty wrestling to save souls. Oh, that all our churches might see and realize the infinite sacrifice of Christ!

Recently, in visions during the night season, a representation passed before me. Among God's people there seemed to be a great reformatory movement. Many were praising God. The sick were healed, and other miracles were wrought. A spirit of intercession was seen, even as was manifested before the great day of Pentecost. Hundreds and thousands were seen visiting families and opening before them the Word of God. Hearts were convicted by the power of the Holy Spirit, and a spirit of genuine conversion was manifest. On every side doors were thrown open to the proclamation of the truth. The world seemed to be lightened with a heavenly influence. Great blessings were received by the true and humble people of God. I heard voices of thanksgiving and praise, and there seemed to be a reformation such as we witnessed in 1844.[1]

He who does nothing, but waits to be compelled by some supernatural agency, will wait on in lethargy and darkness. God has given His word. God speaks in unmistakable language to your soul. Is not the word of His mouth sufficient to show you your duty, and to urge its fulfillment?[2]

When God appoints means for a certain work, we are not to neglect these means, put them aside, and then pray and expect that He will work miracles to supply our neglect. To every man God has appointed His work, according to his capacities and capabilities.[3]

# The Manifestation of the Spirit

*"The manifestation of the Spirit is given to every man to profit with-al. For to one is given by the Spirit the word of wisdom. . . . To another the working of miracles" (1 Corinthians 12:7, 8, 10).*

Like the twelve apostles, the seventy disciples whom Christ sent forth later received supernatural endowments as a seal of their mission. When their work was completed, they returned with joy, saying, "Lord, even the devils are subject unto us through Thy name." Jesus answered, "I beheld Satan as lightning fall from heaven" (Luke 10:17, 18).

Henceforth Christ's followers are to look upon Satan as a conquered foe. Upon the cross, Jesus was to gain the victory for them; that victory He desired them to accept as their own. "Behold," He said, "I give unto you power to tread on serpents and scorpions, and over all the power of the enemy: and nothing shall by any means hurt you" (Verse 19).

The omnipotent power of the Holy Spirit is the defense of every contrite soul. No one who in penitence and faith has claimed His protection will Christ permit to pass under the enemy's power. It is true that Satan is a powerful being; but, thank God, we have a mighty Saviour, who cast out the evil one from heaven. Satan is pleased when we magnify his power. Why not talk of Jesus? Why not magnify His power and His love?[4]

He who does nothing until he feels especially compelled to do something for God, will never do anything. God has given His word, and is this not sufficient? Can you not hear His voice in His word? If you will use God's appointed means, and diligently search the Scriptures, having a determined purpose to obey the truth, you will know the doctrine whether it be of God; but God will never work a miracle to compel you to see His truth. God . . . has made it possible for all men to be saved. Christ died for a ruined world, and through the merit of Christ, God has elected that man should have a second trial, a second probation, a second test as to whether he will keep the commandments of God, or walk in the path of transgression.[5]

# Victory by Supernatural Means

*"Remember what the Lord thy God did unto Pharaoh, and unto all Egypt; the great temptations which thine eyes saw, and the signs, and the wonders, and the mighty hand, and the stretched out arm, whereby the Lord thy God brought thee out: so shall the Lord thy God do unto all the people of whom thou art afraid. Moreover the Lord thy God will send the hornet among them, until they that are left, and hide themselves from thee, be destroyed. Thou shalt not be affrighted at them: for the Lord thy God is among you, a mighty God and terrible" (Deuteronomy 7:18–21).*

Anciently God went before His people to battle against their enemies, but holy and consecrated ones bore the ark containing the ten precepts of Jehovah, and if any had transgressed any one of these ten commandments in the decalogue God turned His face from His people and suffered the enemy to make a dreadful slaughter. If Israel kept the ten precepts, a copy of which was contained in the ark they bore with them, God's angels fought with the armies of Israel, and although their numbers were ever so small, He turned back their enemies and gave them a triumphant victory.[6]

The world's Redeemer presents to His followers the plan of the battle in which they are called to engage, and He bids them count the cost. He assures them that angels who excel in strength shall be in His army, and will enable those who trust in Him to fight valiantly. One shall chase a thousand, and two put ten thousand to flight—not through their own strength, but through the power of Omnipotence. They are to be more than conquerors through Him that loved them. He shows them the vast confederacy of evil that is arrayed against them; but He also cheers them with the proclamation that they are fighting in company with the hosts of heaven, and that One mightier than all the heavenly intelligences is in the ranks of those who battle for truth and righteousness. . . . The captain of the Lord's host will lead them forward in every conflict against natural and supernatural foes. Jesus says, "Be of good cheer; I have overcome the world' (John 16:33). Your Leader is a conqueror. Advance to victory.[7]

# The Same Power as Anciently

*"[The living God] worketh signs and wonders in heaven and in earth, who hath delivered Daniel from the power of the lions" (Daniel 6:27).*

Daniel in the lions' den was the same Daniel who stood before the king as chief among the ministers of state and as a prophet of the Most High. A man whose heart is stayed upon God will be the same in the hour of his greatest trial as he is in prosperity, when the light and favor of God and of man beam upon him. Faith reaches to the unseen, and grasps eternal realities.[8]

Jesus does not desire those who have been purchased at such a cost to become the sport of the enemy's temptations. He does not desire us to be overcome and perish. He who curbed the lions in their den, and walked with His faithful witnesses amid the fiery flames, is just as ready to work in our behalf to subdue every evil in our nature. Today He is standing at the altar of mercy, presenting before God the prayers of those who desire His help. He turns no weeping, contrite one away. Freely will He pardon all who come to Him for forgiveness and restoration.[9]

Through an infinite sacrifice, God has made it possible that men shall practice holiness in this life. Those who would ascertain their election for the future life, may ascertain it by their attitude of obedience to the commandments of God. Strong emotions, strong impulses, or desires, for heaven, when listening to a description of the charms of a future life, will not prove that you are elected to sit down with Jesus Christ upon His throne. If you would know the mystery of godliness, you should follow that which has been revealed.[10]

Through the power of Christ, men and women have broken the chains of sinful habit. They have renounced selfishness. The profane have become reverent, the drunken sober, the profligate pure. Souls that have borne the likeness of Satan have become transformed into the image of God. This change is in itself the miracle of miracles. A change wrought by the Word, it is one of the deepest mysteries of the Word. We cannot understand it; we can only believe.[11]

# The Source of True Miracles

*"Ye men of Israel, hear these words; Jesus of Nazareth, a man approved of God among you by miracles and wonders and signs, which God did by him in the midst of you, as ye yourselves also know: Him, being delivered by the determinate counsel and foreknowledge of God, ye have taken, and by wicked hands have crucified and slain: Whom God hath raised up, having loosed the pains of death: because it was not possible that he should be holden of it" (Acts 2:22–24).*

The anguish of Christ on Calvary's cross speaks louder than any argument that can be presented, to prove the immutability of the law. But Jesus bore the penalty of the law, and tasted death for every man. But the tomb could not hold Him. Three days after His crucifixion, the mighty angels of heaven parted the darkness from their track, and rolled the stone from the sepulcher. The seal of the government was broken, and the Roman guards placed there to keep the tomb from all disturbance, lest the disciples might come and steal away the body of Jesus, fell to the earth as dead. The angel of the Lord appeared, whose countenance was like lightning, and his raiment white as snow, and for fear of him, the keepers did quake, and became as dead men. Christ came forth from the tomb a mighty conqueror over death and the grave, and He ascended up on high, there to intercede for us as a merciful and faithful high priest, who is touched with the feeling of our infirmities.

We are not to enter heaven without trial. Jesus has told us that we must strive, agonize, to enter in at the strait gate. We are to wage a continual warfare against principalities and powers, and spiritual wickedness in high places, against the ruler of the darkness of this world. But Jesus knows the plan of the battle, and He comforts us with the assurance that He is at our right hand, that we shall not be moved. He says, "Lo, I am with you alway, even unto the end of the world" (Matthew 28:20). The angels of God are all about us. "Are they not all ministering spirits, sent forth to minister for them who shall be heirs of salvation?" (Hebrews 1:14).[12]

# What About John the Baptist?

*"John did no miracle: but all things that John spake of this man were true" (John 10:41).*

It was not given to John to call down fire from heaven, or to raise the dead, as Elijah did, nor to wield Moses' rod of power in the name of God. He was sent to herald the Saviour's advent, and to call upon the people to prepare for His coming. So faithfully did he fulfill his mission, that as the people recalled what he had taught them of Jesus, they could say, "All things that John spake of this Man were true" (John 10:41). Such witness to Christ every disciple of the Master is called upon to bear.[13]

God does not generally work miracles to advance His truth. If the husbandman neglects to cultivate the soil after sowing his seed, God works no miracle to counteract the sure result of neglect. In the harvest he will find his field barren. God works according to great principles which He has presented to the human family, and it is our part to mature wise plans, and set in operation the means whereby God shall bring about certain results. Those who make no decided effort, but simply wait for the Holy Spirit to compel them to action, will perish in darkness. We would ask those who are waiting for a miracle, What means have been tried which God has placed within your reach? We would ask those who are hoping for some supernatural work to be done, who simply say, "Believe, believe," Have you submitted yourself to the revealed command of God? The Lord has said, "Thou shalt," and, "Thou shalt not." Let all study the parable of the talents, and realize that to every man God has given his work—to every man He has entrusted his talents, that by exercising his ability, he may increase his efficiency. You are not to sit still, and do nothing in the work of God. There is work, earnest work, to be done for the Master in overcoming evil habits that are condemned in the word of God, and in doing those good things that are there commanded. Individually, you must battle against evil, wrench yourself from all hurtful associations, study God's word, and pray for divine aid to war against the world, the flesh, and the devil. You need daily light from God to fight the good fight of faith.[14]

# Five Loaves and Two Fishes

*"Jesus took the loaves; and when he had given thanks, he distributed to the disciples, and the disciples to them that were set down; and likewise of the fishes as much as they would. When they were filled, he said unto his disciples, Gather up the fragments that remain, that nothing be lost. Therefore they gathered them together, and filled twelve baskets with the fragments of the five barley loaves, which remained over and above unto them that had eaten" (John 6:11–13).*

The providence of God had placed Jesus where He was, and He depended on His heavenly Father for means to relieve the necessity. When we are brought into strait places, we are to depend on God. In every emergency we are to seek help from Him who has infinite resources at His command. . . .

When the disciples heard the Saviour's direction, "Give ye them to eat" (Matthew 14:16), all the difficulties arose in their minds. They questioned, "Shall we go into the villages to buy food?" But what said Christ? "Give *ye* them to eat." The disciples brought to Jesus all they had; but He did not invite them to eat. He bade them serve the people. The food multiplied in His hands, and the hands of the disciples, reaching out to Christ, were never unfilled. The little store was sufficient for all. When the multitude had been fed, the disciples ate with Jesus of the precious, heaven-supplied food.

As we see the necessities of the poor, the ignorant, the afflicted, how often our hearts sink. We question, "What avail our feeble strength and slender resources to supply this terrible necessity? Shall we not wait for someone of greater ability to direct the work, or for some organization to undertake it?" Christ says, "Give *ye* them to eat." Use the means, the time, the ability, you have. Bring your barley loaves to Jesus.

Though your resources may not be sufficient to feed thousands, they may suffice to feed one. In the hand of Christ they may feed many. Like the disciples, give what you have. Christ will multiply the gift. He will reward honest, simple reliance upon Him. That which seemed but a meager supply will prove to be a rich feast.[15]

# Seek the Eternal Bread

*"When the people therefore saw that Jesus was not there, neither his disciples, they also took shipping, and came to Capernaum, seeking for Jesus. And when they had found him on the other side of the sea, they said unto him, Rabbi, when camest thou hither? Jesus answered them and said, Verily, verily, I say unto you, Ye seek me, not because ye saw the miracles, but because ye did eat of the loaves, and were filled. Labour not for the meat which perisheth, but for that meat which endureth unto everlasting life, which the Son of man shall give unto you"* (John 6:24–27).

It is a sin to support and indulge in idleness those who are able to labor. Some have been zealous to attend all the meetings, not to glorify God, but for the "loaves and fishes." Such would much better have been at home laboring with their hands, "the thing that is good," to supply the wants of their families and to have something to give to sustain the precious cause of present truth. Now is the time to lay up treasure in heaven and to set our hearts in order, ready for the time of trouble. Those only who have clean hands and pure hearts will stand in that trying time. Now is the time for the law of God to be in our minds, foreheads, and written in our hearts.

The Lord has shown me the danger of letting our minds be filled with worldly thoughts and cares. I saw that some minds are led away from present truth and a love of the Holy Bible by reading other exciting books; others are filled with perplexity and care for what they shall eat, drink, and wear. Some are looking too far off for the coming of the Lord. Time has continued a few years longer than they expected; therefore they think it may continue a few years more, and in this way their minds are being led from present truth, out after the world. In these things I saw great danger; for if the mind is filled with other things, present truth is shut out, and there is no place in our foreheads for the seal of the living God. I saw that the time for Jesus to be in the most holy place was nearly finished and that time can last but a very little longer. What leisure time we have should be spent in searching the Bible, which is to judge us in the last day.[16]

# Much Depends on Our Heart

*"Though [Jesus] had done so many miracles before them, yet they believed not on him: that the saying of Esaias the prophet might be fulfilled, which he spake, Lord, who hath believed our report? and to whom hath the arm of the Lord been revealed? Therefore they could not believe, because that Esaias said again, He hath blinded their eyes, and hardened their heart; that they should not see with their eyes, nor understand with their heart, and be converted, and I should heal them" (John 12:37–40).*

Man-made theories pass from one to another, and the doctrines of men, like evil leaven, work actively till the whole lump is leavened. When the Lord sends a message, He gives sufficient evidence to convince the honest in heart of its truth; but those who would resist the truth call for greater evidence. Should the Lord give them a greater evidence, it would only make their opposition more determined.[17]

That which led the Jews to reject the Saviour's work was the highest evidence of His divine character. The greatest significance of His miracles is seen in the fact that they were for the blessing of humanity.[18]

We were not eyewitnesses of the miracles of Jesus, which attest His divinity; but we have the statements of His disciples who were eyewitnesses of them, and we see by faith through their eyes, and hear through their ears; and our faith with theirs grasps the evidence given.

The apostles accepted Jesus upon the testimony of prophets and righteous men, stretching over a period of many centuries. The Christian world have a full and complete chain of evidence running through both the Old and the New Testament; in the one pointing to a Saviour to come, and in the other fulfilling the conditions of that prophecy. All this is sufficient to establish the faith of those who are willing to believe. The design of God was to leave the race a fair opportunity to develop faith in the power of God and of His Son and in the work of the Holy Spirit.[19]

# Miraculous Strength Available

*"By the hands of the apostles were many signs and wonders wrought among the people" (Acts 5:12).*

Why do we not rely more trustingly upon the grace and power of Christ? Why do we not believe with all our hearts? We have a Friend in the courts of heaven who assures us, "All power is given unto me in heaven and in earth" (Matthew 28:18).

The Christian church began its existence by praying for the Holy Spirit. . . .

Christ has made provision that His church shall be a transformed body. Illumined with the light of heaven, possessing the glory of Immanuel. It is His purpose that every Christian shall be surrounded with a spiritual atmosphere of light and peace. There is no limit to the usefulness of the one who, putting self aside, makes room for the working of the Holy Spirit upon the heart, and lives a life wholly consecrated to God. . . .

The only ambition of the believers was to reveal the likeness of Christ's character and to labor for the enlargement of His kingdom.

Notice that it was after the disciples had come into perfect unity, when they were no longer striving for the highest place, that the Spirit was poured out. . . .

Learning, talent, eloquence, every natural or acquired endowment, may be possessed; but without the presence of the Spirit of God, no heart will be touched, no sinner won to Christ. On the other hand, if they are connected with Christ, if the gifts of the Spirit are theirs, the poorest and most ignorant of His disciples will have power that will tell upon hearts. God makes them channels for the outflowing of the highest influence in the universe. My brethren and sisters, plead for the Holy Spirit. God stands back of every promise He has made.[20]

He who will give himself to God as fully as did Moses, will be guided by the divine hand as verily as was the great leader of Israel. He may be lowly and apparently ungifted; yet if with a loving, trusting heart he obeys every intimation of God's will, his powers will be purified, ennobled, energized, and his capabilities will be increased.[21]

# The Early Church

*"[The early Christian believers] continued stedfastly in the apostles' doctrine and fellowship, and in breaking of bread, and in prayers. And fear came upon every soul: and many wonders and signs were done by the apostles" (Acts 2:42, 43).*

The Holy Spirit especially rested upon the apostles, who were witnesses of Jesus' crucifixion, resurrection, and ascension—important truths which were to be the hope of Israel. All were to look to the Saviour of the world as their only hope, and walk in the way Jesus had opened by the sacrifice of His own life, and keep God's law and live. I saw the wisdom and goodness of Jesus in giving power to the disciples to carry on the same work which caused the Jews to hate and slay Him.[22]

Through the gift of the Holy Spirit the disciples were to receive a marvelous power. Their testimony was to be confirmed by signs and wonders. Miracles would be wrought, not only by the apostles, but by those who received their message.[23]

Said Jesus, "They shall cast out devils; they shall speak with new tongues; they shall take up serpents [as in the case of Paul], and if they drink any deadly thing, it shall not hurt them; they shall lay hands on the sick, and they shall recover" (Mark 16:17, 18).

At that time, poisoning was practiced to quite an extent. Unscrupulous men did not hesitate to remove by this means those who stood in the way of their ambition. Jesus knew that His apostles would be subject to this danger, if not specially protected from it. He knew that there would be many who would be so deluded as to think it would be doing God service to put these witnesses to death by any means. He therefore guarded them against this insidious evil. Thus the Lord assured His servants that they were not to labor in their own strength, but in the strength of the Holy Ghost. Though the disciples received their commission to preach the gospel to all nations, they did not at the time comprehend the vast extent, and wonderful character of the work that was before them—a work that was to descend to their successors, and to be carried on to the end of time.[24]

# Two Kinds of Miracles

*"Beholding the man which was healed standing with [Peter and John], [the Jewish leaders] could say nothing against it. But when they had commanded to go aside out of the council, they conferred among themselves, saying, What shall we do to these men? for that indeed a notable miracle hath been done by them is manifest to all them that dwell in Jerusalem; and we cannot deny it. But that it spread no further among the people, let us straitly threaten them, that they speak henceforth to no man in this name. And they called them, and commanded them not to speak at all nor teach in the name of Jesus. But Peter and John answered and said unto them, Whether it be right in the sight of God to hearken unto you more than unto God, judge ye. For we cannot but speak the things which we have seen and heard" (Acts 4:14–20).*

The Jews were astonished that the disciples could perform miracles similar to those they had seen wrought by Jesus. They had supposed that when He died, all such wonderful manifestations would cease. But here was this man who had been a helpless cripple for forty years, now free from pain, and rejoicing in the full use of his limbs.

The following day Annas and Caiaphas, with the remaining members of the council, came together, and Peter and John were brought before them. In that very room, and before those very men, Peter had shamefully denied his Lord. All this came distinctly before his mind as he now appeared for his own trial. The members of the council remembered Peter's cowardice when his Master was before them, and they flattered themselves that he could be intimidated by threats of imprisonment and death. But the impulsive, self-confident Peter who denied Christ in the hour of his greatest need, was a very different man from the Peter who was then before the Sanhedrim for examination. He was no longer a proud boaster; he had been converted, and had become distrustful of self. He was filled with the Holy Spirit; and through [His] power he had become firm as a rock, and was ready with modest courage to honor the name he had once disowned.[25]

# A Powerful Answer to Prayer

*"[The disciples' fellow believers] lifted up their voice to God with one accord, and said, Lord, . . . behold their threatenings: and grant unto thy servants, that with all boldness they may speak thy word, by stretching forth thine hand to heal; and that signs and wonders may be done by the name of thy holy child Jesus. And when they had prayed, the place was shaken where they were assembled together; and they were all filled with the Holy Ghost, and they spake the word of God with boldness. And the multitude of them that believed were of one heart and of one soul: neither said any of them that ought of the things which he possessed was his own; but they had all things common. And with great power gave the apostles witness of the resurrection of the Lord Jesus: and great grace was upon them all" (Acts 4:24, 29–33).*

As the disciples proclaimed the truths of the gospel in Jerusalem, God bore witness to their word, and a multitude believed. . . . The converts to the gospel were "of one heart and of one soul" (Acts 4:32). One common interest controlled them—the success of the mission entrusted to them; and covetousness had no place in their lives. Their love for their brethren and the cause they had espoused was greater than their love of money and possessions. Their works testified that they accounted the souls of men of higher value them earthly wealth.

Thus it will ever be when the Spirit of God takes possession of the life. Those whose hearts are filled with the love of Christ will follow the example of Him who for our sake became poor, that through His poverty we might be made rich. Money, time, influence—all the gifts they have received from God's hand, they will value only as a means of advancing the work of the gospel. Thus it was in the early church; and when in the church of today it is seen that by the power of the Spirit the members have taken their affections from the things of the world, and that they are willing to make sacrifices in order that their fellow men may hear the gospel, the truths proclaimed will have a powerful influence upon the hearers.[26]

# Stephen, the Deacon

*"Stephen, full of faith and power, did great wonders and miracles among the people" (Acts 6:8).*

The Holy Spirit suggested a method whereby the apostles might be relieved from the task of apportioning to the poor, and similar burdens, so that they could be left free to preach Christ. "Then the twelve called the multitude of the disciples unto them, and said, It is not reason that we should leave the word of God, and serve tables. Wherefore, brethren, look ye out among you seven men of honest report, full of the Holy Ghost and wisdom, whom we may appoint over this business. But we will give ourselves continually to prayer, and to the ministry of the word" (Acts 6:2–4).

The church accordingly selected seven men full of faith and the wisdom of the Spirit of God, to attend to the business pertaining to the cause. Stephen was chosen first; he was a Jew by birth and religion, but spoke the Greek language, and was conversant with the customs and manners of the Greeks. He was therefore considered the most proper person to stand at the head and have supervision of the disbursement of the funds appropriated to the widows, orphans, and the worthy poor. . . .

The seven chosen men were solemnly set apart for their duties by prayer and the laying on of hands. Those who were thus ordained were not thereby excluded from teaching the faith. On the contrary, it is recorded that "Stephen, full of faith and power, did great wonders and miracles among the people" (Verse 8). They were fully qualified to instruct in the truth. They were also men of calm judgment and discretion, well calculated to deal with difficult cases of trial, of murmuring or jealousy.

This choosing of men to transact the business of the church, so that the apostles could be left free for their special work of teaching the truth, was greatly blessed of God.[27]

The Saviour had spoken to Saul through Stephen, whose clear reasoning could not be controverted. The learned Jew had seen the face of the martyr reflecting the light of Christ's glory—appearing as if "it had been the face of an angel" (Acts 6:15).[28]

# Philip in Samaria

*"Philip went down to the city of Samaria, and preached Christ unto them. And the people with one accord gave heed unto those things which Philip spake, hearing and seeing the miracles which he did" (Acts 8:5, 6).*

When [the believers as well as the disciples] were scattered by persecution they went forth filled with missionary zeal. They realized the responsibility of their mission. They knew that they held in their hands the bread of life for a famishing world; and they were constrained by the love of Christ to break this bread to all who were in need. The Lord wrought through them. Wherever they went, the sick were healed and the poor had the gospel preached unto them. Philip, one of the seven deacons, was among those driven from Jerusalem.[29]

When God pointed out to Philip his work, the disciple did not say, "The Lord does not mean that." No; "he arose and went" (Acts 8:27). He had learned the lesson of conformity to God's will. He realized that every soul is precious in the sight of God, and that angels are sent to bring those who are seeking for light into touch with those who can help them.

Today as then angels are waiting to lead men to their fellow men. An angel showed Philip where to find the Ethiopian, who was so ready to receive the truth, and today angels will guide and direct the footsteps of those workers who will allow the Holy Spirit to sanctify their tongues, and refine and ennoble their hearts. The angel sent to Philip could himself have done the work for the Ethiopian, but this is not God's way of working. It is His plan that men are to work for their fellowmen.

In the experience of Philip and the Ethiopian is presented the work to which the Lord calls His people. The Ethiopian represents a large class who need missionaries like Philip—missionaries who will hear the voice of God, and go where He sends them. There are many who are reading the Scriptures, but who cannot understand their import. All over the world, men and women are looking wistfully to heaven. Prayers and tears and inquiries go up from souls longing for light, for grace, for the Holy Spirit. Many are on the verge of the kingdom, waiting only to be gathered in.[30]

# Miracles in the Life of Paul

*"All the multitude [of apostles and elders] kept silence, and gave audience to Barnabas and Paul, declaring what miracles and wonders God had wrought among the Gentiles by them" (Acts 15:12).*

Paul had prided himself upon his Pharisaical strictness; but after the revelation of Christ to him on the road to Damascus, the mission of the Saviour, and his own work in the conversion of the Gentiles, were plain to his mind; and he fully comprehended the difference between a living faith and a dead formalism. Paul still claimed to be one of the children of Abraham, and kept the ten commandments in letter and in spirit as faithfully as he had ever done before his conversion to Christianity. But he knew that the typical ceremonies must soon altogether cease, since that which they had shadowed forth had come to pass, and the light of the gospel was shedding its glory upon the Jewish religion, giving a new significance to its ancient rites.[31]

As the chief priests and rulers witnessed the effect of the relation of Paul's experience, they were moved with hatred against him. They saw that he boldly preached Jesus and wrought miracles in His name, that multitudes listened to him and turned from their traditions and looked upon the Jewish leaders as the murderers of the Son of God. Their anger was kindled, and they assembled to consult as to what was best to be done to put down the excitement. They agreed that the only safe course was to put Paul to death. But God knew of their intention, and angels were commissioned to guard him, that he might live to fulfill his mission.[32]

God's special purpose was fulfilled in the journey of Paul upon the sea; He designed that the ship's crew might thus witness the power of God through Paul and that the heathen also might hear the name of Jesus, and that many might be converted through the teaching of Paul and by witnessing the miracles he wrought. Kings and governors were charmed by his reasoning, and as with zeal and the power of the Holy Spirit he preached Jesus and related the interesting events of his experience, conviction fastened upon them that Jesus was the Son of God.[33]

# All to Glorify God Alone

*"God wrought special miracles by the hands of Paul: so that from his body were brought unto the sick handkerchiefs or aprons, and the diseases departed from them, and the evil spirits went out of them"* (Acts 19:11, 12).

As Paul was brought in direct contact with the idolatrous inhabitants of Ephesus, the power of God was strikingly displayed through him. The apostles were not always able to work miracles at will. The Lord granted His servants this special power as the progress of His cause or the honor of His name required. Like Moses and Aaron at the court of Pharaoh, the apostle had now to maintain the truth against the lying wonders of the magicians; hence the miracles he wrought were of a different character from those which he had heretofore performed. As the hem of Christ's garment had communicated healing power to her who sought relief by the touch of faith, so on this occasion, garments were made the means of cure to all that believed; "diseases departed from them, and evil spirits went out of them" (Acts 19:12). Yet these miracles gave no encouragement to blind superstition. When Jesus felt the touch of the suffering woman, He exclaimed, "Virtue is gone out of *me*" (Luke 8:46). So the scripture declares that the Lord wrought miracles by the hand of Paul, and that the name of the Lord Jesus was magnified, and not the name of Paul.

The manifestations of supernatural power which accompanied the apostle's work were calculated to make a deep impression upon a people given to sorcery, and priding themselves upon their intercourse with invisible beings. The miracles of Paul were far more potent than had ever before been witnessed in Ephesus, and were of such a character that they could not be imitated by the skill of the juggler or the enchantments of the sorcerer. Thus the Lord exalted His servant, even in the estimation of the idolaters themselves, immeasurably above the most favored and powerful of the magicians.[34]

Miracles were daily wrought by the disciples through the power of God; and all whose minds were open to evidence were affected by the convincing power of these things.[35]

# Why No Miracles?

*"Oh my Lord, if the Lord be with us, why then is all this befallen us? and where be all his miracles which our fathers told us of?" (Judges 6:13).*

We need an enlarged faith. The Lord desires His will to be done in the hearts of all who believe in Him. But many who might be laborers together with God will never be, because they cling to their imperfections of character. One clings to a cherished fault. Still another enjoys his hereditary and cultivated defects, and makes it his life work to build himself up and glorify himself, until at last he is found to be filled, not with the Holy Spirit, but with self.

The great day of the Lord is right upon us, and God calls for messengers who will be worked by the Holy Spirit, who will not want to work the Spirit. Such messengers will be guided by the Spirit, molded, refined, and beautified in righteousness because they are willing to be worked. But those who are satisfied to carry with them a vast amount of selfishness, faultfinding, suspicion, distrust, and strife, will be so deceived that they will not know their short measurement. They are filled with their own doings. They have not the least idea of what it means to be crucified with Christ. To humble self is an experience strange to them. Before they can serve God acceptably, self must die.[36]

Unbelievers have inquired, "Why are not miracles wrought among those who claim to be God's people?" Brethren, the greatest miracle that can be wrought is the conversion of the human heart. We need to be reconverted, losing sight of self and human ideas, and beholding Christ, that we may be transformed into His likeness. When this the greatest of all miracles is wrought within our hearts, we shall see the workings of other miracles.

God cannot work through us miraculously while we are unconverted. It would spoil us; for we would take it as an evidence that we were perfect in His sight. . . . "Abide in me, and I in you. As the branch cannot bear fruit of itself, except it abide in the vine; no more can ye, except ye abide in me" (John 15:4). Those who see Christ by living faith, those who abide in Him, will have power to work miracles for His glory.[37]

# Remembering the Seventy

*"The seventy [disciples] returned again with joy, saying, Lord, even the devils are subject unto us through thy name. And he said unto them, I beheld Satan as lightning fall from heaven. Behold, I give unto you power to tread on serpents and scorpions, and over all the power of the enemy: and nothing shall by any means hurt you. Notwithstanding in this rejoice not, that the spirits are subject unto you; but rather rejoice, because your names are written in heaven" (Luke 10:17–20).*

It was not part of the mission of Christ to exercise His divine power for His own benefit, to relieve Himself of suffering. This He had volunteered to take upon Himself. He had condescended to take man's nature, and He was to suffer the inconveniences, ills, and afflictions of the human family. He was not to perform miracles on His own account; He came to save others. The object of His mission was to bring blessings, hope, and life to the afflicted and oppressed. He was to bear the burdens and griefs of suffering humanity.[38]

The seventy had not, like the twelve, been constantly with Jesus, yet they had often heard His lessons of instruction. They were sent forth under His direction, to work as He Himself was working. Wherever they went, they were to sound the message, "The kingdom of God is come nigh unto you. All may be admitted into His kingdom who will receive His message and His Messenger. This is the day of your visitation." They were to present the truth of God in such a manner that the people might be led to lay hold upon the blessings placed within their reach.[39]

The seventy were sent out with the warning, "Behold, I send you forth as lambs among wolves" (Luke 10:3). But though sent out to meet opposition, they were not to be spiritless, powerless, and feeble. They were to exercise every proper means that was consistent with the commission they were given, and spend and be spent in seeking to win souls to the kingdom of Jesus Christ. A new and mighty movement was to be inaugurated, a new epoch was to be ushered in, advancing the truth to the world.[40]

# Keeping a Christlike Attitude

*"John answered [Jesus], saying, Master, we saw one casting out dev-ils in thy name, and he followeth not us: and we forbad him, because he followeth not us. But Jesus said, Forbid him not: for there is no man which shall do a miracle in my name, that can lightly speak evil of me"* *(Mark 9:38, 39).*

During their early evangelistic labors, James and John met one who, while not an acknowledged follower of Christ, was casting out devils in His name. The disciples forbade the man to work and thought they were right in doing this. But when they laid the matter before Christ, He reproved them, saying, "Forbid him not: for there is no man which shall do a miracle in My name, that can lightly speak evil of Me" (Mark 9:39). None who showed themselves in any way friendly to Christ were to be repulsed. The disciples must not indulge a narrow, exclusive spirit, but must manifest the same far-reaching sympathy which they had seen in their Master. James and John had thought that in checking this man they had in view the Lord's honor; but they began to see that they were jealous for their own. They acknowledged their error and accepted the reproof.[41]

The fact that one does not in all things conform to our personal ideas or opinions will not justify us in forbidding him to labor for God. Christ is the Great Teacher; we are not to judge or to command, but in humility each is to sit at the feet of Jesus, and learn of Him. Every soul whom God has made willing is a channel through which Christ will reveal His pardoning love. How careful we should be lest we discourage one of God's light bearers, and thus intercept the rays that He would have shine to the world!

Harshness or coldness shown by a disciple toward one whom Christ was drawing—such an act as that of John in forbidding one to work miracles in Christ's name—might result in turning the feet into the path of the enemy, and causing the loss of a soul. Rather than for one to do this, said Jesus, "it is better for him that a millstone were hanged about his neck, and he were cast into the sea" (Verse 42).[42]

# Prophecy Fulfilling

*"There shall arise false Christs, and false prophets, and shall shew great signs and wonders; insomuch that, if it were possible, they shall deceive the very elect" (Matthew 24:24).*

It is now too late in the day for men to please and glorify themselves. Ministers of God, it is too late to be contending for the supremacy. The solemn time has come when ministers should be weeping between the porch and the altar, crying, "Spare thy people, O Lord, and give not thine heritage to reproach" (Joel 2:17). It is a day when, instead of lifting up their souls in self-sufficiency, ministers and people should be confessing their sins before God and one another. The law of God is made void, and even among those who advocate its binding claims are some who break its sacred precepts. The Bible will be opened from house to house, and men and women will find access to these homes, and minds will be opened to receive the Word of God; and when the crisis comes, many will be prepared to make right decisions even in the face of the formidable difficulties that will be brought about through the deceptive miracles of Satan. Although these will confess the truth and become workers with Christ at the eleventh hour, they will receive equal wages with those who have wrought through the whole day. There will be an army of steadfast believers who will stand as firm as a rock through the last test. But where in that army are those who have been standard-bearers? Where are those whose voices have sounded in proclaiming the truth to the sinning? Some of them are not there. We look for them, but in the time of shaking they have been unable to stand, and have passed over to the enemy's ranks.

Brethren and sisters, the Lord wants to impart to us increased light . . . When the angel was about to unfold to Daniel the intensely interesting prophecies to be recorded for us who are to witness their fulfillment, the angel said, "Be strong, yea, be strong." We are to receive the very same glory that was revealed to Daniel, because it is for God's people in these last days, that they may give the trumpet a certain sound.[43]

# Beware!

*"If any man shall say to you, Lo, here is Christ; or, lo, he is there; believe him not: for false Christs and false prophets shall rise, and shall shew signs and wonders, to seduce, if it were possible, even the elect"* (Mark 13:21, 22).

Deceivers will come, and while claiming to be doing a special work for God, while professing to have advanced piety, to be sanctified, to see visions, and to have dreams, they will be doing the work of the enemy, and be found breaking the commandments of God. We should be on our guard, and bring these pretenders to the test; for "to the law and to the testimony: if they speak not according to this word, it is because there is no light in them" (Isaiah 8:20). Shall we take heed to the solemn warnings of Christ, of Paul, and of John, upon this point, and not be deceived by the subtle devices of the enemy?[44]

Spiritualists are increasing in numbers. They will come to men who have the truth as Satan came to Christ, tempting them to manifest their power and work miracles and give evidence of their being favored of God and of their being the people who have the truth. Satan said to Christ, "If thou be the Son of God, command that these stones be made bread" (Matthew 4:3). Herod and Pilate asked Christ to work miracles when He was on trial for His life. Their curiosity was aroused, but Christ did not work a miracle to gratify them.

Spiritualists will press the matter to engage in controversy with ministers who teach the truth. If they decline, they will dare them. They will quote Scripture, as did Satan to Christ. "Prove all things," say they. But their idea of proving is to listen to their deceptive reasonings, and in attending their circles. But in their gatherings the angels of darkness assume the forms of dead friends and communicate with them as angels of light.

Their loved ones will appear in robes of light, as familiar to the sight as when they were upon the earth. They will teach them and converse with them. And many will be deceived.[45]

# Miracles of Evil + Persecution

*"[The lamblike beast] doeth great wonders, so that he maketh fire come down from heaven on the earth in the sight of men, and deceiveth them that dwell on the earth by the means of those miracles which he had power to do in the sight of the beast; saying to them that dwell on the earth, that they should make an image to the beast, which had the wound by a sword, and did live" (Revelation 13:13, 14).*

[Revelation 13:13, 14 quoted.] No mere impostures are here foretold. Men are deceived by the miracles which Satan's agents have power to do, not which they pretend to do.[46]

The same masterful mind that plotted against the faithful in ages past is still seeking to rid the earth of those who fear God and obey His law. Satan will excite indignation against the humble minority who conscientiously refuse to accept popular customs and traditions. Men of position and reputation will join with the lawless and the vile to take counsel against the people of God. Wealth, genius, education, will combine to cover them with contempt. Persecuting rulers, ministers, and church members will conspire against them. With voice and pen, by boasts, threats, and ridicule, they will seek to overthrow their faith. By false representations and angry appeals they will stir up the passions of the people. Not having a "Thus saith the Scriptures" to bring against the advocates of the Bible Sabbath, they will resort to oppressive enactments to supply the lack. To secure popularity and patronage, legislators will yield to the demand for a Sunday law. Those who fear God cannot accept an institution that violates a precept of the Decalogue.[47]

Satan will work miracles to confirm minds in the belief that he is God. All the people of God are now to stand on the platform of truth as it has been given in the third angel's message. All the pleasant pictures, all the miracles wrought, will be presented in order that, if possible, the very elect shall be deceived. The only hope for anyone is to hold fast the evidences that have confirmed the truth in righteousness. Let these be proclaimed over and over again, until the close of this earth's history.[48]

# The Threefold Union

*"I saw three unclean spirits like frogs come out of the mouth of the dragon, and out of the mouth of the beast, and out of the mouth of the false prophet. For they are the spirits of devils, working miracles, which go forth unto the kings of the earth and of the whole world, to gather them to the battle of that great day of God Almighty"* *(Revelation 16:13, 14).*

When Protestantism shall stretch her hand across the gulf to grasp the hand of the Roman power, when she shall reach over the abyss to clasp hands with spiritualism, when, under the influence of this three-fold union, our country shall repudiate every principle of its Constitution as a Protestant and republican government, and shall make provision for the propagation of papal falsehoods and delusions, then we may know that the time has come for the marvelous working of Satan and that the end is near.[49]

The prince of darkness, who has so long bent the powers of his mastermind to the work of deception, skillfully adapts his temptations to men of all classes and conditions. To persons of culture and refinement he presents spiritualism in its more refined and intellectual aspects, and thus succeeds in drawing many into his snare. The wisdom which spiritualism imparts is that described by the apostle James, which "descendeth not from above, but is earthly, sensual, devilish" (James 3:15).[50]

It is impossible to give any idea of the experience of the people of God who shall be alive upon the earth when celestial glory and a repetition of the persecutions of the past are blended. They will walk in the light proceeding from the throne of God. By means of the angels there will be constant communication between heaven and earth. And Satan, surrounded by evil angels, and claiming to be God, will work miracles of all kinds, to deceive, if possible, the very elect. God's people will not find their safety in working miracles, for Satan will counterfeit the miracles that will be wrought. God's tried and tested people will find their power in the sign spoken of in Exodus 31:12–18. They are to take their stand on the living word: "It is written." This is the only foundation upon which they can stand securely.[51]

# Take No Pleasure in Unrighteousness

*"The mystery of iniquity doth already work: only he who now let-*
*teth will let, until he be taken out of the way. And then shall that Wicked*
*be revealed, whom the Lord shall consume with the spirit of his mouth,*
*and shall destroy with the brightness of his coming: even him, whose*
*coming is after the working of Satan with all power and signs and lying*
*wonders, and with all deceivableness of unrighteousness in them that*
*perish; because they received not the love of the truth, that they might be*
*saved. And for this cause God shall send them strong delusion, that they*
*should believe a lie: that they all might be damned who believed not the*
*truth, but had pleasure in unrighteousness" (2 Thessalonians 2:7–12).*

If our life is hid with Christ in God, Satan's miracle-working
power, already being manifested, will not deceive us. . . . There are
those who will keep God's charge to the very close of time. They will
know the fellowship of Christ's sufferings. Satan's malignity will be
intensified toward them, as he sees that his time is short. He knows
that he is sure of those who are under his delusions, but those who
will not be deceived by him, he will persecute until the final rebuke
of God is put upon him. He will perform miracles to fasten the deception upon the already deceived, and to deceive others.[52]

Disguised as an angel of light, [Satan] will walk the earth as a
wonder-worker. In beautiful language he will present lofty sentiments. Good words will be spoken by him, and good deeds performed. Christ will be personified, but on one point there will be a
marked distinction. Satan will turn the people from the law of God.
Notwithstanding this, so well will he counterfeit righteousness, that
if it were possible, he would deceive the very elect. Crowned heads,
presidents, rulers in high places, will bow to his false theories.[53]

When those that "believed not the truth, but had pleasure in
unrighteousness" (2 Thessalonians 2:12), shall be left to receive strong
delusion and to believe a lie, then the light of truth will shine upon all
whose hearts are open to receive it, and all the children of the Lord
that remain in Babylon will heed the call: "Come out of her, My people" (Revelation 18:4).[54]

# The Doom of the Deceiver

*"The beast was taken, and with him the false prophet that wrought miracles before him, with which he deceived them that had received the mark of the beast, and them that worshipped his image. These both were cast alive into a lake of fire burning with brimstone" (Revelation 19:20).*

Spiritualists make the path to hell most attractive. Spirits of darkness are clothed by these deceptive teachers in pure robes of heaven, and they have power to deceive those not fortified with Bible truth. Vain philosophy is employed in representing the path to hell as a path of safety. With the imagination highly wrought, and voices musically tuned, they picture the broad road as one of happiness and glory. Ambition holds before deluded souls, as Satan presented to Eve, a freedom and bliss for them to enjoy which they never conceived was possible. Men are praised who have traveled the broad path to hell, and after they die are exalted to the highest positions in the eternal world. Satan, clothed in robes of brightness, appearing like an exalted angel, tempted the world's Redeemer without success. But as he comes to man robed as an angel of light he has better success. He covers his hideous purposes, and succeeds too well in deluding the unwary who are not firmly anchored upon eternal truth.

Riches, power, genius, eloquence, pride, perverted reason, and passion are enlisted as Satan's agents in doing his work in making the broad road attractive, strewing it with tempting flowers. But every word they have spoken against the world's Redeemer will be reflected back upon them, and will one day burn into their guilty souls like molten lead.[55]

When the flood of waters was at its height upon the earth, it had the appearance of a boundless lake of water. When God finally purifies the earth, it will appear like a boundless lake of fire. As God preserved the ark amid the commotions of the Flood, because it contained eight righteous persons, He will preserve the New Jerusalem, containing the faithful of all ages, from righteous Abel down to the last saint which lived.[56]

# A Miracle in the Believer's Heart

*"How shall we escape, if we neglect so great salvation; which at the first began to be spoken by the Lord, and was confirmed unto us by them that heard him; God also bearing them witness, both with signs and wonders, and with divers miracles, and gifts of the Holy Ghost, according to his own will?" (Hebrews 2:3, 4).*

We should now make diligent inquiry of ourselves, Can I, with my present attainments, stand before the face of the holy God? If in the great day of judgment, we come short, we shall have no excuse; for we have access to the Word of God. Take the Bible for your lesson book; for it is by obedience to its truths that we shall be sanctified. To ensure the work of our salvation, God gave to our world the gift of His only begotten Son. Shall we accept the blessing that Christ has bought for us at such infinite sacrifice? He has made it possible for us to be partakers of the divine nature, having escaped the corruption that is in the world through lust.

Let us not give the impression that our religion consists principally in coming to the church on Sabbath, and numbering one among a number who listen to a sermon, and then go back to their homes to continue in sinful practices. . . . Christ has given us the pattern to which we are to work, but unless we make diligent effort with the help of God, we shall miss the mark. We must be sanctified to God, soul, body, and spirit.

Do we learn from Christ every day? If we do not, we shall certainly come short of the knowledge that is essential. We cannot afford to be weaklings in our Christian experience: for we cannot tell when our account may be settled for eternity. We must constantly increase in faith, and in likeness to Jesus Christ. If we will humble ourselves, the Lord will lift us up. We may try to lift ourselves up, but this will not be reckoned in our favor, in the day when Christ estimates character.

Oh, we are, many of us, so filled with self! We are fastened so firmly to our peculiar temperaments and dispositions. Shall we now follow the Word closely, that this great "I" may die, and that Christ may dwell in our hearts by faith?[57]

# Reflecting Christ's Character

*"Behold, I and the children whom the Lord hath given me are for signs and for wonders in Israel from the Lord of hosts, which dwelleth in mount Zion" (Isaiah 8:18).*

The highest evidence that [the Saviour] came from God is that His life revealed the character of God. He did the works and spoke the words of God. Such a life is the greatest of all miracles.

When the message of truth is presented in our day, there are many who, like the Jews, cry, Show us a sign. Work us a miracle. Christ wrought no miracle at the demand of the Pharisees. He wrought no miracle in the wilderness in answer to Satan's insinuations. He does not impart to us power to vindicate ourselves or to satisfy the demands of unbelief and pride. But the gospel is not without a sign of its divine origin. Is it not a miracle that we can break from the bondage of Satan? Enmity against Satan is not natural to the human heart; it is implanted by the grace of God. When one who has been controlled by a stubborn, wayward will is set free, and yields himself wholeheartedly to the drawing of God's heavenly agencies, a miracle is wrought; so also when a man who has been under strong delusion comes to understand moral truth. Every time a soul is converted, and learns to love God and keep His commandments, the promise of God is fulfilled, "A new heart also will I give you, and a new spirit will I put within you" (Ezekiel 36:26). The change in human hearts, the transformation of human characters, is a miracle that reveals an ever-living Saviour, working to rescue souls. A consistent life in Christ is a great miracle. In the preaching of the word of God, the sign that should be manifest now and always is the presence of the Holy Spirit, to make the word a regenerating power to those that hear. This is God's witness before the world to the divine mission of His Son.

Those who desired a sign from Jesus had so hardened their hearts in unbelief that they did not discern in His character the likeness of God. They would not see that His mission was in fulfillment of the Scriptures.[58]

# Gifts Given as Needed

*"If ye then, being evil, know how to give good gifts unto your children: how much more shall your heavenly Father give the Holy Spirit to them that ask him?" (Luke 11:13).*

Were not miracles wrought by Christ and His apostles? The same compassionate Saviour lives today, and He is as willing to listen to the prayer of faith as when He walked visibly among men. The natural cooperates with the supernatural. It is a part of God's plan to grant us, in answer to the prayer of faith, that which He would not bestow did we not thus ask.[59]

Talents used are talents multiplied. Success is not the result of chance or of destiny; it is the outworking of God's own providence, the reward of faith and discretion, of virtue and persevering effort. The Lord desires us to use every gift we have; and if we do this, we shall have greater gifts to use. He does not supernaturally endow us with the qualifications we lack; but while we use that which we have, He will work with us to increase and strengthen every faculty. By every wholehearted, earnest sacrifice for the Master's service our powers will increase. While we yield ourselves as instruments for the Holy Spirit's working, the grace of God works in us to deny old inclinations, to overcome powerful propensities, and to form new habits. As we cherish and obey the promptings of the Spirit, our hearts are enlarged to receive more and more of His power, and to do more and better work. Dormant energies are aroused, and palsied faculties receive new life.

The humble worker who obediently responds to the call of God may be sure of receiving divine assistance. To accept so great and holy a responsibility is itself elevating to the character. It calls into action the highest mental and spiritual powers, and strengthens and purifies the mind and heart. Through faith in the power of God, it is wonderful how strong a weak man may become. . . . He who begins with a little knowledge, in a humble way, and tells what he knows, while seeking diligently for further knowledge, will find the whole heavenly treasure awaiting his demand. The more he seeks to impart light, the more light he will receive.[60]

# The Holy Spirit in Fullness

*"Ask ye of the Lord rain in the time of the latter rain; so the Lord shall make bright clouds, and give them showers of rain, to every one grass in the field" (Zechariah 10:1).*

We have the assurance that in this age of the world the Holy Spirit will work with mighty power, unless by our unbelief we limit our blessings, and thus lose the advantages we might obtain. After one place has been entered, the word comes, add new territory. Press the triumphs of truth. Uplift the cross in the regions beyond. The vineyard is the world. Much money has been wasted by colonizing, when the work of annexing new territory should have been going forward, and the Lord's message sent forth as a lamp that burneth.

In times past holy men of old spake as they were moved by the Holy Spirit. In ancient times the prophets searched what the Spirit of God which was in them signified. The Spirit was not then given in power because Jesus was not yet glorified. Dating from the day of Pentecost, the Holy Spirit was to be poured forth on sons and daughters, on servants and handmaidens. In every hill country, every lowland, every valley, humble workmen for the Lord are to be raised up. The divine, sacred influence of the Holy Spirit working in our world is to be as signs and wonders, because God's people are a peculiar people, an holy nation, shining amid moral darkness as living stones in the Lord's building. The weakest and feeblest, if they exercise faith in God, and improve their entrusted powers, will be elevated, refined and perfected in character under the Holy Spirit's working. Humble and contrite, they submit to the molding of the Spirit, and they will know what His eternal fullness means. . . .

The success of the ministry of Elias was not due to any inherited qualities he possessed, but to the submission of himself to the Holy Spirit, which was given to him as it will be given to all who exercise living faith in God. . . . Candidly and seriously we are to consider the question, Have we humbled ourselves before God, that the Holy Spirit may work through us with transforming power?[61]

# Christ Is Waiting for Empty Vessels

*"Turn you at my reproof: behold, I will pour out my spirit unto you, I will make known my words unto you" (Proverbs 1:23).*

Many heard of Jesus by hearing of the wonderful miracles He performed. When Christ said that His disciples would do greater works that He had done, He did not mean that they would make any more exalted exertion of their powers; He meant that their work would have greater magnitude. He did not refer merely to miracle working, but to all that would transpire under the working of the Holy Spirit.[62]

Christ has promised the gift of the Holy Spirit to His church, and the promise belongs to us as much as to the first disciples. But like every other promise, it is given on conditions. There are many who believe and profess to claim the Lord's promise; they talk *about* Christ and *about* the Holy Spirit, yet receive no benefit. They do not surrender the soul to be guided and controlled by the divine agencies. We cannot use the Holy Spirit. The Spirit is to use us. Through the Spirit God works in His people "to will and to do of His good pleasure" (Philippians 2:13). But many will not submit to this. They want to manage themselves. This is why they do not receive the heavenly gift. Only to those who wait humbly upon God, who watch for His guidance and grace, is the Spirit given. The power of God awaits their demand and reception. This promised blessing, claimed by faith, brings all other blessings in its train. It is given according to the riches of the grace of Christ, and He is ready to supply every soul according to the capacity to receive.[63]

God calls upon men and women to empty their hearts of self. Then His Spirit can find unobstructed entrance. Stop trying to do the work yourself. Ask God to work in and through you until the words of the apostle become yours: "I live; yet not I, but Christ liveth in me" (Galatians 2:20).[64]

Just as surely as you empty your mind of vanity and frivolity, the vacuum will be supplied with that which God is waiting to give you—His Holy Spirit.[65]

# The Spiritual Gift of Faith

*"The manifestation of the Spirit is given to every man to profit with-al. For to one is given by the Spirit the word of wisdom; to another the word of knowledge by the same Spirit; to another faith by the same Spirit" (1 Corinthians 12:7–9).*

The humblest believer, who may regard his talent as of little value will find that, by exercise of his powers, his talents will increase, and using the mites, he may gain pounds by trading with his abilities for the glory of God. Consecrate to God your mental, spiritual, and physical powers, and they will grow as they are used in the service of the Master.[1]

The physical life is to be carefully educated, cultivated, and developed, that through men and women the divine nature may be revealed in its fullness. God expects men to use the intellect He has given them. He expects them to use every reasoning power for Him. They are to give the conscience the place of supremacy that has been assigned to it. The mental and physical powers, with the affections, are to be so cultivated that they can reach the highest efficiency. Thus Christ is represented to the world. By this painstaking effort man is qualified to cooperate with the great Master Workman in saving souls unto life eternal. This is why God entrusted us with talents—that we might have life, eternal life, in the kingdom of heaven.

Is God pleased to see any of the organs or faculties He has given man neglected, misused, or deprived of the health and efficiency it is possible for them to have? Then cultivate the gift of faith. Be brave, and overcome every practice which mars the soul temple. We are wholly dependent on God, and our faith is strengthened by believing, though we cannot see God's purpose in His dealing with us, or the consequence of this dealing. Faith points forward and upward to things to come, laying hold of the only power that can make us complete in Him.[2]

Oh that those who claim to be children of God would invest every talent that God has entrusted to them for His glory! All should educate themselves to exercise faith in the promises of God, in order that faith may grow into perfect trust.[3]

# All Are Given a Measure of Faith

*"For I say, through the grace given unto me, to every man that is among you, not to think of himself more highly than he ought to think; but to think soberly, according as God hath dealt to every man the measure of faith" (Romans 12:3).*

Angels of God who minister unto those who shall be heirs of salvation are acquainted with the condition of all and understand just the measure of faith possessed by each individual.[4]

The grace and righteousness of Christ are offered as a free gift; the subject of justification by faith is to be studied and put into practice. Let us all realize that young and old, if they would behold the glory of Christ, must go into the cleft of the Rock. If we would become Christians, we cannot retain our natural habits and hold fast to the weakness of our character that dishonors our Saviour. We can find no excuse in the plea that this or that sin is the result of "my way." The professed followers of Christ will always be filled with wavering, will always be tossed like the waves of the sea, unless they give up their way and take Christ's way. To cherish our own way, to do those things which naturally please us will bring upon us the sure result of separation from the presence of Christ, and then we shall be without strength.[5]

No one should deceive himself by thinking that his defects are not very grievous. If he does not guard against these defects, they will be his ruin, and will be reproduced in those with whom he associates. Those who do not think that God requires them to watch and pray unceasingly, striving against every imperfection, are deluded by the enemy. Until they change their attitude, they cannot grow in grace. We all need to pray earnestly for determination to overcome every defect of character.[6]

God has given to every man his measure of faith, and each is to walk in faith. He is to show that he has that faith that will rely upon God for help. As God has given to every man his measure of faith, he is to put it into exercise. He is to let his light shine.[7]

# An Illustration of Faith

*"This is the victory that overcometh the world, even our faith"* (1 *John* 5:4).

Monday morning we had a season of prayer in our tent in behalf of my husband. We presented his case to the Great Physician. It was a precious season; the peace of heaven rested upon us. These words came forcibly to my mind: [1 John 5:4 quoted]. . . .

We then took up the work where we had left it on the Sabbath, and the morning was spent in special labor for sinners and backsliders, of whom two hundred came forward for prayers, ranging in years from the child of ten to gray-headed men and women. More than a score of these were setting their feet in the way of life for the first time. . . .

Monday evening I stood in the stand at a tent meeting in progress at Danvers, Mass. A large congregation was before me. I was too weary to arrange my thoughts in connected words; I felt that I must have help, and asked for it with my whole heart. I knew if any degree of success attended my labors, it would be through the strength of the Mighty One.

The Spirit of the Lord rested upon me as I attempted to speak. Like a shock of electricity I felt it upon my heart, and all pain was instantly removed. I had suffered great pain in the nerves centering in the brain; this also was entirely removed. My irritated throat and sore lungs were relieved. My left arm and hand had become nearly useless in consequence of pain in my heart; but natural feeling was now restored. My mind was clear; my soul was full of the light and love of God. Angels of God seemed to be on every side, like a wall of fire.

Before me were a people whom I might not meet again until the judgment; and the desire for their salvation led me to speak earnestly and in the fear of God, that I might be free from their blood. Great freedom attended my effort, which occupied one hour and ten minutes. Jesus was my helper, and His name shall have all the glory. The audience was very attentive.[8]

# Hold Fast as Heroes!

*"Ye should earnestly contend for the faith which was once delivered unto the saints" (Jude 3).*

Among many of the professing followers of Christ there is the same pride, formalism, and selfishness, the same spirit of oppression, that held so large a place in the Jewish heart. In the future, men claiming to be Christ's representatives will take a course similar to that followed by the priests and rulers in their treatment of Christ and the apostles. In the great crisis through which they are soon to pass, the faithful servants of God will encounter the same hardness of heart, the same cruel determination, the same unyielding hatred.

All who in that evil day would fearlessly serve God according to the dictates of conscience, will need courage, firmness, and a knowledge of God and His word; for those who are true to God will be persecuted, their motives will be impugned, their best efforts misinterpreted, and their names cast out as evil. Satan will work with all his deceptive power to influence the heart and becloud the understanding, to make evil appear good, and good evil. The stronger and purer the faith of God's people, and the firmer their determination to obey Him, the more fiercely will Satan strive to stir up against them the rage of those who, while claiming to be righteous, trample upon the law of God. It will require the firmest trust, the most heroic purpose, to hold fast the faith once delivered to the saints.

God desires His people to prepare for the soon-coming crisis. Prepared or unprepared, they must all meet it; and those only who have brought their lives into conformity to the divine standard, will stand firm at that time of test and trial. When secular rulers unite with ministers of religion to dictate in matters of conscience, then it will be seen who really fear and serve God. When the darkness is deepest, the light of a godlike character will shine the brightest. When every other trust fails, then it will be seen who have an abiding trust in Jehovah. And while the enemies of truth are on every side, watching the Lord's servants for evil, God will watch over them for good. He will be to them as the shadow of a great rock in a weary land.[9]

# Creation Out of Nothingness

*"Now faith is the substance of things hoped for, the evidence of things not seen. . . . Through faith we understand that the worlds were framed by the word of God, so that things which are seen were not made of things which do appear" (Hebrews 11:1, 3).*

The work of creation can never be explained by science. What science can explain the mystery of life?

The theory that God did not create matter when He brought the world into existence is without foundation. In the formation of our world, God was not indebted to preexisting matter. On the contrary, all things, material or spiritual, stood up before the Lord Jehovah at His voice and were created for His own purpose. The heavens and all the host of them, the earth and all things therein, are not only the work of His hand; they came into existence by the breath of His mouth.[10]

Better than all other knowledge is an understanding of the word of God. In keeping His commandments there is great reward, and no earthly inducement should cause the Christian to waver for a moment in his allegiance. Riches, honor, and worldly pomp are but as dross that shall perish before the fire of God's wrath.

The voice of the Lord bidding His faithful ones "go forward" frequently tries their faith to the uttermost. But if they should defer obedience till every shadow of uncertainty was removed from their understanding, and there remained no risk of failure or defeat, they would never move on at all. Those who think it impossible for them to yield to the will of God and have faith in His promises until all is made clear and plain before them, will never yield at all. Faith is not certainty of knowledge; it "is the substance of things hoped for, the evidence of things not seen" (Hebrews 11:1). To obey the commandments of God is the only way to obtain His favor. "Go forward" should be the Christian's watchword.[11]

In the mind of God, the ministry of men and women existed before the world was created.[12]

# Two Classes

*"By faith Abel offered unto God a more excellent sacrifice than Cain, by which he obtained witness that he was righteous, God testifying of his gifts" (Hebrews 11:4).*

Cain came before God with murmuring and infidelity in his heart in regard to the promised sacrifice and the necessity of the sacrificial offerings. His gift expressed no penitence for sin. He felt, as many now feel, that it would be an acknowledgment of weakness to follow the exact plan marked out by God, of trusting his salvation wholly to the atonement of the promised Saviour. He chose the course of self-dependence. He would come in his own merits. He would not bring the lamb, and mingle its blood with his offering, but would present *his* fruits, the products of *his* labor. He presented his offering as a favor done to God. . . .

Abel grasped the great principles of redemption. He saw himself a sinner, and he saw sin and its penalty, death, standing between his soul and communion with God. He brought the slain victim, the sacrificed life, thus acknowledging the claims of the law that had been transgressed. . . .

Abel chose faith and obedience; Cain, unbelief and rebellion. Here the whole matter rested.

Cain and Abel represent two classes that will exist in the world till the close of time. One class avail themselves of the appointed sacrifice for sin; the other venture to depend upon their own merits; theirs is a sacrifice without the virtue of divine mediation, and thus it is not able to bring man into favor with God. . . .

The class of worshipers who follow the example of Cain includes by far the greater portion of the world; for nearly every false religion has been based on the same principle—that man can depend upon his own efforts for salvation. It is claimed by some that the human race is in need, not of redemption, but of development—that it can refine, elevate, and regenerate itself. . . . Humanity has no power to regenerate itself. It does not tend upward, toward the divine, but downward, toward the satanic. Christ is our only hope.[13]

# Stepping Out by Faith

*"By faith Abraham, when he was called to go out into a place which he should after receive for an inheritance, obeyed; and he went out, not knowing whither he went" (Hebrews 11:8).*

The word of God came to [Abraham], not with the presentation of flattering prospects in this life of large salary, of great appreciation and worldly honor. . . . He forsook his country, his home, his relatives, and all pleasant associations connected with his early life, to become a pilgrim and a stranger.

It is frequently more essential than many realize, that early associations should be broken up in order that those who are to speak "in Christ's stead" may stand in a position where God can educate and qualify them for His great work. Kindred and friends often have an influence which God sees will greatly interfere with the instructions He designs to give His servants. Suggestions will be made by those who are not in close connection with heaven that will, if heeded, turn aside from their holy work those who should be light bearers to the world. Before God can use him, Abraham must be separated from his former associations, that he may not be controlled by human influence or rely upon human aid. Now that he has become connected with God, this man must henceforth dwell among strangers. His character must be peculiar, differing from all the world. . . .

Abraham's unquestioning obedience was one of the most striking instances of faith and reliance upon God to be found in the Sacred Record. With only the naked promise that his descendants should possess Canaan, without the least outward evidence, he followed on where God should lead, fully and sincerely complying with the conditions on his part, and confident that the Lord would faithfully perform His word. The patriarch went wherever God indicated his duty; he passed through wildernesses without terror; he went among idolatrous nations, with the one thought: "God has spoken; I am obeying His voice; He will guide, He will protect me."

Just such faith and confidence as Abraham had the messengers of God need today.[14]

# Faith Offers No Excuses

*"By faith Abraham, when he was tried, offered up Isaac: and he that had received the promises offered up his only begotten son, of whom it was said, That in Isaac shall thy seed be called: accounting that God was able to raise him up, even from the dead" (Hebrews 11:17–19).*

God had spoken, and His word must be obeyed. Abraham was stricken in years, but this did not excuse him from duty. He grasped the staff of faith and in dumb agony took by the hand his child, beautiful in the rosy health of youth, and went out to obey the word of God. The grand old patriarch was human; his passions and attachments were like ours, and he loved his boy, who was the solace of his old age, and to whom the promise of the Lord had been given.

But Abraham did not stop to question how God's promises could be fulfilled if Isaac were slain. He did not stay to reason with his aching heart, but carried out the divine command to the very letter, till, just as the knife was about to be plunged into the quivering flesh of the child, the word came: "Lay not thine hand upon the lad;" "for now I know that thou fearest God, seeing thou hast not withheld thy son, thine only son from Me" (Genesis 22:12).

This great act of faith is penciled on the pages of sacred history to shine forth upon the world as an illustrious example to the end of time. Abraham did not plead that his old age should excuse him from obeying God. He did not say: "My hairs are gray, the vigor of my manhood is gone; who will comfort my waning life when Isaac is no more? How can an aged father spill the blood of an only son?" No; God had spoken, and man must obey without questioning, murmuring, or fainting by the way.

We need the faith of Abraham in our churches today, to lighten the darkness that gathers around them, shutting out the sweet sunlight of God's love and dwarfing spiritual growth. Age will never excuse us from obeying God. Our faith should be prolific of good works, for faith without works is dead. Every duty performed, every sacrifice made in the name of Jesus, brings an exceeding great reward.[15]

# The Fruit of a Mother's Teaching

*"By faith Moses, when he was come to years, refused to be called the son of Pharaoh's daughter; choosing rather to suffer affliction with the people of God, than to enjoy the pleasures of sin for a season; esteeming the reproach of Christ greater riches than the treasures in Egypt: for he had respect unto the recompense of the reward" (Hebrews 11:24–26).*

Jochebed was a woman and a slave. Her lot in life was humble, her burden heavy. But through no other woman, save Mary of Nazareth, has the world received greater blessing. Knowing that her child must soon pass beyond her care, to the guardianship of those who knew not God, she the more earnestly endeavored to link his soul with heaven. She sought to implant in his heart love and loyalty to God. And faithfully was the work accomplished. Those principles of truth that were the burden of his mother's teaching and the lesson of her life, no after influence could induce Moses to renounce.

From the humble home in Goshen the son of Jochebed passed to the palace of the Pharaohs, to the Egyptian princess, by her to be welcomed as a loved and cherished son. In the schools of Egypt, Moses received the highest civil and military training. Of great personal attractions, noble in form and stature, of cultivated mind and princely bearing, and renowned as a military leader, he became the nation's pride. The king of Egypt was also a member of the priesthood; and Moses, though refusing to participate in the heathen worship, was initiated into all the mysteries of the Egyptian religion. Egypt at this time being still the most powerful and most highly civilized of nations, Moses, as its prospective sovereign, was heir to the highest honors this world could bestow. But his was a nobler choice. For the honor of God and the deliverance of His downtrodden people, Moses sacrificed the honors of Egypt.[16]

Moses was in kingly courts, and a prospective crown was before him. But he turned away from the tempting bribe.[17]

# Committing Our Case to God

*"What shall I more say? for the time would fail me to tell of Gedeon, and of Barak, and of Samson, and of Jephthae; of David also, and Samuel, and of the prophets: who through faith subdued kingdoms, wrought righteousness, obtained promises" (Hebrews 11:32, 33).*

Let all who are afflicted or unjustly used, cry to God. Turn away from those whose hearts are as steel, and make your requests known to your Maker. Never is one repulsed who comes to Him with a contrite heart. Not one sincere prayer is lost. Amid the anthems of the celestial choir, God hears the cries of the weakest human being. We pour out our heart's desire in our closets, we breathe a prayer as we walk by the way, and our words reach the throne of the Monarch of the universe. They may be inaudible to any human ear, but they cannot die away into silence, nor can they be lost through the activities of business that are going on. Nothing can drown the soul's desire. It rises above the din of the street, above the confusion of the multitude, to the heavenly courts. It is God to whom we are speaking, and our prayer is heard.

You who feel the most unworthy, fear not to commit your case to God. When He gave Himself in Christ for the sin of the world, He undertook the case of every soul. . . .

Christ desires nothing so much as to redeem His heritage from the dominion of Satan. But before we are delivered from Satan's power without, we must be delivered from his power within. The Lord permits trials in order that we may be cleansed from earthliness, from selfishness, from harsh, unchristlike traits of character. He suffers the deep waters of affliction to go over our souls in order that we may know Him and Jesus Christ whom He has sent, in order that we may have deep heart longings to be cleansed from defilement, and may come forth from the trial purer, holier, happier. Often we enter the furnace of trial with our souls darkened with selfishness; but if patient under the crucial test, we shall come forth reflecting the divine character.[18]

# Faith Amidst the Flames

*"[Others] were stoned, they were sawn asunder, were tempted, were slain with the sword: they wandered about in sheepskins and goatskins; being destitute, afflicted, tormented; (of whom the world was not worthy:) they wandered in deserts, and in mountains, and in dens and caves of the earth" (Hebrews 11:37, 38).*

[A few years after Wycliffe's death in England] martyrdom succeeded martyrdom. The advocates of truth, proscribed and tortured, could only pour their suffering cries into the ear of the Lord of Sabaoth. The hunted reformers found shelter as best they could among the lower classes, preaching in secret places, and hiding away even in dens and caves.[19]

"Brother Andrews related an instance of a faithful Christian about to suffer martyrdom for his faith. A brother Christian had been conversing with him in regard to the power of the Christian hope—if it would be strong enough to sustain him while his flesh should be consuming with fire. He asked this Christian, about to suffer, to give him a signal if the Christian faith and hope were stronger than the raging, consuming fire. He expected his turn to come next, and this would fortify him for the fire. The former promised that the signal should be given. He was brought to the stake amid the taunts and jeers of the idle and curious crowd assembled to witness the burning of this Christian. The fagots were brought and the fire kindled, and the brother Christian fixed his eyes upon the suffering, dying martyr, feeling that much depended upon the signal. The fire burned, and burned. The flesh was blackened; but the signal came not. His eye was not taken for a moment from the painful sight. The arms were already crisped. There was no appearance of life. All thought that the fire had done its work, and that no life remained; when, lo! amid the flames, up went both arms toward heaven. The brother Christian, whose heart was becoming faint, caught sight of the joyful signal; it sent a thrill through his whole being, and renewed his faith, his hope, his courage. He wept tears of joy."[20]

# A Treasure Almost Extinct

*"When the Son of man cometh, shall he find faith on the earth? (Luke 18:8).*

Let all who can read and discern the signs of the times know that Christ is nigh, even at the door. Let love for God and Christ grow daily, and let love for your brethren be without dissimulation. Let faith be in constant use. Believe God because He is God. Put your human, world-loving spirit under the molding of the Spirit of God. The question is asked, "When the Lord cometh, will He find faith on the earth?" Faith, then, has become almost extinct.[21]

There is no danger that the Lord will neglect the prayers of His people. The danger is that in temptation and trial they will become discouraged, and fail to persevere in prayer.[22]

In the early church Christianity was taught in its purity; its precepts were given by the voice of inspiration; its ordinances were uncorrupted by the device of men. The church revealed the spirit of Christ and appeared beautiful in its simplicity. Its adorning was the holy principles and exemplary lives of its members. Multitudes were won to Christ, not by display or learning, but by the power of God which attended the plain preaching of His word. . . .

There are many flippant talkers of Bible truth, whose souls are as barren of the Spirit of God as were the hills of Gilboa of dew and rain. But what we need is men who are thoroughly converted themselves and can teach others how to give their hearts to God. The power of godliness has almost ceased to be in our churches. And why is this? The Lord is still waiting to be gracious; He has not closed the windows of heaven. We have separated ourselves from Him. We need to fix the eye of faith upon the cross and believe that Jesus is our strength, our salvation.

As we see so little burden of the work resting upon ministers and people, we inquire: When the Lord comes, shall He find faith on the earth? It is faith that is lacking. God has an abundance of grace and power awaiting our demand. But the reason we do not feel our great need of it is because we look to ourselves and not to Jesus.[23]

# Danger of Shipwreck

*"This charge I commit unto thee, son Timothy, according to the prophecies which went before on thee, that thou by them mightest war a good warfare; holding faith, and a good conscience; which some having put away concerning faith have made shipwreck" (1 Timothy 1:18, 19).*

How many are lost by their effort to keep up a name! If one has the reputation of being a successful evangelist, a gifted preacher, a man of prayer, a man of faith, a man of special devotion, there is positive danger that he will make shipwreck of faith when tried by the little tests that God suffers to come. Often his great effort will be to maintain his reputation.

He who lives in the fear that others do not appreciate his value is losing sight of Him who alone makes us worthy of glorifying God. Let us be faithful stewards over ourselves. Let us look away from self to Christ. Then there will be no trouble at all. All the work done, however excellent it may appear to be, is worthless if not done in the love of Jesus. One may go through the whole round of religious activity, and yet, unless Christ is woven into all that he says and does, he will work for his own glory.[24]

As the test comes to every soul, there will be apostasies. Some will prove to be traitors, heady, high-minded, and self-sufficient, and will turn away from the truth, making shipwreck of faith. Why? Because they did not live "by every word that proceedeth out of the mouth of God" (Matthew 4:4). They did not dig deep and make their foundation sure. When the words of the Lord through His chosen messengers are brought to them, they murmur and think the way is made too strait.[25]

God gives sufficient evidence for the candid mind to believe; but he who turns from the weight of evidence because there are a few things which he cannot make plain to his finite understanding will be left in the cold, chilling atmosphere of unbelief and questioning doubts, and will make shipwreck of faith. . . . Jesus never praised unbelief; He never commended doubts.[26]

# Fighting the Good Fight

*"The love of money is the root of all evil: which while some coveted after, they have erred from the faith, and pierced themselves through with many sorrows. But thou, O man of God, flee these things; and follow after righteousness, godliness, faith, love, patience, meekness. Fight the good fight of faith"* (1 Timothy 6:10–12).

Oh, how many flatter themselves that they have goodness and righteousness, when the true light of God reveals that all their lives they have only lived to please themselves![27]

The crimes that are committed through love of display and love of money constitute this world a den of thieves and robbers, and cause angels to weep. But Christians are professedly not dwellers upon the earth; they are in a strange country, stopping, as it were, only for a night. Our home is in the mansions which Jesus has gone to prepare for us. This life is but a vapor, which passes away.

The acquisition of property becomes a mania with some. Every time the golden rule is violated, Christ is abused in the person of His saints. Every advantage that is taken of fellow mortals, be they saints or sinners, will stand as fraud in the Ledger of Heaven. God designed that our lives should represent the life of our great Pattern in doing good to others and in acting a holy part in the elevation of man. About this work there hovers a true dignity and a glory which may never be seen and realized in this life, but which will be fully appreciated in the future life. The record of kindly deeds and generous actions will reach into eternity.[28]

You must fight the good fight of faith. You must be wrestlers for the crown of life. Strive, for the grasp of Satan is upon you; and if you do not wrench yourselves from him, you will be palsied and ruined. The foe is on the right hand, and on the left, before you, and behind you; and you must trample him under your feet. Strive, for there is a crown to be won. Strive, for if you win not the crown, you lose everything in this life and in the future life. Strive, but let it be in the strength of your risen Saviour.[29]

# Radiating Faith

*"I am not ashamed of the gospel of Christ: for it is the power of God unto salvation to every one that believeth; to the Jew first, and also to the Greek. For therein is the righteousness of God revealed from faith to faith: as it is written, The just shall live by faith" (Romans 1:16, 17).*

The faith professed must be the faith acted. Those who have received the light of truth are in the possession of knowledge which they must impart to others. Those who would teach God's Word must themselves receive the divine treasures. They must not be satisfied with repeating set discourses, depending on notes. They are to add to their treasure, constantly improving in their manner of presenting the truth. They are not to be dwarfs in religious knowledge, but are to open their hearts at the first knock of Christ.[30]

The gospel of Christ becomes personality in those who believe, and makes them living epistles, known and read of all men. In this way the leaven of godliness passes into the multitude. The heavenly intelligences are able to discern the true elements of greatness in character; for only goodness is esteemed as efficiency with God.

"Without Me," Christ says, "ye can do nothing" (John 15:5). Our faith, our example, must be held more sacred than they have been held in the past. The word of God must be studied as never before; for it is the precious offering that we must present to men, in order that they may learn the way of peace, and obtain that life which measures with the life of God. Human wisdom so highly exalted among men sinks into insignificance before that wisdom which points out the way cast up for the ransomed of the Lord to walk in.[31]

We entreat the heralds of the gospel of Christ never to become discouraged in the work, never to consider the most hardened sinner beyond the reach of the grace of God. Such may accept the truth in the love of it and become the salt of the earth. He who turns the hearts of men as the rivers of water are turned can bring the most selfish, sin-hardened soul to surrender to Christ.[32]

# Hearing Mixed With Faith

*"Unto us was the gospel preached, as well as unto [the Israelites]; but the word preached did not profit them, not being mixed with faith in them that heard it" (Hebrews 4:2).*

[Hebrews 4:2 quoted.] This opens before us the secret of this matter, the reason why there is so little accomplished by the many discourses that are preached. The words may be indited by the Holy Spirit, but the result lies with the ones who hear. The oft-repeated charge of the Lord in His word is, "He that hath an ear, let him hear" (Revelation 2:7).

It makes every difference whether the word spoken is received into good and honest hearts. The Israelites had the word spoken to them by Jesus Christ from the pillar of cloud, but like many who hear the glad tidings of truth and righteousness in these last days, they did not hear with consecrated ears, and believe. Selfishness and pride, murmuring and unbelief compassed them about as with a garment. They aggravated their guilt by not hearing with faith, and practicing the word spoken.

It was faith that men lacked in the days of Noah. . . . How different would have been the result had they heeded Noah's appeal. . . .

We know and understand the deep poverty of many who are striving for the crown of life. We are not ignorant in regard to the deep working of Satan, which our brethren will have to encounter. Brethren, you must bear in mind that Satan is working with all deceivableness of unrighteousness in them that perish. He moves upon men to make it hard and trying for those who strive for the crown of life. He has come down with great power, working his will, carrying out his plans, that he may keep souls under his control.

I write to the church: Be not unbelieving, but have faith. Receive the message sent to you from God. He has sent you light, not because He would afflict you and cause you pain, but because He loves you and would have you escape from the snares of the enemy which would entangle your souls. Let the good work of purification go forward. Meet the standard the Lord has given you.[33]

# Straightening Up Our Priorities

*"Wherefore, if God so clothe the grass of the field, which to day is, and to morrow is cast into the oven, shall he not much more clothe you, O ye of little faith?" (Matthew 6:30).*

Oh, what are we doing for the Master! When probation shall end, how many will see the opportunities they have neglected to render service to their dear Lord who died for them. And even those who were accounted most faithful will see much more that they might have done, had not their minds been diverted by worldly surroundings.[34]

Is it not time that the members of the church were becoming educated to engage in missionary labor, that when a call is made for men and women to go forth into the harvest field, there may be those who can respond to the call? saying, "We have given ourselves to Christ without reserve. We have educated ourselves and our households to habits of simplicity in dress and living. We are accustomed to self-denial, and realize that we belong to the Lord. We have no other desire than to do His will, and live not to please ourselves, but to win souls for the Master. We are ready to move to distant lands, and lift up the standard of Christ, and in simplicity and humility live out the truth."

Jesus left His home in heaven, and came to this dark world to reach to the very depth of human woe, that He might save those who were ready to perish. This is the love He has shown to fallen man. But is the disciple above his Master, the servant greater than his Lord? If I am indeed a laborer together with God, shall I not be called upon to make some sacrifice for His cause? Will it be too great a sacrifice for any of Christ's followers to make to take the little possession entrusted to their care, and go to the dark places of the earth, where the people have never so much as heard of the truth, and in meekness and lowliness of heart, there make known to men what the Lord has done for the sons of men?

Those who have come together in church capacity can do one hundredfold more than they are now doing to let their light shine forth in the world.[35]

# Exercising Faith by Forgiving

*"Have faith in God. For verily I say unto you, That whosoever shall say unto this mountain, Be thou removed, and be thou cast into the sea; and shall not doubt in his heart, but shall believe that those things which he saith shall come to pass; he shall have whatsoever he saith. Therefore I say unto you, What things soever ye desire, when ye pray, believe that ye receive them, and ye shall have them. And when ye stand praying, forgive, if ye have ought against any: that your Father also which is in heaven may forgive you your trespasses" (Mark 11:22–25).*

The children of the Lord neglect prayer, especially secret prayer, altogether too much; that many do not exercise that faith which it is their privilege and duty to exercise, often waiting for that feeling which faith alone can bring. Feeling is not faith; the two are distinct. Faith is ours to exercise, but joyful feeling and the blessing are God's to give. The grace of God comes to the soul through the channel of living faith, and that faith it is in our power to exercise.

True faith lays hold of and claims the promised blessing before it is realized and felt. We must send up our petitions in faith within the second veil and let our faith take hold of the promised blessing and claim it as ours. We are then to believe that we receive the blessing, because our faith has hold of it, and according to the Word it is ours. "What things soever ye desire, when ye pray, believe that ye receive them, and ye shall have them" (Mark 11:24). Here is faith, naked faith, to believe that we receive the blessing, even before we realize it. When the promised blessing is realized and enjoyed, faith is swallowed up. But many suppose they have much faith when sharing largely of the Holy Spirit and that they cannot have faith unless they feel the power of the Spirit. Such confound faith with the blessing that comes through faith. The very time to exercise faith is when we feel destitute of the Spirit. When thick clouds of darkness seem to hover over the mind, then is the time to let living faith pierce the darkness and scatter the clouds. True faith rests on the promises contained in the Word of God, and those only who obey that Word can claim its glorious promises.[36]

# An Increase in Faith

*"The apostles said unto the Lord, Increase our faith" (Luke 17:5).*

May the Lord increase our faith and help us to see that He desires us all to become acquainted with His ministry of healing and with the mercy seat. He desires the light of His grace to shine forth from many places. He who understands the necessities of the situation arranges that advantages shall be brought to the workers in various places to enable them more effectually to arouse the attention of the people to the truths that make for deliverance from both physical and spiritual ills.

The tender sympathies of our Saviour were aroused for fallen and suffering humanity. If you would be His follower, you must cultivate compassion and sympathy. Indifference to human woes must give place to lively interest in the sufferings of others. The widow, the orphan, the sick and dying, will always need help. Here is an opportunity to proclaim the gospel—to hold up Jesus, the hope and consolation of all men. When the suffering body has been relieved the heart is opened, and you can pour in the heavenly balm. If you are looking to Jesus and drawing from Him knowledge and strength and grace, you can impart His consolation to others, because the Comforter is with you.

You will meet with much prejudice, a great deal of false zeal and miscalled piety; but in both the home and the foreign field you will find more hearts that God has been preparing for the seed of truth than you imagine, and they will hail with joy the divine message when it is presented to them.[37]

When trials come, do not give way to discouragement. Complaining and murmuring weaken the soul and dishonor God. Does it become us to be so ready with complaint? Are not the tokens of God's love sufficient to fill our hearts with thanksgiving and praise? Jesus desires us to trust in Him, bearing patiently the delays we cannot help. He remembers every word He has spoken to lead His children to trust in Him. He is ever mindful of His covenant. His word will never fail. May the Lord increase our faith in our Intercessor.[38]

# He's Rescuing Me—the Lost Sheep

*"Faith cometh by hearing, and hearing by the word of God" (Romans 10:17).*

The moment you grasp God's promises by faith, saying, I am the lost sheep Jesus came to save, a new life will take possession of you, and you will receive strength to resist the tempter. But faith to grasp the promises does not come by feeling. "Faith cometh by hearing, and hearing by the word of God" (Romans 10:17). You must not look for some great change to take place; you must not expect to feel some wonderful emotion. The Spirit of God alone can make a lasting impression on the mind.

Christ longs to see His people resist the adversary of souls; but only by looking away from self to Jesus can we do this. Cease to bemoan your helpless condition; for your Saviour is touched with the feeling of your infirmities, and today He says to you, Be not discouraged, but cast your burdens upon me. I will take them all, and will bring to pass that which is good for your soul. Looking unto Jesus, the Author and Finisher of our faith, we shall be inspired with hope and shall see the salvation of God; for He is able to keep us from falling. When we are tempted to mourn, let us force our lips to utter the praises of God; for He is worthy of praise.[39]

Take the Lord at His word. You must study the promises and appropriate them as you have need. [Romans 10:17 quoted.] Become rooted and grounded in the word, and then you will not renounce the important truths for this time, which are to exert a sanctifying influence upon your life and character.

It is faith that familiarizes the soul with the existence and presence of God; and when we live with an eye single to His glory, we discern more and more the beauty of His character. Our souls become strong in spiritual power; for we are breathing the atmosphere of heaven, and realizing that God is at our right hand, that we shall not be moved. Faith sees that God witnesses every word and action, and that every thing is manifest to Him with whom we have to do. We should live as in the presence of the infinite One.[40]

# There's Hope

*"Behold, Satan hath desired to have you, that he may sift you as wheat: but I have prayed for thee, that thy faith fail not" (Luke 22:31, 32).*

When in the judgment hall the words of denial had been spoken; when Peter's love and loyalty, awakened under the Saviour's glance of pity and love and sorrow, had sent him forth to the garden where Christ had wept and prayed; when his tears of remorse dropped upon the sod that had been moistened with the blood drops of His agony— then the Saviour's words, "I have prayed for thee: . . . when thou art converted, strengthen thy brethren" (Luke 22:32), were a stay to his soul. Christ, though foreseeing his sin, had not abandoned him to despair.

If the look that Jesus cast upon him had spoken condemnation instead of pity; if in foretelling the sin He had failed of speaking hope, how dense would have been the darkness that encompassed Peter! how reckless the despair of that tortured soul! In that hour of anguish and self-abhorrence, what could have held him back from the path trodden by Judas?

He who could not spare His disciple the anguish, left him not alone to its bitterness. His is a love that fails not nor forsakes.

Human beings, themselves given to evil, are prone to deal untenderly with the tempted and the erring. They cannot read the heart, they know not its struggle and pain. Of the rebuke that is love, of the blow that wounds to heal, of the warning that speaks hope, they have need to learn.[41]

To us, as to Peter, the word is spoken, "Satan hath desired to have you, that he may sift you as wheat: but I have prayed for thee, that thy faith fail not" (Luke 22:31, 32). Christ will never abandon those for whom He has died. We may leave Him and be overwhelmed with temptation, but Christ can never turn from one for whom He has paid the ransom of His own life. Could our spiritual vision be quickened, we should see souls bowed under oppression and burdened with grief, pressed as a cart beneath sheaves, and ready to die in discouragement. We should see angels flying quickly to the aid of these tempted ones.[42]

# Living, Not Dead

*"Wilt thou know, O vain man, that faith without works is dead? Was not Abraham our father justified by works, when he had offered Isaac his son upon the altar? Seest thou how faith wrought with his works, and by works was faith made perfect?" (James 2:20–22).*

It is not faith that claims the favor of Heaven without complying with the conditions upon which mercy is to be granted, it is presumption; for genuine faith has its foundation in the promises and provisions of the Scriptures.

Let none deceive themselves with the belief that they can become holy while willfully violating one of God's requirements. The commission of a known sin silences the witnessing voice of the Spirit and separates the soul from God. . . .

We cannot accord holiness to any man without bringing him to the measurement of God's only standard of holiness in heaven and in earth. If men feel no weight of the moral law, if they belittle and make light of God's precepts, if they break one of the least of these commandments, and teach men so, they shall be of no esteem in the sight of Heaven, and we may know that their claims are without foundation.[43]

Our faith should be prolific of good works; for faith without works is dead. Every duty performed, every sacrifice made in the name of Jesus, brings an exceeding great reward. In the very act of duty, God speaks and gives His blessing. But He requires of us an entire surrender of the faculties. The mind and heart, the whole being, must be given to Him, or we fall short of becoming true Christians.[44]

A living faith in Christ will bring every action of the life and every emotion of the soul into harmony with God's truth and righteousness.

Fretfulness, self-exaltation, pride, passion, and every other trait of character unlike our holy Pattern must be overcome; and then humility, meekness, and sincere gratitude to Jesus for His great salvation will continually flow out from the pure fountain of the heart.[45]

# Believing and Doing Blended

*"As the body without the spirit is dead, so faith without works is dead also" (James 2:26).*

We are justified by faith, but judged by the character of our works.[46]

A living faith will be a working faith. Should we go into the garden and find that there was no sap in the plants, no freshness in the leaves, no bursting buds or blooming flowers, no signs of life in stalk or branches, we would say, "The plants are dead. Uproot them from the garden; for they are a deformity to the beds." So it is with those who profess Christianity, and have no spirituality. If there are no signs of religious vigor, if there is no doing of the commandments of the Lord, it is evident that there is no abiding in Christ, the living vine.[47]

Faith and works go together, believing and doing are blended. . . . Let no one take up with the delusion so pleasant to the natural heart, that God will accept of sincerity, no matter what may be the faith, no matter how imperfect may be the life. God requires of His child perfect obedience.

In order to meet the requirements of the law, our faith must grasp the righteousness of Christ, accepting it as our righteousness. Through union with Christ, through acceptance of His righteousness by faith, we may be qualified to work the works of God, to be colaborers with Christ. If you are willing to drift along with the current of evil, and do not cooperate with the heavenly agencies in restraining transgression in your family, and in the church, in order that everlasting righteousness may be brought in, you do not have faith. Faith works by love and purifies the soul. Through faith the Holy Spirit works in the heart to create holiness therein; but this cannot be done unless the human agent will work with Christ. We can be fitted for heaven only through the work of the Holy Spirit upon the heart; for we must have Christ's righteousness as our credentials if we would find access to the Father. In order that we may have the righteousness of Christ, we need daily to be transformed by the influence of the Spirit, to be a partaker of the divine nature.[48]

# Access to God by Faith

*"Being justified by faith, we have peace with God through our Lord Jesus Christ: by whom also we have access by faith into this grace wherein we stand, and rejoice in hope of the glory of God" (Romans 5:1, 2).*

Angels ministered to Jesus, yet their presence did not make His life one of ease and freedom from severe conflict and fierce temptations. He was tempted in all points like as we are, yet without sin. . . .

We are without excuse if we fail to avail ourselves of the ample provisions made for us that we might be wanting in nothing. Shrinking from hardships, complaining under tribulation, makes the servants of God weak and inefficient in bearing responsibilities and burdens.

All who stand unshrinkingly in the forefront of the battle must feel the special warfare of Satan against them. As they realize his attacks, they will flee to the Stronghold. They feel their need of special strength from God, and they labor in His strength; therefore the victories they gain do not exalt them, but lead them in faith to lean more securely upon the Mighty One. Deep and fervent gratitude to God is awakened in their hearts, and they are joyful in the tribulation which they experience while pressed by the enemy. These willing servants are gaining an experience and forming a character which will do honor to the cause of God.

The present is a season of solemn privilege and sacred trust to the servants of God. If these trusts are faithfully kept, great will be the reward of the faithful servant when the Master shall say: "Give an account of thy stewardship" (Luke 16:2). The earnest toil, the unselfish work, the patient, persevering effort, will be rewarded abundantly; Jesus will say: Henceforth I call you not servants, but friends, guests. The approval of the Master is not given because of the greatness of the work performed, because many things have been gained, but because of the fidelity in even a few things. It is not the great results we attain, but the motives from which we act, that weigh with God. He prizes goodness and faithfulness more than the greatness of the work accomplished.[49]

# Pressing Through the Shadows

*"Whatsoever is not of faith is sin" (Romans 14:23).*

Are there not some of us too much like the man who came to the minister, complaining that he had not been blessed, that he felt no joy; God did not answer his prayers although he had prayed again and again for a blessing. "Well," said the minister, "let us kneel right down here and tell the Lord just how the matter stands." After both had prayed, the minister asked him if he felt better. The man answered, "I feel no better than I did before I prayed. I did not expect to be blessed, and I am not blessed." He had made a mockery of prayer. He did not believe the Lord would answer him, and he received just what his faith had claimed. Is it any wonder that such prayers are not answered? "Whatsoever is not of faith is sin" (Romans 14:23). Do you consider this, when you offer up your faithless petitions? Do you stop to consider how you are dishonoring God and impoverishing your own soul? If you could but realize the wrong you are doing, you would cease to make mockery by meaningless devotions.

Come to God in faith and humility. Plead with Him till the break of day, if necessary, till your soul is brought into such close relationship with Jesus, that you can lay your burden at His feet, and say, "I know whom I have believed" (2 Timothy 1:12).[50]

Take God at His word, and work in faith. Satan will come with his suggestions to make you distrust the word of your heavenly Father; but consider, "Whatsoever is not of faith is sin" (Romans 14:23). Press your faith through the dark shadow of Satan, and lodge it upon the mercy seat, and let not one doubt be entertained.[51]

When you surrender yourself entirely to God, when you fall all broken upon Jesus, you will be rewarded by a victory the joy of which you have never yet experienced. As you review the past with a clear vision, you will see that at the very time when life seemed to you only a perplexity and a burden, Jesus Himself was near you, seeking to lead you into the light. Your Father was by your side, bending over you with unutterable love, afflicting you for your good, as the refiner purifies the precious ore.[52]

# The Trial of Your Faith

*"Ye greatly rejoice, though now for a season, if need be, ye are in heaviness through manifold temptations: that the trial of your faith, being much more precious than of gold that perisheth, though it be tried with fire, might be found unto praise and honour and glory at the appearing of Jesus Christ: whom having not seen, ye love; in whom, though now ye see him not, yet believing, ye rejoice with joy unspeakable and full of glory: receiving the end of your faith, even the salvation of your souls" (1 Peter 1:6–9).*

[1 Peter 1:6–9 quoted.] The apostle's words were written for the instruction of believers in every age, and they have a special significance for those who live at the time when "the end of all things is at hand" (1 Peter 4:7). His exhortations and warnings, and his words of faith and courage, are needed by every soul who would maintain his faith "stedfast unto the end" (Hebrews 3:14).[53]

The trial of faith is more precious than gold. All should learn that this is a part of the discipline in the school of Christ, which is essential to purify and refine them from the dross of earthliness. They must endure with fortitude the taunts and attacks of enemies, and overcome all obstacles that Satan may place in their path to hedge up the way. He will try to lead them to neglect prayer and to discourage them in the study of the Scriptures, and he will throw his hateful shadow athwart their path to hide Christ and the heavenly attractions from their view.[54]

Is Satan tempting you again? Is God permitting you to be brought to the same place where you have failed before? Will you now let unbelief take possession of your soul? Will you fail every time, as did the children of Israel? God help you to resist the devil and to come forth stronger from every trial of your faith!

Be careful how you move. Make straight paths for your feet. Close the door to unbelief and make God your strength. If perplexed, hold still; make no move in the dark. I am deeply concerned for your soul. This may be the last trial that God will grant you. Advance not one step in the downward road to perdition. Wait, and God will help you. Be patient, and the clear light will appear.[55]

# The Shield to Quench the Darts

*"Above all, taking the shield of faith, wherewith ye shall be able to quench all the fiery darts of the wicked" (Ephesians 6:16).*

[Ephesians 6:16 quoted.] Stablish your hearts in the belief that God knows of all the trials and difficulties you will encounter in the warfare against evil; for God is dishonored when any soul belittles His power by talking unbelief.

This world is God's great field of labor; He has purchased those that dwell on it with the blood of His only-begotten Son, and He means that His message of mercy shall go to everyone. Those who are commissioned to do this work will be tested and tried, but they are always to remember that God is near to strengthen and uphold them. He does not ask us to depend upon any broken reed. We are not to look for human aid. God forbid that we should place man where God should be. He has promised to help us, and in the Lord Jehovah is "everlasting strength" (Isaiah 26:4).[56]

I asked the angel why there was no more faith and power in Israel. He said, "Ye let go of the arm of the Lord too soon. Press your petitions to the throne, and hold on by strong faith. The promises are sure. Believe ye receive the things ye ask for, and ye shall have them." I was then pointed to Elijah. He was subject to like passions as we are, and he prayed earnestly. His faith endured the trial. Seven times he prayed before the Lord, and at last the cloud was seen. I saw that we had doubted the sure promises, and wounded the Saviour by our lack of faith. Said the angel, "Gird the armor about thee, and above all take the shield of faith; for that will guard the heart, the very life, from the fiery darts of the wicked." If the enemy can lead the desponding to take their eyes off from Jesus, and look to themselves, and dwell upon their own unworthiness, instead of dwelling upon the worthiness of Jesus, His love, His merits, and His great mercy, he will get away their shield of faith, and gain his object; they will be exposed to his fiery temptations. The weak should therefore look to Jesus, and believe in Him; they then exercise faith.[57]

# Building Our Most Holy Faith

*"Beloved, building up yourselves on your most holy faith, praying in the Holy Ghost, keep yourselves in the love of God, looking for the mercy of our Lord Jesus Christ unto eternal life" (Jude 20, 21).*

We desire that everyone should be in a position where he can believe the word of God. How should I feel if my children should be constantly complaining to me, just as though I did not mean well, when my whole life's efforts have been to forward their interests and to give them comfort? Suppose they should doubt my love; my heart would break. I couldn't endure it. How would any of you feel to be thus treated by your children? How can our heavenly Father regard us when we doubt His love, that has led Him to give His only begotten Son that we might have life?[58]

The faith that is required is not a mere assent to doctrines; it is the faith that works by love and purifies the soul. Humility, meekness, and obedience are not faith; but they are the effects, or fruit, of faith.[59]

Should you seek God diligently, He will be found of you; but He will accept no halfhearted repentance. If you will forsake your sins, He is ever ready to forgive. Will you just now surrender to Him? Will you look to Calvary and inquire: "Did Jesus make this sacrifice for me? Did He endure humiliation, shame, and reproach, and suffer the cruel death of the cross because He desired to save me from the sufferings of guilt and the horror of despair, and make me unspeakably happy in His kingdom?" Look upon Him whom your sins have pierced, and resolve: "The Lord shall have the service of my life. I will no longer unite with His enemies; I will no longer lend my influence to the rebels against His government. All I have and am is too little to devote to Him who so loved me that He gave His life for me—His whole divine self for one so sinful and erring." Separate from the world, be wholly on the Lord's side, press the battle to the gates, and you will win glorious victories.[60]

# Looking to Christ's Joy

*"Wherefore seeing we also are compassed about with so great a cloud of witnesses, let us lay aside every weight, and the sin which doth so easily beset us, and let us run with patience the race that is set before us, looking unto Jesus the author and finisher of our faith"* (Hebrews 12:1, 2).

Those who look within for comfort will become weary and disappointed. A sense of our weakness and unworthiness should lead us with humility of heart to plead the atoning sacrifice of Christ. As we rely upon His merits we shall find rest and peace and joy. He saves to the uttermost all who come unto God by Him.

We need to trust in Jesus daily, hourly. He has promised that as our day is, our strength shall be. By His grace we may bear all the burdens of the present and perform its duties. But many are weighed down by the anticipation of future troubles. They are constantly seeking to bring tomorrow's burdens into today. Thus a large share of all their trials are imaginary. For these, Jesus has made no provision. He promises grace only for the day. He bids us not to burden ourselves with the cares and troubles of tomorrow. . . .

The habit of brooding over anticipated evils is unwise and unchristian. In thus doing we fail to enjoy the blessings and to improve the opportunities of the present. The Lord requires us to perform the duties of today and to endure its trials. We are today to watch that we offend not in word or deed. We must today praise and honor God. By the exercise of living faith today we are to conquer the enemy. We must today seek God and be determined that we will not rest satisfied without His presence. We should watch and work and pray as though this were the last day that would be granted us. How intensely earnest, then, would be our life. How closely would we follow Jesus in all our words and deeds.[61]

The joy set before Christ, which sustained Him in all His sufferings, was the salvation of poor sinners. This should be our joy and the spur of our ambition.[62]

# Accountable and Active

*"Be not slothful, but followers of them who through faith and patience inherit the promises" (Hebrews 6:12).*

So long as we choose the easy path of self-indulgence and are frightened at self-denial, our faith will never become firm, and we cannot know the peace of Jesus nor the joy that comes through conscious victory. The most exalted of the redeemed host that stand before the throne of God and the Lamb, clad in white, know the conflict of overcoming, for they have come up through great tribulation. Those who have yielded to circumstances rather than engage in this conflict will not know how to stand in that day when anguish will be upon every soul, when, though Noah, Job, and Daniel were in the land, they could save neither son nor daughter, for everyone must deliver his soul by his own righteousness.

No one need say that his case is hopeless, that he cannot live the life of a Christian. Ample provision is made by the death of Christ for every soul. Jesus is our ever-present help in time of need. Only call upon Him in faith, and He has promised to hear and answer your petitions.[63]

The pleasing fable that all there is to do is to believe has destroyed thousands and tens of thousands, because many have called that faith which is not faith, but simply a dogma. Man is an intelligent, accountable being; he is not to be carried as a passive burden by the Lord, but is to work in harmony with Christ. Man is to take up his appointed work in striving for glory, honor, and immortality. God calls upon men for the use of every talent He has lent them, the exercise of every power He has given; for man can never be saved in disobedience and indolence. Christ wrestled in earnest prayer; He offered up His supplications to the Father with strong crying and tears in behalf of those for whose salvation He had left heaven, and had come to this earth. Then how proper, yea, how essential that men should pray and not faint! How important that they should be instant in prayer, petitioning for the help that can come only from Christ our Lord! If you will find voice and time to pray, God will find time and voice to answer.[64]

# Worth the While

*"For what if some did not believe? shall their unbelief make the faith of God without effect?" (Romans 3:3).*

If we would have wisdom and knowledge to enable us to go through the time of trouble that is before us, we must be gathering it now by daily exercise of faith. We do not desire that you should be anxious about the time of trouble, but we want you to take up your work right where it is, and do it faithfully day by day. There are souls in your own church and neighborhood that need help.[65]

In comparison to the number that reject the truth, those who receive it will be very small, but one soul is of more value than worlds besides. We must not become discouraged, although our work does not seem to bring large returns. It is written of Christ, "He shall not fail nor be discouraged" (Isaiah 42:4). Shall we talk of failure or discouragement? Let us think of the price our Lord has paid that man should not perish, but have everlasting life. Although the greatest portion of the world will reject the truth, some will accept it, some will respond to the drawing power of Christ. Those in whose hands the reading matter is placed may turn from the light, and refuse to obey the convictions of conscience, but the messenger that they despise, through the providence of God may fall into the hands of others, and be as meat in due season to them. They will be aroused to search the Scriptures, to pray to know what is truth, and they will not ask in vain. Angels of God will minister to their necessities. Many who are in harmony with the truth, whose hearts are full of peace and gladness because of the light for these last days, have received their knowledge from the pages that others rejected. Those who are susceptible to the evidences of truth will yield to the convictions of the Spirit of God.[66]

As your experience grows, you will have increased ardor of soul and warmer love for the service of God, because you have oneness of purpose with Jesus Christ. Your sympathies are begotten of the Holy Spirit. You wear the yoke with Christ, and are laborers together with God.[67]

# A Welcome Gift in a Diseased World

*"The manifestation of the Spirit is given to every man to profit with-al. For to one is given by the Spirit the word of wisdom; to another the word of knowledge by the same Spirit; to another faith by the same Spirit; to another the gifts of healing by the same Spirit" (1 Corinthians 12:7–9).*

We want our medical students to be men and women who are most thorough, and who feel it their duty to improve every talent lent them, that they may finally double their entrusted capital.

The light that God has given in medical missionary lines will not cause His people to be regarded as inferior in scientific medical knowledge, but will fit them to stand upon the highest eminence. God would have them stand as a wise and understanding people because of His presence with them. In the strength of Him who is the source of all wisdom, all grace, defects and ignorance may be overcome.[1]

The Lord calls for the best talents to be united . . . for the carrying on of the work as He has directed—not the talent that will demand the largest salary, but the talent that will place itself on the side of Christ to work in His lines. We must have medical instructors who will teach the science of healing without the use of drugs.[2]

Those who have not had special training in one of our medical institutions may think that they can do very little; but, my dear fellow workers, remember that in the parable of the talents, Christ did not represent all the servants as receiving the same number. To one servant was given five talents; to another, two; and to still another, one. If you have but one talent, use it wisely, increasing it by putting it out to the exchangers. Some cannot do as much as others, but everyone is to do all he can to roll back the wave of disease and distress that is sweeping over our world. Come up to the help of the Lord, to the help of the Lord against the mighty powers of darkness. God desires every one of His children to have intelligence and knowledge, so that with unmistakable clearness and power His glory shall be revealed in our world.[3]

# Working Hand in Hand

*"God hath set some in the church, first apostles, secondarily prophets, thirdly teachers, after that miracles, then gifts of healings"* (1 Corinthians 12:28).

The medical missionary work should be a part of the work of every church in our land. Disconnected from the church it would soon become a strange medley of disorganized atoms. It would consume, but not produce. Instead of acting as God's helping hand to forward His truth, it would sap the life and force from the church and weaken the message. Conducted independently, it would not only consume talent and means needed in other lines, but in the very work of helping the helpless apart from the ministry of the word, it would place men where they would scoff at Bible truth.

The gospel ministry is needed to give permanence and stability to the medical missionary work; and the ministry needs the medical missionary work to demonstrate the practical working of the gospel. Neither part of the work is complete without the other.

The message of the soon coming of the Saviour must be given in all parts of the world, and a solemn dignity should characterize it in every branch. A large vineyard is to be worked, and the wise husbandman will work it so that every part will produce fruit. If in the medical missionary work the living principles of truth are kept pure, uncontaminated by anything that would dim their luster, the Lord will preside over the work. If those who bear the heavy burdens will stand true and steadfast to the principles of truth, the Lord will uphold and sustain them.

The union that should exist between the medical missionary work and the ministry is clearly set forth in the fifty-eighth chapter of Isaiah. There is wisdom and blessing for those who will engage in the work as here presented. This chapter is explicit, and there is in it enough to enlighten anyone who wishes to do the will of God. It presents abundant opportunity to minister to suffering humanity, and at the same time to be an instrument in God's hands of bringing the light of truth before a perishing world.[4]

# All Glory to God

*"Bless the Lord, O my soul, and forget not all his benefits: who for-
giveth all thine iniquities; who healeth all thy diseases" (Psalm 103:2, 3).*

Jesus, the divine Master, ever exalted the name of His heavenly
Father. He taught His disciples to pray, "Our Father who art in heav-
en, hallowed be Thy name" (Matthew 6:9, ARV). And they were not
to forget to acknowledge, "Thine is . . . the glory" (Verse 13). So careful was the great Healer to direct attention from Himself to the
Source of His power, that the wondering multitude, "when they saw
the dumb to speak, the maimed to be whole, the lame to walk, and
the blind to see," did not glorify Him, but "glorified the God of
Israel" (Matthew 15:31).[5]

Think of what may be gained by all who seek first the kingdom of
God and His righteousness! There is a great work before all who will
do this. A field of usefulness is open to him who will do good in this
life. The words and works of the one who thus serves God are a savor
of life unto life. He may not be able to speak to congregations, but he
can lead souls to Jesus.

The Lord has more and still more grace and love to give to those
who preach the gospel to sinners. A work is to be done in and for the
churches. They are not merely to be preached to; they are to be educated to receive Christ as their Saviour. The hearts of the members are to
be so softened and humble that they will receive with meekness the
engrafted word, which is able to save their souls. Ministry does not
consist alone in preaching. Those minister who relieve the sick and
suffering, helping the needy, speaking words of comfort to the
desponding and those of little faith. Nigh and afar off, souls are
weighed down by a sense of guilt. It is not hardship, toil, or poverty
that lowers and degrades humanity. It is guilt, wrongdoing. This
brings unrest and dissatisfaction. Jesus would have His children minister to sin-sick souls. Those that are strong ought to bear the infirmities of the weak until they become strong.[6]

Medical missionary work should have its representative in every
place in connection with the establishment of our churches.[7]

# A Key Part of the Church's Mission

*"The Lord doth build up Jerusalem: he gathereth together the outcasts of Israel. He healeth the broken in heart, and bindeth up their wounds" (Psalm 147:2, 3).*

[Medical missionary] work must be done; the truth must be carried into the highways and byways. And ministers and church members should awake and see the necessity of cooperating in this work.[8]

The sick are to be healed through the combined effort of the human and the divine. Every gift, every power, that Christ promised His disciples He bestows upon those who will serve Him faithfully. And He who gives mental capabilities, and who entrusts talents to the men and women who are His by creation and redemption, expects that these talents and capabilities will be increased by use. Every talent must be employed in blessing others and thus bringing honor to God. But physicians have been led to suppose that their capabilities were their own individual property. The powers given them for God's work they have used in branching out into lines of work to which God has not appointed them.

Satan works every moment to find an opportunity for stealing in. He tells the physician that his talents are too valuable to be bound up among Seventh-day Adventists, that if he were free he could do a very large work. The physician is tempted to feel that he has methods which he can carry independent of the people for whom God has wrought that he might place them above every other people on the face of the earth. But let not the physician feel that his influence would increase if he should separate himself from this work: Should he attempt to carry out his plans he would not meet with success.

Selfishness introduced in any degree into ministerial or medical work is an infraction of the law of God. When men glory in their capabilities and cause the praise of men to flow to finite beings, they dishonor God, and He will remove that in which they glory.[9]

The relief of bodily suffering opens the way for the healing of the sin-sick soul.[10]

# Learning Physical Laws

*"My son, attend to my words; incline thine ear unto my sayings. Let them not depart from thine eyes; keep them in the midst of thine heart. For they are life unto those that find them, and health to all their flesh"* *(Proverbs 4:20–22).*

The Lord is not pleased with ignorance in regard to His laws, either natural or spiritual. We are to be workers together with God for the restoration of health to the body as well as to the soul.

And we should teach others how to preserve and to recover health. For the sick we should use the remedies which God has provided in nature, and we should point them to Him who alone can restore. It is our work to present the sick and suffering to Christ in the arms of our faith. We should teach them to believe in the Great Healer. We should lay hold on His promise and pray for the manifestation of His power. The very essence of the gospel is restoration, and the Saviour would have us bid the sick, the hopeless, and the afflicted take hold upon His strength.

The power of love was in all Christ's healing, and only by partaking of that love, through faith, can we be instruments for His work. If we neglect to link ourselves in divine connection with Christ, the current of life-giving energy cannot flow in rich streams from us to the people.[11]

Sound health lies at the very foundation of the student's success. Without it, he can never see the fruition of his ambitions and his hopes. Hence a knowledge of the laws by which health is secured and preserved is of preeminent importance. The human body may be compared to nicely adjusted machinery, which needs care to keep it in running order. One part should not be subjected to constant wear and pressure, while another part is rusting from inaction. While the mind is taxed, the muscles also should have their proportion of exercise. Every young person should learn how to regulate his dietetic habits— what to eat, when to eat, and how to eat. He should also learn how many hours may be spent in study, and how much time should be given to physical exercise.[12]

# Words as a Healing Balm

*"Pleasant words are as an honeycomb, sweet to the soul, and health to the bones" (Proverbs 16:24).*

Jesus was the healer of the body as well as of the soul. He was interested in every phase of suffering that came under His notice, and to every sufferer He brought relief, His kind words having a soothing balm. None could say that He had worked a miracle; but virtue—the healing power of love—went out from Him to the sick and distressed. Thus in an unobtrusive way He worked for the people from His very childhood. And this was why, after His public ministry began, so many heard Him gladly.[13]

Sympathy and tact will often prove a greater benefit to the sick than will the most skillful treatment given in a cold, indifferent way. When a physician comes to the sickbed with a listless, careless manner, looks at the afflicted one with little concern, by word or action giving the impression that the case is not one requiring much attention, and then leaves the patient to his own reflections, he has done that patient positive harm. The doubt and discouragement produced by his indifference will often counteract the good effect of the remedies he may prescribe.

If physicians could put themselves in the place of the one whose spirit is humbled and whose will is weakened by suffering, and who longs for words of sympathy and assurance, they would be better prepared to appreciate his feelings. When the love and sympathy that Christ manifested for the sick is combined with the physician's knowledge, his very presence will be a blessing.[14]

Let the workers in our medical institutions keep Christ, the Great Physician, constantly before those to whom disease of body and soul has brought discouragement. Point them to the One who can heal both physical and spiritual diseases. Tell them of the One who is touched with the feeling of their infirmities. Encourage them to place themselves in the care of Him who gave His life to make it possible for them to have life eternal. Keep their minds fixed upon the One altogether lovely, the chiefest among ten thousand. Talk of His love; tell of His power to save.[15]

# Humility Is Healing

*"Be not wise in thine own eyes: fear the Lord, and depart from evil. It shall be health to thy navel, and marrow to thy bones" (Proverbs 3:7, 8).*

The church needs to be awakened. When Christ was on this earth trying to reclaim souls, to restore the moral image of God in man by warnings, entreaties, appeals, by a perfect example of obedience to His Father's will, He could not do many mighty works in some of the places He visited because of their unbelief. This is why we do not now see more of the deep moving of the Spirit of God upon human minds, more of His power manifested in healing the sick. Unbelief is the barrier between us and God.

How sad it is that God is disappointed and robbed of His glory because those who minister the word do not realize their privilege, and fail to increase in faith and charity. Bring your sick to God in faith. Humble your hearts before Him, confessing your sins. Then pray earnestly, trustingly. You will see the practical working of God's power, and it will be said, "God hath chosen the foolish things of the world to confound the wise; and God hath chosen the weak things of the world to confound the things which are mighty; and base things of the world, and things which are despised, hath God chosen, yea, and things which are not, to bring to naught things that are" (1 Corinthians 1:27, 28).

Much more of God's light and love and grace should be seen in our churches. Then we should see souls receiving the impress of the image of Christ. Those who keep the love of Christ glowing in the heart will provoke others to good works. A hundredfold will be rendered to God in praise and gratitude, in willing, cheerful obedience. The hearts of God's children will be full of praise and thanksgiving to Him who gave His life for the life of the world.[16]

Medical missionary work is to open the door for the gospel of present truth. The third angel's message is to be heard in all places. Economize! Strip yourselves of pride. . . . [God] will give to you that you may give to others.[17]

# Obedience Is Key

*"If thou wilt diligently hearken to the voice of the Lord thy God, and wilt do that which is right in his sight, and wilt give ear to his commandments, and keep all his statutes, I will put none of these diseases upon thee, which I have brought upon the Egyptians: for I am the Lord that healeth thee" (Exodus 15:26).*

Every law governing the human system is to be strictly regarded; for it is as truly a law of God as is the word of Holy Writ; and every willful deviation from obedience to this law is as certainly sin as a violation of the moral law. All nature expresses the law of God, but in our physical structure Jehovah has written His law with His own finger upon every thrilling nerve, upon every living fiber, and upon every organ of the body. We shall suffer loss and defeat, if we step out of nature's path, which God Himself has marked out, into one of our own devising.[18]

Oh, how many lose the richest blessings that God has in store for them in health and spiritual endowments! There are many souls who wrestle for special victories and special blessings that they may do some great thing. To this end they are always feeling that they must make an agonizing struggle in prayer and tears. When these persons search the Scriptures with prayer to know the expressed will of God, and then do His will from the heart without one reservation or self-indulgence, they will find rest. All the agonizing, all the tears and struggles, will not bring them the blessing they long for. Self must be entirely surrendered. They must do the work that presents itself, appropriating the abundance of the grace of God which is promised to all who ask in faith.

"If any man will come after Me," said Jesus, "let him deny himself, and take up his cross daily, and follow Me" (Luke 9:23). Let us follow the Saviour in His simplicity and self-denial. Let us lift up the Man of Calvary by word and by holy living. The Saviour comes very near to those who consecrate themselves to God. If ever there was a time when we needed the working of the Spirit of God upon our hearts and lives, it is now. Let us lay hold of this divine power for strength to live a life of holiness and self-surrender.[19]

# Mercy for the Afflicted

*"Fools because of their transgression, and because of their iniquities, are afflicted. Their soul abhorreth all manner of meat; and they draw near unto the gates of death. Then they cry unto the Lord in their trouble, and he saveth them out of their distresses. He sent his word, and healed them, and delivered them from their destructions" (Psalm 107:17–20).*

[Psalms 103:13, 14; 107:17–20 quoted.] God is just as willing to restore the sick to health now as when the Holy Spirit spoke these words through the psalmist. And Christ is the same compassionate physician now that He was during His earthly ministry. In Him there is healing balm for every disease, restoring power for every infirmity. His disciples in this time are to pray for the sick as verily as the disciples of old prayed. And recoveries will follow; for "the prayer of faith shall save the sick" (James 5:15). We have the Holy Spirit's power, the calm assurance of faith, that can claim God's promises. The Lord's promise, "They shall lay hands on the sick, and they shall recover" (Mark 16:18), is just as trustworthy now as in the days of the apostles. It presents the privilege of God's children, and our faith should lay hold of all that it embraces. Christ's servants are the channel of His working, and through them He desires to exercise His healing power. It is our work to present the sick and suffering to God in the arms of our faith. We should teach them to believe in the Great Healer. The Saviour would have us encourage the sick, the hopeless, the afflicted, to take hold upon His strength. Through faith and prayer the sickroom may be transformed into a Bethel. In word and deed, physicians and nurses may say, so plainly that it cannot be misunderstood, "God is in this place" to save, and not to destroy. Christ desires to manifest His presence in the sickroom, filling the hearts of physicians and nurses with the sweetness of His love. If the life of the attendants upon the sick is such that Christ can go with them to the bedside of the patient, there will come to him the conviction that the compassionate Saviour is present, and this conviction will itself do much for the healing of both the soul and the body.[20]

# The Supreme Physician

*"When the even was come, they brought unto [Jesus] many that were possessed with devils: and he cast out the spirits with his word, and healed all that were sick: that it might be fulfilled which was spoken by Esaias the prophet, saying, Himself took our infirmities, and bare our sicknesses" (Matthew 8:16, 17).*

Our Lord Jesus Christ came to this world as the unwearied servant of man's necessity. He "took our infirmities, and bare our sicknesses," that He might minister to every need of humanity (Matthew 8:17). The burden of disease and wretchedness and sin He came to remove. It was His mission to bring to men complete restoration; He came to give them health and peace and perfection of character.

Varied were the circumstances and needs of those who besought His aid, and none who came to Him went away unhelped. From Him flowed a stream of healing power, and in body and mind and soul men were made whole.

The Saviour's work was not restricted to any time or place. His compassion knew no limit. On so large a scale did He conduct His work of healing and teaching that there was no building in Palestine large enough to receive the multitudes that thronged to Him.[21]

The Saviour in His miracles revealed the power that is continually at work in man's behalf, to sustain and to heal him. Through the agencies of nature, God is working, day by day, hour by hour, moment by moment, to keep us alive, to build up and restore us. When any part of the body sustains injury, a healing process is at once begun; nature's agencies are set at work to restore soundness. But the power working through these agencies is the power of God. All life-giving power is from Him. When one recovers from disease, it is God who restores him.

Sickness, suffering, and death are work of an antagonistic power. Satan is the destroyer; God is the restorer.

The words spoken to Israel are true today of those who recover health of body or health of soul. "I am the Lord that healeth thee" (Exodus 15:26).[22]

# The Healer That Teaches

*"I taught Ephraim also to go, taking them by their arms; but they knew not that I healed them. I drew them with cords of a man, with bands of love" (Hosea 11:3, 4).*

In the Saviour's manner of healing there were lessons for His disciples. On one occasion He anointed the eyes of a blind man with clay, and bade him, "Go, wash in the pool of Siloam. . . . He went his way therefore, and washed, and came seeing" (John 9:7). The cure could be wrought only by the power of the Great Healer, yet Christ made use of the simple agencies of nature. While He did not give countenance to drug medication, He sanctioned the use of simple and natural remedies.

To many of the afflicted ones who received healing, Christ said, "Sin no more, lest a worse thing come unto thee" (John 5:14). Thus He taught that disease is the result of violating God's laws, both natural and spiritual. The great misery in the world would not exist did men but live in harmony with the Creator's plan.[23]

Many act as if health and disease were things entirely independent of their conduct and entirely outside their control. They do not reason from cause to effect, and submit to feebleness and disease as a necessity. Violent attacks of sickness they believe to be special dispensations of Providence, or the result of some overruling, mastering power; and they resort to drugs as a cure for the evil. But the drugs taken to cure the disease weaken the system.[24]

No truth does the Bible more clearly teach than that what we do is the result of what we are. To a great degree the experiences of life are the fruition of our own thoughts and deeds.

"The curse causeless shall not come" (Proverbs 26:2).[25]

We are to learn to talk to the people intelligently and with power. Then they will call upon Christ, recognizing in Him the One who came to our world to do the work of healing for soul and body. Those who are suffering with disease will be aroused to take hold of the light of health reform. They will leave off their wrong habits, and will stand in a position where they can reach others.[26]

# Without Parade and Show

*"Great multitudes followed [Jesus], and he healed them all; and charged them that they should not make him known: that it might be fulfilled which was spoken by Esaias the prophet, saying, behold my servant, whom I have chosen; my beloved, in whom my soul is well pleased: I will put my spirit upon him, and he shall shew judgment to the Gentiles. He shall not strive, nor cry; neither shall any man hear his voice in the streets" (Matthew 12:15–19).*

On several occasions when the Lord had wrought works of healing, He charged those whom He had blessed to tell His deed to no one. They ought to have heeded His injunctions and realized that Christ had not lightly required silence on their part, but had a reason for His command, and they should in no wise have disregarded His expressed desire. It ought to have been sufficient for them to know that He desired them to keep their own counsel, and had good reasons for His urgent request. The Lord knew that in healing the sick, in working miracles for the restoring of sight to the blind, and for the cleansing of the leper, He was endangering His own life; for if the priests and rulers would not receive the evidences He gave them of His divine mission, they would misconstrue, falsify, and make charges against Him. It is true that He did many miracles openly, yet in some instances He requested that those whom He had blessed should tell no man what He had done for them. When prejudice was aroused, envy and jealousy cherished, and His way hedged up, He left the cities, and went in search of those who would listen to and appreciate the truth He came to impart.[27]

"Seekest thou great things for thyself? seek them not" (Jeremiah 45:5). The Lord has no place in His work for those who have a greater desire to win the crown than to bear the cross. He wants men who are more intent upon doing their duty than upon receiving their reward—men who are more solicitous for principle than for promotion.

Those who are humble, and who do their work as unto God, may not make so great a show as do those who are full of bustle and self-importance; but their work counts for more.[28]

# The Earliest Christian Ministry

*"[Jesus] called unto him the twelve, and began to send them forth by two and two; and gave them power over unclean spirits; and commanded them that they should take nothing for their journey, save a staff only; no scrip, no bread, no money in their purse. . . . And they cast out many devils, and anointed with oil many that were sick, and healed them"* (Mark 6:7, 8, 13).

The gospel ministry is an organization for the proclamation of the truth to the sick and to the well. It combines the medical missionary work and the ministry of the word. By these combined agencies opportunities are given to communicate light and to present the gospel to all classes and all grades of society. God wants the ministers and the church members to take a decided, active interest in the medical missionary work.

To take people right where they are, whatever their position or condition, and help them in every way possible—this is gospel ministry. Those who are diseased in body are nearly always diseased in mind, and when the soul is sick, the body also is affected. Ministers should feel it a part of their work to minister to the sick and the afflicted whenever opportunity presents itself. The minister of the gospel is to present the message, which must be received if the people are to become sanctified and made ready for the coming of the Lord. This work is to embrace all that was embraced in Christ's ministry.

Then why do not all our ministers heartily cooperate with those who are carrying forward medical missionary work? Why do they not carefully study the life of Christ, that they may know how He labored, and then follow His example?[29]

Every church member should be engaged in some line of service for the Master. Some cannot do so much as others, but everyone should do his utmost to roll back the tide of disease and distress that is sweeping over our world. Many would be willing to work if they were taught how to begin. They need to be instructed and encouraged.[30]

# What the World Needs Today

*"Believers were the more added to the Lord, multitudes both of men and women. Insomuch that they brought forth the sick into the streets, and laid them on beds and couches, that at the least the shadow of Peter passing by might overshadow some of them. There came also a multitude out of the cities round about unto Jerusalem, bringing sick folks, and them which were vexed with unclean spirits: and they were healed every one" (Acts 5:14–16).*

The world needs today what it needed nineteen hundred years ago—a revelation of Christ. A great work of reform is demanded, and it is only through the grace of Christ that the work of restoration, physical, mental, and spiritual, can be accomplished.

Christ's method alone will give true success in reaching the people. The Saviour mingled with men as one who desired their good. He showed His sympathy for them, ministered to their needs, and won their confidence. Then He bade them, "Follow Me."

There is need of coming close to the people by personal effort. If less time were given to sermonizing, and more time were spent in personal ministry, greater results would be seen. The poor are to be relieved, the sick cared for, the sorrowing and the bereaved comforted, the ignorant instructed, the inexperienced counseled. We are to weep with those that weep, and rejoice with those that rejoice. Accompanied by the power of persuasion, the power of prayer, the power of the love of God, this work will not, cannot, be without fruit.

We should ever remember that the object of the medical missionary work is to point sin-sick men and women to the Man of Calvary, who taketh away the sin of the world. By beholding Him, they will be changed into His likeness. We are to encourage the sick and suffering to look to Jesus and live. . . . God often reaches hearts through our efforts to relieve physical suffering.

Medical missionary work is the pioneer work of the gospel. In the ministry of the word and in the medical missionary work the gospel is to be preached and practiced.[31]

# The Lycaonians Amazed

*"There sat a certain man at Lystra, impotent in his feet, being a crip-
ple from his mother's womb, who never had walked: the same heard Paul
speak: who stedfastly beholding him, and perceiving that he had faith to
be healed, said with a loud voice, Stand upright on thy feet. And he
leaped and walked. And when the people saw what Paul had done, they
lifted up their voices, saying in the speech of Lycaonia, The gods are
come down to us in the likeness of men" (Acts 14:8–11).*

As Paul recounted the works of Christ in healing the afflicted, he
perceived a cripple whose eyes were fastened upon him, and who
received and believed his words. Paul's heart went out in sympathy
toward the afflicted man, whose faith he discerned; and he eagerly
grasped the hope that he might be healed by that Saviour, who,
although he had ascended to Heaven, was still man's Friend and
Physician, having more power even than when He was upon earth.

In the presence of that idolatrous assembly, Paul commanded the
cripple to stand upright upon his feet. Hitherto he had only been able
to take a sitting posture; but he now grasped with faith the words of
Paul, and instantly obeyed his command, and stood on his feet for the
first time in his life. Strength came with this effort of faith; and he who
had been a cripple walked and leaped as though he had never experienced an infirmity.

This work performed on the cripple was a marvel to all beholders.
The subject was so well known, and the cure was so complete, that
there was no room for skepticism on their part. The Lycaonians were
convinced that supernatural power attended the labors of the apostles, and they cried out with great enthusiasm that the gods had come
down to them from Heaven in the likeness of men. This belief was in
harmony with their traditions that gods visited the earth. . . .

The news of the miraculous cure of the cripple was soon noised
throughout all that region, until a general excitement was aroused,
and priests from the temple of the gods prepared to do the apostles
honor.[32]

# Taking No Credit to Self

*"When the apostles, Barnabas and Paul, heard of [the Lycaonians'*
*plan to offer sacrifice unto them] they rent their clothes, and ran in*
*among the people, crying out, and saying, Sirs, why do ye these things?*
*We also are men of like passions with you, and preach unto you that ye*
*should turn from these vanities unto the living God, which made heav-*
*en, and earth, and the sea, and all things that are therein. . . . And with*
*these sayings scarce restrained they the people, that they had not done*
*sacrifice unto them" (Acts 14:14, 15, 18).*

Notwithstanding the apostles positively denied the divinity attributed to them by the heathen, and Paul endeavored to direct their minds to the true God as the only object worthy of worship, it was still most difficult to turn them from their purpose.

They reasoned that they had with their own eyes beheld the miraculous power exercised by the apostles; that they had seen a cripple who had never before used his limbs, made to leap and rejoice in perfect health and strength, through the exercise of the marvelous power possessed by these strangers. But, after much persuasion on the part of Paul, and explanation as to the true mission of the apostles, the people were reluctantly led to give up their purpose. They were not satisfied, however, and led away the sacrificial beasts in great disappointment that their traditions of divine beings visiting the earth could not be strengthened by this example of their favor in coming to confer upon them special blessings which would exalt them and their religion in the estimation of the world.[33]

There is need for every physician closely and critically to examine himself. What is his religious experience? Does he allow self to rule? Does he make his own wishes and desires supreme? Does he keep the glory of God ever before him?[34]

You should lead the patient to behold Jesus as the physician of the body as well as of the soul. If the physician has the love of Christ in his own heart, he will use his influence to set the Mighty Healer before the afflicted one. He can direct the thoughts, the gratitude, and praise, to the Source of all power, mercy, and goodness.[35]

# Accusations Are No Surprise

*"There came thither certain Jews from Antioch and Iconium, who persuaded the people, and, having stoned Paul, drew him out of the city, supposing he had been dead" (Acts 14:19).*

Now a strange change came upon the fickle, excitable people [of Lystra], because their faith was not anchored in the true God. The opposing Jews of Antioch, through whose influence the apostles were driven from that district, united with certain Jews of Iconium, and followed upon the track of the apostles. The miracle wrought upon the cripple, and its effect upon those who witnessed it, stirred up their envy, and led them to go to the scene of the apostles' labor, and put their false version upon the work. They denied that God had any part in it, and claimed that it was accomplished through the demons whom these men served.

The same class had formerly accused the Saviour of casting out devils through the power of the prince of devils; they had denounced Him as a deceiver; and they now visited the same unreasoning wrath upon His apostles. By means of falsehoods they inspired the people of Lystra with the bitterness of spirit by which they were themselves actuated. They claimed to be thoroughly acquainted with the history and faith of Paul and Barnabas, and so misrepresented their characters and work that these heathen, who had been ready to worship the apostles as divine beings, now considered them worse than murderers, and that whoever should put them out of the world would do God and mankind good service.

Those who believe and teach the truths of God's word in these last days, meet with similar opposition from unprincipled persons who will not accept the truth, and who do not hesitate to prevaricate, and even to circulate the most glaring falsehoods in order to destroy the influence and hedge up the way of those whom God has sent with a message of warning to the world. While one class make the falsehoods and circulate them, another class are so blinded by the delusions of Satan as to receive them as the words of truth. They are in the toils of the archenemy, while they flatter themselves that they are the children of God.[36]

# A Blessed Work for All

*"Beloved, I wish above all things that thou mayest prosper and be in health, even as thy soul prospereth" (3 John 2).*

Let us present the gospel to the sick, connecting Jesus, the Great Healer, with the simple remedies used; and our living faith will be answered. But those who come to the Great Healer must be willing to do His will, to humble their souls, and confess their sins. As we lay hold of divine power with a faith that will not be denied, we shall see the salvation of God.

Christ declared that He came to recover men's lives. This work is to be done by Christ's followers, and it is to be done by the most simple means. Families are to be taught how to care for the sick. The hope of the gospel is to be revived in the hearts of men and women. We must seek to draw them to the Great Healer. In the work of healing let the physicians work intelligently, not with drugs, but by following rational methods. Then let them by the prayer of faith draw upon the power of God to stay the progress of disease. This will inspire in the suffering ones belief in Christ and the power of prayer, and it will give them confidence in our simple methods of treating disease. Such work will be a means of directing minds to the truth, and will be of great efficiency in the work of the gospel ministry.[37]

Every church should be a training school for Christian workers. Its members should be taught how to give Bible readings, how to conduct and teach Sabbath school classes, how best to help the poor and to care for the sick, how to work for the unconverted.[38]

In every city where we have a church there is need of a place where treatment can be given. Among the homes of our church members there are few that afford room and facilities for the proper care of the sick. A place should be provided where treatment may be given for common ailments. The building might be inelegant and even rude, but it should be furnished with facilities for giving simple treatments. These, skillfully employed, would prove a blessing not only to our people, but to their neighbors, and might be the means of calling the attention of many to health principles.[39]

# When Facing Illness

*"Knowing this, that the trying of your faith worketh patience. But let patience have her perfect work, that ye may be perfect and entire, wanting nothing. If any of you lack wisdom, let him ask of God, that giveth to all men liberally, and upbraideth not; and it shall be given him"* *(James 1:3–5).*

We all desire immediate and direct answers to our prayers, and are tempted to become discouraged when the answer is delayed or comes in an unlooked-for form. But God is too wise and good to answer our prayers always at just the time and in just the manner we desire. He will do more and better for us than to accomplish all our wishes. . . .

Those who seek healing by prayer should not neglect to make use of the remedial agencies within their reach. It is not a denial of faith to use such remedies as God has provided to alleviate pain and to aid nature in her work of restoration. . . . When we have prayed for the recovery of the sick, we can work with all the more energy, thanking God that we have the privilege of cooperating with Him, and asking His blessing on the means which He Himself has provided.

We have the sanction of the word of God for the use of remedial agencies. Hezekiah, king of Israel, was sick, and a prophet of God brought him the message that he should die. He cried unto the Lord, and the Lord heard His servant and sent him a message that fifteen years should be added to his life. Now, one word from God would have healed Hezekiah instantly; but special directions were given, "Let them take a lump of figs, and lay it for a plaster upon the boil, and he shall recover" (Isaiah 38:21).[40]

The light which has been given me in reference to several critical cases has been represented to me as a sick child I had in charge, and in every case the directions given were, Do not apply ice to the head (but cool water); apply hot fomentations (to the bowels, stomach, and liver). This will quell the fever much sooner even than cold. The reaction after the cold applications raised the fever, in the place of killing it. This direction has been given me again and again.[41]

# Faithful Ambassadors

*"A wicked messenger falleth into mischief: but a faithful ambassador is health" (Proverbs 13:17).*

True medical missionary work is of divine origin, and has a most glorious mission to fulfill. In all its bearings it is to be in conformity with Christ's work.

At this stage of the medical missionary work nothing will help us more than to understand the mission of the greatest Medical Missionary that ever trod the earth; nothing will help us more than to realize how sacred is this line of service, and how perfectly it corresponds to the lifework of the Great Missionary. The object of our mission is the same as the object of Christ's mission. Why did God send His Son to the fallen world? To make known to mankind His love for them. Christ came as a Redeemer. Throughout His ministry He kept prominent His mission to save sinners. . . .

The Saviour lived on this earth a life that love for God will constrain every true believer in Christ to live. Following His example, in our medical missionary work we shall reveal to the world that we are His representatives, and that our credentials are from above.

Christ knew that His Father had chosen Him to carry out the great plan of redemption by coming to the fallen world to die for sinners. And when He came to fulfill His mission, he was, in every sense of the term, a medical missionary. We can do medical missionary work in a Christlike manner only when we are one with Him. United with Him, we receive spiritual life and power, and learn to be "laborers together with God" (1 Corinthians 3:9), manifesting love for everyone for whom He died, and working earnestly to bring into the heavenly garner a harvest of souls. Filled with His Spirit, men and women are animated with the same desire to save sinners that animated Christ in His lifework as a missionary sent of God.

I am instructed to say that God desires to have the medical missionary work cleansed from the tarnish of earthliness, and elevated to its true position before the world. . . . Those who desire to honor God will not mingle worldly policy plans with His plans.[42]

# Beware of Counterfeit Healers

*"There is that speaketh like the piercings of a sword: but the tongue of the wise is health" (Proverbs 12:18).*

We need to be anchored in Christ, rooted and grounded in the faith. Satan works through agents. He selects those who have not been drinking of the living waters, whose souls are athirst for something new and strange, and who are ever ready to drink at any fountain that may present itself. Voices will be heard, saying, "Lo, here is Christ," or "Lo there;" but we must believe them not. We have unmistakable evidence of the voice of the True Shepherd. . . . He leads His sheep in the path of humble obedience to the law of God, but He never encourages them in the transgression of that law.

"The voice of a stranger" is the voice of one who neither respects nor obeys God's holy, just, and good law. Many make great pretensions to holiness, and boast of the wonders they perform in healing the sick, when they do not regard this great standard of righteousness. But through whose power are these cures wrought? Are the eyes of either party opened to their transgressions of the law? and do they take their stand as humble, obedient children, ready to obey all of God's requirements? . . .

None need be deceived. The law of God is as sacred as His throne, and by it every man who cometh into the world is to be judged. There is no other standard by which to test character. . . . If those through whom cures are performed, are disposed, on account of these manifestations, to excuse their neglect of the law of God, and continue in disobedience, though they have power to any and every extent, it does not follow that they have the great power of God. On the contrary, it is the miracle-working power of the great deceiver. He is a transgressor of the moral law, and employs every device that he can master to blind men to its true character. We are warned that in the last days he will work with signs and lying wonders. And he will continue these wonders until the close of probation, that he may point to them as evidence that he is an angel of light and not of darkness.[43]

# Boastful Miracles Not of God

*"And no marvel; for Satan himself is transformed into an angel of light. Therefore it is no great thing if his ministers also be transformed as the ministers of righteousness; whose end shall be according to their works" (2 Corinthians 11:14, 15).*

[Satan's] agents still claim to cure disease. They profess to employ electricity, magnetism, or the so-called "sympathetic remedies;" but in truth the magnetic power of which they boast is directly attributable to the sorcery of Satan.[44]

Men under the influence of evil spirits will work miracles. They will make people sick by casting their spell upon them, and will then remove the spell, leading others to say that those who were sick have been miraculously healed. This Satan has done again and again.

We need not be deceived. Wonderful scenes, with which Satan will be closely connected, will soon take place. God's Word declares that Satan will work miracles. He will make people sick, and then will suddenly remove from them his satanic power. They will then be regarded as healed. These works of apparent healing will bring Seventh-day Adventists to the test.[45]

[Satan] sometimes comes in the form of a lovely young person, or of a beautiful shadow. He works cures, and is worshiped by deceived mortals as a benefactor of our race.[46]

Some declare their unbelief in the work that the Lord has given me to do because, as they say, "Mrs. E. G. White works no miracles." But those who look for miracles as a sign of divine guidance are in grave danger of deception. It is stated in the Word that the enemy will work through his agents who have departed from the faith, and they will seemingly work miracles, even to the bringing down of fire out of heaven in the sight of men. By means of "lying wonders" Satan would deceive, if possible, the very elect.

Multitudes have heard me speak, and have read my writings, but no one has ever heard me claim to work miracles. I have at times been called upon to pray for the sick, and the word of the Lord has been verified. [James 5:14, 15 quoted.] Christ is the great miracle worker. To Him be all the glory.[47]

# Persevering Patience Needed

*"Except ye see signs and wonders, ye will not believe" (John 4:48).*

Those who refuse to improve the light and knowledge that have been mercifully placed within their reach are rejecting one of the means which God has granted them to promote spiritual as well as physical life. They are placing themselves where they will be exposed to the delusions of Satan.

Not a few in this Christian age and Christian nation resort to evil spirits, rather than trust to the power of the living God. The mother watching by the sickbed of her child, exclaims, "I can do no more. Is there no physician who has power to restore my child?" She is told of the wonderful cures performed by some clairvoyant or magnetic healer, and she trusts her dear one to his charge, placing it as verily in the hands of Satan as if he were standing by her side. In many instances the future life of the child is controlled by a satanic power which it seems impossible to break.

I have heard a mother pleading with an infidel physician to save the life of her child; but when I entreated her to seek help from the Great Physician, who is able to save to the uttermost all who come to Him in faith, she turned away with impatience.[48]

The way in which Christ worked was to preach the Word, and to relieve suffering by miraculous works of healing. But I am instructed that we cannot now work in this way, for Satan will exercise his power by working miracles. God's servants today could not work by means of miracles, because spurious works of healing, claiming to be divine, will be wrought.

For this reason the Lord has marked out a way in which His people are to carry forward a work of physical healing, combined with the teaching of the Word. Sanitariums are to be established, and with these institutions are to be connected workers who will carry forward genuine medical missionary work. Thus a guarding influence is thrown around those who come to the sanitariums for treatment. This is the provision the Lord has made whereby gospel medical missionary work is to be done for many souls.[49]

# Pharmaceutical Sorcery

*"Is there no balm in Gilead; is there no physician there? why then is not the health of the daughter of my people recovered?" (Jeremiah 8:22).*

The use of drugs has resulted in far more harm than good, and should our physicians who claim to believe the truth, almost entirely dispense with medicine, and faithfully practice along the line of *hygiene*, using *nature's remedies*, far greater success would attend their efforts. There is no need whatever to exalt the method whereby drugs are administered. I know whereof I speak. Brethren of the medical profession, I entreat you to think candidly and put away childish things. . . . They resort to drugs when greater skill and knowledge would teach them the *more excellent way*."[50]

Many suffering from fevers have died as the results of the drugs administered. They might have been alive today had they been given water treatment by those competent to administer it.[51]

The Lord has warned me that there will come a great apostasy. There will come a falling away in spirituality. Many will turn away their ears from hearing the truth, and will accept fables. Our sanitariums are to be conducted by wise, God-fearing men, who will teach sound doctrines and show why we believe the truth and why we should practice strict temperance in all things, studying how to avoid all harmful practices and influences. Virtue and holiness shall be practiced.

In view of what the Word warns us is coming upon the earth, I felt that I must urge upon our people the necessity of establishing sanitariums. We cannot pray for the miraculous healing of those who know not the truth. They have prostituted their powers, and were they thus healed, they would not return God the glory, but would continue to dishonor Him by following wrong practices. We are to educate those who come to our sanitariums, teaching them how to bring themselves into right relation with God by following right habits of eating, drinking, and dressing.[52]

Our object in establishing sanitariums is to encourage the sick and suffering to look to Jesus and live.[53]

# Are We Striving Lawfully?

*"The Lord our God hath put us to silence, and given us water of gall to drink, because we have sinned against the Lord. We looked for peace, but no good came; and for a time of health, and behold trouble!" (Jeremiah 8:14, 15).*

The remark is often made, by one and another, "Why depend so much on sanitariums? Why do we not pray for the miraculous healing of the sick, as the people of God used to do?" In the early history of our work many were healed by prayer. And some, after they were healed, pursued the same course in the indulgence of appetite that they had followed in the past. They did not live and work in such a way as to avoid sickness. They did not show that they appreciated the Lord's goodness to them. Again and again they were brought to suffering through their own careless, thoughtless course of action. How could the Lord be glorified in bestowing on them the gift of health?"[54]

Jesus is our perfect pattern; and when we look to Him who for the joy that was set before Him endured the cross, despising the shame, we should be aroused to greater earnestness. . . . He passed through fiercer conflicts than man will ever be able to endure.

"If a man also strive for masteries, yet is he not crowned, except he strive lawfully" (2 Timothy 2:5). A man may make earnest efforts to overcome, while he is not in possession of the physical, mental, and moral power which he might possess were he brought into harmony with the laws which govern his being. If through selfish indulgence he is an intemperate man, every organ in his body becomes enfeebled, and he is robbed of mental and moral power. He is not striving lawfully. . . .

We must strive lawfully, if we would win the boon of eternal life. The path is wide enough, and all who run the race may win the prize. If we create unnatural appetites and indulge them in any degree, we violate nature's laws and enfeebled physical, mental, and moral conditions will result. We are hence unfitted for that persevering, energetic, and hopeful effort which we might have made had we been true to nature's laws.[55]

# Prayer for the Sick

*"Is any sick among you? let him call for the elders of the church; and let them pray over him, anointing him with oil in the name of the Lord: and the prayer of faith shall save the sick, and the Lord shall raise him up; and if he have committed sins, they shall be forgiven him"* (James 5:14, 15).

To those who desire prayer for their restoration to health, it should be made plain that the violation of God's law, either natural or spiritual, is sin, and that in order for them to receive His blessing, sin must be confessed and forsaken.

The Scripture bids us, "Confess your faults one to another, and pray one for another, that ye may be healed" (James 5:16). To the one asking for prayer, let thoughts like these be presented, "We cannot read the heart, or know the secrets of your life. These are known only to yourself and to God. If you repent of your sins, it is your duty to make confession of them."

Sin of a private character is to be confessed to Christ, the only mediator between God and man. . . . Every sin is an offense against God, and is to be confessed to Him through Christ. Every open sin should be as openly confessed. Wrong done to a fellowbeing should be made right with the one who has been offended. If any who are seeking health have been guilty of evilspeaking, if they have sowed discord in the home, the neighborhood, or the church, and have stirred up alienation and dissension, if by any wrong practice they have led others into sin, these things should be confessed before God and before those who have been offended. [1 John 1:9 quoted.]

When wrongs have been righted, we may present the needs of the sick to the Lord in calm faith, as His Spirit may indicate. He knows each individual by name, and cares for each as if there were not another upon the earth for whom He gave His beloved Son. Because God's love is so great and so unfailing, the sick should be encouraged to trust in Him and be cheerful. To be anxious about themselves tends to cause weakness and disease. If they will rise above depression and gloom, their prospect of recovery will be better.[56]

# God's Saving Health to All Nations

*"God be merciful unto us, and bless us; and cause his face to shine upon us; Selah. That thy way may be known upon earth, thy saving health among all nations" (Psalm 67:1, 2).*

The efficiency of the medical missionary work is in pointing sin-sick men and women to the Man of Calvary, who taketh away the sin of the world.[57]

When the light came that we should have a sanitarium, the reason was plainly given. There were many who needed to be educated in regard to healthful living. A place must be provided to which the sick could be taken, where they could be taught how to live so as to preserve health. At the same time light was given that the sick could be successfully treated without drugs.[58]

Christ has empowered His church to do the same work that He did during His ministry. Today He is the same compassionate physician that He was while on this earth. We should let the afflicted understand that in Him there is healing balm for every disease, restoring power for every infirmity.[59]

When the sick are restored to health, the glory is often given to the physician, when it was the divine touch, and healing balm of the Saviour that gave relief and prolonged life. If the one who has been restored gives praise to the physician, it is the physician's duty and privilege to hide self in Christ, pointing to the compassionate Saviour as the One who has spoken the word of life. It is his opportunity to acknowledge the Lord as the Worker and the physician as only the instrument, and to impress upon the minds of those to whom the Saviour has thus given a renewal of life and health, that their lives have been prolonged for a high and holy purpose.[60]

We have come to a time when every member of the church should take hold of medical missionary work. The world is a lazar house filled with victims of both physical and spiritual disease. Everywhere people are perishing for lack of a knowledge of the truths that have been committed to us. The members of the church are in need of an awakening, that they may realize their responsibility to impart these truths.[61]

# Our Healing Saviour

*"O Lord my God, I cried unto thee, and thou hast healed me" (Psalm 30:2).*

Do not turn from the loving, compassionate Redeemer to human friends who, though they may give you the very best they have, may lead you into wrong. Take all your troubles to Jesus. Cast your helpless soul upon Him who will not only take your burdens, but will receive you and strengthen and comfort you. He is the great Healer of all maladies.[62]

The nervous timidity of the sick will be overcome as they are made acquainted with the intense interest that the Saviour has for all suffering humanity. Oh, the depth of the love of Christ! To redeem us from death, He died on the cross of Calvary.[63]

Why do we not present our sick and suffering before God in the arms of our faith? Why do we not teach them to believe in the great Healer? Why do we not lay hold of the promises, and bring the sick to God, praying for His healing power to be revealed? Why do we not plead the promise, "These signs shall follow them that believe" (Mark 16:17)? This is the privilege of God's children, and faith should lay hold of all that it is possible to have as an endorsement of faith.

Christ's promises are just as fresh and strong and trustworthy now as they were in the days of the apostles. Some have carried the matter of faith healing to an extreme, and this has greatly hurt the subject. But the need of faith in God should be kept before the church. The realization of our privileges has become almost extinct. Let this part of the commission be brought into our practical life. It is of as much importance as the preaching of the word.[64]

The Saviour left the courts of glory and came to our world to bear temptation and resist evil that man might have power to take hold of His strength. The soul that comes to Christ by living faith receives His power. and is healed of his disease.[65]

# Rivers of Healing Water

*"It shall come to pass, that every thing that liveth, which moveth, whithersoever the rivers shall come, shall live: and there shall be a very great multitude of fish, because these waters shall come thither: for they shall be healed; and every thing shall live whither the river cometh. . . . And by the river upon the bank thereof, on this side and on that side, shall grow all trees for meat, whose leaf shall not fade, neither shall the fruit thereof be consumed: it shall bring forth new fruit according to his months, because their waters they issued out of the sanctuary: and the fruit thereof shall be for meat, and the leaf thereof for medicine" (Ezekiel 47:9, 12).*

The representation given in Ezekiel 47:1–12 is an illustration of the way in which the truth for this time is to go. A large work is to be done by many who have begun in a small way. Many souls will be reached, not through display, not through any devising on the part of man, but through the working of the Holy Spirit on the hearts of human agencies. The Saviour worked in this way. When His methods become the methods of His followers, His blessings will attend their labors.[66]

[Ezekiel 47:8–12 quoted.] Such a river of life and healing God designs that, by His power working through them, our sanitariums shall be.[67]

When the third angel's message shall go forth with a loud voice, and the whole earth shall be lightened with his glory, the Holy Spirit is poured out upon God's people. The revenue of glory has been accumulating for this closing work of the third angel's message. Of the prayers that have been ascending for the fulfillment of the promise—the descent of the Holy Spirit—not one has been lost. Each prayer has been accumulating, ready to overflow and pour forth a healing flood of heavenly influence and accumulated light all over the world.[68]

When the Lord speaks forgiveness to the repenting soul, he is full of ardor, full of love to God, full of earnestness and energy, and the life-giving spirit which he has received cannot be repressed. Christ is in him a well of water springing up into everlasting life.[69]

# A Pure, Clean, Simple Work

*"I will restore health unto thee, and I will heal thee of thy wounds, saith the Lord" (Jeremiah 30:17).*

The disciples who were called from their nets to follow Christ did not have a college education. Christ did not have it. He lived His human life in simplicity—living and preaching the truth. The light of the gospel was shining upon the pathway of those who heard Him. We are to teach our children and youth the importance of simplicity. The straining that is often done to reach a wonderful height of learning—let it not be encouraged. I have seen many a youth destroyed before his education was completed because of this desire for knowledge.

If we would keep well, we must let reason guide us in our manner of living. If we will place ourselves in right relation to God, our beings will respond to His instruction. . . .

We have a living Healer today. We need not depend upon drugs, but upon the Great Physician. If every sanitarium in our land were in living connection with God, the truth would go forth from our institutions as a lamp that burneth. They would carry mercy and light and compassion to the people. . . .

It is time that we were putting on the armor of light. It is time that we were comprehending our duty to the world at this stage of its history. Oh, such wickedness exists in our cities, and yet many of the people are asleep! Professed Christians are asleep. They do not understand that there is a work for them to do.

The Saviour's work of ministering to the suffering was always combined with His ministry of the Word. He preached the gospel and healed infirmity both by the same mighty power. He will do the same today; but we must do our part by bringing the sick in touch with the mighty Healer.[70]

In almost every community there are large numbers who do not listen to the preaching of God's word or attend any religious service. If they are reached by the gospel, it must be carried to their homes. Often the relief of their physical needs is the only avenue by which they can be approached.[71]

# Helpfulness Is Happiness

*"And God hath set some in the church, . . . gifts of . . . helps" (1 Corinthians 12:28).*

All should find something to do that will be beneficial to themselves and helpful to others. God appointed work as a blessing, and only the diligent worker finds the true glory and joy of life. The approval of God rests with loving assurance upon children and youth who cheerfully take their part in the duties of the household, sharing the burdens of father and mother. Such children will go out from the home to be useful members of society. . . .

Jesus did not shirk care and responsibility, as do many who profess to be His followers. It is because they seek to evade this discipline that so many are weak and inefficient. They may possess precious and amiable traits, but they are nerveless and almost useless when difficulties are to be met or obstacles surmounted. The positiveness and energy, the solidity and strength of character, manifested in Christ are to be developed in us, through the same discipline that He endured. And the grace that He received is for us. . . .

Jesus carried into His labor cheerfulness and tact. It requires much patience and spirituality to bring Bible religion into the home life and into the workshop, to bear the strain of worldly business, and yet keep the eye single to the glory of God. This is where Christ was a helper. He was never so full of worldly care as to have no time or thought for heavenly things. Often He expressed the gladness of His heart by singing psalms and heavenly songs. Often the dwellers in Nazareth heard His voice raised in praise and thanksgiving to God. He held communion with heaven in song; and as His companions complained of weariness from labor, they were cheered by the sweet melody from His lips. . . .

Jesus was the fountain of healing mercy for the world; and through all those secluded years at Nazareth, His life flowed out in currents of sympathy and tenderness. The aged, the sorrowing, and the sin-burdened, the children at play in their innocent joy, the little creatures of the groves, the patient beasts of burden—all were happier for His presence.[1]

# Helpfulness From Eden

*"And the Lord God said, It is not good that the man should be alone; I will make him an help meet for him" (Genesis 2:18).*

God made from man a woman, to be a companion and helpmeet for him, to be one with him, to cheer, encourage, and bless him. And he, in his turn, is to be her strong helper. All who enter the matrimonial life with a holy purpose, the husband to obtain the pure affections of a woman's heart, the wife to soften and improve her husband's character, and give it completeness, fulfill God's purpose for them.[2]

Many ladies, accounted well-educated, having graduated with honors at some institution of learning, are shamefully ignorant of the practical duties of life. They are destitute of the qualifications necessary for the proper regulation of the family, and hence essential to its happiness and well-being. They may talk of woman's rights and of her elevated sphere; yet they themselves fall far below the true sphere of woman.

Ignorance of useful employment is contrary to the design of God in the creation of man, and is by no means an essential characteristic of the true gentleman or lady.[3]

One mother says her husband is an unbeliever. She has children but they are taught by the father to disrespect the mother. She is deeply burdened for her children. She does not know what course she can pursue. She then expresses her anxiety to do something in the cause of God, and inquires whether I think she had a duty to leave her family if she is convinced she can do no good to them.

I would answer, my sister, I cannot see how you could be clear before the Lord and leave your husband and your children. I cannot think you would feel that you could do this yourself. The trials you may have may be of a very trying character. You may be often pained to the heart because disrespect is shown you; but I am sure that it must be your duty to care for your own children. This is your field where you have your appointed work. It may be rocky and discouraging soil to work, but you have a Companion in all your efforts to do your duty unflinchingly, conscientiously, notwithstanding all the discouraging circumstances. Jesus is your helper.[4]

# Help for the Helpful

*"Happy art thou, O Israel: who is like unto thee, O people saved by the Lord, the shield of thy help" (Deuteronomy 33:29).*

Do not, my ministering brethren, allow yourselves to be kept at home to serve tables; and do not hover around the churches, preaching to those who are already fully established in the faith. Teach the people to have light in themselves, and not to depend upon the ministers. They should have Christ as their helper, and should educate themselves to help one another, so that the minister can be free to enter new fields.[5]

Christ will succor those who flee to Him for wisdom and strength. If they meet duty and trial with humility of soul, depending upon Jesus, His mighty angel will be round about them, and He whom they have trusted will prove an all-sufficient helper in every emergency.[6]

The best help that ministers can give the members of our churches is not sermonizing, but planning work for them. Give each one something to do for others. Help all to see that as receivers of the grace of Christ they are under obligation to work for Him. And let all be taught how to work. Especially should those who are newly come to the faith be educated to become laborers together with God. If set to work, the despondent will soon forget their despondency; the weak will become strong, the ignorant intelligent, and all will be prepared to present the truth as it is in Jesus. They will find an unfailing helper in Him who has promised to save all that come unto Him.[7]

God is a shield and helper in every emergency to those who believe and trust in Him. When surrounded by difficulties, dangers, and discouragements, we must not yield faith and principle, but cherish every precious ray of light granted us, and be true to our God-given responsibilities.

You who are perplexed and afflicted, look up and be encouraged. Commit your ways in faith to the sympathizing Redeemer. He has identified His interests with yours, and is afflicted in your affliction. He will help you bear your burdens.[8]

# Adopting God's Attitude

*"Fear thou not; for I am with thee: be not dismayed; for I am thy God: I will strengthen thee; yea, I will help thee; yea, I will uphold thee with the right hand of my righteousness. . . . For I the Lord thy God will hold thy right hand, saying unto thee, Fear not; I will help thee. Fear not, thou worm Jacob, and ye men of Israel; I will help thee, saith the Lord, and thy redeemer, the Holy One of Israel" (Isaiah 41:10, 13, 14).*

When an emergency arises, and help is needed, no worker should say, That is not my work. The helper who has the idea that he is only to do the work assigned him, and no more, who feels no responsibility to help wherever and whenever help is needed, should at once dismiss this idea from his mind. He should never feel that a wrong is done him if in an emergency he is asked to work overtime. When extra help is needed, let the workers assist willingly, in Christian meekness, and they will receive a blessing.

It may be that some will rebel when they are asked to do the small, common duties. But these are the duties they need to know how to perform. It is faithfulness in little things that prepares us for usefulness in larger responsibilities. The most successful toilers are those who cheerfully take up the work of serving God in little things. Every human being is to work with his life thread, weaving it into the fabric to help to complete the pattern. Those who desire to be useful can always find employment. Time will never hang heavy on their hands.[9]

It would be helpful for the youth, and for parents and teachers as well, to study the lesson of cooperation as taught in the Scriptures. Among its many illustrations notice the building of the tabernacle—that object lesson of character building—in which the whole people united, "everyone whose heart stirred him up, and everyone whom his spirit made willing" (Exodus 35:21). Read how the wall of Jerusalem was rebuilt by the returned captives, in the midst of poverty, difficulty, and danger, the great task successfully accomplished because "the people had a mind to work" (Nehemiah 4:6). . . .

"We are members one of another" (Ephesians 4:25).[10]

# Following the Supreme Helper

*"Lord, it is nothing with thee to help, whether with many, or with them that have no power: help us, O Lord our God; for we rest on thee"* *(2 Chronicles 14:11).*

"He that is faithful in that which is least is faithful also in much" (Luke 16:10).

It is conscientious attention to what the world terms "little things" that makes life a success. Little deeds of charity, little acts of self-denial, speaking simple words of helpfulness, watching against little sins—this is Christianity. A grateful acknowledgment of daily blessings, a wise improvement of daily opportunities, a diligent cultivation of entrusted talents—this is what the Master calls for.[11]

Consider the part acted by the disciples in the Saviour's miracle for the feeding of the multitude. The food multiplied in the hands of Christ, but the disciples received the loaves and gave to the waiting throng.[12]

Many have no faith in God and have lost confidence in man. But they appreciate acts of sympathy and helpfulness. As they see one with no inducement of earthly praise or compensation come into their homes, ministering to the sick, feeding the hungry, clothing the naked, comforting the sad, and tenderly pointing all to Him of whose love and pity the human worker is but the messenger—as they see this, their hearts are touched. Gratitude springs up. Faith is kindled. They see that God cares for them, and they are prepared to listen as His word is opened.[13]

Whenever the Lord brings destitute fields to your notice and gives you opportunity to help, you are never to neglect the opportunity.

Heed the call that now comes to you. Your usefulness and helpfulness in this case will depend on the distinctness of the line of demarcation that separates you from the vanity and selfishness of the world. Give back to the Lord His own, and thus acknowledge that a Supreme Will controls your will, filling you with the self-sacrificing spirit of Christ. Do this heartily, as unto the Lord. Do we not believe that the end of all things is at hand?[14]

# From Where Do We Seek Help?

*"Woe to them that go down to Egypt for help; and stay on horses, and trust in chariots, because they are many; and in horsemen, because they are very strong; but they look not unto the Holy One of Israel, neither seek the Lord! Yet he also is wise, and will bring evil, and will not call back his words: but will arise against the house of the evildoers, and against the help of them that work iniquity" (Isaiah 31:1, 2).*

You are not to look to the world in order to learn what you shall write and publish or what you shall speak. Let all your words and works testify, "We have not followed cunningly devised fables." "We have also a more sure word of prophecy; whereunto ye do well that ye take heed, as unto a light that shineth in a dark place" (2 Peter 1:16, 19).[15]

A close and searching work must go on among the people of God. How soon, like ancient Israel, we forget God and His wondrous works, and rebel against Him. Some look to the world and desire to follow its fashions and participate in its pleasures in the same manner that the children of Israel looked back into Egypt and lusted for the good things they had enjoyed there, which God chose to withhold from them to prove them and thereby test their fidelity to Him. He wished to see if His people valued more highly His service, and the freedom He had so miraculously given them, than the indulgences they enjoyed in Egypt while in servitude to a tyrannical, idolatrous people.

Every true follower of Jesus will have sacrifices to make. God will prove them and test the genuineness of their faith.[16]

God forbid that those who profess to teach the sacred, solemn truth that the end of all things is at hand, and who claim to be the repositories of the divine law, should cherish a love for pleasure, and look to the world for favor and approbation! Christ gives them no such example.[17]

Men who claim to believe the truth accept propositions to advance the truth according to worldly methods; but our hope is in God, and we are to make this plain by importuning Him for help, by refusing to be molded by the world's plan.[18]

# Lessons Right at Home

*"Behold, God will not cast away a perfect man, neither will he help the evil doers" (Job 8:20).*

Some talk of going to far-off countries as missionaries; and this is well, if the Lord so directs. A brother under conviction of sin once said, "I want to be converted, that I may go out to the heathen to help them." "Why," said I, "begin at home; become right with God where you are; put away your sins, and be a home missionary." If we cannot be missionaries at home, we can never expect to do good in another field.[19]

Lovingly, tenderly, teach your children to come to God as a heavenly Father. By your example in the management of the home, teach them self-control. Teach them to be helpful in the home. Tell them that Christ lived not to please Himself.[20]

No pleasanter sight is there than a family of young folks who are quick to perform little acts of attention toward their elders. The placing of the big arm chair in a warm place for mamma, running for a footstool for aunty, hunting up papa's spectacles, and scores of little deeds show unsurpassed and loving hearts. But if mamma never returns a smiling "Thank you, dear," if papa's "Just what I was wanting, Susie," does not indicate that the little attention is appreciated, the children soon drop the habit. Little people are imitative creatures, and quickly catch the spirit surrounding them. So, if, when the mother's spool of cotton rolls from her lap, the father stoops to pick it up, bright eyes will see the act, and quick minds make a note of it. By example, a thousand times more quickly than by precept, can children be taught to speak kindly to each other, to acknowledge favors, to be gentle and unselfish, to be thoughtful and considerate of the comfort of the family. The boys, with inward pride in their father's courteous demeanor, will be chivalrous and helpful to their young sisters; the girls, imitating the mother, will be gentle and patient, even when big brothers are noisy and heedless.[21]

# Away From Egyptian Education

*"The Egyptians shall help in vain, and to no purpose: therefore have I cried concerning this, Their strength is to sit still" (Isaiah 30:7).*

It was not the teaching of the schools of Egypt that enabled Moses to triumph over his enemies, but an ever-abiding, unflinching faith, a faith that did not fail under the most trying circumstances. At the command of God, Moses advanced, although apparently there was nothing ahead for his feet to tread upon. More than a million people were depending on him, and he led them forward step by step, day by day. God permitted these lonely travels through the wilderness that His people might obtain an experience in enduring hardship, and that when they were in peril they might know that there was relief and deliverance in God alone. Thus they might learn to know and to trust God, and to serve Him with a living faith.

God is not dependent upon men of perfect education. His work is not to wait while His servants go through such lengthy, elaborate preparations as some of our schools are planning to give. He wants men who appreciate the privilege of being laborers together with Him—men who will honor Him by rendering implicit obedience to His requirements, regardless of previously inculcated theories. There is no limit to the usefulness of those who put self to one side, make room for the working of the Holy Spirit upon their hearts, and live lives wholly consecrated to God, enduring the necessary discipline imposed by the Lord without complaining or fainting by the way.[22]

No recreation helpful only to themselves will prove so great a blessing to the children and youth as that which makes them helpful to others. . . .

A new interest may be given to the work of the garden or the excursion in field or wood, as the pupils are encouraged to remember those shut in from these pleasant places and to share with them the beautiful things of nature.

The watchful teacher will find many opportunities for directing pupils to acts of helpfulness.[23]

# Pairing Up to Be Pioneers

*"Two are better than one; because they have a good reward for their labour. For if they fall, the one will lift up his fellow: but woe to him that is alone when he falleth; for he hath not another to help him up"* *(Ecclesiastes 4:9, 10).*

God calls for Christian families to go into communities that are in darkness and error, and work wisely and perseveringly for the Master. To answer this call requires self-sacrifice. While many are waiting to have every obstacle removed, souls are dying without hope and without God in the world. Many, very many, for the sake of worldly advantage, for the sake of acquiring scientific knowledge, will venture into pestilential regions and endure hardship and privation. Where are those who are willing to do this for the sake of telling others of the Saviour? Where are the men and women who will move into regions that are in need of the gospel, that they may point those in darkness to the Redeemer?[24]

Self-supporting missionaries are often very successful. Beginning in a small, humble way, their work enlarges as they move forward under the guidance of the Spirit of God. Let two or more start out together in evangelistic work. They may not receive any particular encouragement from those at the head of the work that they will be given financial support; nevertheless let them go forward, praying, singing, teaching, living the truth. They may take up the work of canvassing, and in this way introduce the truth into many families. As they move forward in their work they gain a blessed experience. They are humbled by a sense of their helplessness, but the Lord goes before them, and among the wealthy and the poor they find favor and help. Even the poverty of these devoted missionaries is a means of finding access to the people. As they pass on their way they are helped in many ways by those to whom they bring spiritual food. They bear the message God gives them, and their efforts are crowned with success. Many will be brought to a knowledge of the truth who, but for these humble teachers, would never have been won to Christ.[25]

# Fragrant Fellow Laborers

*"I intreat thee also, true yokefellow, help those women which laboured with me in the gospel, with Clement also, and with other my fellowlabourers, whose names are in the book of life" (Philippians 4:3).*

Those to whom light has been given are not to seal up the precious ointment, but are to break the bottle and let the fragrance be shared by all around.[26]

It is love that will constitute the bliss of the heavenly family. Those who cultivate love in the homelife will form characters after Christ's likeness, and they will be constrained to exert a helpful influence beyond the family circle, in order that they may bless others by kind, thoughtful ministrations, by pleasant words, by Christlike sympathy, by acts of benevolence. They will be quick to discern those who have hungry hearts, and will make a feast for those who are needy and afflicted. . . .

When the Lord bids us do good for others outside our home, He does not mean that our affection for home shall become diminished, and that we shall love our kindred or our country less because He desires us to extend our sympathies.[27]

Although some may be restricted to one talent, yet if they will exercise that one, it will increase. God values the service according to what a man has and not according to what he has not. If we perform our daily duties with fidelity and love we shall receive the approval of the Master as if we had performed a greater work. We must cease longing to do great service and to trade on large talents, while we have been made accountable only for small talents and the performance of humble duties. In overlooking the small daily duties, and reaching for higher responsibilities, we utterly fail to do the very work which God has given us.

Oh, that I might impress upon this church the fact that Christ has claims upon their service! My brethren and sisters, have you become servants of Christ? Then if you devote the most of your time to serving yourselves, what answer will you give the Master when He shall bid you render an account of your stewardship?[28]

# Training Good "Phebes"

*"I commend unto you Phebe our sister, which is a servant of the church which is at Cenchrea: That ye receive her in the Lord, as becometh saints, and that ye assist her in whatsoever business she hath need of you: for she hath been a succourer of many, and of myself also" (Romans 16:1, 2).*

The way is open for humble, consecrated women, dignified by the grace of Christ, to visit those in need of help, and shed light into discouraged souls. They can lift up the bowed down by praying with them and pointing them to Christ.[29]

Some are called to what are looked upon as humble duties—it may be, to cook. But the science of cooking is not a small matter. The skillful preparation of food is one of the most essential arts, standing above music teaching or dressmaking. By this I do not mean to discount music teaching or dressmaking, for they are essential. But more important still is the art of preparing food so that it is both healthful and appetizing. This art should be regarded as the most valuable of all the arts, because it is so closely connected with life.[30]

Some mothers, with their own hands, open the door and virtually invite the devil in, by permitting their daughters to remain in idleness, or what is but little better, spend their time in knit edging, crocheting, or embroidering, and employ a hired girl to do those things their children should do. They let them visit other young friends, form their own acquaintances, and even go from their parental watchcare some distance from home, where they are allowed to do very much as they please. Satan improves all such opportunities, and takes charge of the minds of these children.[31]

Children should be instructed from their early years to be helpful and share the burdens of their parents. By thus doing they can be a great blessing in lightening the cares of the weary mother. While children are engaged in active labor, time will not hang heavily upon their hands, and they will have less opportunity to associate with vain, talkative, unsuitable companions, whose evil communications might blight the whole life of an innocent girl, by corrupting her good manners.[32]

# Helping to Inspire Hope

*"Salute Urbane, our helper in Christ, and Stachys my beloved"*
*(Romans 16:9).*

In all our associations it should be remembered that in the experience of others there are chapters sealed from mortal sight. On the pages of memory are sad histories that are sacredly guarded from curious eyes. There stand registered long, hard battles with trying circumstances, perhaps troubles in the home life, that day by day weaken courage, confidence, and faith. Those who are fighting the battle of life at great odds may be strengthened and encouraged by little attentions that cost only a loving effort. To such the strong, helpful grasp of the hand by a true friend is worth more than gold or silver. Words of kindness are as welcome as the smile of angels.

There are multitudes struggling with poverty, compelled to labor hard for small wages, and able to secure but the barest necessities of life. Toil and deprivation, with no hope of better things, make their burden very heavy. When pain and sickness are added, the burden is almost insupportable. Careworn and oppressed, they know not where to turn for relief. Sympathize with them in their trials, their heartaches, and disappointments. This will open the way for you to help them. Speak to them of God's promises, pray with and for them, inspire them with hope.[33]

However low, however fallen, however dishonored and debased others may be, we are not to despise them and pass them by with indifference; but we should consider the fact that Christ has died for them, and that if He had not given His life for us, had not caused His light to shine into our souls, we might have been even worse than those we are inclined to despise. We should remember that Jesus has purchased the fallen man or woman or youth that we are tempted to despise.[34]

The Christian has no desire to live for self. He delights to consecrate all that he has and is to the Master's service. He is moved by an inexpressible desire to win souls to Christ. Those who have nothing of this desire might better be concerned for their own salvation. Let them pray for the spirit of service.[35]

# Avoid the Curse of Meroz

*"Curse ye Meroz, said the angel of the Lord, curse ye bitterly the inhabitants thereof; because they came not to the help of the Lord, to the help of the Lord against the mighty" (Judges 5:23).*

The members of the church are not individually aroused to put forth the earnest effort they are capable of making, and every branch of the work is crippled by the lack of fervent piety, and devoted, humble, God-fearing laborers. Where are the soldiers of the cross of Christ? Let the God-fearing, the honest, the single-hearted, who look steadfastly to the glory of God, prepare themselves for the battle against error. There are too many faint, cowardly hearts in this hour of spiritual conflict. Oh that out of weakness they may be made strong, and wax valiant in fight, and put to flight the armies of the aliens!

There is a class that are represented by Meroz. The missionary spirit has never taken hold of their souls. The calls of foreign missions have not stirred them to action. What account will those render to God, who are doing nothing in His cause—nothing to win souls to Christ? Such will receive the denunciation, "Thou wicked and slothful servant" (Matthew 25:26).

The interest and labors of the church must be extended more earnestly and decidedly to both home and foreign missions. Those who have been successful in using their talents to secure earthly treasures should now employ these capabilities to advance God's cause and build up His kingdom. Their tact and ability sanctified to God will be accepted, and He will make it effective in the grand work of turning men from error to truth. There should be deep heart searching with our young men and women to see if they have not a work to do for the Master. There is a work to be accomplished which money cannot do. Destitute fields must be supplied with earnest laborers, with those whose hearts are warm with the love of Christ and with love for souls. All who enter the missionary field will have hardships and trials to endure; they will find hard work, and plenty of it; but those of the right stamp of character will persevere under difficulties, discouragements, and privations, holding firmly to the arm of the Lord.[36]

# Putting Theory Into Practice

*"Lord, I believe; help thou mine unbelief" (Mark 9:24).*

It is not an abundance of light and evidence that makes the soul free in Christ; it is the rising of the powers and the will and the energies of the soul to cry out sincerely, "Lord, I believe; help Thou mine unbelief" (Mark 9:24).[37]

Take hold of Christ by living, active faith. Come to Him just as you are, helpless and dependent, and say, "Lord, I believe; help thou mine unbelief" (Mark 9:24). Help me to study thy life, thy self-denial and self-sacrifice; help me to become a Christian in every sense of the word.[38]

Our church members are greatly in need of a knowledge of practical godliness. They need to practice self-denial and self-sacrifice. They need to give evidence to the world that they are Christlike. Therefore the work that Christ requires of them is not to be done by proxy, placing on some committee or some institution the burden that they themselves should bear. They are to become Christlike in character by giving of their means and time, their sympathy, their personal effort, to help the sick, to comfort the sorrowing, to relieve the poor, to encourage the desponding, to enlighten souls in darkness, to point sinners to Christ, to bring home to hearts the obligation of God's law.[39]

With earnest, untiring energy those who have felt the burden of the Christian help work have testified by their works that they are not content to be mere theoretical believers. They have tried to walk in the light. They have put their belief into practice. They have combined faith and works. They have done the very work the Lord has specified should be done, and many souls have been enlightened, and convicted, and helped.[40]

In the practical work before us, around us on every side, we have by faith in Christ's strength to do our best for ourselves in drawing nigh to God, for have we not the promise that God will respond and draw nigh unto us? And then we have the blessed assurance [that] we may be a help to all those who are brought within the sphere of our influence.[41]

# Inspired Government

*"For unto us a child is born, unto us a son is given: and the govern-
ment shall be upon his shoulder: and his name shall be called Wonderful,
Counsellor, The mighty God, The everlasting Father, The Prince of Peace.
Of the increase of his government and peace there shall be no end"
(Isaiah 9:6, 7).*

Our Lord is truth, He is love, and His scepter stretcheth over the
universe.[42]

Angels are God's ministers, radiant with the light ever flowing
from His presence and speeding on rapid wing to execute His will.
But the Son, the anointed of God, the "express image of His person,"
"the brightness of His glory," "upholding all things by the word of
His power," holds supremacy over them all (Hebrews 1:3). "A glorious high throne from the beginning," was the place of His sanctuary
(Jeremiah 17:12); "a scepter of righteousness," the scepter of His kingdom (Hebrews 1:8). "Honor and majesty are before Him: strength and
beauty are in His sanctuary" (Psalm 96:6). Mercy and truth go before
His face (Psalm 89:14).

The law of love being the foundation of the government of God,
the happiness of all intelligent beings depends upon their perfect
accord with its great principles of righteousness. God desires from all
His creatures the service of love—service that springs from an appreciation of His character.[43]

The church is to be as God designed it should be, a representative
of God's family in another world.[44]

If there were no church discipline and government, the church
would go to fragments; it could not hold together as a body.[45]

He who is weak and inexperienced, although he is weak, may be
strengthened by the more hopeful and by those of mature experience.
Although the least of all, he is a stone that must shine in the building.
He is a vital member of the organized body, united to Christ.[46]

Unless the churches are so organized that they can carry out and
enforce order, they have nothing to hope for in the future; they must
scatter into fragments.[47]

# Organized for Service

*"And God hath set some in the church, . . . governments" (1 Corinthians 12:28).*

The church is organized for service; and in a life of service to Christ, connection with the church is one of the first steps. Loyalty to Christ demands the faithful performance of church duties. This is an important part of one's training; and in a church imbued with its Master's life, it will lead directly to effort for the world without.[48]

Everyone who is a true soldier in the army of the Lord will be an earnest, sincere, efficient worker, laboring to advance the interests of Christ's kingdom. Let no one presume to say to a brother who is walking circumspectly, "You are not to do the work of the Lord; leave it for the minister." Many members of the church have been deprived of the experience which they should have had because the sentiment has prevailed that the minister should do all the work and bear all the burdens.[49]

Cannot you form companies and, as soldiers of Christ, enlist in the work, putting all your tact and skill and talent into the Master's service, that you may save souls from ruin? Let there be companies organized in every church to do this work.[50]

Let there be in every church well-organized companies of workers to labor in the vicinity of that church. Put self behind you, and let Christ go before as your life and power. Let this work be entered into without delay, and the truth will be as leaven in the earth. When such forces are set to work in all our churches, there will be a renovating, reforming, energizing power in the churches, because the members are doing the very work that God has given them to do. Let all our churches be active, zealous, filled will enthusiasm by the Spirit and power of God. It is the intelligent use of the means, the capabilities, the powers, given you by God, consecrated to His service, that will tell in the communities where you may labor. It may be that you will have to make a very small beginning in some places; but do not be discouraged; the work will grow larger, and you will be doing the work of an evangelist. Look at Christ's manner of working, and strive to labor as He did.[51]

# Despisers of Government

*"The Lord knoweth how to deliver the godly out of temptations, and to reserve the unjust unto the day of judgment to be punished: but chiefly them that walk after the flesh in the lust of uncleanness, and despise government. Presumptuous are they, selfwilled, they are not afraid to speak evil of dignities" (2 Peter 2:9, 10).*

The boastful spiritualist claims great freedom, and in smooth, flowery language seeks to fascinate and delude unwary souls to choose the broad path of pleasure and sinful indulgence, rather than the narrow path and the straight way. Spiritualists call the requirements of God's law bondage, and say those who obey them live a life of slavish fear. With smooth words and fair speeches they boast of their freedom and seek to cover their dangerous heresies with the garments of righteousness. They would make the most revolting crimes be considered as blessings to the race.

They open before the sinner a wide door to follow the promptings of the carnal heart, and violate the law of God—especially the seventh commandment. Those who speak these great swelling words of vanity, and who triumph in their freedom in sin, promise those whom they deceive the enjoyment of freedom in a course of rebellion against the revealed will of God. These deluded souls are themselves in the veriest bondage to Satan and are controlled by his power, and yet promising liberty to those who will dare to follow the same course of sin that they themselves have chosen.

The Scriptures are indeed fulfilled in this, that the blind are leading the blind. For by whom a man is overcome, of the same is he brought in bondage. These deluded souls are under the most abject slavery to the will of demons. They have allied themselves to the powers of darkness and have no strength to go contrary to the will of demons. This is their boasted liberty. By Satan are they overcome and brought into bondage, and the great liberty promised to those they deceive is helpless slavery to sin and Satan.

We are not to attend their circles, neither are our ministers to engage in controversy with them. They are of that class specified whom we should not invite into our houses, or bid them Godspeed.[52]

# The Gift of Orderly Government

*"Order my steps in thy word: and let not any iniquity have domin-ion over me" (Psalm 119:133).*

Order is heaven's first law, and the Lord desires His people to give in their homes a representation of the order and harmony that pervade the heavenly courts. Truth never places her delicate feet in a path of uncleanness or impurity. Truth does not make men and women coarse or rough or untidy. It raises all who accept it to a high level. Under Christ's influence, a work of constant refinement goes on.

Special direction was given to the armies of Israel that everything in and around their tents should be clean and orderly, lest the angel of the Lord, passing through the encampment, should see their uncleanness. Would the Lord be particular to notice these things? He would; for the fact is stated, lest in seeing their uncleanness, He could not go forward with their armies to battle.

He who was so particular that the children of Israel should cher-ish habits of cleanliness, will not sanction any impurity in the homes of His people today. God looks with disfavor on uncleanness of any kind. How can we invite Him into our homes unless all is neat and clean and pure?

Believers should be taught that even though they may be poor, they need not be uncleanly or untidy in their persons or in their homes. Help must be given in this line to those who seem to have no sense of the meaning and importance of cleanliness. They are to be taught that those who are to represent the high and holy God must keep their souls pure and clean, and that this purity must extend to their dress, and to everything in the home, so that the ministering angels will have evidence that the truth has wrought a change in the life, purifying the soul and refining the tastes. Those who, after receiv-ing the truth, make no change in word or deportment, in dress or sur-roundings, are living to themselves, not to Christ. They have not been created anew in Christ Jesus, unto purification and holiness.[53]

# Order as a Principle

*"Let all things be done decently and in order" (1 Corinthians 14:40).*

Some who profess to be followers of Christ, call order and neatness, pride. They seem to consider it a virtue to leave their houses and premises in a disorderly, unimproved condition, thinking that they will thus give evidence of their disregard for temporal things, and their high estimate of spiritual things. But this same neglect and slothfulness, which characterizes their business life, will be imparted to their religious life. Their religious experience will be defective. . . . God requires His people to be neat and orderly. All His directions to the children of Israel were of a character to establish habits of order and cleanliness in their dress, and in their surroundings. This was essential in order for them to preserve health, and to exert a proper influence upon other nations as a people adopted by the living God.[54]

Some are very untidy in person. They need to be guided by the Holy Spirit to prepare for a pure and holy heaven. God declared that when the children of Israel came to the mount, to hear the proclamation of the law, they were to come with clean bodies and clean clothes. Today His people are to honor Him by habits of scrupulous neatness and purity.

Christians will be judged by the fruit they bear. The true child of God will be neat and clean. While we are to guard against needless adornment and display, we are in no case to be careless and indifferent in regard to outward appearance. All about our persons and our homes is to be neat and attractive. The youth are to be taught the importance of presenting an appearance above criticism, an appearance that honors God and the truth. . . .

Mothers, if you desire your children's thoughts to be pure, let their surroundings be pure.[55]

I saw that God would not acknowledge an untidy and unclean person as a Christian. . . .

I saw that these things should meet with an open rebuke, and if there was not a change immediately in some that profess the truth, in these things, they should be put out of the camp.[56]

# Setting the Church in Order

*"For this cause left I thee in Crete, that thou shouldest set in order the things that are wanting" (Titus 1:5).*

I have waited anxiously, hoping that God would put His Spirit upon some and use them as instruments of righteousness to awaken and set in order His church. I have almost despaired as I have seen, year after year, a greater departure from that simplicity which God has shown me should characterize the life of His followers. There has been less and less interest in, and devotion to, the cause of God. I ask: Wherein have those who profess confidence in the *Testimonies* sought to live according to the light given in them? Wherein have they regarded the warnings given? Wherein have they heeded the instructions they have received?

I saw that great changes must be wrought in the hearts and lives of very many before God can work in them by His power for the salvation of others. They must be renewed after the image of God, in righteousness and true holiness. Then the love of the world, the love of self, and every ambition of life calculated to exalt self will be changed by the grace of God and employed in the special work of saving souls for whom Christ died. Humility will take the place of pride, and haughty self-esteem will be exchanged for meekness. Every power of the heart will be controlled by disinterested love for all mankind.[57]

The end is near! God calls upon the church to set in order the things that remain. Workers together with God, you are empowered by the Lord to take others with you into the kingdom. You are to be God's living agents, channels of light to the world, and round about you are angels of heaven with their commission from Christ to sustain, strengthen, and uphold you in working for the salvation of souls.

I appeal to the churches in every conference: Stand out separate and distinct from the world—in the world, but not of it, reflecting the bright beams of the Sun of Righteousness, being pure, holy, and undefiled, and in faith carrying light into all the highways and byways of the earth. Let the churches awake before it is everlastingly too late.[58]

# Discerning of Spirits

*"For to one is given by the Spirit the word of wisdom; . . . to another discerning of spirits" (1 Corinthians 12:8, 10).*

Some have been so blinded by their own unbelief that they could not discern the spirit of Brother B. They might have been helped by him if he had been standing in the counsel of God. . . .

He feels that it is an honor to suggest doubts and unbelief in regard to the established faith of God's commandment-keeping people. The truth that he once rejoiced in is now darkness to him, and, unless he changes his course, he will fall back into a mixture of the views of the different denominations, but will agree in the whole with none of them; he will be a distinct church of himself, but not under the control of the great Head of the church. By bringing his views in opposition to the faith of the body, he is disheartening and discouraging the church.[59]

There are many avenues through which the enemy will work, and those who are placed as watchmen on the walls of Zion must be reliable, discerning every device of the enemy. Christ has given warning of deception and falsehood that will come to us, and His warning should be strictly heeded. The senses of everyone should be awake. They should study from cause to effect, and see the necessities of the situation, not only in one line but in all lines. They should understand what is to be endorsed and what is to be set aside. They should discern the spirit of everything purporting to be a direct message from Heaven. They should see when deceptions are multiplying in the very midst of us. They should see that the education and training of the people in these last days is to be that of firm reliance upon the Word of God, which is Yea and Amen in Christ Jesus.[60]

By studying the Word of God, and carrying out its precepts in all their business transactions, men may carefully discern the spirit that controls the actions. In the place of following human impulse and natural inclination, they may learn, by diligent study, the principles that should control the sons and daughters of Adam.[61]

# The Keen Perception of Christ

*"[The chief priests and scribes] watched [Jesus], and sent forth spies, which should feign themselves just men, that they might take hold of his words, that so they might deliver him unto the power and authority of the governor. And they asked him, saying, Master, we know that thou sayest and teachest rightly, neither acceptest thou the person of any, but teachest the way of God truly: Is it lawful for us to give tribute unto Caesar, or no? But he perceived their craftiness" (Luke 20:20–23).*

Jesus is the fountain of all wisdom. Those who connect with Him receive their counsel from a divine source. And it is only such as have "the wisdom that is from above" who can "walk in wisdom toward them that are without" (James 3:17; Colossians 4:5). If we keep the glory of God ever in view, our eyes will be anointed with the heavenly eyesalve, and we shall be able to see deeper, and to behold afar off what the world is. As we discern its dishonesty, its craftiness, its selfishness, its eye-service, its pretense and boasting and grasping covetousness, we are to take our stand to represent the cause of truth by a revelation of sound principles, a firm integrity, and a holy boldness in acknowledging Christ.[62]

The Lord wants us to have the fullness of His blessing, that we may not be on the side of the questioner and the doubter, but have spiritual discernment, and be able to know the voice of the True Shepherd from the voice of a stranger. We must have an individual experience. Do not flatter yourselves that because you have made a high profession, you are the light of the world. The question is, "Are you the light of the world, or are you the darkness of the world?"

All Heaven has its expectation of you to whom the precious light has been entrusted. The light has shone upon you in clear, bright rays from the throne of the living God. The question of most vital importance to each one is, "Is it well with my soul?" It is not well with anyone unless he has met and responded to the light that Heaven has permitted to shine upon his mind. The light of truth is more precious than anything besides. . . . This light is to test us and to make manifest of what spirit we are.[63]

# Solomon's Prayer for Discernment

*"O Lord my God, thou hast made thy servant king instead of David my father: and I am but a little child: I know not how to go out or come in. And thy servant is in the midst of thy people which thou hast chosen, a great people, that cannot be numbered nor counted for multitude. Give therefore thy servant an understanding heart to judge thy people, that I may discern between good and bad" (1 Kings 3:7–9).*

[Solomon] realized that without divine aid he was as helpless as a little child to fulfill the responsibilities resting on him. He knew that he lacked discernment, and it was a sense of his great need that led him to seek God for wisdom. In his heart there was no selfish aspirations for a knowledge that would exalt him above others. He desired to discharge faithfully the duties devolving upon him, and he chose the gift that would be the means of causing his reign to bring glory to God. Solomon was never so rich or so wise or so truly great as when he confessed, "I am but a little child: I know not how to go out or come in" (1 Kings 3:7). . . .

The God whom we serve is no respecter of persons. He who gave to Solomon the spirit of wise discernment is willing to impart the same blessing to His children today. "If any of you lack wisdom," His word declares, "let him ask of God, that giveth to all men liberally, and upbraideth not; and it shall be given him" (James 1:5). When a burden bearer desires wisdom more than he desires wealth, power, or fame, he will not be disappointed. . . .

So long as he remains consecrated, the man whom God has endowed with discernment and ability will not manifest an eagerness for high position, neither will he seek to rule or control. Of necessity men must bear responsibilities; but instead of striving for the supremacy, he who is a true leader will pray for an understanding heart, to discern between good and evil.

The path of men who are placed as leaders is not an easy one. But they are to see in every difficulty a call to prayer. Never are they to fail of consulting the great Source of all wisdom. Strengthened and enlightened by the Master Worker, they will be enabled to stand firm against unholy influences and to discern right from wrong.[64]

# God's Gifts to Solomon

*"God said unto [Solomon], Because thou hast asked this thing, and hast not asked for thyself long life; neither hast asked riches for thyself, nor hast asked the life of thine enemies; but hast asked for thyself understanding to discern judgment; behold, I have done according to thy words: lo, I have given thee a wise and an understanding heart" (1 Kings 3:11, 12).*

The wisdom that Solomon desired above riches, honor, or long life, God gave him. His petition for a quick mind, a large heart, and a tender spirit was granted. . . .

For many years Solomon's life was marked with devotion to God, with uprightness and firm principle, and with strict obedience to God's commands. He directed in every important enterprise and managed wisely the business matters connected with the kingdom. His wealth and wisdom, the magnificent buildings and public works that he constructed during the early years of his reign, the energy, piety, justice, and magnanimity that he revealed in word and deed, won the loyalty of his subjects and the admiration and homage of the rulers of many lands.

The name of Jehovah was greatly honored during the first part of Solomon's reign. The wisdom and righteousness revealed by the king bore witness to all nations of the excellency of the attributes of the God whom he served. For a time Israel was as the light of the world, showing forth the greatness of Jehovah. Not in the surpassing wisdom, the fabulous riches, the far-reaching power and fame that were his, lay the real glory of Solomon's early reign; but in the honor that he brought to the name of the God of Israel through a wise use of the gifts of Heaven.

As the years went by and Solomon's fame increased, he sought to honor God by adding to his mental and spiritual strength, and by continuing to impart to others the blessings he received. None understood better than he that it was through the favor of Jehovah that he had come into possession of power and wisdom and understanding, and that these gifts were bestowed that he might give to the world a knowledge of the King of kings.[65]

# Discerning Iniquity

*"Is there iniquity in my tongue? cannot my taste discern perverse things?" (Job 6:30).*

Some who have not spiritual discernment will fail to distinguish between the false and the true, and will highly esteem those who have no connection with God. Those who have been indifferent and neglectful, and have failed to grow in grace and in the knowledge of the truth, will be deceived. They do not comprehend the first principles of doctrine and experience which secure to man the perfection of Christian character.

Our duty, our safety, our happiness and usefulness, and our salvation call upon us each to use the greatest diligence to secure the grace of Christ, to be so closely connected with God that we may discern spiritual things, and not be ignorant of Satan's devices. Those who are willing to be instructed will heed the counsels and warnings of the Spirit of God. The Lord gives these admonitions and reproofs in mercy. When His professed people move in blindness, yield to temptation, and lose their hold upon Him, He sends them a message of reproof, of warning, of counsel; if they refuse to be corrected, if they rise up in rebellion, and cast reproach upon the messenger whom He sends, they reject not the messenger, but the Lord. When the people refused to listen to the counsel of Samuel the prophet, the Lord said unto him, "They have not rejected thee, but they have rejected me" (1 Samuel 8:7).

Some have a heart of unbelief, and in their self-confidence and self-deception they cannot see their errors. They are blind to their defects and their dangers. Did they see their sins and errors, and still continue in them, the Lord would give them up to blindness of mind and hardness of heart, to follow their own ways, and be ensnared and ruined. Anciently when any neglected or refused to heed the words of reproof and warning sent them of God, His protection was removed from them, and they were left to be deceived and deluded to their own ruin. Only those who, with tears of contrition, listened to the voice of God and gave heed to the warning, escaped the tempter's snare.[66]

# Perceiving a Chance to Help

*"It fell on a day, that Elisha passed to Shunem, where was a great woman; and she constrained him to eat bread" (2 Kings 4:8).*

Our heavenly Father lays blessings disguised in our pathway, but some will not touch these for fear they will detract from their enjoyment. Angels are waiting to see if we embrace opportunities within our reach of doing good—waiting to see if we will bless others, that they in their turn may bless us.[67]

May God pity those who are so afraid of deception as to neglect a worthy, self-sacrificing servant of Christ. The remark was made as an excuse for this neglect: We have been bitten so many times that we are afraid of strangers. Did our Lord and His disciples instruct us to be very cautious and not entertain strangers, lest we should possibly make some mistake and get bitten by having the trouble of caring for an unworthy person?

Paul exhorts the Hebrews: "Let brotherly love continue" (Hebrews 13:1). Do not flatter yourselves that there is a time when this exhortation will not be needed; when brotherly love may cease. . . . Please read Matthew 25:31 and onward. Read it, brethren, the next time you take the Bible at your morning or evening family devotions. The good works performed by those who are to be welcomed to the kingdom were done to Christ in the person of His suffering people. Those who had done these good works did not see that they had done anything for Christ. They had done no more than their duty to suffering humanity. Those on the left hand could not see that they had abused Christ in neglecting the wants of His people. But they had neglected to do for Jesus in the person of His saints, and for this neglect they were to go away into everlasting punishment. And one definite point of their neglect is thus stated: "I was a stranger, and ye took Me not in" (Matthew 25:43). . . .

I am grieved at the selfishness among professed Sabbathkeepers everywhere. Christ has gone to prepare eternal mansions for us, and shall we refuse Him a home for only a few days, in the person of His saints who are cast out?[68]

# Right or Wrong?

*"They shall teach my people the difference between the holy and pro-fane, and cause them to discern between the unclean and the clean"* *(Ezekiel 44:23).*

In these days of peril we should be exceedingly careful not to reject the rays of light which heaven in mercy sends us; for it is by these that we are to discern the devices of the enemy. We need light from heaven every hour, that we may distinguish between the sacred and the common, the eternal and the temporal.[69]

He who can read the hearts of men as an open book sees that which short-sighted mortals fail to discover. Finite wisdom cannot discern the necessity for sharp rebukes, for urgent warnings and entreaties. Those who are themselves deceived in men and in their purposes will pronounce against the messages of reproof which God sends, and will undertake to interpret the matter to suit their own ideas. They turn aside the counsel of God, that it shall not do the work which He designed. Those who have confidence in them are misled, and through their influence they cast aside the warning which God sends them, and then Satan stands ready with his delusions to ensnare their souls. The Lord would have saved them from the ruin if they had listened to His voice. Those who should have helped them, but who only injured them, must render an account at the bar of God. . . .

God's word represents but two great classes among men. Said Jesus to His disciples, "If ye were of the world, the world would love his own; but because ye are not of the world, but I have chosen you out of the world, therefore the world hateth you" (John 15:19). There are but two classes of religious teachers. Of one class the apostle John declares: "They are of the world; therefore speak they of the world, and the world heareth them" (1 John 4:5). Of the other class he says: "We are of God; he that knoweth God heareth us; he that is not of God heareth not us." "Whatsoever is born of God overcometh the world: and this is the victory that overcometh the world, even our faith" (1 John 4:6; 5:4).[70]

# Accountable for Light

*"Should not I spare Nineveh, that great city, wherein are more than sixscore thousand persons that cannot discern between their right hand and their left hand?" (Jonah 4:11).*

Because the Ninevites heard the message of mercy to some purpose, because they humbled their hearts and repented at the preaching of Jonah, the God of heaven was revered before the heathen world.[71]

Open your heart to Christ's forbearance. Let not a day pass in which you do not realize your accountability to work for God, an accountability placed on you by the death of His Son in your behalf. Let not a day pass on which you do not try to heal the wounds that sin has made. Always be found working on the broad plan of God's love.

We are under obligation to will to do the will of God. The Saviour is working for us. He is our Advocate in the heavenly courts, ever making intercession for us. The cry of the one ready to perish finds swift entrance to His ear. "He shall deliver the needy when he crieth; the poor also, and him that hath no helper" (Psalm 72:12). Shall we not work for Him on the lines He has marked out? Shall we not be Christlike advocates of those who err?

Christ suffered, being tempted; therefore He always sympathizes with the tempted ones whom Satan is seeking to destroy. . . . He has compassion on the ignorant, and on those who are out of the way; for when on this earth He was compassed with infirmity. He is able to help us in our perplexities. As He works for us, let us work for one another. Let us reveal His love for our fellow workers, acting in such a way that they will have full confidence in us.

Many more than we suppose need a helping hand held out to them. There are many to whom words of compassion and sympathy would be as a cup of cold water to a thirsty soul. Are you doing Christ service by ministering to weary, discouraged fellow beings? In love and pity Christ helps us. Shall we not impart His grace to others, by speaking to them words of hope and courage?[72]

# Avoiding False Discernment

*"Then shall ye return, and discern between the righteous and the wicked, between him that serveth God and him that serveth him not"* *(Malachi 3:18).*

The world has no right to doubt the truth of Christianity because there are unworthy members in the church, nor should Christians become disheartened because of these false brethren. . . . Judas Iscariot was numbered with the apostles. The Redeemer does not want to lose one soul; His experience with Judas is recorded to show His long patience with perverse human nature; and He bids us bear with it as He has borne. He has said that false brethren will be found in the church till the close of time.

Notwithstanding Christ's warning, men have sought to uproot the tares. . . .

Not judgment and condemnation of others, but humility and distrust of self, is the teaching of Christ's parable. Not all that is sown in the field is good grain. The fact that men are in the church does not prove them Christians.

The tares closely resembled the wheat while the blades were green; but when the field was white for the harvest, the worthless weeds bore no likeness to the wheat that bowed under the weight of its full, ripe heads. Sinners who make a pretension of piety mingle for a time with the true followers of Christ, and the semblance of Christianity is calculated to deceive many; but in the harvest of the world there will be no likeness between good and evil. Then those who have joined the church, but who have not joined Christ, will be manifest.

The tares are permitted to grow among the wheat, to have all the advantage of sun and shower; but in the time of harvest ye shall "return, and discern between the righteous and the wicked, between him that serveth God and him that serveth Him not" (Malachi 3:18). Christ Himself will decide who are worthy to dwell with the family of heaven. He will judge every man according to his words and his works. Profession is as nothing in the scale. It is character that decides destiny.[73]

# Discerning the Signs

*"O ye hypocrites, ye can discern the face of the sky; but can ye not discern the signs of the times?" (Matthew 16:3).*

The Lord's professing people have been sleeping over their allotted work, and in many places it remains comparatively untouched. God has sent message after message to arouse our people to do something, and to do it now. But to the call, "Whom shall I send?" there have been few to respond, "Here am I; send me" (Isaiah 6:8).

When the reproach of indolence and slothfulness shall have been wiped away from the church, the Spirit of the Lord will be graciously manifested. Divine power will be revealed. The church will see the providential working of the Lord of hosts. The light of truth will shine forth in clear, strong rays, and, as in the time of the apostles, many souls will turn from error to truth. The earth will be lighted with the glory of the Lord.

Heavenly angels have long been waiting for human agents—the members of the church—to cooperate with them in the great work to be done. They are waiting for you. So vast is the field, so comprehensive the design, that every sanctified heart will be pressed into service as an instrument of divine power.

At the same time there will be a power working from beneath. While God's agents of mercy work through consecrated human beings, Satan sets his agencies in operation, laying under tribute all who will submit to his control. There will be lords many and gods many. The cry will be heard, "Lo, here is Christ," and, "Lo, there is Christ." The deep plotting of Satan will reveal itself everywhere for the purpose of diverting the attention of men and women from present duty. There will be signs and wonders. But the eye of faith will discern in all these manifestations harbingers of the grand and awful future, and the triumphs that await the people of God.[74]

Thank God, all will not be rocked to sleep in the cradle of carnal security. There will be faithful ones who will discern the signs of the times. While a large number professing present truth will deny their faith by their works, there will be some who will endure unto the end.[75]

# Increasing Discernment

*"Strong meat belongeth to them that are of full age, even those who by reason of use have their senses exercised to discern both good and evil" (Hebrews 5:14).*

Today, as in Christ's day, odd, strange ideas are springing up. The truth Christ taught was grand and high and exalted. But though the Jewish people had been given great light, they did not bring into the practical life the great principles of love to God and man.[76]

Let church members bear in mind that the fact that their names are registered on the church books will not save them. They must show themselves approved of God, workmen that need not be ashamed. Day by day they are to build their characters in accordance with Christ's directions. They are to abide in Him, constantly exercising faith in Him.[77]

It is positively necessary for those who believe the truth, to be making continual advancement, growing up into the full stature of men and women in Christ Jesus. There is no time for backsliding and indifference. Each one must have a living experience in the things of God. Have root in yourselves. Become grounded in the faith, so that having done all you may stand, with unwavering confidence in God, through the time that will try every man's work and character. Exercise your powers in spiritual things, till you can appreciate the deep things of God's Word, and go on from strength to strength.

There are thousands who claim to have the light of truth who take no steps in advance. They have no living experience, notwithstanding they have had every advantage. They do not know what consecration means. Their devotions are formal and hollow, and there is no depth to their piety. The Word of God offers spiritual liberty and enlightenment to those who seek for it earnestly. Those who accept the promises of God, and act on them with living faith, will have the light of heaven in their lives. They will drink of the fountain of life, and lead others to the waters that have refreshed their own souls.[78]

# A Universal Language

*"The heavens declare the glory of God; and the firmament sheweth his handywork. Day unto day uttereth speech, and night unto night sheweth knowledge. There is no speech nor language, where their voice is not heard" (Psalm 19:1–3).*

Many are the ways in which God is seeking to make Himself known to us and to bring us into communion with Him. Nature speaks to our senses without ceasing.[1]

The beauty that clothes the earth is a token of God's love. We may behold it in the everlasting hills, in the lofty trees, in the opening buds and the delicate flowers. All speak to us of God.[2]

The open heart can be impressed with the love and glory of God as seen in the works of His hand. The listening ear can hear and understand the communications of God through the works of nature. There is a lesson in the sunbeam and in the various objects in nature that God has presented to our view. The green fields, the lofty trees, the buds and flowers, the passing cloud, the falling rain, the babbling brook, the sun, moon, and stars in the heavens, all invite our attention and meditation, and bid us become acquainted with God, who made them all. The lessons to be learned from the various objects of the natural world are these: They are obedient to the will of their Creator; they never deny God, never refuse obedience to any intimation of His will. Fallen beings alone refuse to yield full obedience to their Maker. Their words and works are at variance with God and opposed to the principles of His government. . . . There is enough in the natural world to lead you to love and adore your Creator.[3]

If we will but listen, God's created works will teach us precious lessons of obedience and trust. From the stars that in their trackless courses through space follow from age to age their appointed path, down to the minutest atom, the things of nature obey the Creator's will. And God cares for everything and sustains everything that He has created. He who upholds the unnumbered worlds throughout immensity, at the same time cares for the wants of the little brown sparrow that sings its humble song without fear.[4]

# Diverse Tongues for a Reason

*"The Lord said, Behold, the people is one, and they have all one language; and this they begin to do: and now nothing will be restrained from them, which they have imagined to do. Go to, let us go down, and there confound their language, that they may not understand one another's speech. So the Lord scattered them abroad from thence upon the face of all the earth" (Genesis 11:6–8).*

As Noah's descendants increased in numbers, apostasy manifested itself. Those who desired to cast off the restraint of God's law decided to separate from the worshipers of Jehovah. They determined to keep their community united in one body and to found a monarchy which should eventually embrace the whole earth. In the plain of Shinar they resolved to build a city, and in it a tower . . . so high that no flood could rise to the top, so massive that nothing could sweep it away. Thus they hoped to secure their own safety and make themselves independent of God.

This confederacy was born of rebellion against God. The dwellers on the plain of Shinar established their kingdom for self-exaltation, not for the glory of God. Had they succeeded, a mighty power would have borne sway, banishing righteousness and inaugurating a new religion. The world would have been demoralized. Erroneous theories would have diverted minds from allegiance to the divine statutes, and the law of Jehovah would have been ignored and forgotten. . . . At this time there were men who humbled themselves before God and cried unto Him. "O God," they pleaded, "interpose between Thy cause, and the plans and methods of men." . . . Angels were sent to bring to nought the purposes of the builders. . . .

In our day the Lord desires that His people shall be dispersed throughout the earth. They are not to colonize. . . . When the disciples followed their inclination to remain in large numbers in Jerusalem, persecution was permitted to come upon them, and they were scattered to all parts of the inhabited world.

For years messages of warning and entreaty have been coming to our people, urging them to go forth into the Master's great harvest field and labor unselfishly for souls.[5]

# To Reach All Nations

*"And God hath set . . . in the church . . . diversities of tongues" (1 Corinthians 12:28).*

There is a great work before us. The world is to be warned. The truth is to be translated into different languages, that all nations may enjoy its pure, life-giving influence. This work calls for the exercise of all the talents that God has entrusted to our keeping. He has given us abilities that enable us to exert an influence on other minds. We have talents in the pen, the press, the voice, the purse, and the sanctified affections of the soul. All these talents are the Lord's. He has lent them to us, and He holds us responsible for the use we make of them—for the faithful discharge of our duty to the world.[6]

The warning must be given in all lands and to all peoples. Our books are to be translated and published in many different languages. We should multiply publications on our faith in English, German, French, Danish-Norwegian, Swedish, Spanish, Italian, Portuguese, and many other tongues; and people of all nationalities should be enlightened and educated, that they, too, may join in the work.[7]

It may in some cases be necessary that young men learn foreign languages. This they can do with most success by associating with the people, at the same time devoting a portion of each day to studying the language. This should be done, however, only as a necessary step preparatory to educating such as are found in the missionary field themselves, and who with proper training can become workers. It is essential that those be urged into the service who can speak in their mother tongue to the people of different nations. It is a great undertaking for a man of middle age to learn a foreign language, and with all his efforts it will be next to impossible for him to speak it so readily and correctly as to render him an efficient laborer.[8]

Many students from our schools are going out and educating themselves in the languages, and opening the Scriptures to peoples of other tongues. This is an excellent work, just the work the Lord would have them do.[9]

# Instant Translation

*"[The apostles] were all filled with the Holy Ghost, and began to speak with other tongues, as the Spirit gave them utterance. And there were dwelling at Jerusalem Jews, devout men, out of every nation under heaven. Now when this was noised abroad, the multitude came together, and were confounded, because that every man heard them speak in his own language. And they were all amazed and marvelled, saying one to another, Behold, are not all these which speak Galilaeans? And how hear we every man in our own tongue, wherein we were born?" (Acts 2:4–8).*

The Holy Ghost assuming the form of tongues of fire divided at the tips, and resting upon those assembled, was an emblem of the gift which was bestowed upon them of speaking with fluency several different languages, with which they had formerly been unacquainted. And the appearance of fire signified the fervent zeal with which they would labor, and the power which would attend their words.[10]

During the dispersion the Jews had been scattered to almost every part of the inhabited world, and in their exile they had learned to speak various languages. Many of these Jews were on this occasion in Jerusalem, attending the religious festivals then in progress. Every known tongue was represented by those assembled. This diversity of languages would have been a great hindrance to the proclamation of the gospel; God therefore in a miraculous manner supplied the deficiency of the apostles. The Holy Spirit did for them that which they could not have accomplished for themselves in a lifetime. They could now proclaim the truths of the gospel abroad, speaking with accuracy the languages of those for whom they were laboring. This miraculous gift was a strong evidence to the world that their commission bore the signet of Heaven. From this time forth the language of the disciples was pure, simple, and accurate, whether they spoke in their native tongue or in a foreign language.[11]

# Avoiding Counterfeits

*"What is it then? I will pray with the spirit, and I will pray with the understanding also: I will sing with the spirit, and I will sing with the understanding also. . . . I had rather speak five words with my understanding, that by my voice I might teach others also, than ten thousand words in an unknown tongue" (1 Corinthians 14:15, 19).*

Some . . . have exercises which they call gifts and say that the Lord has placed them in the church. They have an unmeaning gibberish which they call the unknown tongue, which is unknown not only by man but by the Lord and all heaven. Such gifts are manufactured by men and women, aided by the great deceiver. Fanaticism, false excitement, false talking in tongues, and noisy exercises have been considered gifts which God has placed in the church. Some have been deceived here. The fruits of all this have not been good. "Ye shall know them by their fruits" (Matthew 7:16). Fanaticism and noise have been considered special evidences of faith. Some are not satisfied with a meeting unless they have a powerful and happy time. They work for this and get up an excitement of feeling. But the influence of such meetings is not beneficial. When the happy flight of feeling is gone, they sink lower than before the meeting because their happiness did not come from the right source.[12]

Some rejoice in the idea that they have the gifts which others have not, and they exult over the matter. May God deliver His people from such gifts. What do these gifts do for them? Are they brought through the exercise of these gifts into the unity of the faith? And do they convince the unbeliever that God is with them of a truth? These discordant ones, believing all these different views, getting together and having considerable excitement, and the unknown tongue, let their light so shine that unbelievers would say, These people are not sane; they are carried away with a false excitement, and we know that they do not have the truth. Such stand directly in the way of sinners, and their influence is effectual to keep men and women out of the Sabbath. Such will be rewarded according as their works shall be. Would to God they would be reformed or give up the Sabbath. They would not then stand in the way of unbelievers.[13]

# Speaking Clearly

*"If the trumpet give an uncertain sound, who shall prepare himself to the battle? So likewise ye, except ye utter by the tongue words easy to be understood, how shall it be known what is spoken? for ye shall speak into the air" (1 Corinthians 14:8, 9).*

The principle presented by Paul concerning the gift of tongues, is equally applicable to the use of the voice in prayer and social meeting. We would not have any one of you who is defective in this respect cease from offering public prayer, or from bearing witness to the power and love of Christ. I do not write these words to silence you; for there has been already too much silence in our meetings; but I write that you may consecrate your voice to Him who gave you this gift, and realize the necessity of cultivating it so that you may edify the church by what you say. If you have acquired the habit of speaking in a low, indistinct way, you should regard it as a defect, and put forth earnest effort to overcome, that you may honor God and edify His children. . . .

In our devotional social meetings, our voices should express by prayer and praise our adoration of our heavenly Father, that all may know that we worship God in simplicity and truth, and in the beauty of holiness. Precious indeed in this world of sin and ignorance is the gift of speech, is the melody of the human voice, when devoted to the praises of Him who hath loved us, and hath given Himself for us. The gift of speech has been greatly abused, and widely perverted from its intended purpose; but let those who claim to be children of the heavenly King awaken to their responsibility and make more of this precious talent than ever they have done before. Let no one say, "There is no use for me to try to pray, for others do not hear me." Rather say, "I will make earnest efforts to overcome this God-dishonoring habit of speaking in a low, indistinct tone, and I will put myself under discipline until my voice shall be audible, even to those who are hard of hearing." Will it not be worth disciplining yourself to be able to add interest to the service of God, and to edify the children of God?[14]

# Cultivating the Gift of Speech

*"The tongue of the just is as choice silver: the heart of the wicked is little worth. The lips of the righteous feed many: but fools die for want of wisdom" (Proverbs 10:20, 21).*

The voice of thanksgiving, praise, and rejoicing is heard in heaven. The voices of the children of God unite with the voices of the angels of heaven.[15]

Speech needs to be converted and sanctified. The Lord requires that education should be given in the science of conversation. This faculty has been much abused and perverted. It has not been held as a precious gift from God, to be used to glorify His name. The words are a power for good or evil, a savor of life unto life, or of death unto death. Choice words must be spoken by those who would do service for Christ. Haphazard words, hasty, common words, talking for the sake of talking, when silence would be better, is a sin. Those who are the most wordy exercise no wholesome influence upon the society in which they live and move. Bible religion is not to be boastfully paraded, but quietly practiced in good words and works.[16]

There are among us those who, without the toil and delay of learning a foreign language, might qualify themselves to proclaim the truth to other nations. In the primitive church, missionaries were miraculously endowed with a knowledge of the languages in which they were called to preach the unsearchable riches of Christ. And if God was willing thus to help His servants then, can we doubt that His blessing will rest upon our efforts to qualify those who naturally possess a knowledge of foreign tongues, and who with proper encouragement would bear to their own countrymen the message of truth?[17]

As representatives of Christ we have no time to lose. Our efforts are not to be confined to a few places where the light has become so abundant that it is not appreciated. With unmistakable clearness the light of truth is to be revealed to many people and nations and tongues.[18]

# The Tongue of the Learned

*"The Lord God hath given me the tongue of the learned, that I should know how to speak a word in season to him that is weary" (Isaiah 50:4).*

God will impress those whose hearts are open to truth and who are longing for guidance. He will say to His human agent: "Speak to this one or to that one of the love of Jesus." No sooner is the name of Jesus mentioned in love and tenderness than angels of God draw near to soften and subdue the heart.[19]

A true Christian constantly acknowledges Christ. He is always cheerful, always ready to speak words of hope and comfort to the suffering. . . .

One sentence of Scripture is of more value than ten thousand of man's ideas or arguments. Those who refuse to follow God's way will finally receive the sentence, "Depart from Me." But when we submit to God's way, the Lord Jesus guides our minds and fills our lips with assurance. We may be strong in the Lord and in the power of His might. Receiving Christ, we are clothed with power. An indwelling Saviour makes His power our property. The truth becomes our stock in trade. No unrighteousness is seen in the life. We are able to speak words in season to those who know not the truth. Christ's presence in the heart is a vitalizing power, strengthening the entire being.[20]

By diligent effort all may acquire the power to read intelligibly, and to speak in a full, clear, round tone, in a distinct and impressive manner. . . .

Every Christian is called to make known to others the unsearchable riches of Christ; therefore he should seek for perfection in speech. He should present the word of God in a way that will commend it to the hearers. God does not design that His human channels shall be uncouth. It is not His will that man shall belittle or degrade the heavenly current that flows through him to the world.

We should look to Jesus, the perfect pattern; we should pray for the aid of the Holy Spirit, and in His strength we should seek to train every organ for perfect work.[21]

# With Grace, Seasoned With Salt

*"Let your speech be alway with grace, seasoned with salt, that ye may know how ye ought to answer every man" (Colossians 4:6).*

The conversation of the Christian should be in heaven, whence we look for the Saviour. Meditation upon heavenly things is profitable, and will ever be accompanied with the peace and comfort of the Holy Spirit. Our calling is holy, our profession exalted. God is purifying unto Himself a peculiar people, zealous of good works. He is sitting as a refiner and purifier of silver. When the dross and tin are removed, then His image will be perfectly reflected in us. . . . When the truth has a sanctifying influence upon our hearts and lives, we can render to God acceptable service and can glorify Him upon the earth, being partakers of the divine nature and having escaped the corruption that is in the world through lust.

Oh, how many will be found unready when the Master shall come to reckon with His servants! Many have meager ideas of what constitutes a Christian. Self-righteousness will then be of no avail. Only those can stand the test who shall be found having on the righteousness of Christ, who are imbued with His spirit, and walk even as He walked, in purity of heart and life. The conversation must be holy, and then the words will be seasoned with grace.[22]

Some with whom you are brought in contact may be rough and uncourteous, but do not, because of this, be less courteous yourself. He who wishes to preserve his own self-respect must be careful not to wound needlessly the self-respect of others. This rule should be sacredly observed toward the dullest, the most blundering. What God intends to do with these apparently unpromising ones, you do not know. He has in the past accepted persons no more promising or attractive to do a great work for Him. His Spirit, moving upon the heart, has roused every faculty to vigorous action. The Lord saw in these rough, unhewn stones precious material, which would stand the test of storm and heat and pressure. God does not see as man sees. He does not judge from appearances, but searches the heart and judges righteously.[23]

# Ready to Give an Answer

*"Sanctify the Lord God in your hearts: and be ready always to give an answer to every man that asketh you a reason of the hope that is in you with meekness and fear: having a good conscience; that, whereas they speak evil of you, as of evildoers, they may be ashamed that falsely accuse your good conversation in Christ" (1 Peter 3:15, 16).*

We are not to conceal the fact that we are Seventh-day Adventists. The truth may be ashamed of us because our course of action is not in harmony with its pure principles, but we need never be ashamed of the truth. As you have opportunity, confess your faith.[24]

Everyone should seek to understand the great truths of the plan of salvation, that he may be ready to give an answer to everyone who asks the reason of his hope. You should know what caused the fall of Adam, so that you may not commit the same error and lose heaven as he lost paradise. You should study the lives of patriarchs and prophets, and the history of God's dealing with men in the past; for these things were "written for our admonition, upon whom the ends of the world are come" (1 Corinthians 10:11). We should study the divine precepts and seek to comprehend their depth. We should meditate upon them until we discern their importance and immutability. We should study the life of our Redeemer, for He is the only perfect example for men. We should contemplate the infinite sacrifice of Calvary, and behold the exceeding sinfulness of sin and the righteousness of the law. You will come from a concentrated study of the theme of redemption strengthened and ennobled. Your comprehension of the character of God will be deepened; and with the whole plan of salvation clearly defined in your mind, you will be better able to fulfill your divine commission. From a sense of thorough conviction, you can then testify to men of the immutable character of the law manifested by the death of Christ on the cross, the malignant nature of sin, and the righteousness of God in justifying the believer in Jesus, on condition of his future obedience to the statutes of God's government in heaven and earth. Thousands more might have been saved if men had preached the word, instead of the maxims, philosophies, and doctrines of men.[25]

# Watching Our Words

*"Set a watch, O Lord, before my mouth; keep the door of my lips"*
*(Psalm 141:3).*

I was shown the case of Brother U's wife. She has a desire to do right, but has failings which cause herself and her friends much trouble. She talks too much. She lacks experience in the things of God, and unless she is converted and transformed by the renewing of the mind, she will be unable to stand amid the perils of the last days. Heart work is needed. Then the tongue will be sanctified. There is much talking which is sinful and should be avoided. She should set a strict watch before the door of her lips and keep her tongue as with a bridle, that her words may not work wickedness. She should cease talking of others' faults, dwelling upon others' peculiarities, and discovering others' infirmities. Such conversation is censurable in any person. It is unprofitable and positively sinful. It tends only to evil. The enemy knows that if this course is pursued by Christ's professed followers, it is opening a door for him to work.

I saw that when sisters who are given to talk get together, Satan is generally present, for he finds employment. He stands by to excite the mind and make the most of the advantage he has gained. He knows that all this gossip, and tale-bearing, and revealing of secrets, and dissecting of character, separate the soul from God. It is death to spirituality and a calm religious influence. Sister U sins greatly with her tongue. She ought by her words to have an influence for good, but she frequently talks at random. Sometimes her words put a different construction upon things than they will bear. Sometimes there is exaggeration. Then there is misstatement. There is no intention to misstate, but the habit of much talking and talking upon things that are unprofitable has been so long cherished that she has become careless and reckless in her words, and frequently does not know what she is stating herself. This destroys any influence for good she might have. It is time there was an entire reform in this respect.[26]

Say nothing that you would not be willing to say in the presence of Jesus and the angels.[27]

323

# Bridling the Tongue

*"If any man among you seem to be religious, and bridleth not his tongue, but deceiveth his own heart, this man's religion is vain" (James 1:26).*

[James 1:26 quoted.] Many will be weighed in the balance and found wanting in this matter of so great importance. Where are the Christians who walk by this rule? who will take God's part against the evilspeaker? who will please God, and set a watch, a continual watch, before the mouth, and keep the door of the lips? Speak evil of no man. Hear evil of no man. If there be no hearers, there will be no speakers of evil. If anyone speaks evil in your presence, check him. Refuse to hear him, though his manner be ever so soft and his accents mild. He may profess attachment, and yet throw out covert hints and stab the character in the dark.[28]

Christians should be careful in regard to their words. They should never carry unfavorable reports from one of their friends to another, especially if they are aware that there is a lack of union between them. It is cruel to hint and insinuate, as though you knew a great deal in regard to this friend or that acquaintance of which others are ignorant. Such hints go further, and create more unfavorable impressions, than to frankly relate the facts in an unexaggerated manner. What harm has not the church of Christ suffered from these things! The inconsistent, unguarded course of her members has made her weak as water. Confidence has been betrayed by members of the same church, and yet the guilty did not design to do mischief. Lack of wisdom in the selection of subjects of conversation has done much harm. The conversation should be upon spiritual and divine things; but it has been otherwise. If the association with Christian friends is chiefly devoted to the improvement of the mind and heart, there will be no after regrets, and they can look back on the interview with a pleasant satisfaction. But if the hours are spent in levity and vain talking, and the precious time is employed in dissecting the lives and character of others, the friendly intercourse will prove a source of evil, and your influence will be a savor of death unto death.[29]

# Bar the Way to Corrupt Speech

*"Let no corrupt communication proceed out of your mouth, but that which is good to the use of edifying, that it may minister grace unto the hearers" (Ephesians 4:29).*

We are counseled to let no corrupt communication proceed out of our mouth; but a corrupt communication is not simply something that is vile and vulgar. It is any communication that will eclipse from the mind the view of Christ, that will blot from the soul true sympathy and love. It is a communication in which the love of Christ is not expressed, but rather sentiments of an un-Christlike character.[30]

In seeking to correct or reform others we should be careful of our words. They will be a savor of life unto life or of death unto death. In giving reproof or counsel, many indulge in sharp, severe speech, words not adapted to heal the wounded soul. By these ill-advised expressions the spirit is chafed, and often the erring ones are stirred to rebellion. All who would advocate the principles of truth need to receive the heavenly oil of love. Under all circumstances reproof should be spoken in love. Then our words will reform but not exasperate. Christ by His Holy Spirit will supply the force and the power. This is His work.

Not one word is to be spoken unadvisedly. No evil speaking, no frivolous talk, no fretful repining or impure suggestion, will escape the lips of him who is following Christ. The apostle Paul, writing by the Holy Spirit, says, "Let no corrupt communication proceed out of your mouth" (Ephesians 4:29). A corrupt communication does not mean only words that are vile. It means any expression contrary to holy principles and pure and undefiled religion. It includes impure hints and covert insinuations of evil. Unless instantly resisted, these lead to great sin.

Upon every family, upon every individual Christian, is laid the duty of barring the way against corrupt speech. When in the company of those who indulge in foolish talk, it is our duty to change the subject of conversation if possible. By the help of the grace of God we should quietly drop words or introduce a subject that will turn the conversation into a profitable channel.[31]

# Who Made Your Mouth?

*"Moses said unto the Lord, O my Lord, I am not eloquent, neither heretofore, nor since thou hast spoken unto thy servant: but I am slow of speech, and of a slow tongue. And the Lord said unto him, Who hath made man's mouth? or who maketh the dumb, or deaf, or the seeing, or the blind? have not I the Lord? Now therefore go, and I will be with thy mouth, and teach thee what thou shalt say" (Exodus 4:10–12).*

From the burning bush the Lord reproved Moses for unbelief when he pleaded his inability to speak. [Exodus 4:11, 12 quoted.] When the word of Lord came to Jeremiah, he said, "Ah, Lord God! behold, I cannot speak: for I am a child." But the Lord said to him: "Say not, I am a child: for thou shalt go to all that I shall send thee, and whatsoever I command thee thou shalt speak. Be not afraid of their faces: for I am with thee to deliver thee, saith the Lord" (Jeremiah 1:6–8).

The same God who gave His messages to Moses and Jeremiah will give His word to His witnesses in this generation. "For it is not ye that speak," Christ declares, "but the Spirit of your Father which speaketh in you" (Matthew 10:20). This word of the Lord has been verified in all ages, and it will be verified to the close of time in all who hold the beginning of their confidence firm unto the end. The most powerful testimony will be given in defense of the faith once delivered to the saints. The Holy Spirit is close beside those who are called to witness for truth and righteousness.[32]

The divine command given to Moses found him self-distrustful, slow of speech, and timid. He was overwhelmed with a sense of his incapacity to be a mouthpiece for God to Israel. But having once accepted the work, he entered upon it with his whole heart, putting all his trust in the Lord. The greatness of his mission called into exercise the best powers of his mind. God blessed his ready obedience, and he became eloquent, hopeful, self-possessed, and well fitted for the greatest work ever given to man. This is an example of what God does to strengthen the character of those who trust Him fully and give themselves unreservedly to His commands.[33]

# The Communication of Our Faith

*"That the communication of thy faith may become effectual by the acknowledging of every good thing which is in you in Christ Jesus"* *(Philemon 6).*

Faith is the gift of God, but the power to exercise it is yours. A single earnest expression of faith strengthens faith; but every expression of doubt confirms doubt, and helps to gather about your soul the dark shadows of unbelief. Then do not open your soul to Satan's temptations by cherishing and expressing the doubts that he insinuates. Talk faith and courage. Press to the light; and bright beams from the Sun of Righteousness will dispel clouds and darkness, and sweet peace will pervade the soul.[34]

Not only should the prayer meeting be faithfully attended, but as often as once each week a praise meeting should be held. Here the goodness and manifold mercies of God should be dwelt upon. Were we as free to give expression to our thankfulness for mercies received as we are to speak of grievances, doubts, and unbelief, we might bring joy to the hearts of others, instead of casting discouragement and gloom upon them. The complainers and murmurers, who are ever seeing the discouragements in the way, and talking of trials and hardships, should contemplate the infinite sacrifice which Christ has made in their behalf. Then can they estimate all their blessings in the light of the cross. While looking upon Jesus, the Author and Finisher of our faith, whom our sins have pierced and our sorrows have burdened, we shall see cause for gratitude and praise, and our thoughts and desires will be brought into submission to the will of Christ. . . .

We must gather about the cross. Christ and Him crucified must be the theme of contemplation, of conversation, and of our most joyful emotion. We should have these special appointments for the purpose of keeping fresh in our thoughts everything which we receive from God, and of expressing our gratitude for His great love, and our willingness to trust everything to the hand that was nailed to the cross for us. We should learn here to talk the language of Canaan, to sing the songs of Zion.[35]

# Communicating in Song

*"Be filled with the Spirit; speaking to yourselves in psalms and hymns and spiritual songs, singing and making melody in your heart to the Lord" (Ephesians 5:18, 19).*

It is a divine influence that touches the heart and creates the heavenly music that flows forth from the lips in pure thanksgiving and praise.[36]

Those who have the gift of song are needed. Song is one of the most effective means of impressing spiritual truth upon the heart. Often by the words of sacred song the springs of penitence and faith have been unsealed. . . .

Young men and women, take up the work to which God calls you. Christ will teach you to use your abilities to good purpose. As you receive the quickening influence of the Holy Spirit, and seek to teach others, your minds will be refreshed, and you will be able to present words that are new and strangely beautiful to your hearers. Pray, and sing, and speak the word.[37]

Let those who are well established in the truth, go into neighboring places, and hold meetings, giving a cordial invitation to all. Let there be in these meetings, melodious songs, fervent prayers, and the reading of God's Word. And let the ideas expressed, and the words in which they are clothed, be such as the common people can readily comprehend.[38]

Let little companies of workers go out as the Lord's missionaries, and do as Christ commissioned the first disciples to do. Let them go into the different parts of our cities, two and two, and give the Lord's message of warning. Tell the people the story of Creation, and how at the close of His work the Lord rested upon and blessed the Sabbath day, setting it apart as a memorial of His work.

Church members young and old should be educated to go forth to proclaim this last message to the world. If they will go in humility, angels of God will go with them, teaching them to lift up the voice in prayer, how to raise the voice in song, and how to proclaim the gospel message for this time. We have not a moment to lose.[39]

# Charming Oratory Set Aside

*"I, brethren, when I came to you, came not with excellency of speech
or of wisdom, declaring unto you the testimony of God. For I determined
not to know any thing among you, save Jesus Christ, and him crucified.
And I was with you in weakness, and in fear, and in much trembling. And
my speech and my preaching was not with enticing words of man's wisdom, but in demonstration of the Spirit and of power: that your faith
should not stand in the wisdom of men, but in the power of God"* (1
*Corinthians 2:1–5).*

In preaching the gospel at Corinth, the apostle adopted a different
course of action from that which had marked his labors at Athens.
While in the latter place, he had adapted his style to the character of
his audience; and much of his time had been devoted to the discussion of natural religion, matching logic with logic, and science with
science. But when he reviewed the time and labor which he had there
devoted to the exposition of Christianity, and realized that his style of
teaching had not been productive of much fruit, he decided upon a
different plan of labor in the future. He determined to avoid elaborate
arguments and discussions of theories as much as possible, and to
urge upon sinners the doctrine of salvation through Christ.[40]

The apostle did not labor to charm the ear with oratory, nor to
engage the mind with philosophic discussions, which would leave
the heart untouched. He preached the cross of Christ, not with
labored eloquence of speech, but with the grace and power of God;
and his words moved the people.[41]

Paul was an eloquent speaker. Before his conversion he had often
sought to impress his hearers by flights of oratory. But now he set all
this aside. Instead of indulging in poetic descriptions and fanciful representations, which might please the senses and feed the imagination,
but which would not touch the daily experience, Paul sought by the
use of simple language to bring home to the heart the truths that are
of vital importance.[42]

# Great Plainness of Speech

*"Seeing then that we have such hope, we use great plainness of speech" (2 Corinthians 3:12).*

Fanciful representations of truth may cause an ecstasy of feeling, but all too often truths presented in this way do not supply the food necessary to strengthen and fortify the believer for the battles of life. The immediate needs, the present trials, of struggling souls—these must be met with sound, practical instruction in the fundamental principles of Christianity.[43]

Those who walk with God are prepared to call wrongdoing by its right name. Sin is sin, whether practiced by ministers, teachers, medical missionaries, or other workers in the Lord's service. . . . Great plainness of speech is required.[44]

Truth is of God; deception in all its myriad forms is of Satan, and whoever in any way departs from the straight line of truth is betraying himself into the power of the wicked one. Those who have learned of Christ will "have no fellowship with the unfruitful works of darkness" (Ephesians 5:11). In speech, as in life, they will be simple, straightforward, and true.[45]

There should be selected for the work wise, consecrated men who can do a good work in reaching souls. Women also should be chosen who can present the truth in a clear, intelligent, straightforward manner. We need among us laborers who see the need of a deep work of grace to be done in hearts; and such should be encouraged to engage in earnest missionary effort. There has long been the need for more of this class of workers. We must pray most earnestly, "Lord, help us to help one another." Self must be buried with Christ, and we must be baptized with the Holy Spirit of God. Then will be revealed in speech, in spirit, and in our manner of labor the fact that the Spirit of God is guiding.

We need as workers men and women who understand the reasons of our faith and who realize the work to be done in communicating truth, and who will refuse to speak any words that will weaken the confidence of any soul in the Word of God or destroy the fellowship that should exist between those of like faith.[46]

# Words of Continuous Praise

*"My tongue shall speak of thy righteousness and of thy praise all the day long" (Psalm 35:28).*

When I was in Colorado some years since, I visited an art gallery, and there were groups of people standing before the pictures as if entranced, and praising the human artist. At evening as I was walking through the town, I saw the glory of the sunset. The bright beams were shining upon the snowcapped mountains, and it seemed as if the portals of heaven were opened, and its glory were streaming through. Persons were continually passing along the street, but none looked at the sight. My companion and myself were gazing upon it in rapture. I could discern in it heaven's beauty; I could see heaven's glory shining from the gates ajar, that we might conceive the beauty of what was within. But the crowds did not look upon the scene. That is the way God is treated.

How many go out into the garden with their children, and as they point them to the beautiful flowers say, "This is an expression of the love of God to you"? This would lead their minds up through nature to nature's God. Would not this be far more profitable to your children than taking them to all the shows and amusements of a demoralizing nature that would absorb their attention so that they forget God?[47]

When men and women can more fully comprehend the magnitude of the great sacrifice which was made by the Majesty of heaven in dying in man's stead, then will the plan of salvation be magnified, and reflections of Calvary will awaken tender, sacred, and lively emotions in the Christian's heart. Praises to God and the Lamb will be in their hearts and upon their lips. Pride and self esteem cannot flourish in the hearts that keep fresh in memory the scenes of Calvary. This world will appear of but little value to those who appreciate the great price of man's redemption, the precious blood of God's dear Son. All the riches of the world are not of sufficient value to redeem one perishing soul. Who can measure the love Christ felt for a lost world as He hung upon the cross, suffering for the sins of guilty men? This love was immeasurable, infinite.[48]

# Right Thoughts Make Right Words

*"My mouth shall speak of wisdom; and the meditation of my heart shall be of understanding" (Psalm 49:3).*

Success or failure in this life depends much upon the manner in which the thoughts are disciplined. If they are controlled as God directs that they shall be, they will be upon those subjects which lead to greater devotion. If the thoughts are right, the words will be right.[49]

Acquire a habit of self-government, that your thoughts may be brought into subjection to the Spirit of Christ. It is the grace of God that you need in order that your thoughts may be disciplined to flow in the right channel, that the words you utter may be right words, and that your passions and appetites may be subject to the control of reason, and the tongue be bridled against levity and unhallowed censure and faultfinding.[50]

All are to a great extent under the influence of their own words. They act out the sentiments expressed in their words. Thus the government of the tongue is closely bound up with personal religion. Many are by their own words led to believe that a wrong course is right. Thoughts are expressed in words, and the words react upon the thoughts, and produce other words. The influence is felt, not only upon oneself, but upon others. The Lord God alone can undo the mischievous result of unwise words. Often an opinion or decision, having been once expressed, will be acted upon, though it may lead to an entirely wrong course. The iron will changes not, because it would be too humiliating to acknowledge oneself in error. The words hastily spoken, to give vent to strong feelings, produce their evil results in hurting, wounding, and bruising souls for whom Christ died. Satan is pleased, God is dishonored, and many souls are ruined by hastily spoken words.

Speak gently. Speak words of kindness and uplifting, for this is the fruit borne on the Christian tree. Overcome all harshness. Rash speeches do much harm to the souls of those who utter them and to the souls of those who hear. Eternity alone will reveal how greatly those who made these speeches needed to humble their hearts and make confession to God.[51]

# A Converted Tongue

*"My tongue shall speak of thy word: for all thy commandments are righteousness" (Psalm 119:172).*

As we speak of God's power, we show that we appreciate the love that is so constantly shown us, that we are grateful for the mercies and favors bestowed on us, and that the whole soul is awakened to a realization of God's glory.

The absence of praise and thanksgiving pleases the enemy of God. The line of demarcation between those who utter the holy name of God in blasphemy, and those who praise Him with heart and with voice, is clear and distinct.[52]

Christ is cleansing the temple in heaven from the sins of the people, and we must work in harmony with Him upon the earth, cleansing the soul temple from its moral defilement. If we will work thus, we shall find that the sweet influence of God's Spirit will be wrought into our life. Grace and peace and strength will take the place of strife and weakness, and instead of talking of discouragement and gloom, we shall speak of God's light and love and joy.[53]

As you arose from the watery grave at the time of your baptism, you professed to be dead, and declared that your life was changed—hid with Christ in God. You claimed to be dead to sin, and cleansed from your hereditary and cultivated traits of evil. In going forward in the rite of baptism, you pledged yourselves before God to remain dead to sin. Your mouth was to remain a sanctified mouth, your tongue a converted tongue. You were to speak of God's goodness, and to praise His holy name.[54]

Speak of the mercy, the goodness, and the love of Jesus; for "we cannot but speak the things which we have seen and heard" (Acts 4:20). Keep your face heavenward. Look at the heavenly attractions, and then you may in truth "shew forth the praises of him who hath called you out of darkness into his marvellous light" (1 Peter 2:9). With all the precious promises given us from the lips of Jesus, let us act our thankfulness. Let us contemplate our duty in the light of the commandments of God.[55]

# Testimony Meetings

*"They that feared the Lord spake often one to another: and the Lord hearkened, and heard it, and a book of remembrance was written before him for them that feared the Lord, and that thought upon his name"* (Malachi 3:16).

Great interest should be taken by Sabbathkeepers to keep up their meetings and make them interesting. There has been a lack of interest, and there is great necessity of more energy being manifested by the commandment-keepers in their meetings. All should have something to say for the Lord, and by so doing they would be blest. A book of remembrance is written of those who do not forsake the assembling of themselves together, and speak often one to another.

The remnant are to overcome by the blood of the Lamb and the word of their testimony. Some expect to overcome alone by the blood of the Lamb, without making any special effort of their own. I saw that God has been merciful in giving us the power of speech. He has given us tongue and utterance, and we are accountable to Him for it, and we should glorify God with our mouth, speaking in honor of His unbounded mercy, and of the truth, and overcome by the word of our testimony through the blood of the Lamb.

We should not come together to remain silent; those only are remembered of the Lord who come together to honor and glorify Him, to speak of His glory and tell of His power; and upon such the blessing of God will rest, and they will be refreshed. If all moved as I saw they should, no precious time would run to waste, and no reproofs would be needed for long prayers and exhortations; for all the time would be occupied by short, sweet testimonies and prayers to the point. . . . First we should feel needy, and then ask God for the very things we need, and then believe He gives them to us. . . .

Some hold back in meetings because they have nothing new to say and must repeat the same story if they speak. I saw that pride was at the bottom of this, that God and angels witnessed the testimonies of the saints and the Lord was well pleased and was glorified by their testimonies repeated weekly. The Lord and His holy angels love simplicity and humility.[56]

# Talking About God

*"Give thanks unto the Lord, call upon his name, make known his deeds among the people. Sing unto him, sing psalms unto him, talk ye of all his wondrous works" (1 Chronicles 16:8, 9).*

We know that the world is filled with iniquity, but shall we think and talk of that only? Shall we look here and there for defects and evils? Shall we look critically at the characters of our brethren? O let us think of the goodness of God! Let us tell of His power, sing of His love. Let us commit our souls unto God as unto a faithful Creator, and stop worrying and fretting. God will help us to live above the things of this life, and give us an abundance of good things to think about and to talk about. Let us come into the presence of Christ. . . . Provision has been made for our cleansing. A fountain has been opened for sin and uncleanness. Ask in faith for the grace of God, and you will not ask in vain.[57]

Oh, that our tongues might be loosed to speak of [God's] goodness, to tell of His power! If you respond to the drawing of Jesus, you will not fail to have an influence on somebody through the beauty and power of the grace of Christ.[58]

It is Satan's plan to talk about that which concerns himself. He is delighted to have human beings talk of his power, of his working through the children of men, but by indulgence in such conversation the mind becomes gloomy and sour and disagreeable. We may become channels of communication for Satan through which words bring no sunshine to the heart. But let us decide that this shall not be. Let us decide not to be channels through which Satan shall send gloomy disagreeable thoughts. Let our words be not a savor of death unto death, but of life unto life, in the words we speak to the people and in the prayers we offer. God desires us to give unmistakable evidences that we have a spiritual life.[59]

Be affable and compassionate. Let your countenance reflect the joy of the Lord. Speak of His goodness and tell of His power. Then your light will shine more and more distinctly. Above your trials and disappointments will be revealed the reflection of a pure, healthy religious life.[60]

# The Prerequisite for Pure Words

*"Make me to understand the way of thy precepts: so shall I talk of thy wondrous works" (Psalm 119:27).*

It is no marvel that there is not more heavenly-mindedness shown among the youth who profess Christianity, when there is so little attention given to the word of God. The divine counsels are not heeded; the admonitions are not obeyed; grace and heavenly wisdom are not sought, that past sins may be avoided, and every taint of corruption be cleansed from the character. . . .

If the minds of our youth, as well as those of more mature age, were directed aright when associated together, their conversation would be upon exalted themes. When the mind is pure, and the thoughts elevated by the truth of God, the words will be of the same character, "like apples of gold in pictures of silver" (Proverbs 25:11). But with the present understanding, with the present practices, with the low standard which even Christians are content to reach, the conversation is cheap and profitless. It is "of the earth, earthy" (1 Corinthians 15:47), and savors not of the truth, or of heaven, and does not come up, even to the standard of the more cultured class of worldlings. When Christ and heaven are the themes of contemplation, the conversation will give evidence of the fact. The speech will be seasoned with grace, and the speaker will show that he has been obtaining an education in the school of the divine Teacher.[61]

[Psalm 119:27 quoted.] This is the light in which we may regard the law of the Lord. Instead of giving the impression that the yoke of Christ is grievous, we may demonstrate the truthfulness of the words, "My yoke is easy, and My burden is light" (Matthew 11:30).

Satan has arranged matters to suit himself. He has declared the religious life to be a life of exaction, of galling sacrifice. Shall we not strive to counteract this by revealing Christ as He is—a compassionate Redeemer, who is constantly saying, "Come unto Me, all ye that labour and are heavy laden, and I will give you rest" (Verse 28). Show the world that you keep the commandments of God because it is for your happiness to do so, even in this life.[62]

# The Joy of Uttering Praise

*"All thy works shall praise thee, O Lord; and thy saints shall bless thee. They shall speak of the glory of thy kingdom, and talk of thy power" (Psalm 145:10, 11).*

If the brethren and sisters were in the place they should be, they would not be at a loss to find something to say in honor of Jesus, who hung upon Calvary's cross for their sins. If they would cherish more of a realizing sense of the condescension of God in giving His only beloved Son to die a sacrifice for our sins and transgressions, and the sufferings and anguish of Jesus to make a way of escape for guilty man, that he might receive pardon and live, they would be more ready to extol and magnify Jesus. They could not hold their peace, but with thankfulness and gratitude would talk of His glory, and tell of His power. And blessings from God would rest upon them by so doing. Even if the same story were repeated, God would be glorified. The angel showed me those who ceased not day nor night, crying, "Holy, Holy, Lord God Almighty." "Continued repetition," said the angel, "yet God is glorified by it." Although we may tell the same story over and over, it honors God, and shows that we are not unmindful of him and His goodness and mercies to us.

I saw that the nominal churches have fallen; that coldness and death reigns in their midst. If they would follow the Word of God, it would humble them. But they get above the work of the Lord. It is too humiliating for them to repeat the same simple story of God's goodness when they meet together, and they study to get something new, something great, and to have their words exact to the ear and pleasing man, and God's Spirit leaves them. When we follow the humble Bible way, we shall have the movings of the Spirit of God. All will be in sweet harmony if we follow the humble channel of truth, depending wholly upon God, and there will be no danger of being affected by the evil angels. It is when souls get above the Spirit of God, moving in their own strength, that the angels cease watching over them, and they are left to the buffetings of Satan.[63]

# Addressing Kings

*"Beware of men: for they will deliver you up to the councils, and they will scourge you in their synagogues; and ye shall be brought before governors and kings for my sake, for a testimony against them and the Gentiles. But when they deliver you up, take no thought how or what ye shall speak: for it shall be given you in that same hour what ye shall speak. For it is not ye that speak, but the Spirit of your Father which speaketh in you" (Matthew 10:17–20).*

In the days of Paul the gospel for which he was imprisoned was thus brought before the princes and nobles of the imperial city. So on this occasion [at the Diet at Augsburg], that which the emperor had forbidden to be preached from the pulpit was proclaimed from the palace; what many had regarded as unfit even for servants to listen to was heard with wonder by the masters and lords of the empire. Kings and great men were the auditory, crowned princes were the preachers, and the sermon was the royal truth of God. "Since the apostolic age," says a writer, "there has never been a greater work or a more magnificent confession."[64]

The servants of Christ are to prepare no set speech to present when brought to trial for their faith. Their preparation is to be made day by day, in treasuring up in their hearts the precious truths of God's Word, in feeding upon the teaching of Christ, and through prayer strengthening their faith; then, when brought into trial, the Holy Spirit will bring to their remembrance the very truths that will reach the hearts of those who shall come to hear.

God will flash the knowledge obtained by diligent searching of the Scriptures into their memory at the very time when it is needed. But if they neglect to fill their minds with the gems of truth, if they do not acquaint themselves with the words of Christ, if they have never tasted the power of His grace in trial, then they cannot expect that the Holy Spirit will bring His words to their remembrance. They are to serve God daily with their undivided affections, and then trust Him.[65]

# The Witness of Children

*"Lo, children are an heritage of the Lord: and the fruit of the womb is his reward. . . . [The children] shall not be ashamed, but they shall speak with the enemies in the gate" (Psalm 127:3, 5).*

In many places where the power of the clergy was exercised to prevent the preaching of the Advent truth, the Lord was pleased to send the message through little children. As they were under age, the law of the State could not restrain them, and they were permitted to speak freely and unmolested. Thus the warning of the soon-coming Judgment was given to the people. This continued about nine months. After that, the influence upon the children was declared by the authorities to be a disease, and some of them were taken to the hospitals; but their mouths were not stopped; for they preached as long as God chose to use them as witnesses. . . .

An eyewitness, speaking of the work accomplished through these children, says: "People went in masses to the places where these child-preachers were, who were mostly poor cottagers. A little girl began preaching but a few miles from the place were I lived, and as the news of the wonderful movement was noised about, I went with my wife to see and hear for myself. When we arrived at the cottage, it was filled with people. The child, who was six or eight years old, moved around among them, and they asked her questions, which she answered as a child usually does. The people flocked together, till the house was surrounded by a great number. When the last had arrived, her manner changed entirely, both in boldness and movements, clearly indicating that she was moved by an invisible power, and not by her own natural gifts. When she commenced speaking, her voice also changed. She said, "Fear God, and give glory to him; for the hour of his Judgment is come" (Revelation 14:7). She reproved sins, such as drinking, theft, adultery, swearing, and backbiting, and also reproved churchgoers for attending church with worldly business in view, instead of listening to God's word and conforming their lives to it. Her voice and words were impressive. Many were weeping and sighing. They were told that time was given them to repent, but they must do it immediately, and not put it off.[66]

# Living What We Speak

*"My little children, let us not love in word, neither in tongue; but in deed and in truth" (1 John 3:18).*

We need to offer praise and thanksgiving to God, not only in the congregation, but in the home life. Let the voices of His heritage be heard recounting the works of the Lord. Speak of His goodness, tell of His power. Whom have I in heaven but Thee? And there is none upon the earth that I desire but Thee. We need more songs of praise and less murmuring and complaining.[67]

God requires heart service. A service of form, lip service, is wholly inefficient in the work of converting souls to God. A service that comes not from the heart is as sounding brass and a tinkling cymbal. The heart must be stirred with the cooperative energy of the Holy Spirit.[68]

Human wisdom, familiarity with the languages of different nations, is a help in the missionary work. An understanding of the customs of the people, of the location and time of events, is practical knowledge; for it aids in making the figures of the Bible clear, in bringing out the force of Christ's lessons; but it is not positively necessary to know these things. The wayfaring man may find the pathway cast up for the ransomed to walk in, and there will be no excuse found for anyone who perishes through misapprehension of the Scriptures. In the Bible every vital principle is declared, every duty made plain, every obligation made evident.[69]

The requirements of God are plainly set before us in His Word, and there are also presented before us great and precious promises. The question to be settled is, "Are we willing to separate ourselves from the world, that we may become children of God?" This is not the work of a moment, or of a day; it is not accomplished by bowing at the family altar, and there offering up lip service. It cannot be accomplished by merely uniting in the services of the prayer meeting. It is a lifelong work. Love to God must be a living principle, underlying every act and word and thought.[70]

Talk is cheap stuff; it does not cost much. Works, fruits, will determine the character of the tree. What fruits have you borne?[71]

# No Guile

*"And I looked, and, lo, a Lamb stood on the mount Sion, and with him an hundred forty and four thousand, having his Father's name written in their foreheads. . . . And in their mouth was found no guile" (Revelation 14:1, 5).*

It is not the ready speaker, the sharp intellect, that counts with God. It is the earnest purpose, the deep piety, the love of truth, the fear of God, that has a telling influence. A testimony from the heart, coming from lips in which is no guile, full of faith and humble trust, though given by a stammering tongue, is accounted of God as precious as gold; while the smart speech, the eloquent oratory, of the one to whom is entrusted large talents, but who is wanting in truthfulness, in steadfast purpose, in purity, in unselfishness, are as sounding brass and a tinkling cymbal. He may say witty things, he may relate amusing anecdotes, he may play upon the feelings; but the spirit of Jesus is not in it. All these things may please unsanctified hearts, but God holds in His hands the balances that weigh the words, the spirit, the sincerity, the devotion, and He pronounces it altogether lighter than vanity.[72]

Those who have learned of Christ will "have no fellowship with the unfruitful works of darkness" (Ephesians 5:11). In speech, as in life, they will be simple, straightforward, and true, for they are preparing for the fellowship of those holy ones in whose mouth "was found no guile" (Revelation 14:5).[73]

If you have prevaricated, if you have borne false witness, if you have misjudged and misinterpreted your brother, if you have misstated his words, ridiculed him, if you have injured his influence in any way, go right to the persons with whom you have conversed about him, with whom you have united in this work, and take all your injurious misstatements back. Confess the wrong that you have done your brother; for your sin will stand charged against you in the books of record until you do all that lies in your power to correct the evil your words have wrought. When you have done all that God requires of you, pardon will be written against your name.[74]

# A Pure Language

*"Wait ye upon me, saith the Lord, until the day that I rise up to the prey: for my determination is to gather the nations, that I may assemble the kingdoms, to pour upon them mine indignation, even all my fierce anger: for all the earth shall be devoured with the fire of my jealousy. For then will I turn to the people a pure language, that they may all call upon the name of the Lord, to serve him with one consent"* (Zephaniah 3:8, 9).

Our speech should be without deception. No guile must be found in our lips, no impurity allowed in our hearts, no unkindliness in our speech or in our attitude toward one another. Learn the language of Canaan here, which will be in harmony with the language of heaven.[75]

We are not to cultivate the language of the earthy, and be so familiar with the conversation of men, that the language of Canaan will be new and unfamiliar to us. We are to learn in the school of Christ.[76]

Educate yourselves to speak in the language of Canaan, the language spoken in the heavenly school by the members of the royal family. Sternly determine to put away all foolish talking and jesting, all selfish amusements. By faith grasp God's promises, and determine that you will be Christians here below, while preparing for translation.[77]

The word of God, spoken by one who is himself sanctified through it, has a life-giving power that makes it attractive to the hearers, and convicts them that it is a living reality. When one has received the truth in the love of it, he will make this manifest in the persuasion of his manner and the tones of his voice. He makes known that which he himself has heard, seen, and handled of the word of life, that others may have fellowship with him through the knowledge of Christ. His testimony, from lips touched with a live coal from off the altar, is truth to the receptive heart, and works sanctification upon the character. And he who seeks to give light to others will himself be blessed.[78]

# The Goal of the Gifts

*"[The Lord] gave some, apostles; and some, prophets; and some, evangelists; and some, pastors and teachers; for the perfecting of the saints" (Ephesians 4:11, 12).*

God has set in the church different gifts. These are all precious in their place, and all are to act a part in the perfecting of the saints.

This is God's order, and men must labor according to His rules and arrangements if they would meet with success. God will accept only those efforts that are made willingly and with humble hearts, without the trait of personal feelings or selfishness.[1]

In the beginning God created man in His own likeness. He endowed him with noble qualities. His mind was well balanced, and all the powers of his being were harmonious. But the Fall and its effects have perverted these gifts. Sin has marred and well-nigh obliterated the image of God in man. It was to restore this that the plan of salvation was devised, and a life of probation was granted to man. To bring him back to the perfection in which he was first created is the great object of life—the object that underlies every other. . . .

All the varied capabilities that men possess—of mind and soul and body—are given them by God, to be so employed as to reach the highest possible degree of excellence. But this cannot be a selfish and exclusive culture; for the character of God, whose likeness we are to receive, is benevolence and love. Every faculty, every attribute, with which the Creator has endowed us is to be employed for His glory and for the uplifting of our fellow men. And in this employment is found its purest, noblest, and happiest exercise.[2]

Every faithful worker will minister for the perfecting of the saints. All who have been benefited by the labors of God's servant, should, according to their ability, unite with him in working for the salvation of souls. This is the work of all true believers, ministers, and people. They should keep the grand object ever in view, each seeking to fill his proper position in the church, and all working together in order, harmony, and love.

There is nothing selfish or narrow in the religion of Christ.[3]

# A Place for Every Member

*"[The Lord] gave some, apostles; and some, prophets; and some, evangelists; and some, pastors and teachers; . . . for the work of the ministry" (Ephesians 4:11, 12).*

From the light that God has given me, I know that His cause today is in great need of the living representative of Bible truth. The ordained ministers, alone, are not equal to the task. God is calling not only upon the ministers, but also upon physicians, nurses, canvassers, Bible workers, and other consecrated laymen of varied talent who have a knowledge of present truth, to consider the needs of the unwarned cities. There should be one hundred believers actively engaged in personal missionary work where now there is but one. Time is rapidly passing. There is much work to be done before satanic opposition shall close up the way. Every agency must be set in operation, that present opportunities may be wisely improved.[4]

The Lord has given to the lay members as well as to the ministers their gift of reason and intelligence, their share of qualification for his work; and for the use of these talents, each one is responsible. God requires of all wholehearted devotion to His work. . . .

There are souls in the church, who though humble in their endowments and acquirements, are still imbued with the Spirit of the Master, and they are ready to sacrifice life itself should it be required of them. These men cannot be placed upon a salary, but they can be educated so that they can do work for the Master in their limited way. It is the duty of the ministers to see that such men are utilized; for while the Lord has a work for men to do in the sacred desk, this is not the whole of his work. When the church is in need of personal labor, then it is the minister's most essential duty to help the souls for whom he is to watch, as one who must give an account. The minister of the gospel should be an educator, that he may impress upon those for whom he labors, their responsibility to labor for others. He should prayerfully and lovingly help every member of the church to find his place in the work of God, that there may be laborers in the fields that are already white for the harvest.[5]

# Building Up the Body of Christ

*"[The Lord] gave some, apostles; and some, prophets; and some, evangelists; and some, pastors and teachers; . . . for the edifying of the body of Christ" (Ephesians 4:11, 12).*

When consecrated believers assemble, their conversation will not be upon the imperfections of others or savor of murmuring or complaint; charity, or love, the bond of perfectness, will encircle them. Love to God and their fellowmen flows out naturally in words of affection, sympathy, and esteem for their brethren. The peace of God rules in their hearts; their words are not vain, empty, and frivolous, but to the comfort and edification of one another.[6]

The religion of Jesus Christ means progress; it means to be ever reaching upward to a holier and higher standard. The Christian whose heart has been touched with the beauty of the Saviour's character, is to put into practice that which he learns in the school of Christ. We must be apt pupils in the school of Christ, readily learning that which he teaches us from day to day.

The talents which God has given us we are to employ to His honor and glory. The Lord has given us reason and intelligence, and He expects us to use them in the right direction. Thus we shall increase them; for a higher power than that of man's alone works in us to will and to do of God's good pleasure. The ability which we possess is not of our own creating. The apostle asks, "Who maketh thee to differ from another? and what hast thou that thou didst not receive? now if thou didst receive it, why dost thou glory, as if thou hadst not received it?" (1 Corinthians 4:7). Our talents belong to God, and to Him we should render them in joyful service, becoming workmen that need not be ashamed.[7]

Study the effect of your words, whether their influence will be saving upon others. Never talk for the sake of talking, but for the edification of those who hear.[8]

Whatever God has written is for the instruction of all. That which He saw essential to inspire holy men to write is for your edification. Only practice the words of truth, and you are safe; you will be God's light bearers to the world.[9]

# The Unity of the Faith

*"[The Lord] gave some, apostles; and some, prophets; and some, evangelists; and some, pastors and teachers; . . . till we all come in the unity of the faith" (Ephesians 4:11, 13).*

Why are many of us so weak and inefficient? It is because we look to self, studying our own temperaments and wondering how we can make a place for ourselves, our individuality, and our peculiarities, in the place of studying Christ and His character.

Brethren who could work together in harmony if they would learn of Christ, forgetting that they are Americans or Europeans, Germans or Frenchmen, Swedes, Danes, or Norwegians, seem to feel that if they should blend with those of other nationalities, something of that which is peculiar to their own country and nation would be lost and something else would take its place.

My brethren, let us put all this aside. We have no right to keep our minds stayed on ourselves, our preferences, and our fancies. We are not to seek to maintain a peculiar identity of our own, a personality, an individuality, which will separate us from our fellow laborers. We have a character to maintain, but it is the character of Christ. Having the character of Christ, we can carry on the work of God together. The Christ in us will meet the Christ in our brethren, and the Holy Spirit will give that union of heart and action which testifies to the world that we are children of God. May the Lord help us to die to self and be born again, that Christ may live in us, a living, active principle, a power that will keep us holy.

Strive earnestly for unity. Pray for it, work for it. It will bring spiritual health, elevation of thought, nobility of character, heavenly-mindedness, enabling you to overcome selfishness and evil surmisings, and to be more than conquerors through Him that loved you and gave Himself for you. Crucify self; esteem others better than yourselves. Thus you will be brought into oneness with Christ. Before the heavenly universe, and before the church and the world, you will bear unmistakable evidence that you are God's sons and daughters. God will be glorified in the example that you set.[10]

# Reflecting Christ Unto Perfection

*"[The Lord] gave some, apostles; and some, prophets; and some, evangelists; and some, pastors and teachers; . . . till we all come in . . . the knowledge of the Son of God, unto a perfect man, unto the measure of the stature of the fulness of Christ" (Ephesians 4:11, 13).*

Look at the cross of Calvary. It is a standing pledge of the boundless love, the measureless mercy, of the heavenly Father. O that all might repent and do their first works. When the churches do this, they will love God supremely and their neighbors as themselves. Ephraim will not envy Judah, and Judah will not vex Ephraim. Divisions will then be healed, the harsh sounds of strife will no more be heard in the borders of Israel. Through the grace freely given them of God, all will seek to answer the prayer of Christ, that His disciples should be one, even as He and the Father are one. Peace, love, mercy, and benevolence will be the abiding principles of the soul. The love of Christ will be the theme of every tongue, and it will no more be said by the true Witness, "I have somewhat against thee, because thou hast left thy first love" (Revelation 2:4). The people of God will be abiding in Christ, the love of Jesus will be revealed, and one Spirit will animate all hearts, regenerating and renewing all in the image of Christ, fashioning all hearts alike. As living branches of the true Vine, all will be united to Christ, the living head. Christ will abide in every heart, guiding, comforting, sanctifying, and presenting to the world the unity of the followers of Jesus, thus bearing testimony that the heavenly credentials are supplied to the remnant church. In the oneness of Christ's church it will be proved that God sent His only begotten Son into the world.

When God's people are one in the unity of the Spirit, all of Phariseeism, all of self-righteousness, which was the sin of the Jewish nation, will be expelled from all hearts. The mold of Christ will be upon each individual member of His body, and His people will be new bottles into which He can pour His new wine, and the new wine will not break the bottles.[11]

# Many Talents, One Truth

*"Now there are diversities of gifts, but the same Spirit. And there are differences of administrations, but the same Lord. And there are diversities of operations, but it is the same God which worketh all in all" (1 Corinthians 12:4–6).*

In all the Lord's arrangements, there is nothing more beautiful than His plan of giving to men and women a diversity of gifts. The church is His garden, adorned with a variety of trees, plants, and flowers. He does not expect the hyssop to assume the proportions of the cedar, nor the olive to reach the height of the stately palm. Many have received but a limited religious and intellectual training, but God has a work for this class to do if they will labor in humility, trusting in Him.

God has different ways of working, and He has different workmen to whom He entrusts varied gifts. One worker may be a ready speaker; another a ready writer; another may have the gift of sincere, earnest, fervent prayer; another the gift of singing; another may have special skill in explaining the Word of God with clearness. And each gift is to become a power for God, because He works with the laborer. To one God gives the word of wisdom, to another knowledge; but all are to work under the same Head. The diversity of gifts leads to a diversity of operations; but "it is the same God which worketh all in all" (1 Corinthians 12:6).[12]

God is leading a people out from the world upon the exalted platform of eternal truth, the commandments of God and the faith of Jesus. He will discipline and fit up His people. They will not be at variance, one believing one thing, and another having faith and views entirely opposite, each moving independently of the body. Through the diversity of the gifts and governments that He has placed in the church, they will all come to the unity of the faith. . . .

God is leading out a people and establishing them upon the one great platform of faith, the commandments of God and the testimony of Jesus. He has given His people a straight chain of Bible truth, clear and connected. This truth is of heavenly origin and has been searched for as for hidden treasure.[13]

# United in Action

*"As the body is one, and hath many members, and all the members of that one body, being many, are one body: so also is Christ" (1 Corinthians 12:12).*

Those who have taken upon themselves to carry a measuring line that they may measure everybody and say how things shall go, may now be excused from this responsibility.

The cross of Calvary is to be uplifted, and all who will be engaged in drawing the people to the cross, enlarging the circumference of the circle of believers more and more, will have Christ, the power of salvation. Zeal for the glory of God is to be revealed. Let all understand that we are to get rid of every root of bitterness, and through the Holy Spirit's guidance have a sanctified zeal for the saving of souls who are ready to perish.[14]

If our workers had been baptized with the Spirit of Christ, they would have done fifty times more than they have done to train men for laborers. Though one or two, or even many, have not borne the test, we should not cease our efforts; for this work must be done for Christ. The Saviour was disappointed; because of the perversity of human hearts, His efforts were not rewarded with success; but He kept at the work, and so must we. If we had toiled with fidelity, patience, and love, we should have had one hundred workers where there is one. Unimproved opportunities are written against us in the same book that bears the record of envy and rebellion against God. Years have been lost to us in our foreign missions. There have been a few earnest workers; but to a great extent their energies have been employed in keeping men who profess the truth from making shipwreck of faith. Had these men who required so much help to keep them propped up, been working for the salvation of their fellow-men, they would have forgotten their trials, and would have become strong in helping others. We are able to achieve vastly more than we have done, if we will call to our aid all whom we can. . . .

The plan of holding Bible readings was a heaven-borne idea. There are many, both men and women, who can engage in this branch of missionary labor.[15]

# Drinking Into One Spirit

*"By one Spirit are we all baptized into one body, whether we be Jews or Gentiles, whether we be bond or free; and have been all made to drink into one Spirit. . . . If the whole body were an eye, where were the hearing? If the whole were hearing, where were the smelling? But now hath God set the members every one of them in the body, as it hath pleased him" (1 Corinthians 12:13, 17, 18).*

Day by day the soul needs the religion of Christ. Those who drink deeply of His Spirit will not be ambitious for themselves. They will realize that they cannot go beyond the domain of God, for God reigns everywhere.[16]

God has entrusted different gifts to the different members of His body. He has given them such talents and opportunities as will best promote the advancement of His kingdom. In their different lines of work, they have one Head. The same Spirit works through them.[17]

Many more of the lay members, if consecrated to God's service, could give the warning message of mercy to the multitudes who are not acquainted with the truth for this time. All around us there are souls perishing in sin. Every day there is something to do for the Master.

Every Christian is to let his light shine forth in good works. His words are to magnify our Lord Jesus Christ. Instead of waiting for great opportunities before doing anything, he is to do the work lying nearest him. Thus he will increase his talents and gain a preparation for wider service. Wherever he is, there is his field in which he is earnestly to show forth in word and deed the saving power of truth. He is not to wait to see what others do. He has a personality of his own, and he is responsible to Christ, whose servant he is, for every word and act.[18]

All who are followers of Christ . . . will enter into His travail for the saving of the lost. They share in the sufferings of Christ, and they will share also in the glory that shall be revealed. One with Him in His work, drinking with Him the cup of sorrow, they are partakers also of His joy.[19]

# Branches of One Body

*"If [the church] were all one member, where were the body? But now are they many members, yet but one body" (1 Corinthians 12:19, 20).*

The world needs to see worked out before it the miracle that binds the hearts of God's people together in Christian love.[20]

The gospel ministry is needed to give permanence and stability to the medical missionary work; and the ministry needs the medical missionary work to demonstrate the practical working of the gospel. Neither part of the work is complete without the other.

The message of the soon coming of the Saviour must be given in all parts of the world, and a solemn dignity should characterize it in every branch. A large vineyard is to be worked, and the wise husbandman will work it so that every part will produce fruit. . . . If those who bear the heavy burdens will stand true and steadfast to the principles of truth, the Lord will uphold and sustain them.

The union that should exist between the medical missionary work and the ministry is clearly set forth in the fifty-eighth chapter of Isaiah. There is wisdom and blessing for those who will engage in the work as here presented. This chapter is explicit, and there is in it enough to enlighten anyone who wishes to do the will of God. It presents abundant opportunity to minister to suffering humanity, and at the same time to be an instrument in God's hands of bringing the light of truth before a perishing world. If the work of the third angel's message is carried on in right lines, the ministry will not be given an inferior place, nor will the poor and sick be neglected. In His word God has united these two lines of work, and no man should divorce them.[21]

We have enlisted in the army of the Lord, and we are not to fight on the enemy's side, but on the side of Christ, where we can be a united whole, in sentiment, in action, in spirit, in fellowship. Those who are Christians indeed will be branches of the true vine, and will bear the same fruit as the vine. They will act in harmony, in Christian fellowship.[22]

# No Schism in the Body

*"The eye cannot say unto the hand, I have no need of thee: nor again the head to the feet, I have no need of you. Nay, much more those members of the body, which seem to be more feeble, are necessary: and those members of the body, which we think to be less honourable, upon these we bestow more abundant honour; and our uncomely parts have more abundant comeliness. For our comely parts have no need: but God hath tempered the body together, having given more abundant honour to that part which lacked: that there should be no schism in the body; but that the members should have the same care one for another"* (1 Corinthians 12:21–25).

The Lord desires His church to respect every gift that He has bestowed on the different members. Let us beware of allowing our minds to become fixed on ourselves, thinking that no one can be serving the Lord unless he is working on the same lines as those on which we are working.

Never is a worker to say, "I do not want to work with such a one, because he does not see things as I do. I wish to work with some one who will agree with all I say, and follow out all my ideas." The one the worker thus refuses to connect with may have truths to present that have not yet been presented. Because of the worker's refusal to accept the help provided by the Lord, the work is made one-sided.

The work is hurt unless there are brought into it all the gifts that God has bestowed. Many times the progress of the work has been hindered because the laborers thought their gifts all that were necessary for its advancement. The Lord has not done for His people what He would have done if so many of the workers had not limited the development of the work by refusing to cooperate with laborers who should have been given standing room and encouragement. In self-sufficiency, men have ignored and pushed aside those to whom God has given a special work. . . .

No one is to disparage another's gifts. No one is to suppose that he is the only one who can bring truth from the treasure house of God.[23]

# A United Whole

*"Whether one member suffer, all the members suffer with it; or one member be honoured, all the members rejoice with it. Now ye are the body of Christ, and members in particular" (1 Corinthians 12:26, 27).*

Let us not think that our churches can enjoy God's blessing while in a state of disunion. In this world we are to be representatives of Christ. He has called us to glory and virtue. As He represented the Father, so we are to represent Christ to the world, for in representing Him we are representing the Father, who is in every place to help where help is needed.

We have a great work to perform for the Master. After Jesus has sacrificed so much in our behalf, giving His life for our salvation, shall we by our course of action make Him ashamed of us?[24]

Every church member should feel an interest in all that concerns the human brotherhood and the brotherhood in Christ.[25]

Love for one another is not to be manifested by praise and by flattery of one another, but by true fidelity. The love of Christ will lead us to watch for souls, and if we see one in danger, we will tell him so, plainly and kindly, even at the risk of his displeasure. The religion of Christ is not to be controlled by impulse. We need to pray much and lean wholly upon God. We need to hold the truth with firmness, and in all righteousness and truth; but while we speak the truth with fidelity, we should speak it in love.[26]

Strive earnestly for unity. Pray for it, work it. It will bring spiritual health, elevation of thought, nobility, heavenly mindedness. You will overcome selfishness and evil surmising, and will be more than conquerors through Him that loved you and gave Himself for you. Crucify self. Esteem others better than yourselves. Thus you will be brought into oneness with Christ.[27]

Those who have come together in church capacity can do one hundredfold more than they are now doing to let their light shine forth in the world. They are to come out from the world and to be separate, and to touch not the unclean, but to set their affections on things that are above. They are to live, not to please themselves, but to follow the example of Him who died for their redemption.[28]

# Zealous of Gifts to Do Good

*"Forasmuch as ye are zealous of spiritual gifts, seek that ye may excel to the edifying of the church" (1 Corinthians 14:12).*

There is a great work to be done. The world will not be converted by the gift of tongues, or by the working of miracles, but by preaching Christ crucified. The Holy Spirit must be allowed to work. God has placed instrumentalities in our hands, and we must use every one of them to do His will and way. As believers we are privileged to act a part in forwarding the truth for this time. As far as possible we are to employ the means and agencies that God has given us to introduce the truth into new localities.[29]

There is much talking, much professed love for perishing souls; but talk is cheap stuff. It is earnest Christian zeal that is wanted—a zeal that will be manifested by doing something. All must now work for themselves, and when they have Jesus in their hearts they will confess Him to others. No more could a soul who possesses Christ be hindered from confessing Him than could the waters of Niagara be stopped from flowing over the falls.[30]

Christ has given to the church a sacred charge. Every member should be a channel through which God can communicate to the world the treasures of His grace, the unsearchable riches of Christ. There is nothing that the Saviour desires so much as agents who will represent to the world His Spirit and His character. There is nothing that the world needs so much as the manifestation through humanity of the Saviour's love. All heaven is waiting for men and women through whom God can reveal the power of Christianity.

The church is God's agency for the proclamation of truth, empowered by Him to do a special work; and if she is loyal to Him, obedient to all His commandments, there will dwell within her the excellency of divine grace. If she will be true to her allegiance, if she will honor the Lord God of Israel, there is no power that can stand against her.

Zeal for God and His cause moved the disciples to bear witness to the gospel with mighty power. Should not a like zeal fire our hearts with a determination to tell the story of redeeming love, of Christ and Him crucified?[31]

# A More Excellent Way

*"Covet earnestly the best gifts: and yet shew I unto you a more excellent way. Though I speak with the tongues of men and of angels, and have not charity, I am become as sounding brass, or a tinkling cymbal. And though I have the gift of prophecy, and understand all mysteries, and all knowledge; and though I have all faith, so that I could remove mountains, and have not charity, I am nothing"* (1 Corinthians 12:31–13:1, 2).

In the judgment the use made of every talent will be scrutinized. How have we employed the capital lent us of Heaven? Will the Lord at His coming receive His own with usury? Have we improved the powers entrusted us, in hand and heart and brain, to the glory of God and the blessing of the world? How have we used our time, our pen, our voice, our money, our influence? What have we done for Christ, in the person of the poor, the afflicted, the orphan, or the widow? God has made us the depositaries of His holy word; what have we done with the light and truth given us to make men wise unto salvation? No value is attached to a mere profession of faith in Christ; only the love which is shown by works is counted genuine. Yet it is love alone which in the sight of Heaven makes any act of value. Whatever is done from love, however small it may appear in the estimation of men, is accepted and rewarded of God.[32]

In view of what Christ has done for us, and what He has suffered for sinners, we should, out of pure, disinterested love for souls, imitate His example by sacrificing our own pleasure and convenience for their good. . . . Love, true love for our fellow men, evinces love to God. We may make a high profession, yet without this love it is nothing.[33]

You love the truth and are anxious for its advancement. You will be placed in various circumstances in order to try and prove you. You may develop a true Christian character if you will submit yourself to discipline. Your vital interests are at stake. What you most need is true holiness and a spirit of self-sacrifice. We may obtain a knowledge of the truth and read its most hidden mysteries, and even give our bodies to be burned for its sake; yet if we have not love and charity, we are as sounding brass and a tinkling cymbal.[34]

# Outwitting the Enemy's Strategy

*"That we henceforth be no more children, tossed to and fro, and carried about with every wind of doctrine, by the sleight of men, and cunning craftiness, whereby they lie in wait to deceive" (Ephesians 4:14).*

The great enemy of the church is determined to introduce among God's people that which will result in disunion and variance. Schism and division are not the fruit of righteousness; they are of the evil one. The great hindrance to our advancement is the selfishness that prevents believers from having true fellowship with one another.[35]

[Satan] controls the minds of unconsecrated Sabbathkeepers, and leads them to be jealous of one another, faultfinding, and censorious. It is his special work to divide hearts that the influence, strength, and labor of God's servants may be kept among unconsecrated Sabbathkeepers and their precious time be occupied in settling little differences when it should be spent in proclaiming the truth to unbelievers.[36]

If the love of Christ is in the hearts of the members of the church, through the abundant grace of Christ, there will be oneness, unity, among brethren. We must close the door of the heart to every suggestion that shall have the least tendency toward keeping us from this state of harmony. We must not hamper the soul and cripple its powers by the indulgence of selfishness. Selfishness is sin, and it grieves away the Spirit of Christ. When we cherish unkind thoughts, and harbor suspicions against our brethren, we are cutting ourselves off from the channel of God's light and love. . . . Those who keep the truth will be found faithful to God and to one another.[37]

I was shown God's people waiting for some change to take place—a compelling power to take hold of them. But they will be disappointed, for they are wrong. They must act, they must take hold of the work themselves and earnestly cry to God for a true knowledge of themselves. The scenes which are passing before us are of sufficient magnitude to cause us to arouse and urge the truth home to the hearts of all who will listen. The harvest of the earth is nearly ripe.[38]

# A Unit Edified by Love

*"Speaking the truth in love, [we] may grow up into him in all things, which is the head, even Christ: From whom the whole body fitly joined together and compacted by that which every joint supplieth, according to the effectual working in the measure of every part, maketh increase of the body unto the edifying of itself in love" (Ephesians 4:15, 16).*

Oh, how much the workers need the spirit of Jesus to change and fashion them as clay is molded in the hands of the potter! When they have this spirit, there will be no spirit of variance among them; no one will be so narrow as to want everything done his way, according to his ideas; there will be no inharmonious feeling between him and his brother laborers who do not come up to his standard. The Lord does not want any of His children to be shadows of others; but He would have each one be his own simple self, refined, sanctified, ennobled by imitating the life and character of the great Pattern.[39]

A living church is a working church. The precious light of Bible truth, like a lamp that burneth, is to shine forth from every church member. The precious light of Bible truth, like a lamp that burneth, is to shine forth from every church member. God will use His believing ones as His instrumentalities; through them He will minister to souls fainting for the bread of life. Words of hope and cheer falling from lips that have been touched with a live coal from God's altar will revive and comfort those who are weary and distressed.

Time is precious. The destiny of souls is in the balance. At infinite cost a way of salvation has been provided. Shall Christ's great sacrifice be in vain? Shall the earth be entirely controlled by Satanic agencies? The salvation of souls is dependent upon the consecration and activity of God's church. The Lord calls all who believe in Him to be workers together with Him. While their life shall last, they are not to feel their work is done. Until the time comes when Christ shall say, "It is finished," His work for the saving of souls is not to decrease, but is to grow in extent and importance.[40]

# Not Just to Please Ourselves

*"We then that are strong ought to bear the infirmities of the weak, and not to please ourselves. Let every one of us please his neighbour for his good to edification" (Romans 15:1, 2).*

The efficiency that the Lord designs to see in His people has been sadly lacking in the church. How can we account for this? Have those who profess the name of Christ been truly converted? Have they consecrated to God their reason, their knowledge, their affections, their thoughts? Have they employed their talents of means and ability in the service of the Master? or have they devoted all their energies of mind and body to the building up of worldly enterprises? Jesus says to those who would be His disciples, "If any man will come after me, let him deny himself, and take up his cross, and follow me. For whosoever will save his life shall lose it; and whosoever will lose his life for my sake, shall find it" (Matthew 16:24, 25). He who is a child of God henceforth should look upon himself as a part of the cross of Christ, a link in the chain let down to save the world, one with Christ in His plan of mercy, going forth with Him to seek and save the lost. He is ever to realize that he has consecrated himself to God, and that in character he is to reveal Christ to the world. The self-denial, the self-sacrifice, the sympathy, the love that was manifested in the life of Christ, is to reappear in the life of the worker for God. Those who are laborers together with God will feel the need of wrestling in prayer for the endowment of the Holy Spirit. They will manifest the most tender solicitude for the erring, make most earnest appeals to those who are out of Christ, and will bear much fruit to the glory of God, and will be known as the disciples of Christ.[41]

Christian zeal will not exhaust itself in talk, but will feel and act with vigor and efficiency. Yet Christian zeal will not act for the sake of being seen. Humility will characterize every effort and be seen in every work. . . .

May the Lord open your eyes to see and your heart to feel, and cause you to manifest Christian zeal. Oh, how few feel the worth of souls! How few are willing to sacrifice to bring souls to the knowledge of Christ![42]

# Good and Pleasant Dwelling

*"Behold, how good and how pleasant it is for brethren to dwell together in unity!" (Psalm 133:1).*

The last prayer that Christ offered for His disciples before His trial was that they might be one in Him. Satan is determined that this oneness shall not be, for it is the strongest witness that can be borne that God gave His Son to reconcile the world to heaven. But the union for which Christ prayed must exist among God's people before He can bestow on the church the enlargement and power that He longs to bestow on it.

Unity should be recognized as the element of preservation in the church. Those who are united in church capacity have entered into a solemn covenant with God to obey His word, and to unite in an effort to strengthen the faith of one another. They are to be one in Him, even though they are scattered the world over. This is God's purpose concerning them, and the heart of the Saviour is set upon His followers fulfilling this purpose. But God cannot make them one with Christ and with one another unless they are willing to give up their way for His way.[43]

Brethren, when you humble your hearts before God, you will see that there is danger of Phariseeism in every church, danger of thinking and praying as did the self-righteous pharisee: "I thank God that I am not as other men are." Oh, that there may be a breaking up of the fallow ground of the heart, that the seeds of truth may take deep root and spring up and bear much fruit to the glory of God! My brethren, when you would accuse one of the brethren, consider the words of Jesus, "He that is without sin among you, let him first cast a stone" (John 8:7). Your sin may not be the particular sin that is under consideration, but Jesus' words mean that when you are free from sin you may cast the first stone. When Jesus spoke these words to the accusers, their guilty consciences were aroused. They could not answer Him; they were convicted each in his own conscience, and they went out one by one, beginning at the oldest even to the youngest.[44]

# Being Made Perfect in One

*"That they all may be one; as thou, Father, art in me, and I in thee, that they also may be one in us: that the world may believe that thou hast sent me. . . . I in them, and thou in me, that they may be made perfect in one" (John 17:21, 23).*

[In the prayer of John 17, Jesus Christ] is speaking of the oneness and that unity that shall exist with Christ and His disciples. In that unity, in that oneness, Christ is glorified in us. Now I would have you consider how very light a matter many of us make of seeking to preserve this unity. Why, this unity with believers in and through Christ is the great strength of the church! The oneness, the love which through their faith and unity exists with God's people through faith in Christ, is a power.

How earnest, how decided, how determined should be our efforts to answer the prayer of Christ that we may have that harmony one with another for which Christ died to perfect; that we may be one with Christ; for, unless we are constantly laboring for this harmony and this unity, we shall certainly fail of answering the prayer of being one with Christ as He was one with the Father.[45]

When as individual members of the church, you love God supremely and your neighbor as yourself, there will be no need of labored efforts to be in unity, for there will be oneness in Christ as a natural result. The ears will no longer be open to reports that will injure your neighbor, and no one will take up a reproach against his neighbor. The members of the church will cherish love and unity, and be as one great family. Then we shall bear the divine credentials to the world, that will testify that God has sent His Son into the world. Christ has said, "By this shall all men know that ye are My disciples, if ye have love one to another" (John 13:35). The divinity of Christ is acknowledged in the unity of the children of God. . . .

What can Christ who is so forgiving, so patient with all our mistakes, so rich in mercy and love, think of our hardhearted criticism and faultfinding? Love for your erring brethren will produce far greater effect in reforming them than all your harsh criticisms.[46]

# Of One Mind, Living in Peace

*"Be perfect, be of good comfort, be of one mind, live in peace; and the God of love and peace shall be with you" (2 Corinthians 13:11).*

I have been and am still fellowshiping as brethren and sisters those who have been guilty of grave sins and who even now do not see their sins as God sees them. But the Lord bears with these persons, and why should not I? He will yet cause His Spirit so to impress their hearts that sin will appear to them as it appeared to Paul, exceedingly sinful.

We know but little of our own hearts and have but little sense of our own need of the mercy of God. This is why we cherish so little of that sweet compassion which Jesus manifests toward us and which we should manifest toward one another. We should remember that our brethren are weak, erring mortals like ourselves. Suppose that a brother has through unwatchfulness been overborne by temptation and contrary to his general conduct has committed some error, what course shall be pursued toward him? We learn from the Bible that men whom God had used to do a great and good work committed grave sins. The Lord did not pass these by unrebuked, neither did He cast off His servants. When they repented, He graciously forgave them. . . . Let poor, weak mortals consider how great is their own need of pity and forbearance from God and from their brethren. Let them beware how they judge and condemn others. . . .

Every man must at last stand or fall for himself, not according to the opinion of the party that sustains or opposes him, not according to the judgment of any man, but according to his real character in the sight of God. The church may warn, counsel, and admonish, but it cannot compel any to take a right course. Whoever persists in disregarding the word of God must bear his own burden, answer to God for himself, and suffer the consequences of his own course.

The Lord has given us in His word definite, unmistakable instructions, by obedience to which we may preserve union and harmony in the church. Brethren and sisters, are you giving heed to these inspired injunctions? Are you Bible readers and doers of the word? Are you striving to fulfill the prayer of Christ that His followers might be one?[47]

# The Burden of Epaphras for Today

*"Epaphras, who is one of you, a servant of Christ, saluteth you, always labouring fervently for you in prayers, that ye may stand perfect and complete in all the will of God. For I bear him record, that he hath a great zeal for you, and them that are in Laodicea, and them in Hierapolis." (Colossians 4:12, 13).*

Paul writes to his Colossian brethren: "As ye also learned of Epaphras our dear fellow servant, who is for you a faithful minister of Christ; who also declared unto us your love in the Spirit. [Not an unsanctified love of the smartness, ability, or oratory of the preacher, but a love born of the Spirit of God, which His servant represented in his words and character]" (Colossians 1:7, 8).[48]

Much excellent labor was bestowed upon the Laodicean church. To them was given the exhortation, "Be ye therefore perfect, even as your Father which is in heaven is perfect" (Matthew 5:48). But the church did not follow up the work begun by God's messengers. They heard, but they failed to appropriate the truth to themselves, and to carry out the instruction given them. The result that followed is the result always sure to follow the rejection of the Lord's warnings and entreaties.[49]

We are in continual danger of getting above the simplicity of the gospel. There is an intense desire on the part of many to startle the world with something original, that shall lift the people into a state of spiritual ecstasy, and change the present order of experience. There is certainly great need of a change in the present order of experience; for the sacredness of present truth is not realized as it should be, but the change we need is a change of heart, and can only be obtained by seeking God individually for His blessing, by pleading with Him for His power, by fervently praying that His grace may come upon us, and that our characters may be transformed. This is the change we need today, and for the attainment of this experience we should exercise persevering energy and manifest heartfelt earnestness. We should ask with true sincerity, "What shall I do to be saved?" We should know just what steps we are taking heavenward.[50]

# Perfectly Christlike

*"The disciple is not above his master: but every one that is perfect shall be as his master" (Luke 6:40).*

Those who receive the seal of the living God and are protected in the time of trouble must reflect the image of Jesus fully.[51]

Pure thoughts, noble aspirations, clear perceptions of truth, elevated purposes of action, yearnings to attain to perfection, will be the experience of every real Christian. These have fellowship with the Father and with the Son. They are constantly increasing in the knowledge of God. They grow in reverence and trust and love; but while they are coming nearer and nearer to perfection of character, they will feel more and more deeply their unlikeness to Christ, and have greater distrust of themselves and greater dependence upon God. As these are growing up to the full stature of men and women in Christ Jesus, they will be sought by others, and will be a help and blessing to all with whom they associate. The most Christlike professors are those who are the most kind, pitiful, and courteous; their convictions are firm and their characters strong; nothing can swerve them from their faith or allure them from their duty.[52]

If we build in cooperation with [God], the structure that we rear will day by day grow more beautiful and more symmetrical under the hand of the Master Builder, and through all eternity it will endure.

Sanctification is a progressive work. It is a continuous work, leading human beings higher and still higher. It does not leave love behind, but brings it into the life as the very essence of Christianity.

Christ says to us, "Be ye therefore perfect, even as your Father which is in heaven is perfect" (Matthew 5:48). He is our example. During His life on earth, He was ever kind and gentle. His influence was ever fragrant; for in Him dwelt perfect love. He was never sour and unapproachable, and He never compromised with wrong to obtain favor. If we have His righteousness, we shall be like Him in gentleness, in forbearance, in unselfish love. Shall we not, by dwelling in the sunshine of His presence, become mellowed by His grace?[53]

363

# Going on Unto Perfection

*"Let us go on unto perfection" (Hebrews 6:1).*

In order to perfect Christian character, we should not cultivate merely a life of quiet, prayerful abstraction, nor a life of all outward zeal and busy excitement, while personal piety is neglected. But the present time requires us to be waiting for the coming of the Lord and vigilantly working for the salvation of our fellowmen.[54]

There is no safety for any of us except as we daily receive a new experience in looking unto Jesus, the Author and Finisher of our faith. Day by day we are to behold Him, and to become changed into His image. We are to represent the divine attributes, and follow the footsteps of Jesus at whatever cost to ourselves. We are to place ourselves under divine guidance, consulting the word of God, and daily inquiring, Is this the way of the Lord? There are various erratic characters that are wholly unlike Jesus, and that are within the church of Christ; but unless they will submit to become as clay in the hands of the potter, and will be willing to receive the heavenly mold, and be shaped into such vessels as God shall choose to make them, they will always bear their deformity of character, always be vessels unto dishonor, and will never receive the finishing touch of immortality. No deficiency of character will be immortalized and mar heaven with its imperfection. . . .

The wild, trailing vine which lies prone on the ground, catches at twigs and stumps, and fastens its tendrils about the things of the earth; and in order to have it twine about a proper support, its tendrils must be cut loose from the false supports to which it has attached itself. So it is with the soul. Earthly supports must be removed, and the thoughts and affections must be trained to find their support in God.[55]

We are nearing the end of this earth's history. We have only a short time now in which to perfect Christian character. But those who love Jesus will love those who are the purchase of His blood. Far more patience must be exercised, more earnest efforts must be made to save the erring.[56]

# Perfection Comes Through Patience

*"Knowing this, that the trying of your faith worketh patience. But let patience have her perfect work, that ye may be perfect and entire, wanting nothing" (James 1:3, 4).*

Life is disciplinary. While in the world, the Christian will meet with adverse influences. There will be provocations to test the temper; and it is by meeting these in a right spirit that the Christian graces are developed. If injuries and insults are meekly borne, if insulting words are responded to by gentle answers, and oppressive acts by kindness, this is evidence that the Spirit of Christ dwells in the heart, that sap from the living Vine is flowing to the branches. We are in the school of Christ in this life, where we are to learn to be meek and lowly of heart; and in the day of final accounts we shall see that all the obstacles we meet, all the hardships and annoyances that we are called to bear, are practical lessons in the application of principles of Christian life. If well endured, they develop the Christlike in the character and distinguish the Christian from the worldling.

There is a high standard to which we are to attain if we would be children of God, noble, pure, holy, and undefiled; and a pruning process is necessary if we would reach this standard. How would this pruning be accomplished if there were no difficulties to meet, no obstacles to surmount, nothing to call out patience and endurance? These trials are not the smallest blessings in our experience. They are designed to nerve us to determination to succeed. We are to use them as God's means to gain decided victories over self instead of allowing them to hinder, oppress, and destroy us.

Character will be tested. Christ will be revealed in us if we are indeed branches of the living Vine. We shall be patient, kind, and forbearing, cheerful amid frets and irritations. Day by day and year by year we shall conquer self and grow into a noble heroism. This is our allotted task; but it cannot be accomplished without continual help from Jesus, resolute decision, unwavering purpose, continual watchfulness, and unceasing prayer.[57]

# "If Thou Wilt Be Perfect"

*"If thou wilt be perfect, go and sell that thou hast, and give to the poor, and thou shalt have treasure in heaven" (Matthew 19:21).*

[God] could send means from heaven to carry on His work; but this is out of His order. He has ordained that men should be His instruments, that as a great sacrifice was made to redeem them, they should act a part in this work of salvation, by making a sacrifice for one another, and by thus doing show how highly they prize the sacrifice that has been made for them.

I was directed to James 5:1–3: "Go to now, ye rich men, weep and howl for your miseries that shall come upon you. Your riches are corrupted, and your garments are motheaten. Your gold and silver is cankered; and the rust of them shall be a witness against you, and shall eat your flesh as it were fire. Ye have heaped treasure together for the last days."

I saw that these fearful words apply particularly to the wealthy who profess to believe the present truth. The Lord calls them to use their means to advance His cause. Opportunities are presented to them, but they shut their eyes to the wants of the cause, and cling fast to their earthly treasure. Their love for the world is greater than their love for the truth, their love for their fellow men, or their love for God. He calls for their substance, but they selfishly, covetously, retain what they have. They give a little now and then to ease their conscience, but have not overcome their love for this world. They do not sacrifice for God. The Lord has raised up others that prize eternal life, and that can feel and realize something of the value of the soul, and they have freely bestowed their means to advance the cause of God. The work is closing; and soon the means of those who have kept their riches, their large farms, their cattle, etc., will not be wanted. I saw the Lord turn to such in anger, in wrath, and repeat these words: "Go to now, ye rich men." He has called, but you would not hear. Love of this world has drowned His voice. Now He has no use for you, and lets you go, bidding you: "Go to now, ye rich men."[58]

The Lord will require of us personally a faithful record of how we have used our talents of means.[59]

# Strengthened Unto Perfection

*"It is God that girdeth me with strength, and maketh my way perfect" (Psalm 18:32).*

All have defects of character. All need the help of God every hour, or they will decidedly fail.[60]

I long to address the young men and women who are so willing to reach only cheap standards. O that the Lord might influence their minds to see what perfection of character is! O that they might know the faith that works by love, and purifies the soul! We are living in days of peril. Christ alone can help us and give us the victory. Christ must be all in all to us; He must dwell in the heart; His life must circulate through us, as the blood circulates through the veins. His Spirit must be a vitalizing power that will cause us to influence others to become Christlike and holy.[61]

Heart and soul and voice are to be consecrated to [God] that they may reach the highest degree of excellence—a likeness to the character of God. Every faculty, every attribute with which the Lord has endowed us is to be employed for the uplifting of our fellow men. If we will do our best, working with unselfish spirit, the Lord will accept our service.[62]

The Saviour is by the side of His tempted and tried ones. With Him there can be no such thing as failure, loss, impossibility, or defeat; we can do all things through Him who strengthens us.[63]

All the favors and blessings we enjoy are alone from [God]; we are stewards of His grace and of His temporal gifts; the smallest talent and the humblest service may be offered to Jesus as a consecrated gift, and with the fragrance of His own merits He will present it to the Father. If the best we have is presented with a sincere heart, in love to God, from a longing desire to do service to Jesus, the gift is wholly acceptable. Everyone can lay up a treasure in the heavens. All can be "rich in good works, ready to distribute, willing to communicate; laying up in store for themselves a good foundation against the time to come, that they may lay hold on eternal life" (1 Timothy 6:18, 19).[64]

# Firmly Established and Settled

*"The God of all grace, who hath called us unto his eternal glory by Christ Jesus, after that ye have suffered a while, make you perfect, stablish, strengthen, settle you. To him be glory and dominion for ever and ever. Amen" (1 Peter 5:10, 11).*

We must, through fervent prayer and deep and earnest research, become established and settled, rooted and grounded in the faith, and know, each for himself, that we have the truth. If we are thus established, we shall not depart from the faith when tested and tried. . . .

You are to pray, and search for the truth on every point of faith and doctrine. You will be brought before critical, opposing councils. You will be tried for your faith, and you will want to know that you have good ground for every point of doctrine.[65]

With what earnest effort should we seek for unity, for oneness. The church is to be perfected through sufferings after the example of Christ. Being conformed to His image, we shall be one with Him.

We are to pray for divine enlightenment, but at the same time we should be careful how we receive everything termed new light. We must beware lest, under cover of searching for new truth, Satan shall divert our minds from Christ and the special truths for this time. I have been shown that it is the device of the enemy to lead minds to dwell upon some obscure or unimportant point, something that is not fully revealed or is not essential to our salvation. This is made the absorbing theme, the "present truth," when all their investigations and suppositions only serve to make matters more obscure than before, and to confuse the minds of some who ought to be seeking for oneness through sanctification of the truth.[66]

It is the privilege of everyone to be grounded and settled in the faith. No one who exercises that faith which works by love and purifies the soul will be moved away from the hope of the Gospel.[67]

The Christian who will not exercise his God-given powers not only fails to grow up into Christ, but he loses the strength which he already has; he becomes a spiritual paralytic. It is those who, with love for God and their fellow men, are striving to help others that become established, strengthened, settled, in the truth.[68]

# Made Perfect in Love

*"Herein is our love made perfect, that we may have boldness in the day of judgment: because as he is, so are we in this world. There is no fear in love; but perfect love casteth out fear: because fear hath torment. He that feareth is not made perfect in love" (1 John 4:17, 18).*

Even as Christ was in the world, so are His followers. They are the sons of God, and joint heirs with Christ; and the kingdom and dominion belong to them. The world understand not their character and holy calling; they perceive not their adoption into the family of God. . . . They are strangers. The world know them not, and appreciate not the motives which actuate them.

The world is ripening for its destruction. God can bear with sinners but a little longer. They must drink the dregs of the cup of His wrath unmixed with mercy. Those who will be heirs of God, and joint heirs with Christ to the immortal inheritance, will be peculiar. Yes, so peculiar that God places a mark upon them as His, wholly His. . . . It is soon to be known who is on the Lord's side, who will not be ashamed of Jesus. Those who have not moral courage to conscientiously take their position in the face of unbelievers, leave the fashions of the world, and imitate the self-denying life of Christ, are ashamed of Him, and do not love His example.[69]

The Master calls for gospel workers. Who will respond? Not all who enter the army are to be generals, captains, sergeants, or even corporals. Not all have the care and responsibility of leaders. There is hard work of other kinds to be done. Some must dig trenches and build fortifications; some are to stand as sentinels, some to carry messages. While there are but few officers, it requires many soldiers to form the rank and file of the army; and yet its success depends upon the fidelity of every soldier. One man's cowardice or treachery may bring disaster upon the entire army.

He who has appointed "to every man his work" (Mark 13:34), according to his ability, will never let the faithful performance of duty go unrewarded. Every act of loyalty and faith will be crowned with special tokens of God's favor and approbation.[70]

# God's Glory Seen

*"Arise, shine; for thy light is come, and the glory of the Lord is risen upon thee. For, behold, the darkness shall cover the earth, and gross darkness the people: but the Lord shall arise upon thee, and his glory shall be seen upon thee" (Isaiah 60:1, 2).*

The Lord is calling upon men and women who have the light of the truth for this time to engage in genuine, personal missionary work. . . . There are great blessings in store for those who fully surrender to the call of God. As such workers undertake to win souls to Jesus, they will find that many who never could be reached in any other way will respond to intelligent personal effort.[71]

Those who consecrate their all to God will not be left unmolested by the enemy of souls. Satan will come to them with his specious temptations, designing to allure them from their loyalty to God. He will present to them his bribe, as he did to Christ in the wilderness of temptation, saying, "All these things will I give thee, if thou wilt fall down and worship me" (Matthew 4:9). But what should be the answer of the Christian to all the temptations of the evil one? He should say, "I will not lend my influence in any way to the advancement of anything save the cause of Christ. I am not my own; I have been bought with a price. I am not to live to please myself; for I have been purchased, ransomed by the blood of Christ. It is not possible for me to give to Christ more than that which belongs to Him; for every moment of my life belongs to Him. I am His possession, a servant employed to do the will of my Master." This is the only position that is safe for us to occupy; and if the individual members of the church felt in this way, what a power would the church exert to draw and win souls to Christ. It is this halfhearted work, the effort to serve God and the devil at the same time, that leaves the church so destitute of the Spirit of God. Were the members of the church consecrated to God, were they in the unity of the Spirit, in the bond of peace, were they organized for the purpose of imparting to others an influence of good, the church would be indeed the light of the world.[72]

# Talents Surrendered to God's Spirit

*"I will pour water upon him that is thirsty, and floods upon the dry ground: I will pour my spirit upon thy seed, and my blessing upon thine offspring" (Isaiah 44:3).*

The Lord has said, "Pray ye therefore the Lord of the harvest, that he will send forth labourers into his harvest" (Matthew 9:38). On every hand, fields of usefulness are opening up; but a burden of perplexity rests upon those who should appoint laborers to go to the various stations of usefulness; for they look in vain for men and women fitted for these responsibilities of the work. Is it not time that the members of the church were becoming educated to engage in missionary labor, that when a call is made for men and women to go forth into the harvest field, there may be those who can respond to the call? saying, "We have given ourselves to Christ without reserve. We have educated ourselves and our households to habits of simplicity in dress and living. We are accustomed to self-denial, and realize that we belong to the Lord. We have no other desire than to do His will, and live not to please ourselves, but to win souls for the Master. We are ready to move to distant lands, and lift up the standard of Christ, and in simplicity and humility live out the truth."

Jesus left His home in heaven, and came to this dark world to reach to the very depth of human woe, that He might save those who were ready to perish. This is the love He has shown to fallen man. But is the disciple above his Master, the servant greater than His Lord? If I am indeed a laborer together with God, shall I not be called upon to make some sacrifice for His cause? Will it be too great a sacrifice for any of Christ's followers to make to take the little possession entrusted to their care, and go to the dark places of the earth, where the people have never so much as heard of the truth, and in meekness and lowliness of heart, there make known to men what the Lord has done for the sons of men?[73]

God has a positive ownership of every power He has committed to the human agent. By His own wisdom He makes the terms of man's use of every gift of God. He will bless the proper use of every power put forth for His own name's glory.[74]

# The Promise Is Sure

*"Also upon the servants and upon the handmaids in those days will I pour out my spirit"* (Joel 2:29).

To us today, as verily as to the first disciples, the promise of the Spirit belongs. God will today endow men and women with power from above, as He endowed those who on the Day of Pentecost heard the word of salvation. At this very hour His Spirit and His grace are for all who need them and will take Him at His word.

Notice that it was after the disciples had come into perfect unity, when they were no longer striving for the highest place, that the Spirit was poured out. They were of one accord. All differences had been put away. And the testimony borne of them after the Spirit had been given is the same. Mark the word: "The multitude of them that believed were of one heart and of one soul" (Acts 4:32). The Spirit of Him who died that sinners might live animated the entire congregation of believers.

The disciples did not ask for a blessing for themselves. They were weighted with the burden of souls. The gospel was to be carried to the ends of the earth, and they claimed the endowment of power that Christ had promised. Then it was that the Holy Spirit was poured out, and thousands were converted in a day.

So it may be now. Let Christians put away all dissension and give themselves to God for the saving of the lost. Let them ask in faith for the promised blessing, and it will come. The outpouring of the Spirit in the days of the apostles was "the former rain" (Joel 2:23), and glorious was the result. But the latter rain will be more abundant. . . .

Why do we not hunger and thirst for the gift of the Spirit, since this is the means by which we are to receive power? Why do we not talk of it, pray for it, preach concerning it? The Lord is more willing to give the Holy Spirit to us than parents are to give good gifts to their children. . . .

The presence of the Spirit with God's workers will give the presentation of the truth a power that not all the honor or glory of the world could give. The Spirit furnishes the strength that sustains striving, wrestling souls in every emergency.[75]

# Time for the Refreshing

*"Repent ye therefore, and be converted, that your sins may be blotted out, when the times of refreshing shall come from the presence of the Lord; and he shall send Jesus Christ, which before was preached unto you: whom the heaven must receive until the times of restitution of all things, which God hath spoken by the mouth of all his holy prophets since the world began" (Acts 3:19–21).*

We call upon you to take your stand on the Lord's side, and act your part as a loyal subject of the kingdom. Acknowledge the gift that has been placed in the church for the guidance of God's people in the closing days of earth's history. From the beginning the church of God has had the gift of prophecy in her midst as a living voice to counsel, admonish, and instruct. We have now come to the last days of the work of the third angel's message, when Satan will work with increasing power because he knows that his time is short. At the same time there will come to us through the gifts of the Holy Spirit, diversities of operations in the outpouring of the Spirit. This is the time of the latter rain.[76]

Do we individually realize our true position, that as God's hired servants we are not to bargain away our stewardship? We have an individual accountability before the heavenly universe, to administer the trust committed us of God. Our own hearts are to be stirred. Our hands are to have something to impart of the income that God entrusts to us. The humblest of us may be agents for God, using our gifts for His name's glory. He who improves his talents to the best of his ability may present to God his offering as a consecrated gift that shall be as fragrant incense before Him. It is the duty of everyone to see that his talents are turned to advantage as a gift that he must return, having done his best to improve it.[77]

All the wonders which God has wrought for His people have been performed by the most simple means. When the people of God are wholly consecrated to Him, then He will employ them to carry forward His work on the earth. But we should remember that whatever success may attend us, the glory and honor belongs to God; for every faculty and every power is a gift from Him.[78]

# SOURCE REFERENCES

## JANUARY

1 *Thoughts From the Mount of Blessing*, p. 77.
2 *Christ's Object Lessons*, p. 141.
3 *Testimonies*, vol. 9, p. 284.
4 *The Signs of the Times*, December 16, 1889.
5 *Manuscript Releases*, vol. 10, p. 56.
6 *The Health Reformer*, December 1, 1877.
7 *The Review and Herald*, April 4, 1912.
8 Ibid., September 20, 1898.
9 *Bible Training School*, December 1, 1908.
10 *The Review and Herald*, March 26, 1895.
11 *Sons and Daughters of God*, p. 361.
12 *This Day With God*, p. 187.
13 *Testimonies*, vol. 2, p. 582.
14 *The Review and Herald*, September 24, 1895.
15 *The Upward Look*, p. 240.
16 *Pacific Union Recorder*, August 14, 1902.
17 *Christian Education*, pp. 195, 196.
18 *Christ's Object Lessons*, pp. 346–348.
19 *The Ministry of Healing*, pp. 411, 412.
20 *The Desire of Ages*, pp. 20, 21.
21 *The Upward Look*, p. 52.
22 *The Review and Herald*, January 10, 1899.
23 *The Ministry of Healing*, pp. 207, 208.
24 *Steps to Christ*, pp. 32, 33.
25 *Testimonies*, vol. 5, p. 392.
26 Ibid., vol. 4, p. 221.
27 *The Signs of the Times*, January 23, 1893.
28 *Manuscript Releases*, vol. 17, p. 203.
29 *The Review and Herald*, June 23, 1885.
30 *Selected Messages*, bk. 1, p. 298.
31 *An Appeal to the Youth*, pp. 50, 51.
32 *The Sanctified Life*, p. 76.
33 *The Review and Herald*, November 6, 1900.
34 *Steps to Christ*, pp. 43, 44.
35 Ibid., pp. 28, 29.
36 *Testimonies*, vol. 8, p. 291.
37 *Thoughts From the Mount of Blessing*, pp. 8, 9.
38 *The Ministry of Healing*, p. 77.
39 *Steps to Christ*, pp. 49, 50.
40 Ibid., pp. 51, 52.
41 Ibid., pp. 37, 38.
42 Ibid., p. 41.
43 *The Ministry of Healing*, pp. 71, 72.
44 *The Spirit of Prophecy*, vol. 2, pp. 60, 61.
45 *This Day With God*, p. 184.
46 *The Signs of the Times*, April 16, 1902.
47 *Christ's Object Lessons*, p. 51.
48 *Testimonies*, vol. 4, p. 285.
49 *The Upward Look*, p. 359.
50 *Testimonies*, vol. 3, p. 373.
51 *The Review and Herald*, November 19, 1908.
52 *The Desire of Ages*, p. 240.
53 *Sketches From the Life of Paul*, p. 300.
54 *The Signs of the Times*, February 16, 1882.
55 *That I May Know Him*, p. 248.
56 *Testimonies*, vol. 5, pp. 426, 427.
57 *The General Conference Bulletin*, October 1, 1899.
58 *Sons and Daughters of God*, p. 299.
59 *The Signs of the Times*, April 8, 1889.
60 *Testimonies*, vol. 1, p. 482.
61 *The Signs of the Times*, May 15, 1893.
62 *Child Guidance*, pp. 141, 142.
63 *The Review and Herald*, May 6, 1902.
64 *Selected Messages*, bk. 2, p. 261.
65 *Testimonies*, vol. 3, pp. 46, 47.
66 *The Review and Herald*, November 25, 1884.
67 *Lift Him Up*, p. 250.
68 *The Review and Herald*, May 20, 1884.
69 *Testimonies*, vol. 4, p. 259.
70 *The Review and Herald*, July 18, 1882.
71 *The Signs of the Times*, May 20, 1903.
72 *The Home Missionary*, November 1, 1897.
73 *The Review and Herald*, June 23, 1885.

## FEBRUARY

1 *Testimonies*, vol. 6, p. 163.
2 *The Review and Herald*, June 17, 1890.
3 *Bible Training School*, March 1, 1906.
4 *The Signs of the Times*, March 31, 1890.
5 *The Desire of Ages*, p. 181.
6 *Patriarchs and Prophets*, p. 372.
7 *The Ministry of Healing*, p. 181.
8 *Reflecting Christ*, p. 45.
9 *The Review and Herald*, April 25, 1893.
10 *Testimonies to Ministers*, p. 65.
11 *The Review and Herald*, April 25, 1893.
12 *Testimonies to Ministers*, p. 402.
13 *Testimonies*, vol. 5, p. 83.
14 *Steps to Christ*, pp. 69, 70.
15 *Testimonies*, vol. 4, p. 655.
16 *The Signs of the Times*, September 5, 1895.
17 *The Review and Herald*, October 11, 1892.
18 *Selected Messages*, bk. 1, p. 121.
19 *The Signs of the Times*, April 17, 1893.
20 *The Youth's Instructor*, August 17, 1893.
21 *The Review and Herald*, September 17, 1895.
22 *Selected Messages*, bk. 1, p. 217.
23 *The Review and Herald*, March 8, 1906.
24 *The Youth's Instructor*, November 30, 1893.
25 Ibid., July 5, 1894.
26 *The Signs of the Times*, December 28, 1891.
27 *The Desire of Ages*, p. 672.
28 *Testimonies*, vol. 5, p. 434.
29 *Reflecting Christ*, p. 131.
30 *Gospel Workers*, pp. 285, 286.
31 Ibid., p. 287.
32 Ibid., pp. 286, 287.
33 *The Review and Herald*, January 11, 1887.
34 *Testimonies*, vol. 5, p. 46.
35 *The Desire of Ages*, pp. 489, 490.
36 *Christ's Object Lessons*, p. 337.
37 *Selected Messages*, bk. 2, p. 18.
38 *The Home Missionary*, June 1, 1897.
39 *Education*, pp. 126, 127.
40 *Our High Calling*, p. 159.
41 *The Review and Herald*, July 19, 1887.
42 *The Youth's Instructor*, February 7, 1895.

43 *The Desire of Ages*, p. 189.
44 *Manuscript Releases*, vol. 2, p. 125.
45 *Special Testimonies on Education*, p. 79.
46 *The Review and Herald*, February 21, 1893.
47 *Early Writings*, pp. 59, 60.
48 *Testimonies*, vol. 8, p. 95.
49 Ibid., vol. 4, p. 232.
50 *The Signs of the Times*, April 13, 1888.
51 *Testimonies*, vol. 5, p. 691.
52 *Christ's Object Lessons*, p. 419.
53 *Testimonies*, vol. 7, pp. 90, 91.
54 *The SDA Bible Commentary* [E. G. White Comments], vol. 2, p. 1037.
55 *The Review and Herald*, June 14, 1892.
56 *The Signs of the Times*, October 3, 1895.
57 *The Review and Herald*, September 27, 1892.
58 *The Youth's Instructor*, August 24, 1899.
59 Ibid., February 2, 1893.
60 Ibid., September 17, 1895.
61 *The Signs of the Times*, April 2, 1896.
62 *Testimonies*, vol. 5, p. 648.
63 *The Signs of the Times*, December 28, 1891.
64 *Gospel Workers*, p. 287.
65 *The Southern Review*, December 5, 1899.
66 *The Review and Herald*, December 2, 1875.
67 *Fundamentals of Christian Education*, pp. 537, 538.
68 *The Southern Review*, December 5, 1899.
69 Ibid., August 26, 1890.
70 *Fundamentals of Christian Education*, p. 538.
71 *Gospel Workers* (1892), p. 393.
72 *Testimonies*, vol. 6, pp. 54, 55.
73 *Selected Messages*, bk. 1, p. 225.
74 *The Youth's Instructor*, August 16, 1894.
75 *Testimonies*, vol. 2, p. 166.

## MARCH

1 *Patriarchs and Prophets*, p. 33.
2 Ibid., p. 43.
3 *The Review and Herald*, January 25, 1898.
4 Ibid., September 15, 1896.
5 *The Signs of the Times*, July 23, 1902.
6 *Manuscript Releases*, vol. 19, pp. 265, 266.
7 *The Review and Herald*, December 19, 1893.
8 *Counsels to Parents, Teachers, and Students*, p. 484.
9 *The Kress Collection*, p. 5.
10 *The Gospel Herald*, December 1, 1899.
11 *The Review and Herald*, March 2, 1911.
12 *Testimonies*, vol. 6, p. 13.
13 *The Review and Herald*, October 23, 1900.
14 *Testimonies*, vol. 1, pp. 162, 163.
15 *The Signs of the Times*, February 15, 1892.
16 *Manuscript Releases*, vol. 12, pp. 125, 126.
17 *Christ's Object Lessons*, pp. 86, 87.
18 *The Review and Herald*, April 30, 1895.
19 Ibid., November 30, 1897.
20 *The Great Controversy*, p. 465.
21 *The Signs of the Times*, December 1, 1887.
22 *The Review and Herald*, October 11, 1892.
23 *Counsels to Parents, Teachers, and Students*, p. 357.
24 *Manuscript Releases*, vol. 6, p. 188.
25 *Life Sketches*, p. 84.
26 *Historical Sketches*, p. 213.
27 *The Review and Herald*, October 11, 1892.
28 *Early Writings*, pp. 124, 125.
29 *The Review and Herald*, September 9, 1909.
30 Ibid., October 11, 1892.
31 *The General Conference Bulletin*, April 23, 1901.
32 *The Signs of the Times*, April 30, 1896.
33 *Testimonies*, vol. 4, pp. 360–362.
34 *The Signs of the Times*, April 30, 1896.
35 *Education*, p. 126.
36 *Thoughts From the Mount of Blessing*, p. 97.
37 *The SDA Bible Commentary* [E. G. White Comments], vol. 1, p. 1081.
38 *Thoughts From the Mount of Blessing*, p. 129.
39 *The Review and Herald*, March 20, 1888.
40 Ibid., July 5, 1892.
41 *The Review and Herald*, December 23, 1890.
42 *The Signs of the Times*, June 16, 1890.
43 *The SDA Bible Commentary* [E. G. White Comments], vol. 1, p. 1120.
44 *The Review and Herald*, August 16, 1892.
45 *Notebook Leaflets*, vol. 1, p. 104.
46 *Prophets and Kings*, p. 252.
47 *The Review and Herald*, October 16, 1883.
48 *The Youth's Instructor*, February 15, 1900.
49 *The Review and Herald*, November 13, 1900.
50 *The Signs of the Times*, March 17, 1887.
51 *Manuscript Releases*, vol. 7, p. 153.
52 *The Review and Herald*, September 30, 1909.
53 *The Signs of the Times*, April 6, 1891.
54 *The Review and Herald*, September 30, 1909.
55 *Testimonies*, vol. 1, p. 336.
56 *The Review and Herald*, February 23, 1897.
57 *The Signs of the Times*, July 22, 1875.
58 *Manuscript Releases*, vol. 4, p. 355.
59 Ibid., vol. 5, p. 123.
60 *Special Testimonies*, Series B, vol. 2, pp. 12, 13.
61 *The Signs of the Times*, August 21, 1901.
62 *The Youth's Instructor*, December 9, 1897.
63 *The Signs of the Times*, June 24, 1897.
64 *The Home Missionary*, August 1, 1896.
65 *Manuscript Releases*, vol. 14, p. 160.
66 *The Home Missionary*, August 1, 1896.
67 *The Signs of the Times*, August 21, 1901.
68 *The Review and Herald*, June 12, 1913.
69 Ibid.
70 Ibid., August 27, 1903.
71 *My Life Today*, p. 233.
72 *Testimonies*, vol. 7, pp. 23, 24.
73 *The Review and Herald*, August 26, 1902.
74 *The Acts of the Apostles*, pp. 598–600.
75 *Testimonies*, vol. 1, pp. 60, 61.

## APRIL

1 *The Acts of the Apostles*, pp. 17–19.
2 *Gospel Workers* (1892), p. 11.
3 Ibid., pp. 12, 13.
4 Ibid., pp. 21, 22.
5 *The Acts of the Apostles*, pp. 361, 362.
6 *Testimonies*, vol. 3, p. 54.
7 *Early Writings*, pp. 102, 103.
8 *The SDA Bible Commentary* [E. G. White Comments], vol. 4, p. 1164.
9 *Testimonies*, vol. 2, pp. 507, 508.
10 *The Acts of the Apostles*, p. 328.
11 *The Review and Herald*, April 15, 1902.
12 *The Acts of the Apostles*, p. 209.

13 Ibid., pp. 164, 165.
14 *The Review and Herald*, March 13, 1900.
15 *The Acts of the Apostles*, p. 352.
16 *Sketches From the Life of Paul*, pp. 177–179.
17 Ibid., pp. 148, 149.
18 *The Acts of the Apostles*, pp. 369, 370.
19 *The Review and Herald*, September 11, 1888.
20 *The Acts of the Apostles*, pp. 370, 371.
21 *The Review and Herald*, August 30, 1892.
22 *Testimonies*, vol. 6, pp. 411–413.
23 Ibid., vol. 5, pp. 617, 618.
24 Ibid., p. 619.
25 Ibid., vol. 4, pp. 406, 407.
26 *Patriarchs and Prophets*, p. 28.
27 *Gospel Workers*, pp. 125, 126.
28 *Early Writings*, p. 101.
29 *Sermons and Talks*, vol. 1, p. 77.
30 *The Adventist Home*, p. 32.
31 *My Life Today*, p. 33.
32 *Manuscript Releases*, vol. 1, p. 92.
33 *Testimonies*, vol. 4, pp. 376, 377.
34 *Testimonies to Ministers*, pp. 142, 143.
35 *The Review and Herald*, November 20, 1894.
36 *Testimonies*, vol. 6, p. 412.
37 *The Review and Herald*, September 2, 1909.
38 *Testimonies*, vol. 6, p. 343.
39 *Notebook Leaflets*, vol. 1, p. 140.
40 *Testimonies*, vol. 2, p. 645.
41 Ibid., vol. 4, pp. 405–407.
42 *Gospel Workers*, p. 76.
43 *Manuscript Releases*, vol. 6, p. 37.
44 Ibid., vol. 20, p. 248.
45 *Testimonies*, vol. 3, pp. 486, 487.
46 Ibid., vol. 1, p. 471.
47 *Special Testimonies*, Series A, No. 4, p. 23.
48 *Testimonies*, vol. 3, p. 217.
49 Ibid., vol. 1, p. 375.
50 *The Ministry of Healing*, p. 340.
51 *Gospel Workers*, p. 271.
52 *Testimonies*, vol. 7, p. 250.
53 Ibid., pp. 208, 209.
54 *Early Writings*, p. 102.
55 *Testimonies*, vol. 6, p. 120.
56 Ibid., vol. 5, p. 618.
57 *Manuscript Releases*, vol. 5, pp. 449, 450.
58 *Gospel Workers*, p. 206.
59 *Testimonies*, vol. 1, pp. 473, 474.
60 *The Review and Herald*, October 8, 1889.
61 *The Acts of the Apostles*, p. 203.
62 *Manuscript Releases*, vol. 9, p. 61.
63 *The Acts of the Apostles*, p. 361.
64 *Testimonies to Ministers*, pp. 143, 144.
65 *The Kress Collection*, p. 153.
66 *The Review and Herald*, February 18, 1909.

MAY

1 *The Spirit of Prophecy*, vol. 3, p. 182.
2 *Acts of Apostles*, p. 263.
3 *Testimonies*, vol. 4, pp. 594, 595.
4 Ibid., vol. 1, pp. 230–232.
5 *The Review and Herald*, June 26, 1900.
6 Ibid., August 25, 1885.
7 Ibid., February 6, 1900.
8 *The Signs of the Times*, June 16, 1881.
9 Ibid., July 20, 1882.
10 Ibid., April 22, 1889.
11 *Patriarchs and Prophets*, pp. 712, 713.
12 *Testimonies*, vol. 3, p. 494.
13 *Medical Ministry*, p. 158.
14 *General Conference Bulletin*, April 1, 1903.
15 *Testimonies*, vol. 4, p. 167.
16 *The Signs of the Times*, February 17, 1898.
17 *Thoughts From the Mount of Blessing*, pp. 33, 34.
18 *The Acts of the Apostles*, pp. 599, 600.
19 *This Day With God*, p. 296.
20 *Testimonies*, vol. 8, pp. 301, 302.
21 Ibid., vol. 4, p. 185.
22 *Prophets and Kings*, pp. 444–446.
23 *Patriarchs and Prophets*, p. 168.
24 *Prophets and Kings*, pp. 669, 670.
25 Ibid., p. 535.
26 *Testimonies*, vol. 5, pp. 753, 754.
27 *Gospel Workers*, pp. 332, 333.
28 *The Spirit of Prophecy*, vol. 4, pp. 207, 208.
29 *Patriarchs and Prophets*, pp. 527, 528.
30 *Testimonies*, vol. 4, p. 15.
31 *The Youth's Instructor*, August 3, 1899.
32 *The Review and Herald*, June 21, 1892.
33 *Special Testimonies on Education*, pp. 150, 151.
34 *The Signs of the Times*, April 16, 1896.
35 Ibid., February 18, 1897.
36 *Testimonies to Ministers*, p. 421.
37 *Manuscript Releases*, vol. 2, pp. 278, 279.
38 *Testimonies*, vol. 8, pp. 221, 222.
39 *The Desire of Ages*, p. 104.
40 *Christ's Object Lessons*, p. 278.
41 *Early Writings*, pp. 154, 155.
42 *Testimonies*, vol. 3, pp. 61, 62.
43 *Manuscript Releases*, vol. 1, p. 364.
44 *Sermons and Talks*, vol. 1, p. 391.
45 *Testimonies*, vol. 4, pp. 147, 148.
46 *Early Writings*, pp. 123, 124.
47 *Selected Messages*, bk. 2, pp. 113, 114.
48 *The Review and Herald*, March 22, 1892.
49 *Manuscript Releases*, vol. 14, pp. 190, 191.
50 Ibid., pp. 189, 190.
51 *The Paulson Collection*, pp. 128, 129.
52 *Special Testimonies on Education*, pp. 106–108.
53 *Selected Messages*, bk. 3, p. 338.
54 Ibid., vol. 2, p. 114.
55 Ibid., vol. 1, p. 41.
56 *Fundamentals of Christian Education*, p. 336.
57 *The Signs of the Times*, July 26, 1883.
58 *Selected Messages*, bk. 3, p. 83.
59 *Special Testimonies*, Series A, No. 1b, p. 9.

JUNE

1 *Medical Ministry*, p. 300.
2 *The Review and Herald*, October 7, 1909.
3 *The Southern Work*, pp. 39, 40.
4 *Evangelism*, p. 346.
5 *The Acts of the Apostles*, pp. 526, 527.
6 *Testimonies*, vol. 7, p. 37.
7 Ibid., vol. 6, pp. 314, 315.
8 *Sketches From the Life of Paul*, p. 300.
9 *Testimonies*, vol. 6, pp. 335, 336.
10 *Education*, pp. 73, 74.
11 Ibid., pp. 78, 79.

[12] *The Review and Herald*, December 22, 1904.
[13] *Testimonies*, vol. 4, pp. 415, 416.
[14] *The Review and Herald*, June 8, 1886.
[15] *The Great Controversy*, pp. 594, 595.
[16] *Testimonies*, vol. 8, p. 295.
[17] *Gospel Workers*, pp. 312, 313.
[18] Ibid., pp. 311, 312.
[19] *Testimonies*, vol. 7, p. 289.
[20] *The Acts of the Apostles*, pp. 573, 574.
[21] *The Retirement Years*, p. 21.
[22] *Evangelism*, p. 470.
[23] *Manuscript Releases*, vol. 21, pp. 269, 270.
[24] *Testimonies*, vol. 5, p. 117.
[25] *The Acts of the Apostles*, p. 574.
[26] *A Solemn Appeal*, p. 148.
[27] *Testimonies*, vol. 2, pp. 187, 188.
[28] *The Review and Herald*, January 3, 1893.
[29] *The Ministry of Healing*, p. 106.
[30] *The Acts of the Apostles*, p. 587.
[31] *Education*, p. 79.
[32] *Testimonies*, vol. 6, pp. 117, 118.
[33] *The Review and Herald*, May 9, 1899.
[34] *Testimonies*, vol. 6, p. 119.
[35] Ibid., vol. 2, pp. 462, 463.
[36] Ibid., p. 464.
[37] *Historical Sketches*, p. 232.
[38] *Testimonies*, vol. 2, pp. 242, 243.
[39] Ibid., vol. 3, p. 483.
[40] *Manuscript Releases*, vol. 8, pp. 434, 435, 437.
[41] Ibid., vol. 21, pp. 97, 98.
[42] *Testimonies*, vol. 2, p. 306.
[43] *Manuscript Releases*, vol. 8, pp. 435-437.
[44] *The Review and Herald*, November 13, 1883.
[45] Ibid., June 16, 1891.
[46] *Loma Linda Messages*, pp. 313, 314.
[47] *Patriarchs and Prophets*, p. 592.
[48] *Testimonies*, vol. 3, p. 137.
[49] *Education*, pp. 186, 187.
[50] Ibid., pp. 187, 188.
[51] Ibid., p. 54.
[52] *Manuscript Releases*, vol. 1, p. 317.
[53] Ibid., p. 318.
[54] *Christian Education*, pp. 39, 40.
[55] Ibid., p. 40.
[56] *Selected Messages*, vol. 3, pp. 209, 210.
[57] *Counsels to Parents, Teachers, and Students*, pp. 204, 205.
[58] Ibid., pp. 205-207
[59] *Gospel Workers*, p. 29.
[60] *Testimonies*, vol. 8, p. 16.

## JULY

[1] *Special Testimonies*, Series B, No. 8, pp. 3, 4.
[2] *Christian Education*, p. 117.
[3] *The EGW 1888 Messages*, p. 111.
[4] *The Ministry of Healing*, p. 94.
[5] *The Review and Herald*, September 28, 1897.
[6] *Manuscript Releases*, vol. 7, pp. 111, 112.
[7] *The Youth's Instructor*, December 20, 1894.
[8] *Prophets and Kings*, p. 545.
[9] *The Ministry of Healing*, p. 90.
[10] *The Review and Herald*, September 28, 1897.
[11] *The Acts of the Apostles*, p. 476.
[12] *The Review and Herald*, July 19, 1892.

[13] *The Desire of Ages*, pp. 219, 220.
[14] *The Review and Herald*, September 28, 1897.
[15] *The Ministry of Healing*, pp. 48–50.
[16] *Early Writings*, pp. 57, 58.
[17] *The Review and Herald*, October 18, 1892.
[18] *The Desire of Ages*, p. 406.
[19] *The Spirit of Prophecy*, vol. 3, p. 182.
[20] *The Review and Herald*, April 30, 1908.
[21] Ibid., August 31, 1911.
[22] *Spiritual Gifts*, vol. 1, pp. 86, 87.
[23] *The Desire of Ages*, p. 821.
[24] *The Spirit of Prophecy*, vol. 3, p. 248.
[25] *The Signs of the Times*, January 22, 1885.
[26] *The Acts of the Apostles*, pp. 70, 71.
[27] *The Spirit of Prophecy*, vol. 3, pp. 292, 293.
[28] *The Acts of the Apostles*, p. 116.
[29] Ibid., p. 106.
[30] *The Review and Herald*, March 2, 1911.
[31] *Sketches From the Life of Paul*, p. 65.
[32] *Early Writings*, p. 202.
[33] Ibid., p. 207.
[34] *Sketches From the Life of Paul*, pp. 135, 136.
[35] Ibid., p. 53.
[36] *The Southern Review*, December 5, 1899.
[37] *Manuscript Releases*, vol. 4, p. 113.
[38] *Confrontation*, pp. 42, 43.
[39] *This Day With God*, p. 113.
[40] *The Signs of the Times*, December 10, 1894.
[41] *The Acts of the Apostles*, pp. 543, 544.
[42] *The Desire of Ages*, p. 438.
[43] *The Review and Herald*, December 24, 1889.
[44] *The Youth's Instructor*, September 27, 1894.
[45] *The Review and Herald*, April 1, 1875.
[46] *The Great Controversy*, p. 553.
[47] *Testimonies*, vol. 5, pp. 450, 451.
[48] *The Review and Herald*, August 9, 1906.
[49] *Testimonies*, vol. 5, p. 451.
[50] *The Great Controversy*, pp. 553, 554.
[51] *Testimonies*, vol. 9, p. 16.
[52] *The Review and Herald*, September 22, 1896.
[53] Ibid., August 17, 1897.
[54] *The Great Controversy*, p. 390.
[55] *The Review and Herald*, April 1, 1875.
[56] *Spiritual Gifts*, vol. 3, p. 87.
[57] *The Review and Herald*, August 15, 1907.
[58] *The Desire of Ages*, p. 407.
[59] *The Great Controversy*, p. 525.
[60] *Christ's Object Lessons*, pp. 353, 354.
[61] *The Southern Work*, December 5, 1899.
[62] *The Home Missionary*, July 1, 1897.
[63] *The Desire of Ages*, p. 672.
[64] *The Southern Work*, December 5, 1899.
[65] *The Review and Herald*, March 15, 1892.

## AUGUST

[1] *The Review and Herald*, September 10, 1895.
[2] Ibid., November 6, 1900.
[3] *The Youth's Instructor*, July 26, 1894.
[4] *Testimonies*, vol. 2, p. 125.
[5] *The Youth's Instructor*, September 14, 1893.
[6] *The Review and Herald*, June 11, 1901.
[7] *Sermons and Talks*, vol. 2, p. 133.
[8] *Life Sketches*, pp. 226, 227.
[9] *The Acts of the Apostles*, pp. 431, 432.

10 *Testimonies*, vol. 8, pp. 258, 259.
11 Ibid., vol. 4, pp. 27, 28.
12 *Manuscript Releases*, vol. 18, p. 380.
13 *Patriarchs and Prophets*, pp. 72, 73.
14 *Testimonies*, vol. 4, pp. 523, 524.
15 Ibid., pp. 144, 145.
16 *Education*, pp. 61, 62.
17 *Testimonies*, vol. 3, p. 406.
18 *Christ's Object Lessons*, pp. 174, 175.
19 *The Spirit of Prophecy*, vol. 4, pp. 89, 90.
20 *Testimonies*, vol. 1, pp. 657, 658.
21 *Special Testimonies*, Series A, No. 6, p. 23.
22 *Christ's Object Lessons*, p. 175.
23 *Testimonies*, vol. 5, pp. 166, 167.
24 *The SDA Bible Commentary* [E. G. White Comments], vol. 7, p. 958.
25 *Testimonies*, vol. 6, pp. 132, 133.
26 Ibid., vol. 4, pp. 232, 233.
27 Ibid., vol. 3, p. 475.
28 Ibid., vol. 4, p. 490.
29 *Christian Education*, p. 114.
30 *The Signs of the Times*, March 8, 1899.
31 *The Review and Herald*, December 15, 1891.
32 *Testimonies*, vol. 4, p. 537.
33 *The Paulson Collection*, pp. 44, 45.
34 *Testimonies*, vol. 4, p. 537.
35 *The Home Missionary*, October 1, 1892.
36 *Early Writings*, pp. 72, 73.
37 *The Review and Herald*, December 17, 1914.
38 *The Southern Work*, March 13, 1902.
39 *The Review and Herald*, September 15, 1896.
40 Ibid., January 24, 1888.
41 *Education*, pp. 89, 90.
42 *Prophets and Kings*, pp. 175, 176.
43 *The Great Controversy*, pp. 472, 473.
44 *Testimonies*, vol. 4, p. 145.
45 Ibid., pp. 527, 528.
46 *The Review and Herald*, April 21, 1896.
47 *The Youth's Instructor*, September 13, 1894.
48 *Selected Messages*, bk. 1, pp. 373, 374.
49 *Testimonies*, vol. 2, pp. 509–511.
50 *The Signs of the Times*, February 24, 1888.
51 *The Youth's Instructor*, August 9, 1894.
52 *Testimonies*, vol. 4, p. 220, 221.
53 *The Acts of the Apostles*, p. 518.
54 *Testimonies*, vol. 5, p. 578.
55 Ibid., p. 572.
56 *The Signs of the Times*, September 17, 1896.
57 *Early Writings*, p. 73.
58 *The Signs of the Times*, March 18, 1889.
59 *The Watchman*, March 24, 1908.
60 *Testimonies*, vol. 5, pp. 438, 439.
61 Ibid., p. 200.
62 Ibid., vol. 2, p. 115.
63 Ibid., vol. 5, p. 215.
64 *The Review and Herald*, April 1, 1890.
65 Ibid., June 11, 1889.
66 *The Home Missionary*, February 1, 1890.
67 *The Youth's Instructor*, August 9, 1894.

## SEPTEMBER

1 *Medical Ministry*, p. 65.
2 Ibid., p. 75.
3 *The Review and Herald*, June 9, 1904.
4 *Testimonies*, vol. 6, pp. 289, 290.
5 *Prophets and Kings*, p. 69.
6 *The Review and Herald*, July 19, 1898.
7 *Medical Ministry*, p. 322.
8 *Testimonies*, vol. 6, p. 299.
9 Ibid., pp. 243, 244.
10 *Medical Ministry*, p. 322.
11 *Counsels on Health*, p. 31.
12 *The Signs of the Times*, August 26, 1886.
13 *The Desire of Ages*, p. 92.
14 *The Ministry of Healing*, pp. 244, 245.
15 *Counsels on Health*, pp. 528, 529.
16 *The Review and Herald*, July 19, 1898.
17 Ibid., December 10, 1901.
18 Ibid., December 18, 1881.
19 *Testimonies*, vol. 9, pp. 165, 166.
20 *The Ministry of Healing*, p. 226.
21 Ibid., p. 17.
22 Ibid., pp. 112, 113.
23 *The Desire of Ages*, p. 824.
24 *Medical Ministry*, pp. 296, 297.
25 *Education*, p. 146.
26 *The Review and Herald*, January 21, 1909.
27 *Testimonies to Ministers*, p. 35.
28 *The Ministry of Healing*, pp. 476, 477.
29 *Testimonies*, vol. 6, pp. 300, 301.
30 *The Ministry of Healing*, p. 149.
31 Ibid., pp. 143, 144.
32 *Sketches From the Life of Paul*, pp. 56, 57.
33 Ibid., pp. 58, 59.
34 *Medical Ministry*, p. 47.
35 Ibid., p. 150.
36 *Sketches From the Life of Paul*, pp. 59, 60.
37 *Medical Ministry*, p. 29.
38 *The Ministry of Healing*, p. 149.
39 *Testimonies*, vol. 6, p. 113.
40 *The Ministry of Healing*, pp. 230–232.
41 *Manuscript Releases*, vol. 20, p. 278.
42 *The Review and Herald*, June 16, 1904.
43 Ibid., November 17, 1885.
44 *Sketches From the Life of Paul*, p. 139.
45 *Selected Messages*, bk. 2, p. 53.
46 *Testimonies*, vol. 1, p. 296.
47 *Selected Messages*, bk. 2, pp. 53, 54.
48 *Christian Temperance and Bible Hygiene*, pp. 111, 112.
49 *Selected Messages*, bk. 2, p. 54.
50 *The Place of Herbs in Rational Therapy*, p. 29.
51 *Loma Linda Messages*, p. 30.
52 *Manuscript Releases*, vol. 6, p. 378.
53 *Counsels on Health*, p. 528.
54 *Loma Linda Messages*, p. 30.
55 *The Review and Herald*, October 18, 1881.
56 *Gospel Workers*, pp. 216, 217.
57 *Counsels on Health*, p. 528.
58 *Loma Linda Messages*, p. 30.
59 *Counsels on Health*, p. 210.
60 *Pacific Health Journal*, February 1, 1901.
61 *Testimonies*, vol. 7, p. 62.
62 *The Review and Herald*, November 19, 1901.
63 Ibid., February 2, 1905.
64 Ibid., July 19, 1898.
65 Ibid., January 21, 1909.
66 *Manuscript Releases*, vol. 20, p. 102.
67 *Testimonies*, vol. 6, p. 228.
68 *Manuscript Releases*, vol. 2, p. 206.

[69] *Evangelism*, pp. 288, 289.
[70] *The Review and Herald*, January 21, 1909.
[71] *The Ministry of Healing*, p. 144.

## OCTOBER

[1] *The Desire of Ages*, pp. 72–74.
[2] *The Signs of the Times*, September 6, 1899.
[3] Ibid., August 26, 1886.
[4] *Manuscript Releases*, vol. 3, p. 369.
[5] *Historical Sketches*, p. 139.
[6] *Testimonies*, vol. 4, p. 599.
[7] Ibid., vol. 6, pp. 49, 50.
[8] *The Signs of the Times*, February 28, 1878.
[9] *The Medical Missionary*, pp. 176, 177.
[10] *Education*, p. 286.
[11] *Messages to Young People*, p. 143.
[12] *Education*, p. 286.
[13] *The Ministry of Healing*, p. 145.
[14] *Medical Ministry*, January 1, 1903.
[15] *Selected Messages*, bk. 2, p. 371.
[16] *Spiritual Gifts*, vol. 4b, p. 78.
[17] *The Review and Herald*, June 20, 1882.
[18] Ibid., August 23, 1892.
[19] *Sermons and Talks*, vol. 1, p. 370.
[20] *The Spalding Magan Collection*, p. 185.
[21] *The Health Reformer*, February 1, 1874.
[22] *Counsels to Parents, Teachers, and Students*, pp. 408, 409.
[23] *Education*, pp. 212, 213.
[24] *Testimonies*, vol. 9, p. 33.
[25] Ibid., vol. 7, p. 23.
[26] *The Spalding Magan Collection*, p. 125.
[27] *The Review and Herald*, October 15, 1895.
[28] *Testimonies*, vol. 4, p. 619.
[29] *Testimonies*, vol. 6, p. 285.
[30] *The Southern Watchman*, October 30, 1901.
[31] *An Appeal to Mothers*, p. 14.
[32] Ibid., p. 16.
[33] *The Ministry of Healing*, p. 158.
[34] *The Review and Herald*, October 15, 1895.
[35] Testimonies, vol. 7, p. 10.
[36] *Historical Sketches*, p. 290.
[37] *Messages to Young People*, p. 109.
[38] *The Review and Herald*, February 17, 1910.
[39] *Testimonies*, vol. 6, pp. 263, 264.
[40] Ibid., p. 299.
[41] *Manuscript Releases*, vol. 18, p. 126.
[42] *General Conference Daily Bulletin*, February 17, 1897.
[43] *Patriarchs and Prophets*, p. 34.
[44] *Selected Messages*, bk. 3, p. 17.
[45] *Testimonies*, vol. 3, p. 428.
[46] *Selected Messages*, bk. 3, p. 16.
[47] *Testimonies*, vol. 1, p. 270.
[48] *The General Conference Bulletin*, July 1, 1902.
[49] *The Review and Herald*, July 9, 1895.
[50] *The Signs of the Times*, May 29, 1893.
[51] *The Review and Herald*, September 29, 1891.
[52] Ibid., April 15, 1875.
[53] Ibid., June 10, 1902.
[54] *The Signs of the Times*, April 22, 1880.
[55] *The Review and Herald*, June 10, 1902.
[56] *Manuscript Releases*, vol. 5, p. 377.
[57] *Testimonies*, vol. 2, p. 484.

[58] Ibid., vol. 6, pp. 436, 437.
[59] Ibid., vol. 3, p. 441.
[60] *Manuscript Releases*, vol. 14, pp. 197, 198.
[61] *The Upward Look*, p. 187.
[62] *The Review and Herald*, October 7, 1909.
[63] Ibid., October 1, 1889.
[64] *Prophets and Kings*, pp. 30, 31.
[65] Ibid., pp. 31–33.
[66] *The Review and Herald*, January 8, 1884.
[67] *Testimonies*, vol. 2, p. 68.
[68] Ibid., vol. 1, pp. 679, 680.
[69] *The Review and Herald*, October 16, 1883.
[70] Ibid., January 8, 1884.
[71] *The Youth's Instructor*, September 23, 1897.
[72] *Pacific Union Recorder*, March 13, 1902.
[73] *Christ's Object Lessons*, pp. 72–74.
[74] *Testimonies*, vol. 9, pp. 46, 47.
[75] Ibid., vol. 5, p. 10.
[76] *Manuscript Releases*, vol. 14, p. 59.
[77] Ibid., vol. 9, p. 48.
[78] *The Review and Herald*, January 10, 1888.

## NOVEMBER

[1] *Christian Education*, p. 54.
[2] *Patriarchs and Prophets*, p. 48.
[3] *Testimonies*, vol. 3, pp. 333, 334.
[4] *Steps to Christ*, pp. 85, 86.
[5] *Testimonies*, vol. 8, pp. 213–215.
[6] *The Review and Herald*, May 13, 1884.
[7] *Testimonies*, vol. 7, p. 160.
[8] Ibid., vol. 5, p. 392.
[9] *The Review and Herald*, March 25, 1909.
[10] *The Spirit of Prophecy*, vol. 3, p. 266.
[11] *The Acts of the Apostles*, pp. 39, 40.
[12] *Testimonies*, vol. 1, p. 412.
[13] *Spiritual Gifts*, vol. 4b, p. 159.
[14] *Christian Education*, pp. 130, 131.
[15] Ibid., pp. 130, 131.
[16] *The Voice in Speech and Song*, pp. 30, 31.
[17] *Testimonies*, vol. 5, p. 391.
[18] *The Review and Herald*, July 7, 1903.
[19] *Testimonies*, vol. 6, p. 339.
[20] Ibid., vol. 7, pp. 70, 71.
[21] *Christ's Object Lessons*, pp. 335, 336.
[22] *Testimonies*, vol. 2, pp. 317, 318.
[23] *Gospel Workers*, pp. 122, 123.
[24] *Testimonies*, vol. 6, p. 81.
[25] *The Review and Herald*, April 24, 1888.
[26] *Testimonies*, vol. 2, pp. 185, 186.
[27] *The Youth's Instructor*, January 1, 1903.
[28] *Testimonies*, vol. 2, p. 54.
[29] Ibid., pp. 186, 187.
[30] *The SDA Bible Commentary* [E. G. White Comments], vol. 6, p. 1117.
[31] *Christ's Object Lessons*, p. 337.
[32] *The Review and Herald*, May 24, 1898.
[33] *Patriarchs and Prophets*, p. 255.
[34] *The Signs of the Times*, March 5, 1885.
[35] *Testimonies*, vol. 4, pp. 461, 462.
[36] *This Day With God*, p. 169.
[37] *The Review and Herald*, June 6, 1912.
[38] Ibid., November 19, 1914.
[39] *The Upward Look*, p. 91.
[40] *Sketches From the Life of Paul*, p. 102.

[41] Ibid., p. 105.
[42] *The Acts of the Apostles*, pp. 251, 252.
[43] Ibid., p. 252.
[44] *Manuscript Releases*, vol. 16, p. 1.
[45] *Prophets and Kings*, p. 252.
[46] *Evangelism*, p. 472.
[47] *The Bible Echo*, November 19, 1894.
[48] *Testimonies*, vol. 2, p. 212.
[49] *The Review and Herald*, April 6, 1886.
[50] *Testimonies*, vol. 4, p. 235.
[51] *The Signs of the Times*, March 1, 1905.
[52] *The Review and Herald*, November 20, 1900.
[53] Ibid., February 11, 1890.
[54] *The SDA Bible Commentary* [E. G. White Comments], vol. 7, p. 908.
[55] *The Signs of the Times*, December 7, 1891.
[56] *Christian Experience and Views of Ellen G. White* (1854), pp. 34-36.
[57] *The Review and Herald*, May 28, 1889.
[58] *The Signs of the Times*, February 22, 1892.
[59] *Loma Linda Messages*, p. 537.
[60] *Manuscript Releases*, vol. 8, p. 333.
[61] *The Review and Herald*, August 21, 1888.
[62] *The Signs of the Times*, April 28, 1898.
[63] *Early Writings*, pp. 115, 116.
[64] *The Great Controversy*, p. 208.
[65] *Testimonies on Sabbath School Work*, pp. 106, 107.
[66] *Historical Sketches*, pp. 205, 206.
[67] *Manuscript Releases*, vol. 20, p. 269.
[68] *The Review and Herald*, September 6, 1892.
[69] Ibid., December 1, 1891.
[70] Ibid., October 23, 1888.
[71] *Testimonies*, vol. 2, p. 685.
[72] *The SDA Bible Commentary* [E. G. White Comments], vol. 6, p. 1091.
[73] *The Review and Herald*, December 3, 1908.
[74] Ibid., May 28, 1889.
[75] *Manuscript Releases*, vol. 12, p. 83.
[76] *The Youth's Instructor*, June 28, 1894.
[77] *The Review and Herald*, August 27, 1903.
[78] *The Desire of Ages*, p. 142.

## DECEMBER

[1] *Selected Messages*, bk. 3, p. 25.
[2] *Patriarchs and Prophets*, p. 595.
[3] *The Review and Herald*, November 12, 1908.
[4] Ibid., April 7, 1910.
[5] *The Home Missionary*, October 1, 1892.
[6] *Testimonies*, vol. 1, p. 509.
[7] *The Youth's Instructor*, September 13, 1894.
[8] *Manuscript Releases*, vol. 18, p. 371.
[9] *Special Testimonies*, Series A, No. 7, p. 14.
[10] *Testimonies*, vol. 9, pp. 187, 188.
[11] *The Review and Herald*, March 20, 1894.
[12] *The Signs of the Times*, March 15, 1910.
[13] *Testimonies*, vol. 3, pp. 446, 447.
[14] *Atlantic Union Gleaner*, January 8, 1902.
[15] *The Review and Herald*, December 15, 1885.
[16] *Testimonies*, vol. 8, pp. 140, 141.
[17] *The Review and Herald*, February 16, 1911.
[18] *Pacific Union Recorder*, November 5, 1903.

[19] *Thoughts From the Mount of Blessing*, p. 13.
[20] *Counsels on Health*, pp. 514, 515.
[21] *Gospel Workers*, p. 392.
[22] *Testimonies*, vol. 9, p. 188.
[23] *Pacific Union Recorder*, December 29, 1904.
[24] *The Upward Look*, p. 172.
[25] *Testimonies*, vol. 7, p. 292.
[26] *The Signs of the Times*, February 7, 1895.
[27] *Bible Training School*, May 1, 1903.
[28] *The Home Missionary*, October 1, 1892.
[29] *Special Testimonies*, Series A, No. 10, p. 13.
[30] *Testimonies*, vol. 2, p. 233.
[31] *The Acts of the Apostles*, p. 600.
[32] *The Great Controversy*, p. 487.
[33] *Testimonies*, vol. 2, pp. 115, 116.
[34] Ibid., vol. 4, p. 133.
[35] *The Review and Herald*, May 12, 1903.
[36] *Testimonies*, vol. 1, p. 261.
[37] *The Signs of the Times*, April 13, 1891.
[38] *Testimonies*, vol. 1, p. 261.
[39] *The Review and Herald*, April 13, 1886.
[40] *Pacific Union Recorder*, November 5, 1903.
[41] *The Home Missionary*, October 1, 1892.
[42] *Testimonies*, vol. 2, p. 233.
[43] *The Review and Herald*, May 12, 1903.
[44] *Manuscript Releases*, vol. 11, p. 267.
[45] *Sermons and Talks*, vol. 1, p. 194.
[46] *Manuscript Releases*, vol. 11, pp. 266–268.
[47] *Testimonies*, vol. 5, pp. 246–248.
[48] Ibid., vol. 4, p. 316. [Comments in brackets are in the original text.]
[49] *The SDA Bible Commentary* [E. G. White Comments], vol. 7, p. 964.
[50] *The Review and Herald*, March 22, 1892.
[51] *Early Writings*, p. 71.
[52] Ibid., September 8, 1885.
[53] Ibid., January 14, 1904.
[54] *Testimonies*, vol. 2, p. 673.
[55] *The Review and Herald*, November 20, 1894.
[56] *Manuscript Releases*, vol. 10, p. 11.
[57] *Testimonies*, vol. 5, pp. 344, 345.
[58] Ibid., vol. 1, pp. 174, 175.
[59] *The Review and Herald*, February 6, 1879.
[60] *The Signs of the Times*, July 27, 1882.
[61] *The Youth's Instructor*, October 31, 1895.
[62] *This Day With God*, p. 71.
[63] *The Desire of Ages*, p. 490.
[64] *The Review and Herald*, June 20, 1893.
[65] Ibid., September 4, 1888.
[66] *Manuscript Releases*, vol. 14, p. 178.
[67] *The Signs of the Times*, September 4, 1901.
[68] *Testimonies*, vol. 5, p. 393.
[69] Ibid., vol. 1, p. 287.
[70] *The Review and Herald*, May 23, 1912.
[71] Ibid., April 7, 1910.
[72] *The Home Missionary*, October 1, 1892.
[73] Ibid.
[74] *Our High Calling*, p. 40.
[75] *Testimonies*, vol. 8, pp. 20, 21.
[76] *Manuscript Releases*, vol. 5, pp. 151, 152.
[77] *Special Testimonies*, Series A, No. 9, pp. 18, 19.
[78] *The Signs of the Times*, June 30, 1881.

# SCRIPTURE INDEX

4:11, 12 . . . . . . . . . . . . Dec. 2
4:11, 12 . . . . . . . . . . . . Dec. 3
4:11, 13 . . . . . . . . . . . . Dec. 4
4:11, 13 . . . . . . . . . . . . Dec. 5
4:14 . . . . . . . . . . . . . . Dec. 14
4:15, 16 . . . . . . . . . . . Dec. 15
4:29 . . . . . . . . . . . . . . Nov. 13
5:18, 19 . . . . . . . . . . . Nov. 16
6:14 . . . . . . . . . . . . . . Mar. 24
6:16 . . . . . . . . . . . . . . Aug. 27

### PHILIPPIANS
4:3 . . . . . . . . . . . . . . . Oct. 10
4:11-13 . . . . . . . . . . . . Jan. 28

### COLOSSIANS
4:6 . . . . . . . . . . . . . . . Nov. 9
4:12, 13 . . . . . . . . . . . Dec. 20

### 1 THESSALONIANS
4:7, 8 . . . . . . . . . . . . . Feb. 23
5:2, 3 . . . . . . . . . . . . . May 29

### 2 THESSALONIANS
2:7-12 . . . . . . . . . . . . . July 25

### 1 TIMOTHY
1:18, 19 . . . . . . . . . . . Aug. 13
3:1 . . . . . . . . . . . . . . . Apr. 13
3:2 . . . . . . . . . . . . . . . Apr. 14
3:2 . . . . . . . . . . . . . . . Apr. 16
3:2 . . . . . . . . . . . . . . . Apr. 17
3:2 . . . . . . . . . . . . . . . Apr. 18
3:2 . . . . . . . . . . . . . . . Apr. 19
3:2 . . . . . . . . . . . . . . . Apr. 20
3:2 . . . . . . . . . . . . . . . Apr. 21
3:2, 3 . . . . . . . . . . . . . Apr. 24
3:2, 3 . . . . . . . . . . . . . Apr. 25
3:2, 4, 5 . . . . . . . . . . . Apr. 26
3:2, 6, 7 . . . . . . . . . . . Apr. 27
4:10, 11 . . . . . . . . . . . June 29
4:14, 15 . . . . . . . . . . . . Apr. 5
4:16 . . . . . . . . . . . . . . June 30
6:6 . . . . . . . . . . . . . . . Jan. 27
6:10-12 . . . . . . . . . . . Aug. 14

### 2 TIMOTHY
1:7 . . . . . . . . . . . . . . . Jan. 13
3:16, 17 . . . . . . . . . . . June 9
4:2 . . . . . . . . . . . . . . . June 7
4:5 . . . . . . . . . . . . . . . June 5

### TITUS
1:5 . . . . . . . . . . . . . . . Oct. 20
1:7 . . . . . . . . . . . . . . . Apr. 23
1:7 . . . . . . . . . . . . . . . Apr. 28
1:7, 8 . . . . . . . . . . . . . Apr. 22
2:1 . . . . . . . . . . . . . . . June 10
2:2 . . . . . . . . . . . . . . . June 11
2:2 . . . . . . . . . . . . . . . June 12
2:3 . . . . . . . . . . . . . . . June 13
2:3 . . . . . . . . . . . . . . . June 14
2:3 . . . . . . . . . . . . . . . June 15
2:4 . . . . . . . . . . . . . . . June 16
2:4 . . . . . . . . . . . . . . . June 17
2:4 . . . . . . . . . . . . . . . June 18
2:4 . . . . . . . . . . . . . . . June 20
2:4, 5 . . . . . . . . . . . . . June 19
2:6, 7 . . . . . . . . . . . . . June 21
2:8 . . . . . . . . . . . . . . . June 22

### PHILEMON
6 . . . . . . . . . . . . . . . . Nov. 15

### HEBREWS
1:8 . . . . . . . . . . . . . . . Jan. 4
2:3, 4 . . . . . . . . . . . . . July 27
4:2 . . . . . . . . . . . . . . . Aug. 16
5:14 . . . . . . . . . . . . . . Oct. 31
6:1 . . . . . . . . . . . . . . . Dec. 22
6:12 . . . . . . . . . . . . . . Aug. 30
10:15 . . . . . . . . . . . . . Feb. 7
11:1, 3 . . . . . . . . . . . . Aug. 5
11:4 . . . . . . . . . . . . . . Aug. 6
11:8 . . . . . . . . . . . . . . Aug. 7
11:17-19 . . . . . . . . . . . Aug. 8
11:24-26 . . . . . . . . . . . Aug. 9
11:32, 33 . . . . . . . . . . Aug. 10
11:37, 38 . . . . . . . . . . Aug. 11
12:1, 2 . . . . . . . . . . . . Aug. 29

### JAMES
1:3, 4 . . . . . . . . . . . . . Dec. 23
1:3-5 . . . . . . . . . . . . . Sep. 19

1:17 . . . . . . . . . . . . . . Jan. 1
1:18 . . . . . . . . . . . . . . Mar. 14
1:26 . . . . . . . . . . . . . . Nov. 12
2:20-22 . . . . . . . . . . . Aug. 22
2:26 . . . . . . . . . . . . . . Aug. 23
5:10 . . . . . . . . . . . . . . May 9
5:14, 15 . . . . . . . . . . . Sep. 26

### 1 PETER
1:6-9 . . . . . . . . . . . . . Aug. 26
1:13, 14 . . . . . . . . . . . Feb. 22
3:15, 16 . . . . . . . . . . . Nov. 10
5:6, 7 . . . . . . . . . . . . . Jan. 21
5:10, 11 . . . . . . . . . . . Dec. 26

### 2 PETER
1:19-21 . . . . . . . . . . . May 30
2:9 . . . . . . . . . . . . . . . Jan. 25
2:9, 10 . . . . . . . . . . . . Oct. 17

### 1 JOHN
1:8 . . . . . . . . . . . . . . . Mar. 10
1:9 . . . . . . . . . . . . . . . Jan. 18
2:4 . . . . . . . . . . . . . . . Mar. 21
2:21 . . . . . . . . . . . . . . Mar. 22
3:18 . . . . . . . . . . . . . . Mar. 23
3:18 . . . . . . . . . . . . . . Nov. 28
3:24 . . . . . . . . . . . . . . Feb. 6
4:13 . . . . . . . . . . . . . . Feb. 24
4:17, 18 . . . . . . . . . . . Dec. 27
5:4 . . . . . . . . . . . . . . . Aug. 3
5:11, 12 . . . . . . . . . . . Jan. 26

### 3 JOHN
2 . . . . . . . . . . . . . . . . Sep. 18

### JUDE
3 . . . . . . . . . . . . . . . . Aug. 4
20, 21 . . . . . . . . . . . . Aug. 28

### REVELATION
13:13, 14 . . . . . . . . . . July 23
14:1, 5 . . . . . . . . . . . . Nov. 29
16:13, 14 . . . . . . . . . . July 24
19:20 . . . . . . . . . . . . . July 26